MILTON IN GOVERNMENT

MILTON

— IN —

GOVERNMENT

ROBERT THOMAS FALLON

The Pennsylvania State University Press
University Park, Pennsylvania

Frontispiece: Towers of the Public Record Office, Chancery Lane, by David Gentleman. Courtesy, Public Record Office. Crown copyright, reproduced with the permission of the Controller of Her Majesty's Stationery Office, London.

Library of Congress Cataloging-in-Publication Data

Fallon, Robert Thomas.
    Milton in government / Robert Thomas Fallon.

    p.   cm.
    Includes bibliographical references and index.
    ISBN 0-271-00904-7 (acid-free)
    1. Milton, John, 1608–1674—Political and social views.
    2. Great Britain—Politics and government—1649–1660.
    3. Great Britain—Foreign relations—1649–1660. I. Title.
    PR3592.P64F35   1993
    821'.4—dc20   92-17716
                                                         CIP

Published by The Pennsylvania State University Press,
Barbara Building, Suite C, University Park, PA 16802-1003

It is the policy of The Pennsylvania State University Press to use acid-free paper for the first printing of all clothbound books. Publications on uncoated stock satisfy the minimum requirements of American National Standard for Information Sciences—Permanence of Paper for Printed Library Materials, ANSI Z39.48–1984.

Contents

To John T. Shawcross
Fond Friend
and
Kind Mentor

Preface

> *But he . . . must not be long in Prefacing.*
> (Prose 8:86)

The study of Milton's politics is not uncharted ground, of course. Since 1667, when the King's Licenser, Roger L'Estrange, examined *Paradise Lost* for seditious material, readers have pored over the poet's works for keys to his political art and thought, tracing their development through the turbulent decades of the mid-seventeenth century.[1] The principal sources for this inquiry have been not only the words Milton wrote but also the words Milton read, for he schooled himself diligently in politics and history. This book will add yet a third source—the poet's experience as a public servant to the English Republic—in the conviction that his daily labors close to his country's centers of political power were of comparable importance to the shaping of his art.

One of Milton's chief duties, indeed his only duty after the fading of his sight in 1652, was the preparation of official documents for the heads of state of the English Republic.[2] These State Papers have been published frequently since his death, the earliest volume, the *Literae Pseudo-Senatus Anglicani Cromwelii*, appearing in 1676, and the most recent, the fifth volume, part 2, of the *Complete Prose Works of John Milton*, edited by J. Max Patrick, in 1971. For a number of reasons, however, these documents are seldom cited by Miltonists, and, one suspects, infrequently read. It must be admitted that for one unfamiliar

---

1. The list is long; but certainly seminal to our understanding are Don Wolfe, *Milton in the Puritan Revolution* (1941); Arthur Barker, *Milton and the Puritan Dilemma, 1641–1660* (1942); and Christopher Hill, *Milton and the English Revolution* (1977). More recent and highly recommended are Stevie Davies, *Images of Kingship in Paradise Lost* (1983), and Joan Bennett, *Reviving Liberty* (1989). The scholarly introductions to the volumes of the Yale *Prose* are singularly valuable.

2. There is some question whether the *Second Defence* was commissioned by the government. The *Defence of Himself* was not.

with the historical context of the letters, an afternoon's reading of them would be a long one indeed; but, more important, there are doubts whether the wording and style of the papers can be attributed to Milton. They were for the most part prepared originally in English, and it was his task to translate them into Latin, the accepted language of diplomatic discourse at the time; hence one cannot say with any assurance that he composed them or that they represent his sentiments on the events they record. For this reason it is generally accepted that one should be wary of citing the text of a letter to support conclusions about Milton's political thought or art; and as a consequence they are largely ignored. William Riley Parker best expresses Miltonists' reservations about the papers when he characterizes the poet as "little more than a translator for monolingual bosses" and dismisses any conjecture about attributing additional documents to him: "If one set about seriously collecting on this basis, it should not be difficult to double or triple the now accepted number of letters! And to what end?"[3] If a scholar of Parker's stature finds them contributing little to Milton's biography, others may well feel justified in dismissing them as of slight consequence to his poetry.

To what end, then? The purpose of this book is to gain an understanding of what Milton *knew* about the international events of his time. It offers a close examination of his role in government, little understood to date; and through a narrative of the historical events to which his letters respond, it makes accessible to Miltonists who might not otherwise consult them a long-neglected body of the poet's works. The basic premise of this book is that Milton was more intimately involved in the preparation of official papers than is currently acknowledged; and to this effect I offer evidence to support three propositions: First, he was responsible for many more papers than have hitherto been credited to him. Further, the wording of a number of the letters was indeed his and hence they may confidently be included among his "works." Lastly, as translator and composer of a substantial body of official papers, he was intimately acquainted with both the events that precipitated the correspondence and the consequences that flowed from it. The accumulated weight of this evidence, it is hoped, will persuade the reader that Milton's experience in government left a telling impression on his creative imagination.

It is hoped that this volume will prove of value to scholars of several disciplines. Although largely historical in content, it is intended princi-

---

3. William R. Parker, *Milton: A Biography*, 2:945, 1014.

pally for an audience of literary students and scholars, with a narrative of events designed chiefly to make the letters intelligible. Again, having read the accounts, they will then know what Milton knew. Historians will take pleasure in, and profit from, the insights to be gained by a close reading of letters between heads of state, the accounts of treaty negotiations, the description of the Republic's secretariats, and the overall picture of the government bureaucracy within which the poet worked, with dedication and diligence, from roughly his fortieth to his fifty-first year. Historiographers will find the survey of Public Record Office holdings of value, particularly the detailed listing of the contents of the State Papers Foreign (SP 71–113); and the various appendixes offer reference material as well as food for thought.

Literary scholars will be disappointed that these pages do not address their central concern, that is, the influence of Milton's political experience on his poetry; and some explanation is owed them. Several years ago I published a book, *Captain or Colonel*, in which I traced Milton's knowledge of the military events of his time and discussed how that experience affected the military imagery of his poetry. Since Milton was not involved directly in the wars, it was a relatively simple matter to describe the events with which he as a citizen of London would have been familiar and at the same time to analyze the parallels between the history and the art. Both fit nicely between the covers of a single volume. Milton's political involvement, however, was far more pervasive and complex, and his experience of it more immediate, hence it has filled a volume of its own. Literary analysis will fill yet another, by either the present author or the readers themselves. Quotations from Milton's poetry will be found scattered throughout the text but at this juncture certainly no claim can be made that the events under discussion were a source for the lines. They are offered here simply as intriguing parallels between life and art, a more studied analysis of which must await another day.

A consideration of the dynamics of influence, that is, just how Milton's knowledge of England's foreign affairs shaped his poetry, must await that same day. There can be little doubt that it did. His lines abound with courtiers, generals, diplomats, dictators, counselors, and kings, all engaged in debate, negotiation, ceremony, conquest, and the play of political power, mirroring the actions of figures he encountered, either through correspondence or within council chambers, during his decade of service. In collecting the evidence of that experience, these pages lay the foundation for literary analysis, leaving to a later time the more familiar task of tracing the influence of those years on his art.

Admittedly, this study of Milton's political experience could not appear at a less auspicious time. For literary scholars it will be of value chiefly insofar as it casts light on his great works; but for decades the critical community has had little patience with notions arising from the premise that life influences art, and especially since the appearance of Ezra Pound's *Pisan Cantos*, that political life influences political art. Further, at this moment in the postmodern world, literary scholars are enchanted by theory and hence may find a historical study, if not entirely marginal to their interests, perhaps a bit pedestrian. One may hope that they will find these pages useful, although my labors will appeal most to that dwindling group of scholars who hold that the author is to be valued as well as his text, and that his stated intent can be honored as a gloss on his art.

A new school of critics has appeared of late who profess that a work of art does indeed arise from the culture that gives it birth and that the artist weaves into the fabric of his work threads from his life experiences; and they are most welcome for that, whatever one's view of their method.[4] The advocates of the "New Historicism," as they call it, find fault with the play of power exercised by the political institutions of a ruling class and often discover in an artist's work heavily encoded messages subversive to that authority; hence they may welcome a study of the most accomplished encoders of them all, the composers of diplomatic discourse, for whom a single word can encapsule a world of meaning.

These pages examine the State Letters from several perspectives: First, they offer a narrative of the historical context of the documents so that the reader may encounter them in the sequence in which they were written. The historical accounts offer only sufficient detail to allow for an appreciation of the events that occasioned the letters. For the sake of clarity, the documents are organized into country studies, ten in all, each of which examines as a corpus the bulk of the letters written to a single state or in response to an historical event. Second, frequent quotations from the documents are included to give the reader some flavor of the language (at times quite delicious) and to aid in an evaluation of their impact on Milton's imagination. Third, the book addresses disputed attributions of certain letters to Milton, questioning some, confirming others, and adding a number not hitherto accounted his.

The introductory chapter offers a survey of the premises of the book and the aspects of Milton's government activity that will be more fully

---

4. Two essays highly critical of the New Historicists have appeared recently in *PMLA*: Edward Pechter, "The New Historicism and Its Discontents: Politicizing Renaissance Drama," and Richard Levin, "The Poetics and Politics of Bardicide."

developed in the pages to follow. Chapters 1 through 3 are a study of the State Papers, and Chapter 4 an analysis of the influence of this experience on his concept of government as he articulated it in the tracts written during the Anarchy in his quixotic attempt to rescue England from the threat of a restored monarchy.

A Note on Sources

In *Complete Prose Works of John Milton*, J. Max Patrick offers comprehensive historical headnotes to Milton's State Papers. His principal sources for this material are the Nalson and the Thurloe papers in the Bodleian Library, Oxford, which provide considerable information on the activities of the Interregnum governments. Since these sources have already been thoroughly documented, the present study refers to them only occasionally and relies more heavily on the official records of the English government deposited in the Public Record Office, London, in particular the State Papers Foreign (SP 71–113). It is evident that none of Milton's modern editors have consulted these files, which will be found at times to complement, at others to amplify, and on occasion to correct alternate sources.[5]

In an effort to capture as closely as possible the flavor of diplomatic language of the time, contemporary translations are used wherever available, chiefly Edward Phillips's *Letters of State*, published some twenty years after the poet's death. Phillips was the second to print them in English, the first being the unknown editor of the unreliable *Milton's Republican Letters* in 1682; but *Letters of State* has a number of advantages. First, it is readily available to readers in the Columbia edition of Milton's works; and, further, Phillips's close relationship to Milton and the distinct possibility that he helped the poet prepare his official correspondence would seem to make his versions the most authentic.[6] They have the additional virtue of being seventeenth-century translations of seventeenth-century documents, whose purpose was to

5. Patrick cites only SP 82/7, 94/1 (once), 96/6, and 103/69 (once, the only reference to a document dated after 25 May 1655). Patrick's last citation of the Order or Letter Books is the letter to the Swiss, dated 28 November 1653 (W40, P63), after which Milton no longer worked for the Council of State. W. Douglas Hamilton used the files in his *Original Papers* (1859) but left no record of the location of the letters.

6. *The Works of John Milton* 13:600. Phillips, it is noted, was "a contemporary and in Milton's confidence."

reflect accurately the tone and intent of letters originally drafted in seventeenth-century English by the leaders of the Republic. Most of these men had either no Latin at all or an insufficient command of the language for the purpose, which accounts in part for the critical role played by John Milton, whose Latin had the grace and precision necessary to the conduct of international affairs.

The reader will find that, although this book deals with historical documents, it is content at times to interpret them with such qualified language as "seems to be," "in all likelihood," and an occasional "perhaps," reflecting a historian's wariness about his sources, especially those in translation.

A complete list of Milton's State Papers is included as Appendix E.

A Note on Dating

Controversies over the dating of letters are for the most part relegated to footnotes, where they will not unduly intrude on the narrative. The governments of the Republic continued to use the Julian calendar, although Continental states had largely converted to the Gregorian; indeed, it was not until 1752 that England adopted modern dating. Parliament refers specifically to this practice in Milton's earliest letters, noting that the date inscribed is in the "English" or "old" style. The Julian year began on 25 March, and England's correspondence occasionally made a concession to the different practice of its Continental neighbors by dating a letter written prior to that day with both years, thus, "January 30, 1650/51." It frequently did not, however; hence in these pages all annual dates have been changed to reflect the Gregorian year, that is, a letter dated "January 30, 1650" in the seventeenth-century sources is referred to as written on "January 30, 1651."

At the time the two calendars differed by ten days; and on occasion the English deferred to the difference by citing both dates, as in "16/6 August."[7] More frequently, again, they did not. Since the daily dates in the Order Books of the Council of State, the *Calendar of State Papers, Domestic Series*, and documents in the State Papers files are all Julian, it seems wiser to use the earlier of the two days.

Many of the letters bear no dates, and various editors have supplied

---

7. The order varied widely, at times "6/16," at others "16/6." The earlier date is always Julian.

them by reference to other sources. J. Max Patrick is quite thorough in this matter. Those which appear in the seventeenth-century sources represent documents at various stages of their evolution, since Milton did not keep on file all the drafts of any single letter he worked on, nor did he necessarily retain the final version. In preparing an edition of the State Letters, Patrick was quite properly concerned with the specific version that has come down to us, whether an early or penultimate draft or final copy, and his dating of documents identifies when Milton actually wrote the words before us. Hence some documents appear in their final form, others are versions approved by the Council of State but later amended by Parliament, and yet others are drafts written at one stage or another of their history. Patrick lists the copies of any single letter available in various archives, identifies which stage of its evolution the printed version appears to represent, and dates it according to when Milton wrote that version, whether draft or final copy. Since this study is chiefly concerned with the historical context of the letters, it more often cites the date when the letter was finally approved for dispatch, regardless of the version we have, in order to accurately place it in the sequence of correspondence. Any discussion of dates will be to that end, with occasional notes when the State Papers Foreign offer a convincing alternative to Patrick's dating.

A Note on Documentation

Of the two most recent editions of the State Papers, the Columbia volumes are cited as *Works* and the Yale as *Prose*.

Intertextual documentation is restricted to (1) the identification of the State Papers, cited by reference to the numbers assigned them in *Works* and *Prose*, e.g., "(W1, P5)," and (2) quotations from Milton's works other than the Papers, cited by reference to the volume and page number in *Prose*, e.g., "(1:501)." Quotations of the poetry are from Merritt Y. Hughes, *John Milton, Complete Poems and Major Prose*.

For the most part, references to the Order Books and Letter Books of the Council of State cite the *Calendar of State Papers, Domestic Series, Commonwealth* (*CSPD*), which has proven entirely reliable.[8] Where precise wording is important, the original documents in SP 18 and 25

---

8. G. E. Aylmer observes: "Points of procedure and provenance of documents apart, there is little to glean from the originals which is not in the *Calendar*" (*State's Servants* 352).

are identified. Where dates are cited in the text, providing ready reference to the volumes of *CSPD*, footnotes are omitted.

Citations of documents in the Public Record Office follow the form: file number/bundle/folio pages, e.g., "SP 25/66/54–57."

The Public Record Office has many of the files in the State Papers Domestic, including SP 25, on microfilm, but none as yet in the State Papers Foreign. Some of the latter have been published elsewhere, however, and wherever possible those sources are given, as a convenience to those who do not have access to the Public Record Office but wish to consult the original documents.

No attempt is made to duplicate the exhaustive list of manuscript and printed copies of letters provided by Patrick in *Prose*. He offers documentation for each letter in the Tanner, Nalson, Rawlinson, Skinner, and Columbia MSS,[9] and in published sources such as Morland (1658), *Literae* (1676), *Milton's Republican Letters* (1682), Phillips (1694), Birch (1738), Thurloe (1742), Hamilton (1859), Stern (1877–79), Masson (1875–94), *Works* (1931–38), Abbott (1937–47), and French (1949–59). Since he cites the State Papers Foreign on so few occasions, letters found therein are fully documented.

Since this book is neither a bibliography nor an edition, no effort is made to record the exhaustive bibliographical data available in the works of John T. Shawcross or the meticulous examination of texts by Leo Miller. Tireless and inspired digging by both of these remarkable scholars has unearthed countless copies of Milton's letters in foreign archives, as well as a number of published collections, giving us an appreciation of how widely admired they were in the years after his death. Of particular value are John Shawcross's citation of the 50 letters in Gregorio Leti's *Historia* (1692) and Leo Miller's report on the 113 in Johan Christian Lünig's *Literae Procurem Europae* (1712), many of which contain significant variants in address, closing, text, and dating. Both scholars find it unlikely that these collections were transcribed from Milton's original files or from *Literae*; hence they tell us little of the size or composition of those files and cast only a flickering light on the occasion of an individual letter.[10] This study draws gratefully on their work whenever it enhances an understanding of Milton's working

9. Patrick cites Tanner 52–56 and Rawlinson MS A 260–61 almost exclusively, and Nalson X and XVIII chiefly.

10. See John Shawcross, "A Survey of Milton's Prose Works," 357–58, and *Milton, A Bibliography for the Years 1624–1700*, xii, 101–2, 106. Of Lünig, Leo Miller observes that "he used a different manuscript collection from any hitherto known" ("Milton's State Letters: The Lünig Version" 413).

environment and the historical setting of his letters. The hope is that the sum of our separate efforts will persuade readers of their value.

I am grateful to the University of Pittsburgh Press for permission to use excerpts from my "Filling the Gaps: New Perspectives on Mr. Secretary Milton," which appeared in *Milton Studies 12*; to the editors of *SEL*, who agreed to my including a radically revised "Milton in the Anarchy: A Question of Consistency" in Chapter 4; and to Roy Flannagan, the editor of *Milton Quarterly*, who consented to the inclusion of major sections of "Milton in Government: Denmark and Savoy."

This study had its genesis a decade and a half ago, and in the intervening years it has incurred many debts. I am grateful to the National Endowment for the Humanities for the fellowship, which gave me the luxury of a year in which to put the material into manuscript form, and to my colleagues at La Salle University for their support from the very beginning. The work has taken me to many collections, but I owe a special debt of gratitude to the Deputy Keeper and his staff at the Public Record Office, Chancery Lane, London, whose courtesy and efficiency, once again over the years, have made researching a pleasure. I am also obliged to Hilton Kelliher of the Student's Manuscript Room of the British Library for his generosity in making available to me the Weckherlin papers in the Trumbull MS, to the Rare Book and Manuscript Library in Butler Library for allowing access to the Columbia MS, and to Albert C. Labriola for his courtesy in permitting me to examine the manuscript of Leo Miller's book on the Dutch negotiations. I am indebted also to Francine Lottier and Dana Bielicki for their help with the manuscript and index.

Many individuals, although somewhat marginally concerned with the subject, have offered gracious support and encouragement over the past two decades. Among those too numerous to mention, three deserve particular thanks: Roland M. Frye, whose sympathy and scholarly example have guided these efforts; my colleague, chair, and good friend, James A. Butler, who has offered a willing ear in times of uncertainty and shared my joy during moments of success; and John S. Morrill, whose friendship has been an unanticipated and most welcome bonus of these efforts.

Two others, both Milton scholars already mentioned as eminently knowledgeable in the substance of this study, deserve my special thanks. The first, Leo Miller, has offered invaluable counsel and challenge over the years. I am much indebted to his books on the Oldenburg Safeguard and the Dutch negotiations, upon which I draw liberally here. His death, in April 1990, has deprived us of a unique colleague. To the

second, John T. Shawcross, I owe the most. To praise his scholarship
and express my gratitude adequately would exhaust my vocabulary and
cause him embarrassment. As but a token of my regard and affection,
therefore, this book is dedicated to him.

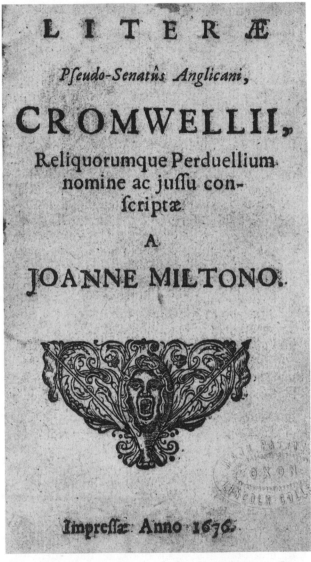

Title page, 1676 edition of the State Letters. Courtesy, Department of Special Collections, Van Pelt–Dietrich
Library Center, University of Pennsylvania.

INTRODUCTION
The Secretary for Foreign Languages

> . . . *only add*
> *Deeds to thy knowledge serviceable.*
> (PL 12:581–82)

On 13 March 1649, the newly organized Council of State of the Commonwealth of England called John Milton from private life to employ him, as he later put it, "especially in connection with foreign affairs" (4:628). Two days later, he was appointed to the post of Secretary for Foreign Languages, a position he held for over ten years, until the eve of the Restoration. The office was vacant at the time because the Council decided to replace Georg Weckherlin, who had served similar Parliamentary executive bodies in that capacity since 1644. Why Milton was chosen can only be a matter of conjecture. Aside from Weckherlin, there were others available with a great deal more experience, men such as Theodore Haak, an accomplished linguist, fluent in German, Dutch, and the Scandinavian languages, who had translated documents and performed diplomatic missions for Parliament in the 1640s.[1] Milton's

---

1. Sketches of Haak and others named appear in Appendix D.

friend, Samuel Hartlib, was available, as was René Augier, who had served as Parliament's agent in Paris. Perhaps it was thought that Weckherlin, at sixty-five, was too old, or that so many of them, Weckherlin included, were foreign born. It may have been that those with the desirable experience had gained it in the service of the Presbyterian-dominated Parliament of the 1640s, which Colonel Pride had purged the previous December, and that the new government preferred to make a clean break with the past. Milton roundly condemned that body; and although his *Character of the Long Parliament* was not published until after his death, he was never modest about expressing his views and surely did so privately at the time, perhaps to Council members of his acquaintance, men such as John Bradshaw, the president, who had acted as his solicitor in litigation, or Luke Robinson, a fellow student at Christ's College, who could also attest to his mastery of Latin.[2] The publication in February of *The Tenure of Kings and Magistrates* weighed heavily in his favor. A spirited defense of the trial and execution of Charles I, the tract identified him as a vigorous advocate of the new regime, perhaps tipping the balance in his favor despite his inexperience in public affairs.

The official records of the Council of State refer to their secretary frequently enough to delight the hearts of his many biographers but, unfortunately, not so often as to produce agreement on the scope of his duties or the nature of his day-to-day activities as the servant of that body. Parker's judgment that Milton was "little more than a translator and interpreter for monolingual bosses"[3] is balanced by that of others, such as Don M. Wolfe, who describes him as "a prompt, resourceful coworker in the immense variety of duties imposed upon the Council by the daily issues faced by the new republic."[4] As the distance between "mere translator" and "coworker" seems rather large, it is apparent that a close examination of Milton's political experience is somewhat overdue.

Milton's duties during his long tenure as Secretary for Foreign Lan-

---

2. David Masson, *The Life of John Milton*, 4:79; Parker 1:353. Both biographers agree that it could have been any number of Council members.

3. Parker 2:945. He is somewhat ambivalent, however, elsewhere elevating Milton to "secretary for foreign affairs . . . theoretically a post of equal power and importance to that of General Secretary [Gualter Frost, Sr.] or secretary for domestic affairs" (2:1022).

4. *Prose* 4:144. Wolfe goes on to describe him "as a vivid, cherished personality in the midst of the executive body of the nation" (145). For other comment see Denis Saurat, *Milton, Man and Thinker*, 85; Kenneth Muir, *John Milton*, 85; and George F. Sensabaugh, *That Grand Whig Milton*, 3. James H. Hanford's view is nicely balanced (*John Milton, Englishman* 137–38).

guages went far beyond those implied by that title alone, for in addition to his responsibilities as official translator and interpreter he was at one time or another called upon to act as diplomat, licenser, investigator, political polemicist, censor, and secretary to committees. Evidence of these activities is to be found in a variety of sources, including biographies, comments by contemporary political and literary figures, and, of course, the works of John Milton himself—since, happily for over three centuries of scholars, it was his habit to write at some length about himself as he was excoriating Bishop Hall, Salmasius, More, or whoever was the target of the moment.

The two most important source documents, however, are those letters of state which have been identified, by one means or another, as composed or translated by Milton, and the *Calendar of State Papers, Domestic Series,* which contains condensed minutes from the Order Books of the Council of State and several of its committees,[5] some diplomatic correspondence, and a variety of other government documents. It is to these two collections that most modern scholars turn in evaluating Milton's role in the English government.

These records are, however, incomplete. Despite the dedicated efforts of several generations of scholars, from W. Douglas Hamilton to J. Max Patrick, we still do not have a complete list of the State Letters for which Milton was responsible; and in the Order Books there are long periods during which there is no mention of Mr. Secretary Milton at all, particularly during the Protectorate. It is these gaps in the record which are most intriguing, and a brief glance at how they have been interpreted in the past will help to put the study into perspective. William Riley Parker's judgments on the State Letters are illustrative. His general practice is to accept as the product of Milton's hand only those documents for which there is inarguable corroborative evidence, dismissing a number of papers that have hitherto been accepted as Miltonic, since, as he puts it, he "can see no valid reason" to consider them.[6] He surveys what is left and concludes confidently that Milton was not very busy. Similar judgments are made on the evidence of the Order Books. Parker, for example, observes that during the Protectorate Milton was relieved of most of his duties to the Council of State; and more recently Austin Woolrych has proposed that Milton performed only "a few

5. SP 25/1–61 (Draft Order Books), SP 25/62–79 (Fair Order Books).
6. Parker 1:360. For similar comments see 2:1014, 1016, and 1039. Patrick also omits a number of documents included in former editions. Shawcross lists as arguable additions nine letters of state, the Dutch Declaration of 1652, and the Spanish Declaration of 1655 ("Survey" 353, 360–63).

tasks for the Council of State" during that period.[7] Both survey the record and, once more, conclude that he was not very active in his office.

Anyone examining the pages of the Order Books for the years 1654 to 1659 may well reach the same conclusion, for the record of the daily proceedings of the Council is all but empty of reference to their secretary. Save for mention of salary and position in Cromwell's funeral procession, one can find no evidence to indicate that Milton was doing anything to earn that salary or justify that position.[8] And yet, the State Papers show that during the second half of his tenure he was preparing more letters than ever for his government. If numbers suggest anything, the thirty-two letters in 1656 and the twenty-two in both 1657 and 1658, to mention only those listed by J. Max Patrick in *Prose* as most likely the product of his hand, reflect a respectable level of involvement and activity. It therefore seems more reasonable to suggest that during those years John Milton was working quite hard indeed, but apparently *not for the Council.*

The present study seeks to offer a clear picture of Milton's position in the English government through a careful examination of the two sources mentioned, the State Letters and the *Calendar of State Papers, Domestic Series*. To fill out the picture left by these incomplete records, yet a third source will be added to the inquiry, the State Papers Foreign in the Public Record Office, London (SP 71–113). It is puzzling that these archives have been so long neglected by students of a man employed "especially in connection with foreign affairs." Scholars may have been dissuaded by the editors of *Works*, who over fifty years ago reported that "the Public Record Office can now find no original drafts or copies claimed as Milton's sent by the Commonwealth." It is evident that the official consulted was not entirely devoted to the search, for in fact those files hold numerous copies of his letters.[9]

The advantage of the public records, of course, is that they are the official archives, which frequently include the working papers of the officials responsible for them. The State Papers Foreign, for example, contain lengthy summaries of events, which place Milton's letters clearly in context. It was Parliament's practice to hear periodic progress reports on negotiations; and for that purpose all relevant documents,

---

7. Parker 1:481; Austin Woolrych, "Milton and Cromwell," 198.

8. *CSPD* 6:386, 458; 8:128; 12:131; 13:256.

9. *Works* 13:597. Fallon, "Miltonic Documents," is a report of the search of the State Papers Foreign conducted in the summer of 1977, one which found a number of copies of Milton's letters not listed in published sources.

Milton's among them, were collected into a single file for easy reference, often supplemented by a narrative of events, as in the abortive deliberations toward treaties with Spain and Denmark in 1652. Further, there are significant benefits, as we shall see, to examining his letters in their archival environment, which can provide persuasive evidence for additional attributions, as in the case of papers associated with the Piedmont Massacre.

A careful examination of these records will help clarify the scope and quality of Milton's public service. It will become apparent that he was not a mover and shaker in the governments of the English Republic, but that, although he did not make policy, he had a critical role in articulating it. Further it will be seen that as a public official he was close to his country's centers of political power, performing essential duties as a highly respected servant of England's ruling bodies; and he was more active and more creative in his office than has been hitherto acknowledged. Finally, his tracts on government composed during the months prior to the Restoration will offer insight into his response to the experience of these ten years of public service. These later works reflect a distrust of parliamentary government and a preference for limited authority delegated to a body of select, godly men.

It is hoped that students of Milton will emerge from a reading of these pages persuaded that the duties of his office required him to be intimately aware of the international events of his time, that this knowledge left a significant imprint on his creative imagination, and therefore that the documents which record his experience in government deserve consideration in the study of his art. But before examining the individual letters themselves, something must first be said of the surviving records of his work, and of the bodies he served.

The Fragmentary Record of Service

As has been noted, conclusions about Milton's involvement in his government office have been based largely on two points of evidence: the appearance of his name in the Order Books of the Council of State, and the number of his State Papers. Both sources are valuable in determining the *type* of activity Milton was engaged in at any specific time but neither is reliable in determining the *level* of his activity over a longer period. In fact, both records are incomplete. It has been suggested that the virtual disappearance of his name from the Order Books for the years 1654–59 offers significant evidence that he was voluntarily withdrawing from participation in government. Some have gone so far as to interpret this withdrawal as a reflection of his distaste for Cromwell and the Protectorate,[10] and others that his "silence" during that period is evidence of a growing disillusionment with public life itself.[11] As will be shown later in these pages, however, during those years the various Latin Secretaries were responsible, not to the Council of State, *but to a different office entirely*, that of the Secretary of State; hence the paucity of reference in the records of the Council tells us nothing whatsoever about either the extent of his government activity or his attitude toward that government. It will be further shown that the absence of his name from other records of the Republic is not so much evidence of a lack of activity as an indication that the record of such activity is simply not available.

The same may be said of the number of Milton's State Papers that have come down to us, which seem very few indeed for a decade of public service.[12] Again, any conclusions about the poet's level of activity or his political sentiments based on the number of his *published* State Papers must be questioned.[13] Such conclusions are argued from two largely unexamined and highly doubtful premises: that he kept copies of all the papers he worked on, and that the surviving transcripts of his letters contain all the papers he kept. A quick glance at the number of his published letters will shake confidence in both these notions. Milton

10. Barker remarks that "his official work for the Council was not however reduced until 1655, though he had actually been doing little" (381). Christopher Hill observes that "Milton was easing himself out of government service" (*Milton and the English Revolution* 191); and this suggests to him that the poet disapproved of Protectorate policies. Hugh Trevor-Roper, who accepts Woolrych's judgment in these matters, concludes that Milton had "lost faith in the Protectorate" (*Catholics, Anglicans, and Puritans* 277).

11. Woolrych refers to "the silence of the state papers" ("Milton and Cromwell" 204), Barker "the five years' silence between 1654 and 1659" (196).

12. Patrick indexes 178 papers but includes a number of these, such as the Dutch (P47) and the Spanish (P84) Declarations, only to reject them as Miltonic. His statement that "Milton was responsible for the Latin of at least two hundred state papers" (*Prose* 5:469) is accurate if one includes the 35 exchanged in the Portuguese negotiations of 1651 (P26).

13. Hill remarks that "he was employed from about 1654 only as an occasional translator" ("Milton and the English Revolution" 29). Austin Woolrych agrees: "He continued to draw his salary and to perform a few tasks for the Council of State, but the gaps between the occasional state letters that he composed were often months long, and he withdrew his interests more and more from state affairs" ("Milton and Cromwell" 198). As has been noted, however, the number of letters actually *increased* during these years. To consider only those listed in *Prose*, he was responsible for only eight in each of the relatively slow years, 1653–54, but thirteen in 1655, thirty-two in 1656, and twenty-two in 1657 and again in 1658.

was responsible for the translation, from Latin into English, of papers addressed to the Republic's executive bodies. Although there are but ten of these to be found in the seventeenth-century sources, all in the Columbia MS, one may safely assume that he worked on more than the average of one a year that this figure would seem to reflect. The same may be said of his Latin letters, which average about sixteen a year. When one examines additional sources, such as the Order Books, the State Papers, Foreign and Domestic, and other collections that fill in the record of his activity, these figures appear ridiculously small. He was obviously responsible for a great many more; but when the time came to have the letters transcribed for publication, he had to select from the number he had kept during his ten years of service to fit the size and purpose of the intended volume. It is clear from the evidence of Brabazon Aylmer, Milton's printer, that he had in mind a single volume. He was preparing a book of both his public and private Latin letters but was prevented by the censor from publishing the State Papers and substituted his youthful *Prolusions* for them in the volume that finally appeared.[14]

We may gain some insight into the purpose of the projected volume by considering, again, how few of Milton's English translations are available to us. He quite reasonably saw no need to have such letters transcribed, since they were not to be included in the volume. His letters were to be offered to the public, not so much as a biographical or historical record, but as a literary work designed to demonstrate the poet's mastery of Latin. Only in this context could he hope to have them licensed for publication; and even at that they failed. His intent is reflected in the letter addressed to the readers of the 1676 *Literae*, in which the editor, after deploring Milton's politics, states the objective of the volume as follows: "What alone we wish to commend to you is the embellishment of what is written and the elegance of the Latin style" (*Works* 13:3). In brief, the English letters did not fit the purpose of the volume; nor, we may assume, did many of the Latin letters he had at his disposal.

Once it is accepted that Milton was responsible for considerably more than the average of sixteen or seventeen letters a year that the seventeenth-century sources record, one can consider the editorial decisions required of an author who must select letters for publication from among the many accumulated over a decade of service. If Milton in-

14. Masson 6:721. See Appendix B for a detailed discussion of the early manuscripts.

tended a single volume, or as in this case a half-volume, he would have had to weigh a number of considerations in determining which letters to publish. To suggest but a few:

He would select the most important documents, those addressed to a king or chief minister, for example. The bulk of Milton's State Papers are letters from Parliament and the Lord Protector to foreign heads of state.

He would select those which reflect the scope of the correspondence. The printed letters are addressed to some twenty-six different nations, states, and cities.

He would select those which illustrate the diversity of the correspondence. Milton's papers are indeed varied. Aside from those of more momentous occasion, they include petitions from shipowners and merchants, credentials for and instructions to English envoys, protests of murders, attempted murders, and abductions, introductions for English soldiers enlisting in the service of a foreign prince, pleas for the release of captives, thanks for services rendered, as well as one ordering a ship's captain home for disciplinary action and another offering congratulations on the birth of an heir.

He would want to avoid having too many letters on the same subject or of the same type. Some groups were included, of course, to demonstrate his dexterity in composing variations on a theme, prominent among them the nine letters to European heads of state concerning the Piedmont Massacre. Although markedly similar in theme and content, they were appropriate for inclusion because of the importance of the occasion and impassioned rhetoric of the prose.

He would exclude documents of excessive length, treaties or extended declarations, because of both space limitations and the sensitivity of the material. The Swedish treaty, for example, is quite long (*Works* 13: 564–91); and it was, moreover, a legal document of international accord, hence inappropriate and probably illegal for a private citizen to publish. Milton may well have been so apprehensive about the censor (quite justifiably, as it turned out) that he omitted any such documents. He apparently had a number in his files, for Daniel Skinner reported that he possessed copies of treaties with Spain, Portugal, France, and the United Netherlands, which he could only have obtained from Milton.[15]

He would select documents associated with widely publicized events, concerning which prospective readers would be knowledgeable and nat-

15. Masson 6:796. Again, see Appendix B.

urally curious, letters, for example, dealing with the assassination of Anthony Ascham, the attempt on Philip Meadows's life, the Piedmont Massacre, and the War in the North.

This is not to suggest that Milton was wholly methodical in his choice of documents. The above list is offered merely to illustrate that any one or a combination of factors could have influenced his editorial strategy. There is, then, every reason to believe that the documents Milton had transcribed for publication represent but a fraction of those for which he was responsible. In the examination of individual letters in later chapters, evidence will be offered for the inclusion, as by his hand, of additional documents that are available in the public records today, and even more that are known to have been written, but have not been located (see Appendix F).

Some readers may find assertions that Milton "wrote" this or that letter so loose an employment of the term that it begs the question of how much of their wording was in fact his. Certainly the issue of Milton as "composer" of correspondence must be addressed, and it is no small matter. Parker's insistence that he was a mere "translator and interpreter for monolingual bosses" has led many to dismiss the State Papers on the basis that the events occasioned by Milton's letters would have had little impact upon the imagination of one engaged in so menial a task, and hence they need not be taken into account by literary scholars considering his poetry. It must be said at the outset of any discussion of the issue that there is no direct, tangible evidence that Milton composed any of the letters attributed to him. He was certainly employed frequently as a translator of other men's words, and the generic "wrote" is intended to include that activity, whatever additional role he may have had in the preparation of documents.

The word "composer," however, implies considerably more than "translator" and deserves closer study. A suggestive feature of the State Papers is that many survive in pairs or groups. The most conspicuous example of the former is the series of companion letters to Louis XIV and Cardinal Mazarin, and of the latter the aforementioned nine on the Piedmont Massacre. Although each letter in any pair or group was no more than a reiteration of the message of the others, they all had to be couched in distinctly individual language. It was assumed that a respectable head of state would have the resources at his disposal to prepare a different text for each addressee, even though the occasion and the matter were the same for all.[16]

---

16. There is one exception to this rule of different wording. In the Council of State's

Thus, since different phrasing was to be employed in preparing any single group of letters, a certain linguistic ingenuity was required. When, for example, William Jephson was sent as an envoy to the king of Sweden in August 1657, his route of travel called for him to pass through Hamburg, Bremen, Brandenburg, Holstein, and Lübeck; and the protocol of the time required that he present himself to the ruling body of each city, armed with letters from the Lord Protector asking that he be extended what aid and protection might be required along the way (W95–97, P129–30). These are short letters, presenting no particular problems in composition, all saying the same thing but in different Latin; and one must wonder if it was really necessary for John Thurloe to prepare five different, individual letters *in English* for his Secretary for Foreign Languages to translate into Latin. In eight years at such tasks Milton had routinely prepared many similar documents and knew what was required of them. In a far more likely scenario the busy Secretary of State would draft *one* and ask his experienced assistant to compose the others in the same vein. Or, equally as likely, he may have been asked to compose them all.

There are times also when one comes upon a passage that ignites a flash of recognition, lighting a conviction, though there is no substantial evidence for it, that Milton left his mark on a document. One such instance is Parliament's first letter to the duke of Tuscany (W17, P29) written in answer to his overture of friendship, a reply characteristically tardy for Parliament's cumbersome machinery for foreign affairs. The Council of State ordered Milton to bring in "the letter to Tuscany" on 2 January 1652, some eight months after receipt of the duke's.[17] It opens, without apology for the delay, acknowledging his of 22 April, and cites the warm testimony of English merchants who have enjoyed his hospitality. But it goes on to mention yet another group who can affirm the duke's affection for the English, "certain of our young Nobility, either Travelling through your cities, or residing there for the improvements of their Studies"; and apparently pleased with the notion, the composer repeats it in this very short letter, citing the "Citizens of our Republic, Travelling through *Tuscan* territories." Was Milton given a free hand in the preparation of this letter and as he wrote did his memory drift back

---

two letters to the governors of Galicia and Andalusia thanking them for their assistance to English ships (W14, P19), the only differences are the names of the addressee in the heading and of the state in the body. They are otherwise identical. Patrick draws attention to the fact that W14, as printed, names the governor of Andalusia in the heading but the province of Galicia in the body.

17. *CSPD* 4:89.

to his own pleasant stay in Florence some thirteen years prior? It is certainly difficult to resist the thought.[18]

That some of the pairs and groups are of the same substance and have the same date adds weight to the position that Milton was responsible for more letters than have survived. For example, when Richard Cromwell succeeded his father as Lord Protector in September 1658, it was important that the nations of Europe be assured that the transition had been peaceful, that normal relations would be uninterrupted, that all treaties would be honored, and that all envoys would remain accredited. Two of his letters to this effect are included in Milton's State Papers, the pair to Louis XIV and Cardinal Mazarin (W124–25, P159–60). Another such occasion was the restoration of the Rump in May 1659, and we have two letters written on that event, those to the kings of Sweden and Denmark (W135–36, P174–75). There can be little question that on both occasions many more letters to the same effect were sent to the other nations of Europe and that all Latin Secretaries at Thurloe's disposal were mobilized for the task. We may safely assume that Milton wrote more than two for each transition, but that in selecting representative letters for the proposed volume, he chose only those few for publication.

These features of Milton's State Papers lead to an important conclusion: If a companion to any single known letter is found, then it must be assumed to be by Milton's hand. It defies reason to suggest that Thurloe would have had one secretary write a letter to the king of France and another, at the opposite end of Westminster, prepare its companion to Cardinal Mazarin. Further, if a document is found that can be clearly identified as part of a group already known to be Milton's, there is a strong case for acknowledging it as his.

Evidence for the existence of a number of missing letters will be offered later, but whatever the evidence, such claims raise reasonable questions as to where the documents are and why they have not been found. They were first deposited in the Paper Office at Whitehall; and having been delivered to the care of a succession of Keepers since, are now meticulously maintained in the Public Record Office in Chancery Lane, London. The collection, however, has been subject to frequent removals and ravaging fires over the years, resulting in unaccountable losses. The records from the period of most interest to Miltonists, 1649–60, are

18. Patrick remarks of the passage, "Remembering his own reception in Florence, Milton approaches the autobiographical when he notes that young Englishmen who have travelled or resided in Tuscan cities can testify to the duke's esteem for their nation" (*Prose* 5:558).

particularly sparse, due in part to the chaotic administrative practices of the Interregnum governments and perhaps also to the reluctance of public officials of the Republic to turn over potentially incriminating documents to the King's Keepers after the Restoration. Milton, it would appear, was able to retain the documents accumulated during his decade of service. Hence, there are great gaps in the public records that might be expected to throw light on the poet's activities as Latin Secretary.

There are scattered clues suggesting the existence of a body of such records, dating from the early years of the Republic before the onset of Milton's blindness and dealing with foreign affairs, his principal area of responsibility. On 2 February 1650 the Council of State directed its president, John Bradshaw, to issue a warrant instructing Georg Weckherlin, Milton's predecessor as Latin Secretary, "to deliver such letters and papers of state as are in his hands, to Mr. Milton, to be deposited in the Paper Office at Whitehall."[19] Two and a half years later there was a similar and perhaps more important transfer of papers. When Thurloe assumed his duties as general secretary to the Council of State and clerk to the Committee for Trade and Foreign Affairs, he asked with characteristic thoroughness that all of the scattered documents appropriate to the office be made available to him, presumably so that he could read in the area of his new responsibilities. On 17 June and again on 25 October 1652, a sizable number of documents were delivered to him by the Keeper, Ambrose Randolph (or Randall, as he is identified in the documents), including copies of treaties, diplomatic instructions, and records of negotiations accumulated in a half-century of dealings with Continental powers: Denmark, Spain, Sweden, Germany, the United Netherlands, Switzerland, and "Divers Princes."[20]

Of particular interest is the order to include in the bundle "all the papers that he [Randolph] had from Lord Bradshaw when he was President delivered out of the Library of Lord Bradshaw, and by him to Mr. Thurloe being very many," among which almost certainly were the papers that Milton had received from Weckherlin. Bradshaw was president of the Council from 10 March 1649 until 31 December 1651, when that body initiated the practice of rotating the presidency. It must be assumed that his collection contained documents dealing with foreign affairs, and it is not too sanguine to suggest that these papers, "being very many," may have included a number that could cast some light on Milton's activities during Bradshaw's long presidency.

These Bradshaw papers do not appear to have been recovered. They

19. *CSPD* 1:503; SP 45/20/230–31; Trumbull MS 22:15.
20. Tanner MS 114:90; printed in *Thurloe* 1:xii–xiii.

are not with the Thurloe papers of the Rawlinson MS. That collection contains few diplomatic documents for the period 1649–51, the majority of those included being copies of papers Thurloe collected during his participation in the St. John–Strickland mission to the Dutch in 1651. They do not appear in the Tanner MS or in the appropriate collections of the Public Record Office. There are scattered collections from the period in the State Papers Foreign, such as documents exchanged with Hamburg, Spain, and Oldenburg; but most of the bundle is missing.[21] One further clue to its whereabouts does exist. On 2 October 1660, a King's Warrant was issued directing Thurloe to turn over to the Keeper "all those papers, books, and records of state mentioned in a catalogue hereunto annexed and [sic] were heretofore delivered unto you by Ambrose Randolph Esq., late clerk of said papers, and likewise all those papers, books, and records of state delivered by the said Ambrose Randolph to Bradshaw and by him left with you," as well as all other papers in his possession.[22] Thurloe obviously ignored the last injunction, but he may well have felt compelled to deliver those papers specifically listed in the catalogue mentioned in the warrant, itself perhaps compiled from the letter of transmittal that accompanied the bundles of 17 June and 25 October 1652.

Here, then, is evidence of the existence of an undiscovered body of documents, the Bradshaw papers, whose dates include the period of Milton's most active participation in government. Whether Thurloe kept them after the Restoration to be secreted in the false ceiling of yet another room or delivered them to the King's Keeper to be scattered and lost in the administrative chaos of the period must be left to future scholars to discover. The possibility of their existence surely excites interest. The present study will go no further than to propose that this is an instance when the records of those bodies with which Milton was most likely to have been associated are not available, constituting a clear example of a gap in our evidence of his activity.[23] In light of this gap, comments on the level of his activity during this period, one of

21. Documents exchanged during the Portuguese negotiations of 1651 are in the Nalson collection, Bodleian Library, Oxford. There are no records from the period in SP 75; 78; 84; in SP 103 for Savoy, Switzerland, France, Portugal, Sweden, and Tuscany; in SP 104; or in SP 108 for Denmark, the German States, Hamburg, Savoy, Spain, and Switzerland. The catalog of the Rawlinson MS A, vols. 1–73 (the Thurloe papers) contains no reference to such documents, nor do the indexes of the Rawlinson and Tanner MSS.

22. SP 45/20/238; Tanner MS 118:243.

23. There are other such gaps. See Chapter 3 for the paucity of Exchequer records from the period.

which observes that by the end of 1651 "his official tasks had thinned
to a trickle," or judgments concerning his position in government, such
as that characterizing him as "only for a time a learned hanger-on in a
revolutionary government" must be considered premature, at best.[24]

The Secretariat

The composition and function of the group of men who served the Interregnum governments in the capacity of secretary changed constantly
over the years as a result of illness, death, dismissal, promotion, or reorganization. In *The State's Servants*, G. E. Aylmer gives highly useful
biographical sketches of the men appointed to positions on the secretariats of the English Republic; and they are discussed below as they
enter the narrative of Milton's service.[25] For the moment, it will be of
value to survey two groups closely associated with Milton, the Latin
Secretaries themselves and the group of linguists who assisted them in
the translation of official documents. First, it is clear that John Milton
was the only officially designated Secretary for Foreign Languages to
the Council of State from 15 March 1649 to 8 September 1653, the first
four-and-one-half years of the English Republic.[26] On the latter date
Philip Meadows was appointed to the post, not, however, to replace the
poet, but to share the duties of the office with him, for official documents continued to refer to Milton as "Latin Secretary" until as late as
Cromwell's funeral in September 1658. Meadows soon impressed his
superiors, who recognized in him a man fit for higher diplomatic responsibilities. In February 1656 he was appointed ambassador to Portugal, a post he filled with distinction until July of that year, when he
returned to England to recover from injuries received from an attempt
on his life in Lisbon. The following February Meadows was alerted for
a mission to Denmark, although because of Cromwell's indecision over
his policy toward Sweden he was not actually appointed as envoy nor
did he leave for Copenhagen, until August 1657.

On 8 September 1657 a "Mr. Sterry" was appointed "in the absence

---

24. Woolrych, "Milton and Cromwell," 188; Howard, "Flying Through Space," 3.

25. See Aylmer on John Thurloe (258–60 and *passim*), Gualter Frost, Sr. (254–56),
Henry Scobell (256–58), and William Jessop (234–38). He says little of Georg
Weckherlin, however, who enters the narrative at the onset of Milton's blindness.

26. Georg Weckherlin was engaged in March 1652; but after some consultation he was
appointed "assistant secretary to the Committee for Foreign Affairs," not Latin Secretary
(*CSPD* 4:172, 175).

e staff were responsible for correspondence with a
area of interest. The able John Thurloe would cer-
d the advantages of utilizing the same person in
of negotiations, especially when correspondence
ate, repetitive, and prolonged, for such a practice
of briefing a new assistant each time a new docu-
sed. And if the situation called for the preparation
nts on any single occasion, it would simply not
the task to two or three different assistants. Milton
d by his superiors to act in this capacity on at least
ns, during the negotiations with Portugal in 1651
nann Mylius in 1652.

analogy to modern practice, available evidence
at during the Protectorate John Milton manned the
dealt with correspondence necessitated by the War
e was called upon to write the documents associated
Massacre because his talents and convictions were
ted to the occasion. And, save for a period of sev-
when he seemed to be the only Latin Secretary on
eft to others.

the conduct of foreign affairs will be explored in
neral overview of the manner in which the Republic
with foreign powers will be of value at the outset.
onwealth period Parliament delegated that respon-
cil of State; but the Rump proved a jealous parent
any concentration of power in institutions that
ent of its immediate control. In their zeal for reform
out to dismantle such bodies, replacing them with *ad*
re closely accountable to them. As Mary Ann Ev-
s in her introduction to the first volume of the Inter-

civil war, and more especially after the death of
the whole routine of regal government was swept
y Council, Exchequer and Admiralty departments,
ber, Court of Wards, Court of Requests, Prerogative
d Chancellor, Treasurer and Chancellor of the Ex-
ecretaries of State, &c.; and in place thereof, the
cutive government was represented by one single
MMITTEE.[34]

of Mr. Phillip Meadows [to] officiate in the employment of Mr.
Meadow, under Mr. Secretary."[27] There is some question which Sterry
this was. The Order Books make frequent reference to a Peter Sterry,
who in one of the Council's earliest acts was appointed their "preacher"
with a salary of £100 a year, very shortly thereafter raised to £200.[28] He
later became Cromwell's personal chaplain and was designated a
"Trier," one of a board of commissioners entrusted to approve public
ministers for the church. It seems unlikely, however, that a well-known
preacher who already had two important posts appropriate to his divine
calling would be engaged to assume yet a third, especially a purely administrative position that would make scant use of his talents. It is more
reasonable to assume that it was his brother, Nathaniel Sterry, who
received the appointment.[29] Little is known about Nathaniel but there is
evidence for the identification, a record of payment on 31 August 1658
of £100, "to Mr. Peter Sterry for ye use of his brother Nathaniel Sterry
being so much due for his attendance one half year in ye publique service," that is, the salary for six months of the £200 a year allocated for
the position.[30]

Meadows remained in Scandinavia until the Restoration, and it is
unclear whether Sterry was ever officially appointed Secretary for Foreign Languages or simply brought on to "officiate in the employment of
Mr. Meadow," as the order reads. It is highly possible that six months
is all he lasted, for by September 1658 Andrew Marvell is clearly identified, as is Milton, as "Latin Secretary" in the order for Cromwell's funeral and Nathaniel Sterry is not mentioned.[31] Both Marvell and Milton
remained in their positions during Richard Cromwell's Protectorate and
the rule of the restored Rump. One of the last acts of the Council, on 25

27. *CSPD* 11:89.
28. Ibid. 1:177.
29. Vivian Pinto agrees that Nathaniel was the Sterry appointed (*Peter Sterry* 33–34). I
am endebted to Pinto for much of the information on this obscure figure. It appears that
there was confusion on the identity from the very beginning; the secretary who kept the
Order Books left a blank space where Sterry's first name would appear (SP 25/78/132).
30. Rawlinson MS A 62:38.
31. In that order Peter Sterry *is* listed, but as a "preacher" along with Hugh Peters and
Thomas Lockyer. There is some evidence that Nathaniel eventually joined Meadows's
embassy in Denmark. On 8 March 1660 Pepys met a Mr. Sterry who had just returned to
England from his post as "secretary to the plenipotentiary in Denmark" (Pinto 33n).
Further, there is a record of £30 granted to Nathaniel Sterry on 29 March 1660 "toward
charge of his journey to the Sound" (*CSPD* 13:595). Parker, citing evidence from Thurloe's pay records, proposes that Marvell was appointed in September 1657 (Rawlinson
MS A 62:49), but he does not conjecture whether it was in conjunction with Sterry or in
place of him (2:1092).

October 1659, the day it adjourned as a consequence of Lambert's coup, was an order that both be paid £86 12s. of their annual salaries of £200 a year.[32]

Even though Milton was the only Latin Secretary recognized by the Council for many years, it is quite clear he was not the sole public servant engaged in composing, translating, or otherwise preparing documents related to the conduct of England's international affairs. The Council of State, and later the Secretary of State, made use of a number of other figures who shared translation duties with Milton, though they do not seem to have received official appointments. They were called in from time to time when the need arose and were rewarded irregularly for their services. Less is known about the duties performed by these men, who seemed to hover about on the periphery of the bureaucracy; but since they were employed in tasks similar to Milton's and, we must assume, were frequently in consultation with him, some knowledge of their function is important to a full understanding of the poet's position in government. This "shadow secretariat," as I have labeled it, was composed of some highly talented men with whom Milton shared intellectual interests as well as secretarial duties. The list includes Samuel Hartlib, John Dury, Theodore Haak, Andrew Marvell (before his appointment as Latin Secretary), and later, John Dryden. A full report on these figures will be found in Appendix D.

The presence of so many others engaged in translations has important implications for our understanding of Milton's role. A general survey of the State Papers, although they may represent only a fraction of those he worked on, leaves the clear impression that he was employed by his superiors quite selectively. His addressees were many and varied and, as mentioned, he doubtless chose letters to be transcribed precisely to demonstrate the diversity of his Latin. In fact, however, his activities were sharply focused. During the years 1649–51, for example, he was chiefly preoccupied with the war and negotiations with Portugal and the difficulties with Hamburg. In 1652 he concentrated his energies on the Oldenburg Safeguard, the Danish negotiations, and correspondence with Spain. It is the last half of his career, however, that is most revealing. From 1655 to 1659 John Thurloe engaged him quite selectively in three areas: the Piedmont Massacre, the War in the North, and correspondence with France. A full 70 percent of his letters in those years relate to these matters alone, and we can assume that he was conversant with the many turns and counter-turns of diplomatic maneuvering that

32. *CSPD* 13:256; SP 25/107/143.

---

marked their p
turned to the sl
century manusc
leading up to tl
Design. There is
than Savoy, Tu
German states o
from 1653 on th
loomed large in
for the two on tl

The evidence
men is suggestiv
monwealth's con
seems to have o
principles that ap
tary of state pres
sponsible for a s
ship, politics, eco
familiar. Were th
has subordinates
"Romanian desk,
remain current or
such an arrangem
whose concerns a
nation, he has at
made it his busin
able to act or adv
draft corresponde
and provide lines
when the need ari
takes.

The secretariat
period had nothing
tion; and although
torate may have b
primitive bodies to
of the imagination.

33. Of the hundred
thirty-two deal with the
There are five to France,
this duplication into acc

---

certain members of tl
designated nation or
tainly have recognize
any single sequence
promised to be intri
obviates the necessity
ment must be comp
of multiple docume
make sense to assign
was clearly designate
two separate occasic
and those with Herr

Thus, to use the
strongly indicates th
"French desk" and
in the North. And h
with the Piedmont
particularly well sui
eral months in 1656
duty, the rest were
Milton's role in
detail later, but a ge
pursued its relation:
During the Comme
sibility to the Cour
body, suspicious o
might act independ
the members set ab
hoc committees m
erett Green observe
regnum *Calendar*:

During the
Charles I.,
away—Pri
Star Cham
Court, Lo
chequer, S
whole exe
word—C(

34. *CSPD* 1:vii.

This restructuring applied to Parliament's internal organization as well. As William Bidwell notes, "By April, 1653 only six of the fourteen major standing committees which were functioning in the early days of the Rump remained." The Council of State, as a creature of Parliament, acted in concert with its parent body. Bidwell estimates that the first three Councils appointed an average of eighty *ad hoc* committees per year.[35] It was their customary way of doing business: when an issue arose, they appointed a committee; when the issue was resolved, the committee disbanded. Each of these temporary bodies required the services of a secretary and Milton is recorded as having served in this capacity for two such bodies, in the aforementioned negotiations with Portugal and those with Mylius. It was not until December 1651 that the Council provided for a permanent body responsible for relations with other states, the Committee for Trade and Foreign Affairs.

During the Protectorate, Cromwell, assisted by his Secretary of State, John Thurloe, kept the conduct of foreign affairs in his own hands, consulting the Council only on larger matters of peace and war.[36] Mention of the Committee for Trade and Foreign Affairs all but disappears from the Order Books; and when it is referred to, the emphasis is on "Trade." In 1654, for example, three of only five references to foreign affairs deal with the release of captured ships, whereas the other two are a petition from a captured sea captain and provisions for the "sea poor."[37] In the 1655 Order Books there are no references to the committee. Further, of the 472 committees appointed by Council from 20 December 1653 to 27 June 1654, only a handful were charged with foreign affairs, and these were largely colonial matters such as the administration of Barbados and Virginia. Again, the 149 appointed from 2 October 1655 to 26 March 1656 dealt mostly with trade, with Europe mentioned only in connection with the embargo on Spanish goods.[38] The overwhelming impression of the available records remains that the Council was not in the business of determining foreign policy for the Protectorate, hence they had little occasion to employ Milton's skills.

35. Bidwell, "Committees and Legislation," 70, 138.
36. Peter Gaunt argues convincingly that there was a "secret" Order Book where minutes of the Council's meetings devoted to foreign affairs were recorded, but until it becomes available there is no way to determine just what influence Council had upon the designs of the Lord Protector ("The Councils of the Protectorate" 69).
37. *CSPD* 7:43, 313, 316, 317, 424.
38. SP 25/121–22. On 3 April 1654 one committee was appointed "to examine ye Portugall businesse" (SP 25/121/36).

A Secretary's Duties

I was privileged to serve on the faculty senate of my university for a number of years, where it was the practice to prepare documents by committee consensus. Correspondence from the president or provost was read, and senators debated the proper method and substance of response, at the conclusion of which one member, most frequently the secretary or president, was delegated the task of preparing a draft based on the discussion held. At subsequent meetings further debate ensued during which individual members proposed changes in the wording of the draft, often ending in a proposal that it be revised and resubmitted for approval. It is an unwieldy process at best, but anyone who has sat on a similar academic body will fully appreciate the system under which the secretaries of the English Commonwealth performed their duties.

These clerks, as they were also called, to the Council were employed to gather information and report on it, to keep minutes, to prepare letters based on the resolutions of the body, and to communicate decisions to individuals concerned. In utilizing the secretaries, the Council and its committees called upon them to use a certain amount of independent judgment and initiative. Gualter Frost was frequently asked to "prepare" a letter or report based upon his familiarity with the discussion within the Council. On 28 February 1651, for example, he was directed "to draw up an order, according to the debates now had." Robert Coytmor, the secretary to the Admiralty Committee, received similar instructions, such as that "to write a letter to Col. Deane" and to prepare weekly intelligence reports to be sent to the fleet.[39] Later, Thurloe acted in a comparable fashion. The phrases appear as a refrain among the entries in Council's Order Books: Mr. Thurloe "doe draw up a paper," "do prepare a draft of a letter," "to prepare the draft of an Act," Mr. Thurloe to do this, that, and the other; and the minutes of the Committee for Foreign Affairs include similar instructions, duties he could not have performed competently had he not been present during the debate and aware of the issues.[40]

---

39. *CSPD* 1:99; 2:149.
40. See ibid. 4:342, 346, 364, 419, and *passim*. The following excerpts from SP 25/131, the Order Books of the Committee for Trade and Foreign Affairs, are illustrative: 12 (21 July 1652) "an answer be prepared . . . by Mr. Thurloe"; 41 (8 October 1652) "That Mr. Thurloe doe draw up a paper according to ye Debate now had thereupon"; 48 (27 October 1652) "That Mr. Thurloe doe draw up a paper according to ye Debate now had at this Committee"; 74 (24 November 1652) "That Mr. Thurloe do prepare ye draught of a letter according to ye debate now had"; 75 (26 November 1652) "That Mr. Thurloe doe draw up a paper . . . according to ye debate now had."

This practice has important implications for any discussion of matters such as the degree to which Milton "composed" the letters of state and the frequency of his attendance at meetings of the Council of State, for there is evidence that his superiors employed him in much the same manner. Patrick reports that Milton collaborated with Henry Marten, a Council member, in the preparation of one of Parliament's early letters to Hamburg.[41] On 29 January 1650, the poet was directed "to prepare a letter to the governor of Tetuan in answer to his," and on 2 January 1652, "to prepare a Letter in Latine of the substance of what was now here read in English to be sent to the Duke of Tuscany." "Of the substance" is important, for it clearly implies that he was present in the chamber at the time and that he composed the letter based on what he heard discussed there.[42] He very clearly played a major role in the preparation of the Oldenburg Safeguard, which was drafted originally by Hermann Mylius, for, as Milton writes to him at one point, "Certain things I found it necessary to insert; others I condensed" (4:838). Indeed, any busy executive makes use of assistants in this manner. The phrases are familiar—"Prepare a letter," "Draft a speech," "Give me a summary of this discussion"—and the secretary must be present at meetings and aware of issues to fulfill this function. His presence is particularly necessary in discussion that precedes the composition of diplomatic correspondence, where the exact wording is critical, as it was in many of Milton's early letters. He wrote one, for example, for Richard Bradshaw in Hamburg that had to be returned because the word "Agent" appeared rather than the desired "Resident,"[43] and the delay in the approval of the Oldenburg Safeguard was occasioned by Parliament's refusal to include a brief phrase extending its protection to the count's heirs. These are delicate and sensitive matters and the secretary responsible for correspondence between parties to the negotiations had to be intimately aware of the issues involved.

Once drafted, a document pursued a torturous career, passing under the scrutiny of several bodies before receiving final approval. The administrative procedure for the production of a state paper was cumbersome at best, ably illustrated by the practice in place during 1652. The Council received a letter, either directly or delegated to them from Parliament, and passed it down to the Committee for Foreign Affairs to

---

41. *Prose* 5:478.

42. *CSPD* 4:89. Patrick's remark on this letter is instructive. It shows, he says, that "Milton was no mere translator of other men's words" (*Prose* 5:558). See also Hanford 138.

43. *Prose* 5:519–20.

prepare an answer. That body frequently appointed a subcommittee, which after discussion of the letter directed John Thurloe to prepare a draft based on "the debate now had." Thurloe's English draft was then further discussed and revised at the subcommittee level, passed up to the Council for more discussion and revision, often requiring a new draft before all were satisfied. Parliament, of course, was the ultimate repository of executive authority in the Republic, and a document was frequently referred to that body for further revision or approval. Only when the House had passed on a letter could the Council order it translated into Latin for delivery in both languages to the addressee.

Under the Protectorate this administrative process was somewhat simplified. As we shall see, the Latin Secretaries came under the supervision of the Secretary of State, who was directly responsible to the Lord Protector. Parliament was not a factor in foreign affairs; it sat for less than five months of the first two and a half years of Cromwell's rule and devoted most of its energies during that interval to debate on the constitution. The Council of State was consulted, but it had little influence in the conduct of foreign affairs. The government continued to be somewhat slow in replying to individual letters, which might well go through a number of drafts before dispatch; but this was largely due to Cromwell's indecision rather than a committee wrangling over language. Thurloe and Cromwell were the architects of the Republic's foreign policy; and Milton was answerable to them alone, rather than to a Council crowded with discordant voices.

Understanding this cumbersome practice will cast light on several matters to be discussed below: It explains the often lengthy delays between letters in any single sequence of exchanges. It also has a bearing, as noted, on how much of the wording of any single letter is Milton's. Further, it accounts for the different dates and versions of documents available in the several archives. The letters in the early manuscripts of the State Papers were transcribed from Milton's files, which contained documents at various stages of their evolution from the initial draft to the final copy approved for signature.

1

THE COMMONWEALTH
Before the Darkness

What supports me, dost thou ask?
The conscience, Friend, to have lost them overplied
In liberty's defense, my noble task.

(Sonnet 22)

When John Milton first assumed his duties as Secretary for Foreign Languages in March 1649, he was already blind in his left eye; and three years later he had lost his sight entirely. March 1652 thus marks a transition in the substance and scope of his responsibilities in his office. Of his private life during those early years of public service little is known. Late in 1649 he was assigned an official residence in Scotland Yard, to the north of Whitehall, a short walk from the seat of government at Westminster Palace.[1] In May 1651 Parliament ordered several occupants, including Milton, to vacate the quarters to make way for its own members, and in response the Council of State formed a committee to contest the directive. The incident in no way reflects a change in

---

1. Michael Hanson includes Fisher's map of Whitehall, prepared in 1670 (*2000 Years of London* 120–21). The Palace itself was left unoccupied until the Protectorate, when Cromwell moved in. The Commonwealth Council of State met in old Westminster Palace on the west side of King Street.

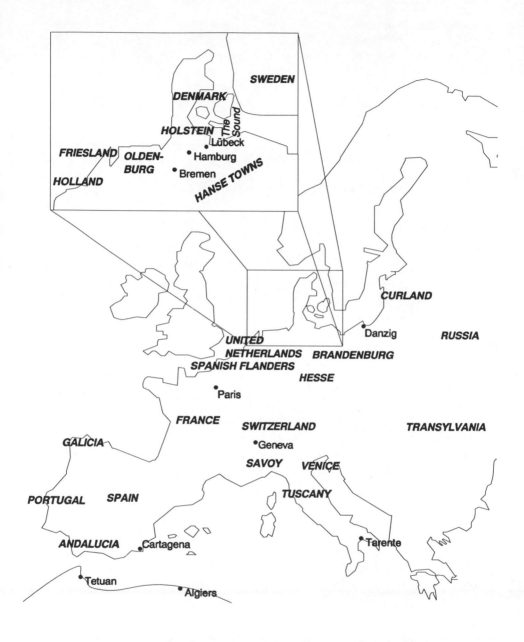

Destinations of Milton's State Letters Courtesy of LaSalle University.

Milton's status in government; he was simply caught in a power struggle between the Council and its parent body. Council prevailed for the moment, and he remained in Scotland Yard until December, when, as he wrote to Hermann Mylius, the family moved for reasons of health.

His new home, as Edward Phillips described it, was "a pretty garden house, in Petty France in Westminster, next door to Lord Scudamore's, and opening into St. James Park."[2] The house, on Birdcage Walk, was well chosen, no further from Westminster Palace than had been the quarters in Scotland Yard; and there he remained until the Restoration. The only other notable event of Milton's personal life in those years was the birth of a son, baptized John, on 16 March 1651.

During the first three years in his official capacity he filled a variety of functions, many of them domestic in nature. He was directed to license Marchmount Needham's *Mercurius Politicus*, a weekly publication which became a semiofficial organ of the Republic. He was additionally ordered to search the papers of suspected enemies of the state, arrange for publication of books favorable to the Commonwealth, and dispose of official records committed to his custody. Aside from these duties, in his critical role as defender of the Republic, he was almost continually engaged in composing tracts addressed to an international audience. In 1649 he published *Observations upon the Articles of Peace with Ireland* and *Eikonoklastes*, and apparently was occupied throughout 1650 with the composition of his first *Defence of the English People*.[3] In the preparation of letters of state, which is the focus of our concern, he was used quite selectively during those years, with fully three-fourths of his published papers occasioned by the difficulties with Hamburg, the Portuguese war, and relations with Spain. Thus, there is no evidence that he was in any way involved in the diplomatic initiative with the United Netherlands in early 1651, or in correspondence with France, matters in which apparently other hands were engaged. Sources other than the seventeenth-century manuscripts reveal his connection with the Oldenburg Safeguard and the 1652 Dutch negotiations, which were just getting under way as his last light dimmed.

When the first Council of State convened on 17 February 1649, however, foreign affairs was low on the agenda. Parliament, having swept aside many of the institutions of the monarchy, struggled with the problem of replacing them with practical alternatives more appropriate to

2. Masson 4:418–19.
3. Although the Council ordered its preparation on 8 January, it was not registered for publication until 31 December 1650.

England's proclaimed status as a republic. Moreover, there were enemies at home to be dealt with. Cromwell set out in May to quell an
incipient Leveller uprising in the southwest, and in July he left with an
army to subdue Ireland. After a successful campaign, he returned the
following year, only to be ordered almost immediately to the north,
where the defiant Scots had declared their allegiance to Charles II. The
threat from that quarter was not eliminated until 3 September 1651,
when Cromwell soundly defeated the young king and his Scottish allies
at Worcester.

When the revolutionary leaders of the English Republic first looked
beyond their shores, they beheld a hostile Europe. They had, after all,
decapitated a king, and so could expect little sympathy from the
crowned heads across the Channel. Parliament's forces at sea had to
contend with a small royalist fleet, preying destructively on Commonwealth shipping, and at the same time conduct undeclared naval wars
with France and Portugal. The Dutch seemed hospitable, although that
in time proved illusory, and, surprisingly, so did the Spanish, who
opened their ports to an English navy engaged in hostilities with their
common enemies, the French and Portuguese.

Parliament's first tentative efforts to establish diplomatic relations
with Continental powers encountered fierce opposition from militant
royalist exiles, who in the name of the as yet uncrowned Charles II
attacked the Republic's envoys wherever they appeared. Dr. Isaac Dorislaus, Parliament's first envoy to the United Netherlands, was murdered in The Hague in May 1649. The following February Charles
Vane embarked upon a mission to Portugal, which ended with his flight
from Lisbon three months later; and in June Anthony Ascham, the English Agent to Spain, was murdered by royalists within hours of his arrival in Madrid. Richard Bradshaw, in Hamburg, went in fear of his life
after public threats by Charles's advocates there. His ironically under-
stated reminder to his superiors on the Council of State may well speak
for all the Republic's envoys abroad in those early years: "I hope it will
please your honours to remember that I live amongst a people with little
affection to the Republic of England."[4]

The first concern of the new government, then, was survival; and
Milton's letters from this period chronicle the Republic's struggle for
legitimacy in a community of nations that abhorred the very thought of
such an England. Many of Parliament's letters open with an eloquent
defense of their right to rule, and others stand in stout defiance of those

4. SP 82/7/220–21.

who question that right, challenging the hostile reception of the Republic's envoys and asserting England's privileges as a sovereign nation.

Europe's attitude toward the English Republic changed markedly after Worcester, where Cromwell crushed the last organized threat to the Commonwealth. Legitimacy was no longer at issue, and Parliament, now securely in power, resolved to flex its economic muscle. In October 1651 they passed the Navigation Act, "For the increase of the shipping and the encouragement of navigation of this nation," to be achieved by requiring that all goods imported into England be carried on English vessels or those from the cargo's country of origin.[5] Impressed with Parliament's now-unchallenged authority at home and stung by the sweeping provisions of the Navigation Act, the nations of Europe rushed diplomats to London, eager to recognize the regime and negotiate relief from the Act's adverse effects upon their own commerce. The Council of State was literally overwhelmed with ambassadors and had to devise new institutions to accommodate its enhanced position in the international community.

In the spring of 1649, however, the men of the Council had little time to concern themselves with events beyond their shores, and their early efforts to provide for diplomatic exchange were perfunctory at best. Committees were established as the need for them arose and on 13 March six members were designated as a "committee to consider what alliances this crown had with foreign states." It was this body that on the same day was directed to invite John Milton to become Secretary for Foreign Languages. Two days later this group, now addressed as the "Committee for Foreign Affairs," was asked to look into the matter of salaries for people employed abroad; but in ensuing months it languished for lack of business. In July the "Committee for Foreign Alliances and Treaties" was revived and Thomas Scott, then director of foreign intelligence, added.[6] It was not until 16 February 1650–a full year after the organization of the government—that a "Committee for Foreign Negotiations" appears as one of the standing committees of the Council of State. The body was apparently not staffed until three months later, when "Sir Henry Mildmay and Messrs. Marten, Challoner, and Scott" were appointed as a "committee to consider foreign alliances" for the purpose of studying a treaty with the Swiss.[7]

Alliances, Negotiations, Agencies, Treaties—the confusion of com-

    5. Samuel Rawson Gardiner, *Constitutional Documents of the Puritan Revolution,* 468–71.
    6. *CSPD* 1:37.
    7. Ibid. 2:165.

mittees and names may well reflect the confusion of the members themselves in assuming these unfamiliar duties; for the men of the Council of
State, as John Milton later characterized them, "were mechanics, soldiers, home-grown, strong and bold enough, [but] in public political
affairs mostly inexperienced," and "not more than three or four had
ever been out of England."[8] Their inexperience can be seen in the elaborate instructions given for the reception of Gerard Schaep, the commis-
sioner from Holland. On 20 May 1650, the meeting of the Council of
State, which was winding down one war and preparing for another,
was almost entirely given over to detailed instructions for the reception
of Schaep, one of the first foreign emissaries to honor the Commonwealth with this level of recognition. The anxiety of the men of the
Council can almost be felt in the meticulous orders given to the able
and sophisticated Master of Ceremonies, Sir Oliver Fleming, instructions including everything from the preparation of barges, the designation of temporary housing, and the allotment of funds, to the appointment of five members as a committee simply to consider how to
entertain the visitor—all arrangements that established governments
carry out as a matter of routine. The following month they even went
so far as to suggest that the busy Cromwell, then on his way to fight the
Scots for the very survival of the Commonwealth, pause to pay Schaep
a courtesy call before departing for the north.[9]

When the third Council of State met in February 1651, they designated, according to their custom, standing committees, seven in all; but
conspicuously absent is any reference to a body charged with foreign
affairs. The Council chose to deal with such matters by appointing *ad
hoc* bodies when the need arose. On 22 January 1651, eleven members
were designated as a committee to examine the relationship with Holland; and on 8 February, four members, Sir Henry Vane, Sir Henry
Mildmay, Dennis Bond, and Thomas Scott, were selected to treat with
the Portuguese minister, João de Guimarães, newly arrived to settle an
undeclared naval war between the two countries. The Council further
ordered that "Mr. Milton, secretary for foreign languages, be appointed
to attend this committee at their meetings, and that Joseph Frost be
employed for such writing as the committee shall have occasion for."[10]
There is good reason to believe that Milton remained in constant attendance with the committee during its four months of fruitless negotiations with Guimarães, for he was still there in May when the Council of

8. Miller, *John Milton and the Oldenburg Safeguard*, 172; French 3:164.
9. *CSPD* 2:211.
10. Ibid. 3:40.

State ordered "Mr. Milton to repair to the public Minister of Portugal, and desire a list of such persons as he wishes to carry with him as his retinue, that the same may be affixed to his pass."[11]

The membership and function of the Portugal committee is of particular significance because of Milton's association with it. During February and March it more than doubled in size; to the original four commissioners appointed on 8 February there were soon added six more, so that it was comprised of some of the most important members of the Council.[12] In addition, it was assigned matters that had nothing to do with Portugal. On 1 April, for example, Council directed that "the order of Parliament concerning the Isle of Scilly [be] referred to the Committee which treats with the agent of Portugal"[13] and, further, that they prepare instructions for the English "Ambassadors now in Holland."[14] Thus, items that had been the concern of the earlier Dutch committee, now apparently dissolved, were being referred to the Portugal committee, six of whose members had sat on the other body anyway.[15] If, as the evidence suggests, Milton continued to serve the committee during these months, these tasks would have fallen to him as well. And it appears that the body remained sitting well after Guimarães's departure in June, for there are further references to the "committee to whom the business of Scilly was referred," and as late as 25 October another to the "Committee for Portugal."[16]

There are references in the *Calendar* to a number of other bodies involved in foreign affairs. One, a committee that met in the "Horse

11. Ibid. 203.

12. Ibid. 40, 46, 50, 69, 95. The committee finally numbered ten members: Sir Henry Vane, Bulstrode Whitelocke, Dennis Bond, Thomas Challoner, Sir Henry Mildmay, Major Richard Salway, Col. George Thompson (or Thomson), Thomas Scott, who directed the Council's intelligence operations at the time, and the two Lords Commissioners of the Great Seal, Henry Marten and Sir James Harrington. Cromwell, of course, was in Scotland.

13. The Scilly Islands, at the most distant southwest tip of Cornwall, were controlled by a royalist, Sir John Glenville, who preyed on shipping without respect for nationality. The States General dispatched a fleet under van Tromp to eliminate the annoyance but they were persuaded to withdraw before he could take action. Blake finally secured the islands for the Commonwealth in May.

14. *CSPD* 3:122. Soon after the arrival of the St. John–Strickland mission at The Hague in March, Prince Edward, Rupert's brother, insulted them to their face; and Col. James Apsley sought an interview with St. John, reportedly with the intention of assassinating him (Gardiner 1:324). The committee was instructed to prepare letters of protest for the ambassadors.

15. *CSPD* 3:19; Vane, Whitelocke, Mildmay, Marten, Challoner, and Scott.

16. *CSPD* 3:209, 243, 493.

Chamber" at Whitehall, is of particular interest.[17] Initially, this does not appear to have been a standing body, but a series of committees that met in that place, each concerned in some way with foreign relations. On 21 September 1650, some papers from Gerard Schaep were carried to the "committee in the Horse Chamber"; the Portugal committee Milton served met there;[18] and in the fall of 1651 several other matters were referred to a body meeting in that room, including one of more than usual importance—the report of George Fisher, the English Agent to Spain, concerning the murder of Anthony Ascham, the Commonwealth's envoy to Spain. It would appear that this body grew out of the old Portugal committee, which met in that chamber and which, as we have seen, was taking on new responsibilities after the negotiations that were its original raison d'être had come to an end. These references suggest that this body became a kind of de facto committee for foreign affairs that the Council called the "Committee that meets in the Horse Chamber" for want of a better name. Further, there is no evidence in the Calendar that there was any standing committee of the Council charged with these concerns from the spring of 1650 until the end of 1651. At the same time, there was a "Committee for Trade that sits in the Horse Chamber."[19] The Council of State had always had a body charged with the responsibility for trade; there is a reference to such a committee as early as March 1649, and a year later the Council designated itself, or any five members sitting, as "a committee for trade and plantations."[20] In the fall of 1651 that body began to take on new importance; on 2 October six members were added, including the Lord General himself, fresh from his victory at Worcester.

The Horse Chamber committee and the Committee for Trade might have been the same body, but in view of the evidence that a group devoted to matters of trade had existed for some time, it appears more likely that the former was a separate group devoted to foreign affairs. Later events clarify the situation. On 17 December 1651, the newly convened fourth Council of State decided to simplify matters by establishing a Committee for Trade and Foreign Affairs. They further directed that "all things referred to the former committee which met in

17. The Horse Chamber was very likely the large room between the Tilt Yard and the Horse Guard Barracks. See Fisher's map (Hanson 120–21).

18. CSPD 3:122.

19. Ibid. 441, 496. There are frequent references in the Calendar to a "Council of Trade." This was an entirely separate body appointed by Parliament and concerned chiefly with inland commerce (3:270).

20. CSPD 1:64; 2:18.

the Horse Chamber be revived and referred to this committee who are to meet there every Wednesday and Friday mornings." England, having settled its domestic problems at Worcester, began to look beyond its borders, and the Council of State found it necessary to designate a standing body charged with responsibility for the conduct of foreign affairs.

The membership of this new committee is revealing. Of the ten members of the Portugal committee, five were appointed to the body immediately, another (Challoner) before the month was out, and yet another (Thomson) the following year. Some, such as Sir Henry Mildmay, did not sit because they were not elected to the fourth Council of State.[21] Of the six named to the Committee for Trade in October, four were members of the new Council, and three of these were appointed to the new committee.[22] The implication is clear that the new committee was an amalgamation of the two older bodies, the Committee for Trade and the unidentified committee that sat in the Horse Chamber, which, as we have seen, seems to have been an outgrowth of the "Committee for Portugal," which Milton had served.

The Committee for Trade and Foreign Affairs, once formed, played an important role in the Commonwealth. From its first sitting there is almost daily reference to it in the *Calendar,* where it is commonly identified in the minutes as the "committee for foreign affairs."[23] With the dissolution of the Rump, however, such references diminish sharply; and with the establishment of the Protectorate in December 1653, they all but cease.

These, then, were the various bodies charged with responsibility for the conduct of foreign affairs during the Commonwealth period. The secretariat that served them was composed of three groups: the permanent secretaries to the Council itself, the secretaries to the standing committees of the Council, and a number of others who were brought in from time to time to perform specific tasks as the need arose.

The central figure of the permanent secretariat until his death in March 1652 was Gualter Frost, Sr., and an examination of his numerous duties could very well lead one to conclude that he died of exhaustion. He was, first, the general secretary of the Council of State, a position that required him to be present at all of its sessions. He was called upon to draw up the orders regulating the conduct of these meet-

21. Ibid. 4:67; 5:2.

22. Ibid. 4:67; Cromwell, Vane, and Wauton.

23. A year later, on 2 December 1652, it was again listed as a standing body of the Council, under the title "Committee for Trade Plantations and Foreign Affairs."

ings, to prepare letters based on the discussions he heard, to develop reports in a variety of areas of foreign and domestic affairs for both the Council and Parliament, and to supervise the operation of the messengers, clerks, and doorkeepers who served the Council. He was, in addition, treasurer to the Council, entrusted with the disbursements of contingency funds amounting to many thousands of pounds each year, designated specifically for expenditure by that body. Very few meetings went by without some directive that he pay various sums for a duty performed for the Council or to a widow deserving of pension. Further, he was general housekeeper and errand boy, charged with providing sufficient chairs, notifying individuals called before the Council, securing doors, and performing numerous other nondescript chores, such as the one to ask "the merchants trading with Guinea whether the gold lately come in has been sold,"[24] as well as keeping the meticulous records of who was present, who not, who arrived early, and who late at the meetings. He had to assist him Gualter Frost, Jr., and Edward Dendy, the Sergeant at arms.

The urbane Sir Oliver Fleming was master of ceremonies to the Council of State, a position comparable to the modern protocol officer. His duties involved reception and entertainment of foreign ambassadors and dignitaries, the arrangement of formal ceremonies, and in general the proper observation of the elaborate ritual of seventeenth-century diplomacy. The scope of his duties can best be defined by reference to a long letter he wrote to the Council of State early in his tenure in which he recommended certain preparations to be made for reception of foreign visitors. His suggestions covered a wide range of subjects, including types of gifts to be exchanged, funds for entertainment, titles of address to be used, the size and composition of escorts, the decoration of barges, and the number of interpreters to be present and volleys of muskets to be fired upon greeting—all, of course, in keeping with the rank and importance of the visitor.[25]

These were the men who made up the permanent secretariat to the Council of State during the first three years of the Commonwealth. So far as is known, John Milton, as Secretary for Foreign Languages, was the *only* member of the body whose designated duties were in the area of foreign affairs. The Council directed Gualter Frost to perform occasional tasks in this area, but, given the general secretary's crowded day, it seems reasonable to assume that he would pass even these infrequent orders on to Milton. Edward Dendy, as Sergeant at arms, had no place

24. *CSPD* 2:117.
25. Ibid. 1:131–33.

in these matters; and although Sir Oliver Fleming acted at times as an intermediary between foreign envoys and English officials, his chief function was the formal reception, entertainment, and accommodations for visitors in London. Thomas Scott was the director of foreign intelligence but he was a member of the Council itself and not the secretariat. Thus, the record names only John Milton as the servant of the executive body of England in this vital area.[26]

The several standing committees were served by secretaries who did not come under the aegis of the ubiquitous Frost. Robert Coytmor was appointed "secretary to the Navy and Admiralty Committee" on 13 March 1649, and served in that capacity with his own staff of a clerk and two messengers for three years, until replaced by Robert Blackborne. William Hawkins was secretary to the Irish and Scotch Committee until replaced by William Rowe, who was provided with the handsome salary of £300 a year.[27] There was in addition a "shadow secretariat," consisting of such figures as Samuel Hartlib, Theodore Haak, and René Augier, who were employed for correspondence, translation, or composition as the occasion required (see Appendix D).

This account of the structure of the committees and the function of the secretariat of the Council of State of the Commonwealth offers insight into the place and function of John Milton in the government he served. As has been noted, until the establishment of the Committee for Trade and Foreign Affairs in December 1651, the Council developed its foreign policy through a series of *ad hoc* bodies; and, further, Milton was the only permanent member of the secretariat charged with responsibility for foreign affairs until the hiring of Georg Weckherlin in March 1652. These two facts alone raise the question of his relationship to these various committees, which were operating in the area of his responsibility. Some of the matters with which he was concerned were referred to such groups; for example, the correspondence with the duke of Tuscany was put in the hands of a committee headed by Thomas Challoner on 10 December 1651. Since the Council's standing committees all had their own secretaries and staff, it must be assumed that someone served these *ad hoc* bodies in a comparable capacity. Milton was hired by one and appointed to another, the Portugal committee, in February 1651; but the Order Books do not say who filled the role for the larger and more prestigious group designated to deal with the United Netherlands at about the same time.

The record in the *Calendar* of the Council and its committees is valu-

26. Ibid. xx–xxi.
27. Ibid. 6:459.

able to an understanding of how these bodies used their secretaries and, therefore, will cast some light on other matters of interest: What were the day-to-day activities of the Secretary for Foreign Languages? Was he present in the chambers during debate? To what degree were his letters of state mere translations of others' words, and how much of them was of his own composition? The Mylius correspondence, which will be discussed in detail in the section on Oldenburg, offers insight into Milton's duties and reveals the inadequacy of the *Calendar* as a guide to the *level* of his activity. That record for the period 16 October 1651–2 March 1652 contains only one clear reference to Milton's presence in Council, that of 1 January when he took the oath, and one that implies his presence, the reference to the letter to Tuscany on the following day. The Mylius papers provide at least twelve clear references to his presence during those six months at Council meetings on the safeguard alone, including the reception and the farewell audience.[28] This activity, moreover, came during a period when he was ordered to investigate and report on a book by a Mr. White, to defend himself for the licensing of the Racovian Catechism, to prepare the letter to Tuscany, and to involve himself in the activities that followed the arrival of the Dutch ambassadors on 19 December 1651. It is safe to say that Milton attended additional meetings of the Council in carrying out these duties.

The *Calendar* is helpful to understanding the *type* of activity Mr. Secretary Milton engaged in, however. His correspondence with particular cities and states reveals him as something more than the minor clerk and translator that some would have him. At least until his blindness was total, like the other secretaries who served the Council and its various committees, he attended meetings, heard debate, and performed numerous functions that brought him into frequent, sometimes daily, contact with the men who shaped the destiny of his country.

Hamburg

The first state letter for which John Milton was responsible he addressed to the city of Hamburg (W151, P1). This was not his first letter to Hamburg, of course. As he worked on his translation he may have recalled the earlier *Elegia Quarta*, which he had written to his old tutor, Thomas Young, during the Thirty Years War, in which Milton seized

---

28. *Prose* 4:828–50; French 3:75–205. The dates are 16, 20, and 25 October and 31 December 1651; 2, 6, 8, and 19 January; 4, 9, and 22 February; and 2 March 1652.

upon the rumor of approaching armies to assure his friend, then chaplain to the English colony there, that his faith would protect him from harm. Milton somewhat exaggerated that earlier threat but it provided the occasion for some rousing and elegant Latin verse. His later letters dealt with yet another threat, calling for more pragmatic but no less elegant Latin prose; and in responding to that threat both Parliament and their Latin Secretary were set to school in the subtle art of diplomatic correspondence.

Hamburg was traditionally a close trading partner of England; and to facilitate commerce the Company of Merchant Adventurers, the English corporation for overseas trade, had established a permanent colony there. The Company was in sympathy with the new government, but had to contend with a militant body of royalist advocates in the city, chief among them John Cochrane, the King's Resident. Within weeks after the execution of Charles I, his angry supporters made their presence known by a series of violent acts against the Merchant Adventurers designed to interrupt trade with the city; and the magistrates of Hamburg found themselves unwilling hosts to two feuding English colonies, both of which claimed to represent the legitimate government of England. Parliament complained for years about the treatment of English merchants subjected to "all manner of ill Language, Threats and naked Swords of Ruffians and Homicides," as Milton's letter puts it.

The history of these troubles is amply documented in the holdings of the Public Record Office, with over 220 folio pages of the State Papers Foreign, Hamburg and the Hanse Towns, devoted to the period 1649–52. The file contains correspondence between English representatives in Hamburg and their superiors in London, as well as several state letters exchanged between the governments, a number of them Milton's.[29] His first letter from Parliament to Hamburg, dated 2 April 1649 (W151, P1), is an eloquent overture by the newly formed revolutionary government, proposing that their mutually beneficial and peaceful trading relationship continue. It opens with a lengthy justification for Parliament's

---

29. SP 82/7/122–200; SP 82/8/1–144. These documents cover the period April 1649–June 1652. The only state letters from Parliament in the files, *all Milton's*, are W151, P1; W1, P5; W18, P37; W25, P43; and W26, P42. Also to be found are eight letters from Hamburg to England, including one dated 11 December 1649 in answer to Milton's of 10 August, one dated 16 June 1650 in answer to his of 31 May, and one dated 11 June 1652 in answer to his of 12 March. The majority of the documents in the files are letters from Richard Bradshaw, the English Resident in Hamburg, to his superiors in Westminster and a number he received from James Waynwright, his agent in London. The files are catalogued in *The Sixth Report of the Royal Commission on Historical Documents*, appendix, pp. 426–44.

assumption of power, which is characteristic of many of the Republic's initial contacts with Continental states: "Having by the grace of God come through so many trials . . . and many vain efforts to preserve the liberty which had been entirely taken from us but won again by force of arms," the letter proclaims, the decision was made "to convert the haughty domination of a kingdom into the form of a free state." It goes on to cite their common experience in the religious wars, pledges that Hamburg traders in England will receive the full protection of the new regime, and asks that English citizens in that city receive reciprocal treatment. It appoints Isaac Lee, the president of the Merchant Adventurers in Hamburg, as Parliament's envoy there, and requests in vague but unmistakable terms that English merchants be protected "against the violence and abuse of wicked men who, being in their own country attached to the party of tyrants and driven from home on account of many resultant villanies," are now attacking "their countrymen who love political liberty."[30]

This letter suffered the fate of a number over which Milton labored—it was never delivered. Isaac Lee, who valued his health, declined the honor and subsequently returned the letter along with the set of instructions accompanying it.[31] He did, however, deliver to the Senate of Hamburg a second letter, which he had received in the same post (P2), one that unlike its more vaguely worded companion is filled with specific complaints that "English nationals are being treated unlawfully if they are thought to be a little too zealous for the general freedom of our native land," that their traditional "immunities and privileges" are being infringed upon, and that they are denied "the free exercise of religion." Particular mention is made of "John Cochrane, a Scot," who, it claims, had attempted with the aid of accomplices to assassinate the Company's minister, Dr. Ebury, and would indeed have succeeded "if [their] arms . . . had fired."[32]

The Senate of Hamburg replied in June with a complaint of their own about the shoddy quality of recent shipments of English woolens.[33] In Milton's letter of 10 August (W1, P5) Parliament promises to look into

30. SP 82/7/122–23. For other instances of initial letters to foreign states defending an assumption of power, see Parliament's to Spain (W4, P11) and Portugal (W5, P10), and the Council of State's to the duke of Holstein (W38, P62). When the Rump was reinstated in May 1659, their initial letters were much less effusive (W135–36, P174–75).

31. SP 82/7/142.

32. P2 does not appear in the seventeenth-century sources, hence the translation is a modern one by Paul W. Blackford. It was discovered by C. M. Williams in the Brotherton Collection (Leeds University), Marten and Loder MSS, 3S, XI, f. 2 (*Prose* 5:481).

33. SP 82/7/124–25.

the matter but quickly turns to more recent indignities suffered by English merchants, who, they protest, have been subjected to further "Injuries of a most Profligate People," in particular the infamous Cochrane. At his instigation, certain "Ruffians and Homicides" kidnapped "Two or Three of the Merchants, together with the President of the Society" on the "River, of which your city is the Mistress [the Elbe]"; and their fellow merchants, after asking in vain for help from the city, had to rescue them "by Force of Arms" from an "Ignominious Captivity." Parliament demands that Hamburg punish, or at least expel, the criminals, again mentioning Cochrane by name and "those who lately assaulted the Preacher."

The seventeenth-century sources record only one letter to Hamburg written by Milton in the period between August 1649 and the following April, that of 4 January. There were apparently further exchanges during those months, however, for in the April letter (W11, P14) Parliament complains that their protests about the incident have gone unanswered, although Hamburg had replied on 11 December to the only one in the record, that of 10 August.[34] Milton's letter of 4 January deals with a separate issue entirely (W2, P6). The revolutionary leaders, faced with a wall of hostility from almost all the nations of Europe and an effective campaign of sabotage by exiled royalists, were anxious to know who their real friends were, and to that end required all Englishmen eighteen years or over, at home or abroad, to subscribe to the "Engagement," an oath of allegiance to the Commonwealth.[35] The Hamburg Senate issued a decree forbidding English residents from doing so, and Parliament wrote to ask why. In the letter they protest, citing the United Provinces as a country that had raised no objection to the practice, and blame Hamburg's reluctance on "certain Vagabond *Scots*" who, they suggest, have intimidated some of the city magistrates. The matter was eventually resolved, and by May the English merchants had all taken the oath.[36]

England's problems with Hamburg, and John Cochrane, were far from over, however. The revolutionary leaders, few of whom had experience in international affairs, and their Latin Secretary, himself a novice in the field, were soon to receive a lesson in the subtle distinctions of diplomatic protocol. In Milton's letter of 2 April 1650 (W11, P14), Parliament, after further complaints about "Sedicious Persons . . . sent to your city by [Charles Stuart]," announces the appointment of Rich-

---

34. Ibid. 144, 147–49.
35. Gardiner, *Constitutional Documents*, 391.
36. As reported by Richard Bradshaw (SP 82/7/180).

ard Bradshaw as England's permanent envoy to Hamburg. They had hoped perhaps to impress the Hamburgers with the seriousness of their concern by naming to the post a nephew of John Bradshaw, who had presided over the trial of Charles I and was serving as president of the Council of State; but young Bradshaw's arrival only provided a convenient focus for royalist agitators. He was immediately embroiled in a controversy with the city precipitated by a single word in Milton's letter, that designating his diplomatic rank.

It was an uncertain time for the new government, then making its first tentative efforts to establish diplomatic relations with foreign powers. Exiled royalists had murdered Dorislaus in The Hague and Ascham in Madrid, and a hostile John IV had sent Vane packing from Lisbon. Bradshaw was to receive an comparably unpleasant reception. The Hamburg Senate, trying to maintain a balance between the strong royalist elements and the English merchants in the city, were less than enthusiastic about his arrival; and as a device to mollify the angry royalists they raised the question of his diplomatic rank.

> Orders and Degrees
> Jar not with liberty, but well consist.
> (*PL* 5:792–93)

A third of Milton's letters cite the rank of the envoy concerned. As Latin Secretary, he was responsible for the preparation of the formal documents, called "Letters of Credence," which notify the host state of the appointment of an envoy, as well as routine letters requesting hospitality for traveling diplomats, and those releasing an envoy for return home at the end of a mission, as was required by the protocol of the time. Since so many of these letters identify the envoy by rank, some knowledge of these grades will be useful to an understanding of the issues involved.

There were essentially three diplomatic grades. The lowest was *internuntius*, literally "messenger," "negotiator," or "go-between," most frequently translated by Phillips as "Agent." Next came *orator*, Latin for "spokesman for an embassy," rendered for the most part as "Resident." The highest rank was *legatus*, or "Embassador." Where no grade is indicated, the envoy was identified generically as a *publicus minister*. In practice the Republic was quite conservative in the ranks it assigned emissaries. During the Commonwealth, Parliament, always jealous of its powers, designated no ambassadors; and Cromwell named but few. When the restored Rump assumed powers in May 1659, it resumed its old parsimonious policies, reducing Philip Meadows, whom Cromwell had designated *legatus* the previous year (W127, P163), to the lesser rank of *internuntio extraordinario* (W135–36, P174–75).

On the evidence of Milton's State Papers, it would appear that the English government departed from this pattern as frequently as they adhered to it. When, for example, William Jephson undertook his mission to the Swedish king in August 1657, the six letters he carried assigned him four different ranks.[37] This confusion may be explained in part by the fact that many of the documents Milton kept on file were drafts in various stages of their development, and as the letter evolved the governments of the Republic seemed to have frequently vacillated over what rank to assign envoys. In a number of the early letters they avoided the issue altogether by assigning none at all (W4, P11). A further difficulty is that Phillips's translation is erratic in these matters— *orator* is at times Agent (W87, P119; W98, P133), at others Resident (W49, P71), and *legatus* is at one point reduced to Resident (W127, P163)—which would suggest that he was simply unfamiliar with the fine distinctions involved. Another confusing factor is the occasional use of the neologisms *agentis* rather than *internuntius* for Agent and *residens* in place of *orator* for Resident. In his study of the Dutch negotiations, Leo Miller demonstrates persuasively that Milton made every effort to use classical Latin in his translations and that he was frequently overruled by his superiors in favor of more contemporary constructions. The designation of diplomatic rank is surely an instance of such disagreement, particularly in the Hamburg controversy, where his superiors insisted on the neologism *residens* over his preferred *orator*. It appears that Milton finally prevailed in the issue, for the classical *internuntius* and *orator* were consistently used after 1652.

The designation of rank was not simply a matter of diplomatic posturing. In the case of the host country it determined the dignity of the envoy's reception, the privilege and precedence afforded him, and, of prime importance, the level of government to which he had easy access. In assigning the envoy a grade his nation signaled the seriousness attached to his mission, the relative importance of the state to which he was accredited, and the range of issues he was empowered to negotiate. Bradshaw's problems are illustrative. In Milton's letter of credence the envoy is designated *internuntium* and Bradshaw soon discovered that as a consequence he was extended fewer of the dignities appropriate to the

---

37. For Sweden he is *internuntii extraordinarii* (W92, P127); for Brandenburg and Hamburg no rank is mentioned (W94–95, P128–29); for Bremen he is *oratis munere* (W96, P130); for Lübeck he is *publico munere* (W97, P131); and for Holstein he is *legationem* (W99, P132).

position he assumed Parliament intended him to have. He was denied access to important officials; and he reported in May that the "Burgermaster" refused to attend a funeral for the secretary of the Merchant Adventurers "because he will not meet with the English Resident to give him place" and so sent a senator of inferior rank in his stead.[38] He informed the Council of State that the Hamburgers "now dispute the word *Internuncius* [*sic*], which they will not understand to reach so high as Resident"; and he requested that they write again and "adde to the Word *Internuncium, & Legatum nostrum.*"[39] Parliament was unwilling to allow Bradshaw the dignity of *legatum* but they did promptly dispatch a letter in which he is referred to as *residentem* and, to be safe, *oratem* as well (W12, P16).[40] Two years later they were still anxious about his status, for in Milton's letter of 12 March 1652 various forms of *residens* are repeated no less than four times, in so many different cases as to virtually decline the noun (W18, P37).

In time, the leaders of the English Republic became quite punctilious, when it suited their purpose, in their observation of the privileges each grade carried with it, particularly in relation to access. When the Dutch ambassadors arrived in December 1651, they were greeted with elaborate ceremony and given immediate audience by the Parliament and Council of State, but Hermann Mylius, who had been in London for four months, could not even gain access to their Latin Secretary; and the Swedish envoy, Peter Spiering, Lord Silvercrone, whose questionable credentials delayed his reception, died before seeing anyone. When, in December 1650, the Portuguese envoy, João de Guimarães, arrived at Southampton to negotiate an end to the war with England, the Council detained him in that city until he had submitted his credentials so that they could determine his rank, "whether of Embassador, or Agent, or Envoy" ["*sive Legati, sive Agentis, sive Internuntii*"] (W16, P20).

While the two governments squabbled over Bradshaw's rank, royalist agitation continued unabated, as the Hamburg magistrates searched for neutral ground between the wrangling factions of Englishmen. They delayed resolution initially by haggling over legal niceties, claiming that

38. SP 82/7/178.

39. Ibid. 178–79.

40. There were problems with this letter, however. Either the Council failed to inform Milton of the policy or he simply erred, for Bradshaw returned yet another earlier version (not available) because, as he complained, "in the beginninge it titles me Resident and toward the end Agent." The printed version is obviously a final draft, for the error has been corrected. Milton uses both *residentem* and *oratem* so that there will be no mistake. Bradshaw had to remind the Council continually that "Agent is farr inferior to Resident" (SP 82/7/203). Patrick is confusing about this letter (cf. *Prose* 5:520 and 5:584).

the attack on Dr. Ebury, although intended, had not in fact taken place, and that the kidnapping had occurred on the river, hence outside their jurisdiction. On 21 May 1650, however, Bradshaw was able to report that after all this legalistic foot-dragging, the royalists had finally been brought before a judge and sentenced to banishment. When the English objected to the mildness of the punishment, they were reminded that the court was merely following the advice of Parliament's 10 August letter to "command 'em to depart your Territories." To incite the English even further, the Hamburg authorities were apparently lax in carrying out that moderate sentence. Bradshaw reported that the criminals "absent not the Citty"[41] and on 31 May a concerned Parliament wrote again, protesting in Milton's Latin that the Resident had received further insults and threats from the same quarter and demanding that the city provide for "the safety of his Person, and the honour due his Quality" (W12, P16).

The controversy remained unresolved, for in Milton's letter of 12 March 1652, almost two years later, Parliament was still demanding justice for the kidnapping and the assault upon the "Preacher," and objecting to "the Insolencies of one *Garmes* who has carry'd himself contumeliously toward this Republic" (W18, P37). In 1652, however, it was a far more confident and secure English government responding to slights to its citizens abroad, and apparently there were some voices calling for more forceful action. In the State Papers Foreign is an early version of the 12 March letter, one offering a glimpse of the debate that frequently took place in committee over the wording of correspondence.[42] As originally drafted, the letter had a decidedly belligerent tone, including a thinly veiled threat that Parliament would "make use of such meanes as God hath put into their power to repaire such Indignities and dammage which through your Care and Justice Wee wish and desire may bee prevented." Calmer heads prevailed, it would seem, as the final version gives notice only that, should the abuse continue, "Reparations" might be called for. The threat of force implied in "such meanes as God hath put into their power" was apparently deemed an overreaction.

This was Milton's last letter of protest to Hamburg, for events rather than words had turned the balance in England's favor. After Cromwell defeated Charles II at Worcester and Parliament passed the Navigation Act, Hamburg joined the parade of nations who hurried envoys to London. In April 1652, Parliament acknowledged the arrival of Leo ab

41. SP 82/7/207.
42. SP 82/8/128.

Aitzema as the Resident for both Hamburg and the Hanseatic League (W25–26, P42–43).[43] There were no complaints voiced in the letter to Hamburg, simply a statement that Aitzema had been courteously received and a request "that the same Equity be returned" for the English Resident.

The early manuscripts of Milton's State Papers include seventeen letters to Hanseatic League cities, eleven to Hamburg, two each to Danzig and Bremen, one to Lübeck and one to the Senate of the League. Five of the Hamburg letters, those written during his first three years in office when the events in that city most troubled England, appear in the Public Record Office file; and they are the only ones addressed *from* Parliament to Hamburg in its entire 220 pages. The archival evidence, thus, gives reason to believe that he was the only secretary engaged in the Hamburg correspondence over that period, and there can be little question that he translated replies from their Senate into English. If it is discovered that there were more letters exchanged, which is implied by the language of those available, they can reasonably be attributed to him.[44]

The Council labored long over language, their deliberations often focusing on a few words, as in the letter of 12 March 1652, where a moderate demand for reparations replaced a more bellicose threat of force. As we have seen, gaining final approval for any single letter was a cumbersome process, for after perhaps twenty men in Council had decided on its wording, the document was then placed before the House, where any one of a hundred members or more might have his own ideas about what to say. The *Calendar* records an illustrative incident occasioned by the preparation of Bradshaw's credential letter of 2 April 1650. Once Council had agreed on the wording, the Lords Commissioners of the Great Seal had to present it to Parliament for final ap-

43. Ibid. 122–38. The Hanseatic League was a loose organization of German cities and groups of traders abroad originally formed in defense of commercial interests. At the height of its influence in the fourteenth century, it numbered some hundred cities on the Baltic coast and the Rhine, including Riga, Danzig, Hamburg, Lübeck, Bremen, and Cologne. By the end of the sixteenth century it had diminished in importance and, although still a legal entity, actually existed in name only. In English records the League is referred to as the "Hanse Towns."

44. Miller argues for the attribution of a letter from the Council of State to Aitzema, dated 8 April 1652, an answer to his delivered to the Council at his audience on 27 February. The envoy, like many others in London at the time, was negotiating for relief from the Navigation Act, and the Council characteristically refused to budge. Miller is persuaded by certain linguistic parallels between Milton's letter of 13 April to the Hanse Towns (W25, P43) and the Council's of 8 April ("New Milton Texts" 283).

proval, and Milton was instructed to attend them, waiting outside the doors of Parliament in case there were further changes decided upon.[45] One of the revisions he had to make was the designation of Bradshaw's rank, for although the Council had clearly intended Resident, Parliament characteristically opted for the lowest grade available, the troublesome *internuntius*.

Such instances illustrate the advantages of employing the same secretary from the beginning to the end of a series of letters dealing with the same set of events, one who was familiar with the points at issue and the subtleties of language required, and who had learned from hard experience, as in the present instance, such nice distinctions as that between *internuntius* and *orator*.

Portugal

how couldst thou hope
Long to enjoy it quiet and secure,
Between two such enclosing enemies?
(PR 3:359–61)

During the first years of the Republic, England's relations with Portugal were acrimonious, largely because the king, John IV, was sympathetic to the royalists. The immediate source of friction was a small fleet of warships, some eight to thirteen in number at various times, commanded by Prince Rupert, the able and adventurous nephew of the late Charles I. In 1649, Rupert preyed upon Commonwealth shipping in the waters around England and France with some success. In October of that year he escaped from the port of Kinsale in Ireland, eluding a Commonwealth fleet under Admiral Robert Blake, and in December entered Lisbon harbor, where he was offered haven by the Portuguese. He brought with him several captured prizes, whose cargoes he was allowed to sell there, enabling him to refit his small fleet.

Parliament responded quickly and aggressively to what it considered a threat to its sovereignty. Milton's first letter to Portugal on 4 February 1650 (W5, P10) opens with an eloquent justification for the establishment of the Republic and introduces Charles Vane as the Commonwealth's envoy to Lisbon. It mentions only briefly the source of conten-

45. *CSPD* 2:67, 73.

tion between the two nations, the "Pyrates and Revolters of our Nation," who have been offered "Refuge in your Ports" and permitted "to
sell their Goods [i.e., from the English prizes] by Publick Outcries at
Lisbon." In a companion letter, Parliament is more specific about grievances (W6, P7): After giving a brief history of Rupert's fleet, they object
to the sanctuary offered the royalists, citing the "furious Pyracy" and
"notorious and infamous Robberies" of those same "Pyrates and Revolters" (the Portuguese correspondence draws heavily on the vocabulary of invective). Parliament further threatens that "there will be a final
end to that vast Trade" between the two nations unless Rupert is ordered "to depart the Territories of *Portugal*" and warns the king not to
receive "any pretended Embassadors" from Charles Stuart.[46]

In March, Parliament took decisive action. A Commonwealth fleet
under Admiral Blake anchored off the mouth of the Tagus River, effectively blockading the harbor of Lisbon, where Rupert's ships rode safely
in refuge, protected by the guns of Portuguese forts commanding the
entrance. The blockade was clearly an act of war; and in an effort to
calm fears Parliament wrote assuring John IV that the action was not
directed against Lisbon but "the same Rabble of Fugitives" anchored
there, whose "Flagitious manners," the letter goes on to say, will have
surely by now convinced the Portuguese of "their Audaciousness, their
Fury and their Madness" (W10, P15). It announces the impending arrival of a "New Fleet" under Admiral Edward Popham, sent to reinforce Blake in subduing "those detested Freebooters . . . the Pests of
Commerce and Violators of the Law of Nations." Further, should the
king for some reason be unwilling to expel the royalists, Parliament
asks leave "to assail our own Revolters and Sea Robbers" in the harbor.

Since several of Milton's Spanish papers relate directly to Blake's
campaign in Portuguese waters, it will be helpful to consider them in
context. Spain had been at war with Portugal since 1640, when after
sixty years of Spanish rule that small country had broken away and
asserted its independence. King Philip IV, consequently, had opened his
ports to Blake's fleet, thus making it possible for him to remain on
station for extended periods; and Parliament took care to announce

---

46. W5 and W6 are similar to the two sent Isaac Lee in Hamburg, the first justifying
Parliament's assumption of power and introducing the envoy, the second lodging protests
in specific terms (W151, P1; P2). W5 is dated 4 February in the sources and Patrick has
W6 as 25 January. Both are probably early drafts of the final letter. The Skinner MS has
W6 as 24 February, which is very close to the date they were eventually placed in Vane's
hands, for he left London shortly thereafter as a passenger in Blake's fleet, which dropped
anchor outside Lisbon on 10 March.

Popham's arrival to the Spanish as well (W137, P8). The letter thanks Philip for his support and requests that the same courtesies he had offered Blake be extended to Popham, that is, "the right of freely and safely putting in, or with raised anchors sailing off, or of temporary stay."[47] To be sure, Philip IV's hospitality to the English was prompted more by animosity toward Portugal than love for the Republic, but it was no less welcome for that. Some months later, in November, the Council of State wrote to the governors of Andalusia and Galicia, the Spanish Atlantic provinces north and south of Portugal, thanking them for their reception of English ships, which had been "civilly receiv'd" in their ports, chiefly Cadiz and Salamanca, and there "assisted with all things necessary to those that perform long voyages" (W14, P19).[48] Parliament's correspondence during this encounter was apparently quite extensive. Another of Milton's letters, addressed to the governor of Tetuan, a Moroccan port on the Mediterranean, requests that in case of need he receive hospitably "our fleet or any part of it which is now on the coast of Portugall near to Lisbon awaiting for certain pirates & revolters of our owne nation" (W158, P18).

John IV responded aggressively in September, ordering English merchants in Portugal imprisoned and sending a fleet against Blake. The English destroyed the Portuguese in that encounter, whereupon Blake, his point made, raised the blockade and sailed for Cadiz to refit his fleet. Properly impressed, the king declared Rupert no longer welcome in Lisbon. The royalists put to sea in October and, sailing eastward

47. There is some question about the dating of W137. *Works* has 27 April, *Prose* a much earlier 25 January. Patrick, using internal evidence (5:501), clarifies matters by showing that the printed document is an earlier draft of one later revised and approved on 27 April (no copy of which is presently available). Milton included the draft in the transcript, a not uncommon occurrence, probably because he had not kept a copy of the later version. *Work's* 27 April, suggested by Masson (4:233), is entirely plausible as the date of the final approved version, as it appears to be a companion to W10, which is so dated. The two letters, one each to the kings of Spain and Portugal, both announce the dispatch of Popham's fleet to their waters and were very likely to have been composed together and approved at the same time.

Patrick's internal evidence is certainly of interest. During its first year in power Parliament could not make up its mind what to call itself. In W137 it is "the Supreme States of the whole nation in Parliament"; hence the draft, as we have it, had to be prepared before 30 January, the day it was finally decided that "Parliament of the Commonwealth of England" (*Parliamentum Republicae Angliae*) would be more fitting (*CSPD* 1:497).

48. As noted earlier, the Council of State's two letters to the governors of Galicia and Andalusia are identical, save for the names of the addressee in the heading and of the state in the body. Patrick draws attention to the fact that W14, as printed, names the governor of Andalusia in the heading but the province of Galicia in the body (5:527).

through the Straits of Gibraltar, attacked English ships in harbors along
the Malaga coast, enraging the Spanish. Blake finally hunted Rupert
down and soundly defeated him the following month, whereupon the
prince with the remnant of his fleet, two men-of-war and three prizes,
sought refuge in the Spanish port of Cartegena, on the Mediterranean
coast. Of the letters Milton translated into English he retained three
arising from this situation, all written in November 1650 by the king of
Spain, two of them addressed to the governor of Cartegena and one to
Blake (W155–57, P21–23). In his letters to the governor Philip IV orders that the prizes be seized and returned to their owners, that Rupert
be excluded from Spanish ports where he has "giv'n any offence," and
that the Parliamentary fleet be everywhere welcomed. Blake, who had
pursued the royalists to the harbor, demanded that the entire fleet of
five ships be surrendered to him; but the king in his reply agreed to
hand over only the prizes, making no mention of the men-of-war. Blake
repeated his demands but apparently to no avail.[49] The resourceful
Rupert somehow escaped and found refuge in Toulon, where he gathered another small fleet with which he sailed off to the West Indies.

Blake continued operations in Portuguese waters and in December
John IV sent an envoy, João de Guimarães, to England in an effort to
work out a peaceful settlement of their differences. Parliament's reception was decidedly cool. They placed the envoy under guard in Southampton and prepared a letter to him sternly requesting that he submit
his "Credential Letters from the King" so that they can determine by
what authority he had appeared on their shores (W16, P20). Parliament, better schooled now in such matters as a consequence of Richard
Bradshaw's experience in Hamburg, demanded that Guimarães identify
his diplomatic rank, "whether of Embassador, or Agent, or Envoy"
("*sive Legatis, sive Agentis, sive Internuntii*"). The letter, further, gave
prior notice of Parliament's position in any negotations; they would
demand "Reparations for the Damage which your King has done this
Republick, protecting our Enemy all the last Summer in his Harbors,
and prohibiting the *English* Fleet, then ready to assail Rebels and Fugitives, which our Admiral had pursu'd so far." In the end, Guimarães

---

49. George Fisher gave a detailed account of the incident to the Council of State in a
letter of 20 December 1650 (SP 94/43/47, 69–84). *Works* dates the three letters in November 1650; *Prose* has 7 January 1651, the day, it is explained, on which Milton delivered the translations. These letters are the only evidence I have been able to find that
Milton had Spanish. According to Patrick, on 24 December the ambassador submitted
them to Parliament *in Spanish*, and Milton translated them into English presumably from
that language (*Prose* 5:532, 534, 537).

It records yet another step, however, in the long process
toward a peace treaty between the two nations. A Por-
led by the Conde de Penaguião, returned to London in
again, but he had no more success than Guimarães. Two
Portuguese found Cromwell more receptive, and a treaty
whereupon according to protocol Cromwell released
a cordial letter to King John IV, dated 25 July 1654, in
"prayers to God for your Majesty's safety, the welfare
and the prosperous success of your Affairs" (W65,

were slow to ratify the treaty, however, as they were
English merchants in Lisbon freedom of worship and
raising the reparations agreed upon, eventually re-
In March 1656 Cromwell sent Philip Meadows, then
to Lisbon to spur ratification, which left Milton alone
some months. He was, therefore, responsible for a con-
of correspondence not customarily assigned him, into Portugal from July to October. Three of these, all
concern the treaty and an unfortunate incident that
On 11 May, Meadows was wounded in the
unsuccessful attempt on his life, not this time by royal-
he was reportedly the victim of a plot orchestrated by
who was seeking revenge for the earlier execution of
London.[60] Despite his injury, Meadows stayed on and
on 30 May. The first of the three letters deals with
Cromwell applauds the fact that "there is now a firm
between both Nations" but warns the king not to
of the document, which he states firmly "would be the
to annul the whole" (W76, P105). The next deals with
Meadows, regarding which Cromwell insists that "the
Encouragers of this Abominable Fact" be
and Encouragers of this Abominable Fact" be
justice (W77, P106). In the third, to John IV's chief
Conde d'Odemira, Cromwell thanks him for his part in
and urges that the "conceal'd Authors" of the attempted
"intended piece of Inhumanity," be sought out and pun-
P107).
returned home in July, to receive a handsome pension from

moirs of the Life of . . . Cromwell (1740), Francis Peck attributes the
wello Scripti (1654) to Milton; but there appears to be no basis for the
013; French 3:373; Works 18:638).
:238.

was spared the humiliation of reading such a letter, for it was not sent
and he was allowed to proceed to London. The question of his credentials was not left to die, however. In February the Council demanded to
see "the originals of the powers he has from the King," rather than the
copies Guimarães had presented, deemed unacceptable by Parliament.[50]
Finally satisfied, the Council allowed him an audience, one carefully
arranged, however, to reflect their displeasure. Sir Oliver Fleming was
specifically directed to attend the envoy "with three coaches," which
was something of an affront—he greeted the Swedish ambassador in
1655 with ten. Indeed, so intent was the Council to create the proper
atmosphere that they went into extraordinary detail in arranging the
reception, even to stipulating that Guimarães "shall be placed in a chair
near the middle of the table, which chair is to be without elbows."[51]

The negotiations that followed are of interest to Miltonists because
they give a brief glimpse of the duties he was called upon to perform as
Latin Secretary.[52] As has been noted, he was ordered to "attend" the
committee appointed to negotiate with Guimarães and evidently remained at that post until the envoy left in June. Milton's presence at
meetings with the Portuguese envoy was essential because the exchanges
between the two parties were conducted in Latin; and though some of
the members of the Portugal committee, like Sir Henry Vane and
Thomas Scott, were learned men, most were not and a translator in
attendance was necessary to the conduct of business. Certainly, all the

50. *CSPD* 3:36.

51. Ibid. 8.

52. Since SP 89/4, State Papers Foreign, Portugal, contains no records relating to the
negotiations, the account given here is documented chiefly from *CSPD* 3:36–211, which
is sufficient for our purposes, and SP 94/43, State Papers Foreign, Spain, supplemented by
reference to the Nalson papers. Those wishing a more detailed account may consult Patrick's summary (*Prose* 5:546–50) or the papers themselves (Bodleian, Nalson 10:6 and
17:123–60). There is a calendar of the collection in *Historical Manuscripts Commission.
Thirteenth Report. Appendix, Part I, The Manuscripts of his Grace the Duke of Portland,
Preserved at Welbeck Abbey.*

SP 89/4 contains material from only one incident in the Portuguese war. English merchants found it profitable to lease ships to Portugal's Brazil Company. On 20 May Blake
seized nine "English Brazil ships"; and though he released them in August, the action
precipitated litigation that dragged on until November of the following year (72–119).
The file also contains papers associated with the negotiations following the arrival of
another Portuguese envoy in August 1652, which resulted in a treaty finally signed on 10
July 1654 (121–52). Copies of the treaty, in English and Latin, are in SP 103/57, Treaty
Papers, Portugal (285–301) and the Portuguese ratification is in SP 108/386, Treaties,
Portugal. There is no evidence that Milton was involved in these later negotiations. His
only letter relevant to the treaty is one from Cromwell to the king, 25 July 1654, releasing
the ambassador for return to Portugal (W65, P67).

documents submitted to Guimarães had to be translated into Latin and those received from him into English before they could be considered by the committee. Young Joseph Frost, the son of the General Secretary to the Council, was "employed for such writing" as was needed, but it was Milton's task to do the actual translating.

And there was a great deal to do. Patrick, in his report on the negotiations based on the Nalson papers, identifies thirty-five documents exchanged, of which ten are accompanied by a Latin translation.[53] Patrick explains the origins of the collection: "Sometime before 1682, Dr. John Nalson, Rector of Doddington and Canon of Ely, took a selection of papers from the office of the Clerk of Parliament and was allowed to make copies of others that were in the Paper Office"; and it would appear that among the documents he "took" were those relating to the 1651 negotiations, for SP 89/4, State Papers Foreign, Portugal, is empty of any reference to Guimarães's embassy, while the record in the Nalson papers is virtually complete. Based on the Order Book entries specifically associating Milton with the Portuguese committee, Patrick is of the opinion that he was responsible for the bulk of the translations of both Latin and English documents required in the negotiations.[54]

Deliberations proceeded on two levels, the satisfaction of English demands and the peace treaty itself, although since the demands were never satisfied, there seems to have been little progress on the latter. There were six, as stipulated in Council's first letter of 12 February: (1) All Englishmen imprisoned in Portugal will be set free and (2) all impounded ships, money, and goods will be released. Further, (3) the killers of English merchants in Lisbon and those who attempted to burn an English ship there will be brought to justice. Parliament demanded (4) reparations amounting to £214,640 (later reduced to £180,000) to defray the cost of maintaining a fleet in Portuguese waters for a year. Finally, (5) all goods and (6) all ships seized by Rupert and still held in Portugal will be restored or reparations paid therefor. Council further stated that not until (1) and (2) had been fully implemented would there be a "cessation of arms and seizures," and then only for three months; nor could there be any discussion of a peace treaty until this was accomplished. The following day, 13 February, Guimarães submitted a paper of his own, demanding an end to hostilities, restoration of trade, and reparations amounting to £900,000. In essence, the negotiations consisted of numerous meetings and a seemingly interminable exchange of documents in which each side successively replied to the other's an-

53. Nalson 10:6 and 17:123–60; *Prose* 5:546–50.
54. *Prose* 5:474; *CSPD* 3:40, 203.

---

swer to their reply. On 10 M[...]
Council's demands and on 18 [...]
glish remained adamant, refusin[...]
until their own had been fully [...]
ing Council, backed by Blake's[...]
trade, Guimarães was forced i[...]
pear, not sufficiently to satisfy [...]

The English grew impatient. [...]
while agreeing to the English [...]
vague about specific measures t[...]
cil noted that his "last letter w[...]
tion"; on 11 April the Council [...]
peremptory insistence that he a[...]
April was considered satisfacto[...]
the English answer was ordered [...]
ered to him, this time with th[...]
days. On 25 April the Council [...]
positive and clear answer to th[...]
"settle both the manner and tin[...]
13 May they declared the Port[...]
Negotiations were promptly b[...]
was ordered to "repair to the [...]
arrangements for his departur[...]
month and in October Parliame[...]
who had relieved Blake, to "dis[...]
take as many of their ships and[...]

One must assume that Mil[...]
named in Council's orders; but [...]
once he had been appointed to [...]
record at least six letters from [...]
from February to May 1651; a[...]
papers include a great many m[...]

Milton was little involved in [...]
five years, during which the ea[...]

55. Nalson 17:127–30, 138–41; C[...]
56. *CSPD* 3:122, 141, 161, 164–65[...]
57. In contrast, during the Dutch ne[...]
designated to prepare certain document[...]
tors involved.
58. The six are those of 6 March, [...]
(*CSPD* 3:72, 128, 140, 164, 182, and [...]

---

that country. [...]
of negotiatio[...]
tuguese emba[...]
1652 to try [...]
years later th[...]
was finally si[...]
Penaguião wi[...]
which he offe[...]
of your King[...]
P67).

The Portug[...]
reluctant to g[...]
they had diff[...]
duced to £50[...]
Latin Secreta[...]
in that post f[...]
siderable amo[...]
cluding six le[...]
dated in Aug[...]
attended its [...]
hand during [...]
ists, however[...]
Penaguião hi[...]
his brother i[...]
secured ratifi[...]
the treaty its[...]
and settl'd P[...]
change a wor[...]
same thing a[...]
the attempt [...]
Authors, Ass[...]
brought to sp[...]
minister, the [...]
the ratificatio[...]
murder, that [...]
ished (W78, [...]

Meadows [...]

59. In his *Me[...]
*Panegyrici Crom[...]
claim (Parker 2:[...]
60. Gardiner [...]

Parliament of £100 per annum for ninety-nine years, which he later wisely requested be changed to a single payment of £1000.[61] It is not clear which hand was injured; but if it was the one he wrote with, it may have been some time before he could return to secretarial duties. Milton continued to be employed in exchanges with Portugal, writing another letter in July and two more in October,[62] after which he seems to have been replaced as the principal translator in correspondence with that country, as the sources credit him with only three more during the balance of his service.[63]

The conclusion that Milton was responsible for the translation of the numerous documents exchanged in the Portuguese negotiations raises an obvious question: Why were none of them included in the seventeenth-century sources? Patrick's suggestion that the clerks were too busy to make copies seems unsatisfactory; surely some of the working documents survived and, as we have seen, the transcriptions of Milton's papers contain many drafts which he included when there was no final version available. It is perhaps more reasonable to suggest that he had the letters on file but deliberately excluded them from the transcripts.

To understand why he may have done so, it will be of value to examine the question of his involvement in treaty negotiations during his tenure as Latin Secretary. Sources other than the early transcripts make it evident that the Council of State, having engaged him to perform duties "especially in connection with foreign affairs," employed him regularly in such negotiations, as an active participant in those with

61. Public Record Office Files, E403/2761/106.

62. W71, P103; W82, P114; W84, P115. W71 is a petition from Cromwell to John IV to recover funds owed English merchants by the Brazil Company. In W82 Cromwell appoints Thomas Maynard "Consul" to Portugal (*consulis munere*), the only occasion in Milton's letters in which an envoy is so designated. Cromwell had been content to call Meadows *internuntius* throughout his mission.

63. W121, P158; W133, P169; W149, P170. The headings of W133 and W149 are puzzling. The one is dated 23 February 1659, the other 19 April 1659; and both are addressed to John IV in all sources. But he had died in November 1656, and was succeeded by his son, Alphonso VI. The date of W133 seems correct, however, for in the letter Richard Cromwell congratulates the king on his victory over the Spanish, doubtless a reference to the defeat of Don Luis de Haro at Elvas in January 1659. In the Lünig collection, a copy of W133 (No. 332) is addressed properly to *Alphonso Portugalliae Regi*; and W121, which names neither king in the early manuscripts, is identified as addressed to Alphonso VI (Miller, "Milton's State Letters," 413–14). Richard also thanks him for payment of certain debts owed English merchants by the Brazil Company, perhaps the same debts for which his father had petitioned John IV in July 1656 (W71, P103). Seventeenth-century states were perpetually short of cash and the settlement of debt was a slow process. One wonders how many of the numerous petitions Milton wrote over the years were successful in securing payment.

Portugal and Oldenburg before his blindness, and thereafter, as we shall
see, as a translator of documents in those with Spain, the United
Netherlands, Denmark, and Sweden. Of the documents exchanged during the course of treaty negotiations, he had very few transcribed: none
from the Portuguese of 1651; and of those conducted the following
year, none from the Oldenburg embassy, only three from the Spanish,
and two from the Danish. One, the fragment of demands, is included
from the Dutch negotiations; but that document appears only in the
Literae, where it is an anomaly, suggesting that it was not a part of the
original manuscript. And again there were none associated with the
lengthy Swedish embassy of 1655–56.[64]

In brief, few of the documents prepared during negotiations with foreign powers, one of Milton's essential functions, were included in the
early sources, and none of the actual treaties. There is evidence that
Milton had in his possession copies of some of the treaties under deliberation at the time. When Daniel Skinner proposed to publish Milton's
letters after his death, the volume was to include copies of several
treaties, the Portuguese among them; and it is difficult to imagine where
Skinner could have secured such documents unless it was from the
poet's archives (see Appendix B). Milton did not have them transcribed,
however, both because they were much too long for the intended volume and because it was impolitic, and probably illegal, for a private
citizen to print such sensitive documents. If he did save the treaties, it is
a reasonable assumption that he saved the correspondence associated
with them as well, and that he decided to omit the letters leading up to
the agreement because they make little sense without access to the final
document. A glance at the counterdemand letter to the Dutch ambassadors (W167E, P38), which he did not include, will attest to just how
lengthy and how puzzling such exchanges can be. The endless debate
over precise wording and obscure issues would have made little sense to
readers, no matter how "fit though few"; and their content allowed
little latitude for the elegant and powerful Latin of letters such as those
on the Piedmont Massacre, the display of which was the express purpose of the contemplated volume. The Skinner MS, which was transcribed for publication, contains only one such letter, that of 30 January
1652 to the Spanish ambassador (W8, P33). Although it refers to the
treaty negotiations under way at the time, it was probably included

64. This count omits documents exchanged prior to the envoy's audience, nor does it
include his *pro forma* release letter, the *recreditif*. The letters cited are: from the Dutch
negotiations—W43a, P39; from the Danish—W29–30, P50–51; and from the Spanish—
W8, P33; W23, P40; and W28, P48.

because it is one of a group of strongly worded letters in the manuscript that protest the murder of Anthony Ascham.

Although the degree of Milton's participation in these various negotiations must remain a question, Patrick's arguments for the Portuguese papers (P26) and Leo Miller's for the Dutch are persuasive;[65] and grounds for the inclusion of the Spanish, Danish, and Swedish treaties will be offered later. Milton was engaged by the Council of State to assist in foreign affairs and certainly the making of treaties is an essential function of any such office.

Oldenburg

In the summer of 1651 Count Anthon Gunther of Oldenburg dispatched Hermann Mylius to London with the mission of securing from the English government a safeguard, or *salva-guardia*, an agreement assuring Oldenburg merchants protection from seizure of their goods and vessels by English warships, at the time engaged in undeclared naval wars with both France and Portugal. The County of Oldenburg, tucked into the northwest corner of Germany between the United Netherlands and the Hanseatic city of Bremen, was not an important state; but the Count had been able to pursue a policy of neutrality during the religious wars, which had wasted central Europe for three decades, and he was determined to maintain that policy in whatever conflicts England might become embroiled. The embassy of Hermann Mylius is of interest to historians because it was a long one, lasting almost seven months from August 1651 to March 1652, and because he kept a detailed diary, or *Tagebuch*, of his activities, contacts, and correspondence over that period. It is of interest to Miltonists because Mylius was limited in his contacts to those public servants with whom the Latin Secretary was most closely associated and because the Council of State assigned Milton the task of shepherding the Oldenburg Safeguard through the labyrinthine processes of the revolutionary government. Mylius, therefore, met with him frequently and was able to give a more intimate account of his function within that government than is available from any other source, at a critical time, moreover, in the poet's life, during the final fading of his eyesight.

For some reason, this relatively insignificant episode in the English

---

65. See Leo Miller, *John Milton's Writings in the Anglo-Dutch Negotiations 1651–1654*, and Chapter 2 herein.

Republic's diplomatic history is abundantly documented in British archives. The State Papers Foreign contain papers associated with Oldenburg embassies in three separate files for the German States and Denmark; and there are additional documents in the Tanner and Nalson MSS at the Bodleian Library.[66] There is another mine of papers in the Oldenburg archives; and Miltonists are much indebted to Leo Miller, who secured a copy of Mylius's diary from the *Niedersächsisches Staatsarchiv* in Oldenburg, laboriously translated the polyglot, often indecipherable script, and published significant abstracts of it in *John Milton and the Oldenburg Safeguard*.[67] Thanks to Miller we have an account of the indefatigable diplomat trying to make his small voice heard by the rulers of England, who were preoccupied at the time with matters more ponderous than the desires of a minor German county, men, moreover, unschooled in the intricate protocol of seventeenth-century diplomacy. Frustrated at every turn, he sought the aid of almost everyone of importance at Westminster and in his daily scribblings provided a vivid picture of the environment in which Milton worked.

At the end of an envoy's mission, it was customary for the host government to write a *recreditif*, a formal letter of thanks and authority for him to return home. Mylius's *recreditif*, addressed to the count, is in Milton's Latin (W39, P34). It is full of praise for the envoy and includes an apology for the long delay, regretting that "at the time the greatest and most weighty Affairs of the Republic were under Debate and serious Negotiation." It was Mylius's ill fortune, and a blessing for historians, that the months of his mission were a watershed for the English Republic, a time when it was able finally to subdue its enemies at home and look beyond its borders to consider its role in the European community. Mylius's small embassy—himself, a secretary, and a servant—was constantly overshadowed by "the greatest and most weighty Affairs of the Republick." He arrived in late August 1651, when Parliament was contending with the invasion of Charles II and his Scottish allies. The royalist threat was eliminated by Cromwell at the battle of Worcester on 3 September; and, after the victors indulged in a short period of celebration, the government immediately became embroiled in

66. For an analysis of the Public Record Office files, see Fallon, "Miltonic Documents," 93–99. The bulk of the papers are to be found in SP 81/54/54–86, State Papers Foreign, German States, and SP 103/24/218–54, Treaty Papers, German States. Additional documents are in SP 103/3/52–53, Treaty Papers, Denmark; Nalson MS 18; and Tanner MS 5.

67. I am particularly indebted to Miller's work for the historical material in this account. Quotations from Mylius's diary are from his book; those from the State Letters are from *Works*, which uses Phillips's translation.

a constitutional issue, the question of new elections for Parliament, which the Rump summarily resolved by voting itself new tenure, to the dissatisfaction of many.

On the heels of these events came the debate over the Navigation Act, and Mylius was overshadowed by the flood of diplomatic activity following its passage, as the great powers of Europe dispatched envoys to London anxious to recognize the new government, now secure after Worcester, and to ameliorate the worst effects of the Act. Mylius's mission was further delayed by the election and subsequent reorganization of a new Council of State, to include the establishment of a permanent body to deal with these additional international responsibilities, the Committee for Trade and Foreign Affairs. Indeed, the Council was not ready for its new role until mid-December, by which time a splendid embassy from the United Netherlands had arrived in London. Mylius looked on enviously as the Dutch ambassadors with an entourage of ninety retainers were greeted with elaborate ceremony, while he languished, virtually ignored, in his small chambers at Westminster.

Even these difficulties might have been overcome had not some members of Parliament raised serious questions about the leanings of the count. As a consequence of the Peace of Westphalia, Oldenburg enjoyed the privilege of collecting tolls on the Weser River, which meant that the count was empowered to impose duties on trade with one of England's more important trading partners, the city of Bremen, which shared the river with Oldenburg. Commercial interests, very strong in Parliament, took strong exception to the privilege and mounted a campaign against the count, accusing him of royalist sympathies, citing contacts with John Cochrane, who had been active against Richard Bradshaw in Hamburg, the earl of Montrose, and the Scot, William McDowell, Charles II's Resident at The Hague. The accusation of royalist sympathies was apparently false but the tolls were very real; and Mylius had to prepare a lengthy "*Memoriale*," defending the count's Weser rights while attempting to answer the slanders of those who feared their effect on trade with Bremen.[68]

Mylius was further hampered in his mission because he was denied contact with those in the seats of power. Early in his stay Parliament directed that, as he put it, "no foreigner may be granted the possibility of access to members of Parliament or the Council of State."[69] Whether this was a practical step taken to protect busy men from the hoards of petitioners who prowled the halls of Westminster, or an expression of

68. SP 103/24/225–26, 237–40.
69. Miller, *Oldenburg*, 69.

revolutionary xenophobia, it is difficult to say, perhaps equal measures
of both; but it had the effect of limiting Mylius to contact with the
members of the secretariat, chiefly Oliver Fleming, Gualter Frost, and
eventually John Milton.

What he sought specifically was approval of two documents, the safeguard itself, a formal agreement between Oldenburg and England, and
a "rescript," a letter in English serving notice of the agreement, one
which the count's merchants could show to the Republic's envoys and
ship captains who might detain them at sea. In the words of the final
document (W152, P35), it directed that "all and every one making
Warre under the Standards of our Common Wealth" shall respect an
Oldenburg merchant's "Rights and Privileges by Sea and Land, freely
and without any molestation to Live, Act, Sayle and Traffique" and
that all English "publique Ministers" abroad shall "bee helpfull unto
him according to the occasion of tyme and place offers with all read-
inesse and willingnesse."

Mylius's method was simplicity itself. He obtained a list of the important people in the English government and, either in person or writing,
made himself known to as many of them as possible. Aside from Frost
and Fleming, whom he pursued tirelessly, he at one time or another
wrote to Bulstrode Whitelocke, Thomas Challoner, Henry Neville, and
Henry Vane, while managing with the help of Fleming to confer with
William Lenthall, the Speaker of the House, and enlisting the aid of
Richard Bradshaw to plead his case with his uncle, John Bradshaw, the
President of Council. Cromwell, who was meticulous about consorting
with "foreigners," he could only see from afar. Mylius conversed with
the Spanish ambassador, Alphonso de Cardenas, the Swedish envoys
Peter Spiering and Benjamin Bonell, the Dutch Gerard Schaep, and Leo
ab Aitzema, the representative of the Hanse Towns; and he gossiped
with each about the others.[70] Of particular interest are his encounters
with a number of lesser figures who hovered about the edge of affairs,
Samuel Hartlib, Georg Weckherlin, Theodore Haak, Hugh Peters, and
most especially, John Dury, who held an official position as Librarian
of St. James Palace but performed important functions that afforded
him access to those in power. Before Milton took over, Dury fostered
Mylius's cause and guided him through the maze that was the revolutionary government.

70. Mylius's energy and persistence may be illustrated by his activities on a representative day, 5 February. Ever an early riser, he was at Hugh Peters's door by 6 A.M., just as
the minister was waking; he then went to confer with Fleming, next to see Milton, and
finally received Richard Bradshaw for further discussions (ibid. 168–69).

From Georg Weckherlin, who had been Latin Secretary under the
monarchy, Mylius learned that Milton now held the post and that he
was out of town, some *"vier meilen von hinnen,"* as he had it in his
diary.[71] The German *meile* is approximately four kilometers, the distance a man can walk in an hour, which suggests that Milton had not
traveled far, although how long he had been absent and for what purpose are unknown. Mylius's affair took a small step forward in mid-
October, when he learned of Milton's return to Westminster. Mylius
promptly wrote to him and then saw him for the first time on the occasion of his official reception by Parliament. The Council of State appointed a committee headed by Bulstrode Whitelocke, Keeper of the
Great Seal, to represent Parliament in receiving Mylius's *creditif*, or letter of credential, in which the count officially designated him as his
envoy to the English government.[72] The audience was conducted in
Latin, and Milton stood behind the Parliamentary representatives,
translating Mylius's remarks into English for them.

The audience took place on 20 October, almost two months after
Mylius's arrival in London, but now he was at least officially authorized to pursue his mission. It was his practice to press draft copies of
the safeguard and rescript into the hands of everyone he encountered.
On 25 October he sent them to Milton, who after discussing the papers
with Bradshaw, returned them two weeks later, noting that he had
"gone through" the text and assuring the envoy that "the matter is
being put in motion by those to whom it has been entrusted," which
apparently did not as yet include himself. Mylius, not to be deterred,
promptly sent them back by return messenger. In his diary Mylius noted
that it was not to his "liking that the matter had been taken out of
[Milton's] hands," though there is no evidence to this point that the
poet had yet been officially appointed to deal with "the matter."[73]

Mylius's efforts in the fall of 1651 proved fruitless. Indeed, he was
little more advanced by the end of December than he had been at the
beginning of September. He wrote a flood of letters and knocked on the
door of everyone in Westminster who he thought might conceivably
further his cause, pleading, pleading, pleading with all that they *get on
with it*, but to no avail. After his audience in mid-October he pressed
Milton for an interview and indeed the Secretary made three appointments to see him, on 25 and 27 October and 7 November, and canceled
all of them, pleading the pressure of business for the Council of State

71. Ibid. 26.
72. Ibid. 26–27, 225–27; SP 81/54/16–17.
73. *Prose* 4:832; Miller, *Oldenburg*, 85–86.

and an unspecified illness. Milton was not being impolite; these were busy days for the Council, and he was probably behind in his work because of his absence. More to the point, he had received no instructions from his superiors to communicate with Mylius and was doubtless restrained by Parliament's order restricting contact between government officials and "foreigners."

Those instructions finally came on 31 December. The Order Books of the Council for that date record the appointment of a committee "to give audience unto the publique Ministers sent from the Duke of Tuscanie and Count of Oldenburgh"; and the same day brought a letter from Milton.[74] It was in fact a response to one he had received from the envoy on 17 December—Mylius had actually not heard from Milton since 24 November. In it the Secretary makes his excuses: "First then, know that ill health, which is almost my perpetual enemy, caused delay; next, for the sake of my health, came a necessary and sudden move to another house, which I had chance to begin on that very day on which your letter was brought to me."[75] Milton was, perhaps, not entirely candid here. The move to new quarters had been proposed as early as the previous June and so may not have been exactly "sudden"; nor may it have been made for reasons of "health," rather because Parliament finally won out in the tug-of-war with the Council for choice government quarters. In a letter of apology for a long silence, such excuses came readily to mind.

At any rate, as Fleming informed Mylius, on the evening of 2 January the Council appointed Milton to see the Oldenburg Safeguard through to its final approval. First, the document had to be revised, chiefly in the interest of brevity; as Milton wrote Mylius, "Certain things I found it necessary to insert, others I condensed; I hardly believe the Council wishes it longer."[76] Then the companion rescript had to be redone and shown to the envoy for his approval. Finally, the two documents were presented to the Council, where they encountered further delays, as opponents continued to raise questions about the Weser tolls and the count's suspected royalist leanings. It was not until 5 February that Oldenburg's supporters felt it safe to bring the matter to a vote, whereupon the Council committed an egregious blunder that almost brought Mylius's five-month vigil to a disappointing end.

On that day, the Council passed the rescript but ignored the more

---

74. SP 25/66/142. The Tuscan envoy appeared at the appointed time; but Mylius did not. No explanation is given for his absence; perhaps the meeting was simply canceled.

75. *Prose* 4:835; Miller, *Oldenburg*, 124.

76. *Prose* 4:838; Miller, *Oldenburg*, 131–33, 257–58.

important safeguard entirely, and then seemed to have misplaced Milton's draft of the latter document. How this happened it is difficult to say; Mylius suspected deception on the part of the count's enemies. Milton was obviously not present at the meeting to prevent the error; and when Mylius inquired about it later, the only satisfaction the Secretary could give him was that "most of them seemed to not have paid enough attention, rather than to have been unwilling to concede what you ask, for they thought that they had granted in that document whatever you wished." In speaking with Mylius he attempted to excuse the blunder by characterizing the Council members in frequently quoted remarks: "Those men were mechanics, soldiers, home-grown, strong and bold enough, in public political affairs mostly inexperienced, of whom the most powerful part of the Commonwealth consisted." Mylius reported the Secretary's advice not to "blame the Commonwealth, nor the sounder men; [for] among the forty persons who were in the Council, not more than three or four had ever been out of England."[77] These remarks have on occasion been cited as evidence of Milton's disrespect for the political leaders he served, especially the soldiers among them; but it is clear from the context that he was apologizing for their mistake by calling attention specifically to their lack of experience *in foreign affairs*, not their fitness to govern England. The resourceful Mylius set about diligently to repair the damage. He prepared an entirely new document, combining the provisions of the safeguard and the rescript into one, and resubmitted it to Council. This is the agreement that Parliament finally approved on 17 February, marking a successful end to his long and frustrating ordeal.

Milton's involvement with the Oldenburg Safeguard may not have ended with the departure of Mylius, however. An additional reason for the long delay was that, until the count of Oldenburg raised the issue, the inexperienced members of the Council of State had not been asked to accede to such an agreement and had to educate themselves concerning its implications. We may conclude from the bungling of 5 February, when they approved the wrong document, that some never did come to understand it. Once they had finally arrived at acceptable wording, it appears that Mylius's, and Milton's, safeguard served as a model for similar agreements with other states.[78] Some time later, for

---

77. *Prose* 4:844; Miller, *Oldenburg*, 172.
78. There are numerous copies of the document, in Latin and English, at various stages of its development. Patrick gives a detailed list of the manuscripts (*Prose* 5:576), as does Miller (*Oldenburg* 239–43), to which now may be added SP 103/24/54–55, 170, 216–17. Shawcross reports on additional copies in the Oldenburg and Schleswig-Holstein archives (*Bibliography* 43–46).

example, a virtually identical document was approved for the duke of Holstein.[79]

In 1653, after the dismissal of the Rump and the seating of the Nominated Assembly, the count of Oldenburg, fearing that the old agreement might no longer be valid, dispatched another embassy, consisting this time of two men, Friedrich Wolzogen and Christopher Gryphiander, with the mission of securing a safeguard from the new government; and they carried with them a request that one be issued to Prince Johan of Anhalt-Zerbst.[80] One wonders how many copies of Milton's safeguard may be found in the surviving archives of other minor German states.

The London stay of the second Oldenburg embassy was no less protracted than the first, delayed by some of the same factors that frustrated Mylius, a government reorganization and English preoccupation with the Dutch. Cromwell, who became Lord Protector in mid-December 1653, received Wolzogen and Gryphiander formally two months later, on 14 February; but in the week following a large embassy from the United Netherlands arrived to negotiate a peace treaty ending the Anglo-Dutch War, and Oldenburg envoys once again found themselves overshadowed by larger events. In May the count sent his son, Anton von Aldenburg, to London with a handsome gift of horses for Cromwell, with the thought perhaps of moving matters along; but it was not until June that the safeguard was finally signed.[81] Milton was responsible for two of Cromwell's letters to the count associated with the negotiations, both dated 29 June. The first confirmed anew "the Letters of safe Conduct lately granted your Lordship by the Parlament" and served as a *recreditif* for the envoys (W44, P64); the second acknowledged the visit of the young Baron Anton and expressed gratitude for the gift (W45, P65).[82] Though there is no evidence that Milton was involved in the later negotiations, the 1654 safeguard was little changed from the one he had prepared two years earlier; and the two letters

79. For the later history of this document see Fallon, "Miltonic Documents," 98–99, and Miller, *Oldenburg*, 275. Copies of the Holstein Safeguard are to be found in SP 103/24/221–22; SP 103/3/52–53; Nalson MS 18:172; and Rawlinson MS A 5:192–94. Shawcross reports on another copy in the Schleswig-Holstein archives (*Bibliography* 45–46). It is printed in Thurloe 1:385–86.

80. Miller, *Oldenburg*, 283.

81. According the Miller, Oldenburg's son was born out of wedlock and the count gave him the title, Baron von Aldenburg (*Oldenburg* 12, 216). One of the horses later threw Cromwell, to his discomfort and the count's dismay. Documents pertinent to the 1654 embassy are in SP 81/54/80–81 and SP 103/24/284–85, 423.

82. The count's letter introducing his son, in Latin, is in SP 81/54/82–85.

serve to associate him with the embassy. The most that can be assumed, however, is that he was consulted in the affair.[83]

Mylius's diary, thus, offers an intimate picture of the internal dynamics of the revolutionary government at a critical juncture in its history. It must be said that up to this time the record of the inexperienced leaders of the Republic in international affairs had been anything but brilliant. The 1651 peace negotiations with Portugal had failed, and the naval war with that nation continued. The St. John–Strickland embassy to the United Netherlands that same year had ended in a humiliating rebuff. Dorislaus had been murdered in Holland and Ascham in Spain; and Bradshaw went in fear of his life in Hamburg. With their domestic enemies finally subdued, however, England's new leaders set out confidently to seek their place among the nations of Europe; and it must have come as a disappointment to discover that one of the most learned, experienced, and respected of their public servants, one whom they had engaged to act "especially in foreign affairs," was all but blind.

> But cloud instead, and ever-during dark
> Surrounds me, from the cheerful ways of men
> Cut off.
>
> (PL 3:45–47)

Mylius's account of his encounters with Milton is frustratingly sketchy about the poet's affliction.[84] In his report on the audience of 20 October he makes no mention of it, perhaps because it was not apparent. The first allusion in the diary is an entry on 24 November, when Mylius reports that Milton has once more expressed regret for not meeting with him because "headache and pain in his eyes made it impossible." The next, in early December, is a remark by Johan Oste, secretary to the Dutch legation, that "Milton is almost blind, so the others were taking on all the business." In his reply to Milton's letter of 31 December, in which the poet had referred vaguely to his "ill health," Mylius offered sympathy, hearing that he suffered "from headache and eye inflammation"; and at their first meeting, on 3 January, he ex-

83. Miller suggests that Theodore Haak performed the diplomatic functions that the poet had for Mylius two years earlier (*Oldenburg* 283).

84. In his diary Mylius mentions meetings on 3, 7, 8, 20, and 28 January; 5, 6, 9, 10, 12, 16, and 24 February; and at his farewell audience on 2 March. The envoy is so meticulous in recording his contacts that we can reasonably assume there were no others.

tended "wishes for recovery of his health, since he suffers from head-ache and suffusion of the eyes." The only other mention is at their parting in March, by which time, Mylius observes, Milton "is wholly deprived of his sight."[85]

Milton's references are also few, none of them specific. Though the plea of "ill health" may in some instances have been a politic excuse for the delays in effecting Mylius's business, it is evident that the affliction was interfering with his ability to carry out his duties. In his letter of 7 November, he regrets not being able to meet with the envoy, offering the pressure of duties and "ill health" as reasons. The next reference, again only to "ill health," appears in the 31 December letter, though he adds that during the previous month "being ill, I was often absent from the Council." On 13 February he writes that he missed the previous day's Council meeting, "detained by yesterday's rain." And that is all we have (4:832, 835, and 848).

Milton's condition seems to have curtailed his attendance at Council meetings. He missed several in December, apparently; he was surely not at the 5 February meeting, where his advice could have prevented Council from voting on the wrong document; and rain kept him home on 13 February. On the other hand, in his frequent communications with Mylius in January and February he specifically mentions atten-dance at Council sessions on five separate occasions and describes the events of two others in such detail as to strongly suggest his presence, this for meetings on the Oldenburg issue alone. There were surely more at a time when he was also engaged in the Tuscan letter, the Dutch negotiations, and the printing of the Racovian Catechism.[86] In his 20 January letter to Mylius he opens with "Yesterday I was present as usual in the Council." Again, during several encounters with Milton, Mylius gives the impression that the Secretary is going about business unhampered by his affliction. On 8 January, for example, he conferred with Milton on the wording of the safeguard and observed that "in my presence he made notes in the margin." The following day he was vis-ited by Milton, who, on his way to London on other business, dropped off a copy of the rescript for approval. On another visit Mylius noted that as he left a member of the Dutch embassy arrived to confer. As late as 24 February the two arranged to meet in St. James Park; but Mylius fails to mention whether Milton needed assistance on that occasion, this

85. Miller, *Oldenburg*, 93, 97, 125, and 214.
86. *Prose* 4:841. Milton referred to his presence in Council on 31 December; 8 and 19 January; and 10 and 23 February; and he reported on the meetings of 3 and 7 January.

but a week before the envoy reported that the poet was "wholly deprived of his sight."[87]

Only one letter arising from the 1652 Oldenburg embassy appears in the seventeenth-century sources, the *recreditif*; and in Mylius's *Tagebuch* there is no evidence that there were others approved for dispatch to either the envoy or the count. The safeguard, which we may be sure was Milton's, is absent, although so many versions of it survive that we may also be sure he had a copy among his papers. He did not have it transcribed probably for the same reasons he omitted the treaties he worked on: it was not a letter but an official state document recording an international agreement. In Daniel Skinner's prospectus he promised to publish "illustrative documents" from Germany and perhaps the safeguard was among them (see Appendix B). Were it not for the Mylius papers, this one letter might be overlooked as yet another routine document of the type Milton was called upon so frequently to prepare.[88] We would have no inkling of the rich and varied events that led to its delivery. One wonders how much more of the bright tapestry of history was open to Milton's imagination, now cast in shadow for us by the curtain of time.[89]

The Mylius papers offer a glimpse of the English Republic's Secretary for Foreign Languages at work. The picture that emerges is a man of energy, devotion, skill, and patience. Of his activities in 1651 there is little knowledge. His absence in the summer and early fall remains unexplained; we know only that in December his move to Petty France preoccupied him for a time, and that he was subject to an unspecified illness, probably a consequence of his eye affliction or, as Miller suggests, his experiments with medication. In the months between Mylius had little contact with him. Once the safeguard was entrusted to Milton's care, however, he is seen heavily engaged in the affairs of his nation. He moved constantly between Council chambers, his home, and the city of London, performing duties that left him little time for leisure, fully occupied with writing, revising, conferring, and advising, always it seems with more to do than the hours allowed. After almost three years

87. Miller, *Oldenburg*, 134, 145–46, 214.

88. Other *recreditifs* are W44, P64; W67, P95; W72, P104; and W104, P138.

89. One would like to know more, for example, about Cromwell's appeal to the duke of Venice on the plight of Thomas Gallilee, held captive by the Turks for five years (W103, P137). In the case of another single letter, that of 14 January 1653 to the duke of Tuscany (W37, P60), happily there are abundant sources, and the tale can be told (see Chapter 2 herein).

in service, he knew his way about the halls of Westminster and spoke personally with Bradshaw, Whitelocke, Neville, Challoner, Frost, and Fleming, to name only those mentioned by Mylius's records. He was well acquainted with what Council would and would not do and advised Mylius accordingly. His remarks about the English leading politicians, the "mechanics" and "soldiers" of the Council of State, reveal a sympathetic understanding of the limitations of his superiors; and he worked patiently within those limitations, adjusting to the slow, laborious processes of republican government.

On the other hand, he was by no means a central figure in that government. There are significant gaps in his meetings with Mylius, at a time when the indefatigable envoy was in almost daily contact with Frost and Fleming, who were obviously the mainstays of the secretariat. By the end of February Milton's efforts on behalf of the Oldenburg Safeguard had much diminished. He saw Mylius but once between 16 February and his farewell audience on 2 March and mentioned attendance at Council only on the twenty-third. When they did communicate, the Secretary often had to admit to ignorance of the safeguard's status, as on 13, 16, and 21 February. It may have been that he was at work on the lengthy documents associated with the Dutch negotiations but it is clear that his fading eyesight was limiting him more and more to such work as he could perform at home.[90]

What is perhaps most impressive is Milton's determination to remain useful despite his growing affliction. There is indeed no mention of it by Milton or Mylius between the envoy's courteous expression of sympathy on 3 January and his farewell audience two months later; and nowhere does Mylius give so much as a hint of impatience that his affairs are being neglected because of Milton's limitations, unlike the Swedish ambassador, Christer Bonde, who complained some years later that

90. From time to time in *John Milton and the Oldenburg Safeguard* Miller pauses to comment on Milton's role in government (see, especially, 75, 259–61, and 297–303), wherein he is sternly critical of the "proliferation of misconceptions as to Milton's status and activities in his secretaryship" (297). He rejects Patrick's frequent assertion that Milton "composed" letters and takes to task the "misguided effort to magnify his role" (302). It is never quite clear who these magnifiers are but I suspect that I am among the more misguided of them, for his arguments challenge, though without attribution, conclusions I arrived at in "Filling the Gaps" and "Miltonic Documents." There is no need to rehearse the issues here; those interested may want to consult my review of Miller's book in *Renaissance Quarterly*. I am most grateful for the debate, which is in essence an honest disagreement over the interpretation of isolated words and phrases. Scholars must extrapolate from frustratingly ambiguous evidence in these matters, and Miller's arguments serve as a useful caution against overstating the case.

only the "blind Miltonius" was available for translations. Milton clearly was determined to remain in his post despite his loss of sight and worked valiantly to demonstrate his continued value to the government he served.

2

THE COMMONWEALTH
After the Darkness

> *Yet I argue not*
> *Against heav'n's hand or will, nor bate a jot*
> *Of heart or hope; but still bear up and steer*
> *Right onward.*
>
> *(Sonnet 22)*

It is ironic that just as the English Republic had set its domestic house in order and was emerging as a principal player on the European stage, when diplomats were flocking to London, eager to recognize the newly confident government, when England stood most in need of public servants skilled in the art of diplomacy, it was discovered that their widely respected Secretary for Foreign Languages, whose three years' experience in his post marked him as knowledgeable and dependable "in the area of foreign affairs," had gone blind. John Milton, however, was determined not to retire from his public office, which might be expected of one so afflicted, but to remain in the service of a cause to which he was devoted; and he strove to demonstrate to his superiors that he could continue to be useful. Even as he set about to do so, however, fate had further blows for him. In May 1652, his daughter, Deborah, was born—and his wife, Mary, died. The following month his year-old son, John, was lost to him as well.

Sympathetic scholars have suggested that this triple blow reduced

Milton to a state of despair; that illness, grief, and the fading of his
eyesight rendered him incapable of performing his duties; and that the
gaps in the chronology of the letters attributed to him in 1651 and 1652
confirm what seems a perfectly human response to these tragedies. Masson remarks on the paucity of reference to Milton in the Order Books
of the Council of State for the period July–November 1651 and suggests that illness and his despair over encroaching blindness might explain the inactivity. Patrick notes that there is no evidence to indicate
Milton's involvement in the preparation of the Dutch Declaration of
July 1652 and suggests that his illness, grief over the loss of his wife and
son, and the failure of his sight probably prevented his participation.[1]

Masson did not have the benefit of the insight provided by Mylius's
Tagebuch, from which we learn that from the middle of October on, at
least, Milton was very busy indeed.[2] Further, according to the early
manuscripts, he was responsible for eleven letters during the weeks
from mid-January to mid-April 1652; and the *Calendar* records several
more that Council ordered him to prepare in connection with the Dutch
negotiations. The last of these orders came on 15 April, and the manuscripts include only one routine letter, of 8 May, between that date and
29 June. A compassionate Council may well have relieved him of some
responsibilities in late April, once John Thurloe had assumed duties as
their General Secretary; but there is other evidence, to be developed
below, to indicate that the poet was not entirely idle during May and
June.

John Milton was a dedicated public servant in an office he considered
important to his vision of the destiny of the English people, and he was
made of sterner stuff than is often credited to him. The trying spring of
1652 and the equally challenging summer of 1660 did much to shape
the character and enrich the imagination of the poet of *Paradise Lost*;
and whereas the latter period is outside our scope, it may be said of the
earlier that his response was a mark of his nature. With the loss of his
wife and son, he was forced to find a new way of living, and with the
loss of his sight, a new way of working. In response to both, he dismissed the impulse to withdraw into the black hole of self, turning
rather, as might any of us, to the therapy of work between vigils of dark
grief by a sickroom door. He reaffirmed his commitment to action in
this world and found a way, remarkable in itself, to remain effective in
his office. Employing his prodigious memory, he digested documents
read to him, revised them as needed, and translated them by dictation

1. Masson 4:323; *Prose* 5:620–21.
2. Miller, *Oldenburg*, 71–121.

into another language, thereby honing skills that later served him well in the collation of the *Christian Doctrine* and the composition of his great epics.

The month of March 1652 was a watershed in the Council's secretariat, for they had to adjust not only to the blindness of their Latin Secretary but to an even more troublesome event, the death of Gualter Frost, their General Secretary. The vacancy was soon filled by John Thurloe. At thirty-six, he was relatively young, eight years Milton's junior, and his experience in government was quite limited. He had an influential patron, however, in Oliver St. John, the Commonwealth's Chief Justice of Common Pleas and member of Council, who had employed Thurloe in his only foreign mission up to the time of his appointment, the abortive embassy to The Hague in March–June 1651. In the midst of those negotiations he was ordered to return to London and report to the Council on the progress of the embassy, and his narrative of events apparently left a very favorable impression on the members. When Council approved his appointment on 30 March 1652, they may not have realized how well they had chosen.[3]

Thurloe received permission to finish some private business in the country, and upon his return at the end of April, he threw himself into his tasks.[4] The minutes of both the Council and the Committee for Foreign Affairs attest to his growing status as an indispensible man. With the passage of time he assumed new responsibilities, in July 1653 as director of intelligence and later as Postmaster-General. Early in the Protectorate Cromwell appointed him Secretary of State, a position that made him the Lord Protector's most trusted advisor in foreign affairs.

Of Milton's official position in the English government, there is no question—he was *the* Secretary for Foreign Languages. After his sight failed, both he and his superiors had to reevaluate his position to determine just what he could and could not do. The Council's first response to Milton's blindness was to call out of retirement old Georg Weckherlin, his predecessor as Latin Secretary, and, on 11 March, appoint him "assistant secretary to the Committee for Foreign Affairs."[5] Weckherlin had had long experience in government. He first entered the royal service in 1625, as Under-Secretary for the German, Latin, and French

---

3. Thurloe was relieved of his predecessor's responsibility as treasurer of the Council's contingency fund, a function assigned to Gualter Frost, Jr.

4. *CSPD* 4:213, 223.

5. Ibid. 175. The wording of the order is ambiguous. He may have been "assistant secretary" to the Council, performing duties for the committee, or "assistant" to the unnamed secretary of the committee.

Tongues; and on occasion he served as personal aide to Charles I, accompanying him on the invasion of Scotland in 1639, for example, while the Secretary of State, Edward Nicholas, remained in London. In 1642, Charles offered him the position of Secretary for the Latin Tongue but he declined and placed himself at the disposal of the Parliament, who two years later appointed him secretary to the Committee for Both Kingdoms, the body delegated to direct the war. Prior to Pride's Purge he served as secretary to the Long Parliament's Council of State, where he performed duties of the type that later fell to John Thurloe under the Protectorate.[6] He corresponded with English envoys abroad, among them William Strickland and Isaac Dorislaus in The Hague, René Augier in Paris, and Theodore Haak in Scandinavia, collecting intelligence and keeping them informed of events in England. He composed letters for the Council, took dictation, translated documents in Latin, French, and German, and at times acted as licenser.[7] He was dismissed in 1649 perhaps because of his association with the Parliament purged by Colonel Pride, although it may well have been simply because of his age.

At the time of his appointment, three years almost to the day after Milton had replaced him, Weckherlin was sixty-eight and in ill health; and despite his experience, it is questionable how active he was in the office.[8] It appears that Thurloe soon found it necessary to take over some of Weckherlin's responsibilities. Beginning in July, the minutes of the Committee for Foreign Affairs reflect Thurloe's presence at meetings, where he was directed to prepare correspondence "according to ye Debate now had," orders which he could only have carried out had he been present to hear "ye Debate." Matters are clarified somewhat by an entry in the Order Books for 1 December, which formalized an arrangement that had apparently been in effect for some time. Thurloe assumed whatever duties Weckherlin had been performing for the committee. His salary was increased by £200, which is what Weckherlin had been

6. In 1648, Isaac Dorislaus, Parliament's envoy to The Hague, wrote frequently to Weckherlin, addressing him as "*Secretaire du Conseil d'Estat du Parliament d'Angleterre*" (Trumbull MS, vol. 22).

7. I am endebted to Mr. Hilton Kelliher of the Student's Manuscript Room in the British Library for his courtesy in allowing me access to the Trumbull papers, which he is presently cataloguing. The information on Weckherlin comes from these documents, as yet unnumbered, and from Peter Beal's catalogue for Southby's, *The Trumbull Papers, Property of the Most Honorable Marquess of Downshire*, 1989, 91–125.

8. On 7 April 1652 the Council ordered that a letter to the king of Denmark be translated by Weckherlin (*CSPD* 4:212) but the task fell to Milton (W24, P41).

earning, and he was appointed "Clerk to the Council and the Committee for Foreign Affairs."[9]

These entries suggest that Milton may well have served as secretary to the Committee for Foreign Affairs from the time of its first sitting in December 1651 until his blindness rendered him incapable of doing so, and that Weckherlin was engaged in March to fill the vacancy. He, in turn, was found inadequate to the task, and Thurloe took over with the old man as assistant, an arrangement that was formalized by the order of 1 December. Thereafter, Weckherlin performed what tasks his health permitted, but apparently in the capacity of Milton's assistant. When he died the following February, Milton wrote to John Bradshaw, then president of the Council, recommending Andrew Marvell as his replacement, "If upon the death of Mr. [Weckherlin], the Councell shall thinke that I shall need any assistant in the performance of my place."[10]

During the first year of his tenure, the only appointed officials Thurloe had to assist him in foreign affairs were Milton and Weckherlin, although he certainly made use of others. With the death of the latter in February 1653, Council passed over Milton's recommendation of Marvell and sometime that summer chose instead young Philip Meadows as his "assistant." In October, Meadows, "now employed as Latin translator," was promoted "to assist Thurloe in foreign affairs" with a handsome increase in salary.[11]

Thus Milton was relieved of many of the duties he had performed when he had his sight. He relinquished whatever role he had with the Committee for Foreign Affairs to Weckherlin; and in that same letter recommending Marvell he acknowledged that he "was no longer fit" for "attendance at conferences with Ambassadors." His activities were limited to the preparation of official documents, but he was no less busy in his office. The early manuscripts and the *Calendar* offer evidence that he became intimately involved in the treaty negotiations that occupied so much of the Council's attention in 1652 and 1653.

9. As Masson notes, the original wording of the order, directing Thurloe to perform "what hath formerly been done by Mr. Weckherlin," was blotted over and his appointment as "Clerk to the Council and the Committee for Foreign Affairs" substituted (4:450–51).

10. *Works* 12:329–30; *Prose* 4:859–60; SP 18/33/75.

11. *CSPD* 6:205–6. His salary was doubled from £100 to £200 and to earn it he was apparently to assist Thurloe as clerk to the Committee for Foreign Affairs. On 18 October, the day after his appointment, the committee was ordered to meet, with "Mr. Meadows to attend them." In the same order, William Jessop was appointed "to assist Mr. Thurloe in the despatch of foreign affairs."

The most significant event on the international scene during those years was England's war with the United Netherlands, declared in July 1652. Many Englishmen, Cromwell and, it would appear, Milton among them, were ambivalent about the conflict, buoyed, on the one hand, by the demonstration of strength, skill, and national purpose in a series of decisive victories over the Dutch fleet, but troubled by a war being waged against a traditional friend and ally, a people who like themselves had ousted their monarchy and professed a strong Protestant faith. Although the principal theater of operations was the Channel and nearby North Sea waters, the war eventually spread to the Mediterranean and Scandinavia, where Denmark joined the Dutch in opposing England.

Relations with the French remained essentially hostile, exacerbated by the hospitality shown the English royal family in Paris and by the navy of the Republic, which continued to prey on French shipping. The first sign of a diplomatic thaw was the arrival in December 1652 of Antoine de Bordeaux as Louis XIV's envoy to London. He was received with due ceremony, but only after an indignant Parliament had required him to resubmit his credentials, in which the king had addressed that body, not as *Parlement*, but perhaps too familiarly for their taste, as *"les Gens du Parlement."*[12]

> Thence to the gates cast round thine eye, and see
> What conflux issuing forth or entering in,
> Praetors, Proconsuls to their Provinces
> Hasting or on return, in robes of State;
>
> . . . .
>
> Or Embassies from Regions far remote
> In various habits on the *Appian* road.
>
> (PL 4:61–68)

The year 1652 was a crowded one in London. Hermann Mylius left in March, having been there for seven months. A large Dutch embassy had arrived the previous December and stayed until July. The Danish ambassadors were in residence from May until November, another Portuguese envoy arrived in August, and Bordeaux in December. The Spanish ambassador was engaged in negotiations until the establishment of the Protectorate. And this is only to mention those nations seeking treaties with England, aside from whom the Council gave audience to

12. Masson 4:382.

newly arrived envoys from Sweden, Venice, Holstein, the Hanseatic League, Switzerland, and a parade of others.[13]

The following year, while all of this diplomatic activity was under way, the Republic endured a period of dramatic transition. During 1653, England was ruled by four different executive bodies. Cromwell dismissed the Rump Parliament on 20 April and appointed an interim Council of State, or "Committee of Thirteen" as it was called, composed chiefly of army officers. This body gave way in July to the Nominated Assembly, or as it has come to be known, the "Barebones" or "Little" Parliament; and they established their own Council of State. This body dissolved itself on 16 December, making way for the establishment of the Protectorate, which constituted the government of England for the next five years. During this turmoil the secretariat remained intact, serving each executive body in turn, pursuing negotiations, composing letters, preparing draft treaties, and performing all of the routine duties of a bureaucracy while waiting for the politicians to sort out their differences.

The United Netherlands

> *League with you I seek,*
> *And mutual amity so strait, so close,*
> *That I with you must dwell, or you with me*
> *Henceforth.*
>
> *(PL 4:375–78)*

The relationship between the English Republic and the United Netherlands was a central concern of English foreign policy throughout the Interregnum.[14] The new government in Westminster held the sturdy Dutch in high esteem because of their devotion to the Reformed Religion and their long struggle for freedom against Spain. Queen Elizabeth had committed English forces on the Continent to support the Dutch, and in later years Holland had sheltered persecuted Puritans, most notably those who eventually emigrated to the New World to establish the

13. For a summary of diplomatic activity in London during 1652–53, see Masson 4:377–83.

14. The nation is often referred to in correspondence as the United Provinces. Holland was but one of the seven so united, though it was the largest and most prosperous. SP 84 is labeled "State Papers Foreign, Holland."

Massachusetts Bay Colony. So close were the two nations in Elizabeth's time that there was even talk of a political union between them, a vision still very much alive in the mid-seventeenth century and, indeed, one destined to become a reality in 1688, although not in the form earlier proposed. Another source of affinity was the compatible form of the Dutch government. With the death of Prince William II in October 1650, the Dutch had managed to set aside the House of Orange, which had strong ties with the Stuarts, and establish a republican form of government, directed by an executive body, the States General, on which each of the seven provinces held seats.

However many and strong the ties binding the two countries, there was one factor that all but canceled them out—the Dutch monopoly over European trade. In the early years of the Republic the new leaders found that, despite the religious and political sympathies between the two republics, their ambitions for expansion of English overseas trade brought them in direct confrontation with their neighbor's dominance at sea. Some measure of that dominance may be seen in contemporary estimates of the size of the Dutch merchant fleet. In 1634 they were said to have 7500 ships engaged in trade, and by 1648, 10,000. In 1669 the French Finance Minister, Jean Baptiste Colbert, reported enviously that out of a total of 20,000 European merchant vessels, the Dutch had a fleet of 15,000–16,000, the English 3000–4000, and his own country a pitiful 500–600.[15] The mercantilist theory of the time held that trade was a fixed sum, a pie of constant size; and if one nation wanted to increase its own share, it had to do so at the expense of another. The imbalance in the merchant fleets of the Dutch and English was an obstacle to amicable union and set the stage for a commercial rivalry that was to spark three Anglo-Dutch wars over the next quarter century.

One of the first concerns of the new government was to establish close diplomatic relations with the United Netherlands. It was an unfortunate beginning. In April 1649, Dr. Isaac Dorislaus arrived in The Hague as the English envoy to the Dutch; but less than a week after his arrival he was assassinated by royalists, the first in what was to be a series of attacks on the Republic's diplomats abroad. Despite his death good relations prevailed between the neighboring nations, and two years later the English dispatched an impressive embassy to The Hague with the mission of proposing a close political union between the states. England's new leaders considered themselves bound to promote an alli-

15. Samuel Rawson Gardiner, *History of the Commonwealth and Protectorate*, 4:198; Tuchman, *The First Salute*, 28–29; Charles Woolsey Cole, *Colbert and a Century of French Mercantilism*, 1:343.

ance of the Protestant nations of northern Europe to oppose the Catholic powers to the south, and they revived the Elizabethan vision of a political union with the United Netherlands to anchor a Protestant League against the Antichrist.

The embassy was the Republic's first serious venture into the international arena, and no cost was spared. It was headed by two distinguished republicans, Chief Justice Oliver St. John and William Strickland, who had been Parliament's Agent to The Hague in the 1640s. The ambassadors entered the city in a splendid procession with 27 coaches and no fewer than 246 retainers, but this impressive array was greeted with unanticipated hostility. Crowds of English royalists and Dutch citizens, loyal to the House of Orange, lined the streets and made their sentiments known by throwing mud at the coaches, abusing the retainers, and breaking the windows of the ambassadors' residence. Further, when the envoys eventually addressed the States General, their proposals met with cold and intransigent opposition. In preference to a political union, the Dutch proposed that the two nations negotiate an alliance on the basis of the *Intercursus Magnus*, a treaty struck between Henry VII and Philip, archduke of Austria, in 1495. In preparation for the mission Milton had been ordered to translate the document, but so uncooperative were the Dutch that little progress was made on it.[16] After a humiliating three months in The Hague, the English returned home empty-handed.

> soon thou shalt have cause
> To wish thou never hadst rejected thus
> Nicely or cautiously my offer'd aid.
>   (PR 4:375–77)

In their revolutionary ardor, the new leaders could not comprehend that the Dutch might prefer to pursue their prosperity rather than join in a crusade against Rome. Further, in their enthusiasm for the grand design, they failed to appreciate how insecure the English government appeared at the time. Charles II was running loose in Scotland, and the campaign to subdue him was stalled by Cromwell's illness, which left him incapacitated for the very months of the embassy. In his farewell speech on 18 June, St. John made specific reference to the situation there, warning that "in a short time you will see our dispute with Scotland at an end, and you will then send envoys to ask what we have now offered you cordially; but, believe me, you will then repent of having

16. *CSPD* 2:116.

rejected our offers."[17] He proved prophetic; within six short months the Dutch were indeed in London, there to "ask" the English again about their "offers."

The English were obviously stung by the sharp rebuke of their first, tentative testing of the waters of international diplomacy, for they did not venture abroad with an embassy of comparable size for years thereafter. Determined not to be seen as weak and insecure again, they undertook to set their own house in order. Cromwell subdued the Scots and, at the battle of Worcester in September 1651, soundly defeated the last serious royalist threat to the Republic. Charles scurried back to the Continent, and the leaders of the Republic, tried and toughened by domestic conflicts, could now turn their attention to the European stage, where they were confronted with that same spectacle of a Dutch shadow over their vision of a prosperous England. The wars and rebellions that had occupied them for the first three years of the Republic may not have developed in them the subtle skills required in international diplomacy, but they had learned to recognize an enemy when they saw one and to seek out his weaknesses. For the Dutch it was obviously trade; and after a brief celebration of the victory at Worcester, Parliament settled down to business. In early October they passed the Navigation Act, which decreed that all goods imported into England could enter only on English ships or on those from the nation of origin, and that the products of English fisheries could be exported only on vessels belonging to "the people of this Commonwealth."[18] It was a dagger pointed at the heart of Dutch commercial hegemony.

Aside from the Council order to translate the *Intercursus Magnus*, there is nothing to connect Milton with Dutch affairs to this point, nor do the seventeenth-century sources reveal much thereafter. Of the eleven documents to the United Netherlands in the manuscripts, ten are dated 1655 or later, and of these seven are routine petitions and credential letters. One document only from the 1652 negotiations appears in these sources, a portion of the demands letter of 15 March, which will be discussed below. The principal evidence of Milton's involvement in the 1652 negotiations are six entries in the Order Books of the Council of State, dating from 21 January to 20 July, which associate him with several of the documents exchanged during the deliberations.[19]

In a comprehensive study of Milton's role in the Dutch negotiations

17. Gardiner, *History*, 1:329.

18. Gardiner, *Constitutional Documents*, 468–71.

19. The entries are all in *CSPD* 4:117 (21 January), 119 (26 January), 121 (28 January), 171 (8 March), 218 (15 April), and 338 (20 July).

from 1651 to 1654, Leo Miller offers evidence for attribution of a number of documents hitherto held questionable; he, further, provides the
text of others known to exist but formerly unavailable, and proposes
still more never before claimed to be Miltonic. Miller discovered a
wealth of material, in both original and transcript, through diligent
search of Dutch archives, which are much more complete than English
holdings for this period. To support his conclusions, Miller cites early
readers of the State Papers who praised them lavishly for the purity of
their Latin expression; and after a careful examination of the language,
he proposes that Milton's letters can be identified by the consistent use
of classic Latin forms, in contrast to the work of other, less-gifted members of the secretariat, who were content to use the vulgate or to coin
neologisms. Miller's contributions, when added to other evidence available, help fill out an otherwise scattered picture of Milton's knowledge
of the issues that precipitated and prolonged the first Anglo-Dutch
war.[20]

In December 1651 the Dutch sent an impressive embassy to London,
headed by Jacob Cats, Gerard Schaep, and Paulus van de Perre, with
the mission to negotiate the repeal of the Navigation Act, or at least to
ameliorate its worst effects. At their first meeting with the commissioners appointed by the Council of State, the ambassadors were informed that the Navigation Act was not negotiable and that any discussions would have to proceed with that understood. Deliberations
between the two parties followed the pattern that became characteristic
of the Republic's negotiations, with letters exchanged on three separate
matters. The first paper submitted by the Dutch, dated 18 January
1652, set out the issues as they saw them (W167B, P30).[21] They pro-

20. Miller's study of the Dutch negotiations has only recently appeared. I am grateful
to Dr. Albert C. Labriola, the editor of the Duquesne Series on Language and Literature,
for allowing me access to the manuscript. Documentation is from the book, which does
not depart from the manuscript in any matters discussed herein. See also Miller, "Lexicographer Milton," 58–62.

The holdings of the Public Record Office are of limited value to this inquiry. On the
earlier negotiations, SP 103/46 includes the narrative prepared by St. John and Strickland,
reporting on their mission to The Hague in 1651 (123–45) and a copy of the Dutch
articles (146–54). Also to be found is Thurloe's summary of Anglo-Dutch relations from
1652 on (220–40), including a copy of the Dutch response to the Declaration in August
of that year (195–204, in Dutch; 204–13, in English). There are some few documents on
the 1653 negotiations, which led to the treaty the following year (SP 84/159/156–63), a
copy of the treaty itself, dated "April 5/15 1654" (SP 108/300), and Parliament's ratification, dated 30 May 1656 (SP 108/286). Also to be found is the States General ratification
of the Treaty of The Hague, 11 May 1659 (SP 108/301).

21. CSPD 4:117 (21 January): "Mr. Milton to translate the paper sent to Council

posed that negotiations for a treaty proceed on the basis of the thirty-six articles left in abeyance at the end of the St. John–Strickland mission. They protested English interference in the Dutch herring fleet and, even more strongly, the "letters of marque and reprisal" that the English government had issued to certain of its citizens. These "letters of marque" authorized a merchant whose property had been seized by the ships of a foreign power to make up the losses by seizing in turn the property of citizens of that power, by any means at his disposal. In effect, they officially sanctioned acts of piracy, and most nations of the time resorted to this device to redress such grievances, as a measure short of war.

The Council replied with two letters, dated 29 January, both of which Milton was ordered to translate into Latin (W167C–D, P31–32).[22] In the answer to the ambassadors' letter of 18 January, the Council, still smarting from the rebuff of their earlier embassy, finds the treaty "left not performed at the Hague . . . to be of noe Consideration."[23] They dismiss the complaint about the herring fleet with a sentence and continue at length to justify the authorization of the letters of marque. The second letter, in answer to another Dutch complaint, is an even more extended justification for the seizure of Dutch vessels and Council's refusal to release them. In the preparation of these letters Milton had occasion to deal directly with members of the embassy, for according to the entry in Hermann Mylius's diary for 20 January, "As I was leaving, one of the Dutch came to him."[24]

While this exchange was going on, both sides were preparing for the principal business of the embassy. On 11 February the Dutch ambassadors submitted the treaty, based on the *Intercursus Magnus*, as it had stood at the close of the St. John–Strickland mission. It was no more agreeable to the English than it had been earlier when they had been seeking a political union rather than a commercial agreement, but they consented to it as a basis for negotiations. On 15 March the Council

---

from the Holland Ambassadors." This is a clear example of a letter Milton translated *into English*, of which no copy has been found. *Prose* dates the letter 24 January, presumably the day Milton submitted the translation.

22. Printed in *Works* 18:80–95. On 26 January, the Council ordered "Mr. Milton to translate into Latin the answer of Council to the first paper of the Holland Ambassadors, containing three articles" (*CSPD* 4:119); this is W167C. On 28 January, Council ordered "the Answer to the paper from the Dutch Ambassadors approved, and Milton to translate it into Latin, to be signed by the Lord President" (*CSPD* 4:121); this is 167D.

23. Miller, *John Milton's Writings*, 101–2. Where available, quotations will be from the original documents, as printed in Miller.

24. Miller, *Oldenburg*, 146.

replied with a long, article-by-article rebuttal, setting out their conditions for the proposed alliance (W167E, P38; referred to hereafter as the "Rebuttal" letter).[25] The document reveals the English ambivalence toward the Dutch embassy, for while it imposes difficult conditions upon them, at the same time it continues to express hope of a political union. The phrases to this effect are ubiquitous and more pointed than customary for such documents: "an even closer and more intimate alliance and covenant than heretofore has been entered into," "bound by ties of permanent alliance," "closer bonds of association and union than ever before."[26] The phrases disappear in the later sections, which enter into details; but it is clear that the English have not abandoned their vision of political union. The Dutch found little to please them in this reply, but much had happened in the months since the treaty had last been discussed in The Hague. This time it was the Dutch who were seeking concessions, as St. John had predicted; and when they later balked at the English revisions, the Council replied pointedly, "Wee think fit to remember your Excies That this Treatie was first desired by You and consented to by Parliament."[27]

Meanwhile, the English were preparing another document that would require negotiations entirely separate from the issue of the letters of marque or the treaty itself. On 15 March, along with the Rebuttal letter, the Council presented the ambassadors with a complex series of documents, listing grievances stretching back to 1618, instances in which the Dutch had captured, sunk, or otherwise disposed of English ships and killed English sailors and merchants. By each item is a price, the whole totaling more than £1.5 million (W43a, P39; referred to hereafter as the "Demands" letter). Moreover, to apply further pressure, the English announced that the bill would have to be settled before deliberations on the treaty could proceed. The demands should not have come as a complete surprise to the Dutch, for Council's letter of 29 January

25. Miller, *John Milton's Writings*, 154–79. The attribution to Milton is based on a Council order of 8 March: "The remainder of the articles to be offered the Dutch ambassadors to be considered to-morrow. So many of the articles as are already passed to be translated into Latin by Mr. Milton" (*CSPD* 4:171).

26. McCrea's translation. One article, the twelfth, is of interest to American historians. On the basis that they were "the first to plant colonies on the continent of North America," the English claimed "the district of Virginia stretching far to the south from the 37th degree of North Latitude all the way to Newfoundland and the 52nd degree." The Dutch settlements in New York are dismissed, "since we do not know whether any Dutch colony is there with the exception of the very few who dwell on the banks of the Hudson River."

27. Miller, *John Milton's Writings*, 183.

(W167C, P32) had informed them of a forthcoming list of "divers
Cases of wrongs and Dammages to a great value. . . . The particulars
whereof will be presented to your Excellencies in Order to a due satisfaction and Reparation to the Parties wronged"; but they must have
been distressed at the size of the bill.

Several meetings and exchanges ensued, until on 16 April the Council
wrote to express their annoyance that there had been no response to the
Demands letter and to repeat their position that the question of reparations must have "priority of consideration before any voluntary Proposalls."[28] This letter is a reply to one received, probably on 12 April,
from the Dutch ambassadors, concerning which there has been some
misunderstanding. In modern editions this Dutch letter, identified as *Ut
Tandem*, is said to be one *from the Council of State* to the ambassadors,
and editors speculate whether Milton wrote it or not (W167F, P44).[29]
The internal evidence shows conclusively, however, that it is a letter
from the Dutch, one in which the ambassadors reduce the points in
contention to three and ask for further consultations. Milton's Rebuttal
letter of 15 March closes with a phrase that much disturbed the ambassadors: "What still remains to be expressed on our part to bring the
discussion to completion shall be presented to your Excellencies at a
convenient time." The Dutch, still recovering from the Demands letter
delivered at the same time, were anxious to ensure that the English were
not planning any further surprises. *Ut Tandem* makes specific reference
to that closing remark, in which, as the ambassadors interpret it, the
English had expressed "certain reservations . . . which must later be
presented for the completion of the treaty"; and they are requesting
uneasily that whatever the English have in mind "be now laid before
us" so that "all the points which can in any way relate to the making of
a treaty between us may be duly analyzed." Council's reply of 16 April
assures the Dutch that they are unduly concerned about the language
"in the close of their Answer to your 36. Articles," which, as they put
it, is "no more then what is tacitly implyed in all Treaties." In brief, the
English presented the Rebuttal letter on 15 March; the Dutch replied
with *Ut Tandem* on or about 12 April, asking if more demands were

28. Miller prints the letter (ibid. 180–84). It is certainly the one referred to in the
Council's order of 15 April, "that the paper now read to be sent to the Dutch Ambassadors, be approved & sent to Mr. Milton to be translated into Latine" (*CSPD* 4:218).

29. It is printed in *Works* (18:124–27) but rejected by *Prose* (P44) on the basis of
French's argument that it is not the one delivered on 20 April (*CSPD* 4:220; French
3:216–17). All accept it erroneously as a Council letter. Studying Dutch archives, Miller
concurs that it was not (*Dutch* 36).

forthcoming; and Council answered on 16 April, attempting to reassure them. Whatever its date, *Ut Tandem* is a Dutch document; hence, the Latin is clearly *not* Milton's.

> Whether to settle peace, or to unfold
>   The drift of hollow states hard to be spell'd
>   Then to advise how war may best, upheld,
> Move by her two main nerves, Iron and Gold.
> (Sonnet 17)

The deliberations continued, and indeed the English began to relax some of their positions, giving promise of agreement; but chance events beyond the control of either party intervened to determine the outcome of the negotiations. On 19 May, there was a short but sharp encounter between an English fleet under Admiral Robert Blake and a much larger Dutch force under Marteen van Tromp in the Dover Downs, that is, in English waters. The battle was precipitated by a momentary misunderstanding on the part of each admiral as to the intentions of the other, but it was an almost inevitable consequence of the controversy that had raged for months over which of the two nations had sovereignty in the narrow channel that separates them. With two proud fleets prowling these contested waters, often in sight of one another, it was only a matter of time before the issues that divided the diplomats at Westminster would be mirrored in the clash of their forces at sea.

Parliament responded with indignation, accusing the ambassadors of all manner of duplicity; and in defense of the English, it must be said that the dominant size of the Dutch fleet and the site of the battle would seem to justify their view that van Tromp was the aggressor. The Dutch tried to calm the storm, to no avail. They dispatched a fourth ambassador, Willem Nieupoort, and yet a fifth, the distinguished Adrian Pauw, who after three fruitless weeks attempting to conciliate the English, took his leave on 30 June. In a trenchant farewell address he takes note of "the strange and unthought of accidents," the encounter "between the two Fleets without Design, but by mere chance," which have brought the negotiations to an end, and prays that God will "in his Mercy prevent the Destructions and Miseries of Wars."[30]

> They ended parle, and both address'd for fight
> Unspeakable.
> (PL 6:296–97)

---

30. *Works* 18:72–79.

Even as Pauw was speaking, John Thurloe was gathering material for the *Declaration of the Parliament of the Commonwealth of England, Relating to the Affairs and Proceedings between this Commonwealth and the States General of the United Provinces of the Low-Countreys,* which was, in effect, a declaration of war. It is actually a collection of documents, including a long account of past grievances and of the negotiations and events of 1652, Parliament's response to Dutch letters concerning "the late Fight between the Fleets," an account of the battle from the English point of view, and a series of exchanges between Pauw, Parliament, and the Council of State in June. This last is a curious choice for a declaration of war, for it includes Pauw's opening speech, a persuasive defense of his country's actions, and the one he delivered just prior to his departure, which is an eloquent plea for peace.[31] For a document intended to show that the English had been negotiating in good faith and the Dutch had not, the *Declaration* is singularly even-handed, as if the leaders of the Republic, in their ambivalence, felt obliged to be fair to their neighbor. It was made public on 9 July, and the Latin translation, *Scriptum Parlamenti Reipublicae ANGLIAE,* was published shortly thereafter.

In the last century, both Hamilton and Masson argued for the acceptance of the *Scriptum* as Milton's Latin, on the basis of the entries in the Council's Order Books directing him to translate documents during the negotiations, and the one of 20 July in particular, which instructs "Mr. Dugard to speak with Mr. Milton as to printing the Declaration" (Dugard was Parliament's official printer).[32] *Works* prints it (18:8–79), convinced that Milton was responsible for the Latin *Scriptum* as well as portions of the English *Declaration. Prose* omits it on the basis that "the objective evidence is slight" and that Milton's personal problems—infirm health, the loss of eyesight, and the death of his wife in May and son in June—would have "prevented him" from doing the work (P47). Miller, citing textual parallels between the Latin of the *Scriptum* and other documents accepted as Miltonic, presents a cogent argument for attribution of some portions of it; he therefore offers the complete text in both Latin and English.[33]

The premises of this study would persuade toward Miller's position: If Milton was indeed responsible for many of the papers that lead up to the *Declaration,* it would be reasonable to conclude that he would be employed in translating the document that represents the culmination

31. Ibid. 44–55, 72–79.
32. Hamilton 20; Masson 4:482–83; *CSPD* 4:338.
33. Miller, *John Milton's Writings,* 196–269.

of the negotiations. Other factors favor attribution. The *Declaration*, not a short document, had to be translated immediately into Latin, French, and Dutch and in later weeks into German, Italian, and Danish.[34] Such an effort would have required Thurloe to mobilize his entire staff of translators. Even if those at his disposal had not been so heavily engaged, he would have naturally turned to his accomplished Secretary for the Latin of such a critical document, the Republic's first declaration of war. His skills would be especially valuable, as it was not an easy matter for England, a champion of the Protestant cause, to justify war with a nation that should more properly have been its closest ally. It was a conflict that Catholic states could only look upon with satisfaction and Protestant, with distress.

The publication of the *Declaration* in July 1652 may well have marked the end of Milton's close involvement in correspondence between the two nations. In the months to follow their differences were to be resolved on the high seas rather than around the conference table. The time for writing of letters was for the moment over; and it would seem that when that time returned, Thurloe sought elsewhere for a Latin translator of Dutch correspondence. Miller argues, once again from the Latin, that Milton was responsible for two more letters to the Dutch in 1653; but whether or not he was, the war was the most dramatic event in the foreign affairs of the Republic during the years 1652–54, of such prominence that it surely left a lasting impression on the imagination of England's Secretary for Foreign Languages.[35] Hence, it will be of value to trace the sequence of events to their end.

The war at sea went well for the English—there was no land action. Victories over the Dutch at the battles of Kentish Knock (28 September 1652), Portland Bill and Beachy Head (18–20 February 1653), and the Gabbard Banks (2 June 1653), together with an effective blockade

34. On 13 July the Council ordered the Latin, French, and Dutch translations prepared (*CSPD* 4:331). Although there is no evidence that Thurloe had the document translated into German, Italian, and Danish, it seems reasonable that the English would prefer to distribute their own wording of such an important document to foreign powers. Theodore Haak was fluent in the Scandinavian languages, Weckherlin in German, and, of course, Milton in Italian. Shawcross lists the various editions in *Milton, A Bibliography*, 35–43. The English version cites 9 July as the official date of the *Declaration* (items 126, 127). The title pages of the Danish (132), German (147), and one of the Dutch editions (155) indicate that it was officially printed in London by order of Parliament on 28 July. A copy was enclosed in Parliament's letter to the duke of Tuscany, dated 29 July (W27, P46), and their letter of 8 July to the Danish ambassadors promises that a copy will be forwarded (Miller, *John Milton's Writings*, 270–72).

35. For a discussion of the influence of the Dutch negotiations on *Paradise Regained*, see Fallon, *Captain or Colonel*, 189–99.

of their ports, soon returned the Dutch to the negotiating table.[36] Their embassy, headed by Jerome Beverning, arrived in London in June 1653 to find a government in transition. Cromwell had dissolved the Long Parliament in April and clearly dominated the interim Council of Thirteen that presided over the nation's affairs until the Barebones Parliament met on 4 July. To the ambassadors' dismay, the Council appointed by that body revived once again the vision of a political union between the two states. On 25 July the Dutch were presented with an ultimatum, one which alarmed Beverning: "The Council did in express terms propose not the establishment of a league and union between two sovereign states and neighbors, but the making of two sovereign states one";[37] and as if to underline their demands, six days later an English fleet under Monk soundly defeated the Dutch at the battle of the Texel, an encounter in which their great admiral, van Tromp, lost his life.

The Dutch were no more enthusiastic about the proposal for union than they had been in 1651, fearing, quite realistically, that they would become but another province of the much larger England, relegated to a servile status comparable to that of Scotland, which had been incorporated into the Commonwealth by the Tender of Union the year before.[38] Cromwell shared the Council's vision of "making the two sovereign states one" and indeed pressed it on the ambassadors; but once he realized the depth of the Dutch resolve against such a union, he abandoned the plan in favor of peace between the two powers. For the moment, however, the two sides were obviously at a deadlock, and the negotiations dragged on through July and August, with the Council insisting on union and the Dutch resisting it adamantly. The English applied pressure by presenting the Dutch with yet a third bill for reparations, updating the claim for damages suffered since thay had submitted the Demands letter in March, and a subsequent one to Adrian Pauw in June of the previous year. And the war went on.

There is no evidence that Milton played any role in these later negotiations, although we can be assured that he followed closely the progress of events that promised to end a war he regretted as much as did Cromwell.[39] Leo Miller has identified eight letters exchanged during the

36. The sole Dutch victory of the war was at Dungeness on 28 November.

37. Gardiner, *History*, 3:44.

38. Masson 4:360–66, although the union was not officially consummated until Cromwell's proclamation in 1654.

39. Two years later, in his *Pro Se Defensio*, Milton said of himself that no one in England "would less desire a war with [the Dutch], would wage one which had begun more pacifically, or rejoice more seriously when it was concluded" (*Prose* 4:742).

summer of 1653 and proposes that two of them can be attributed to Milton on the basis of the Latin employed; the other six, he suggests, were prepared by Philip Meadows, who was appointed to assist in Latin translation at about that time.[40] Miller's conclusions seem at odds with with what we know of Thurloe's practice of using the same translator throughout any single set of negotiations. The matter of the two, however, lies well outside the orb of the central issues under deliberation—the union, the treaty, and reparations—and Milton may have been called upon in isolated instances to relieve some of the pressure on Meadows.

The first, from the Council to the ambassadors, dated 13 July, is an extended quibble over who was responsible for "the first occasion of Jealousie," specifically, who first ordered whose fleet to prepare for war. It is a question tangentially relevant to the issue of reparations; the Council concludes that "the preparations of the States General had their beginning sooner, than those of the Commonwealth," and therefore the English demands are justified. The letter of 1 August, much shorter, deals with the question of who is treating whose prisoners more humanely. Council accuses the Dutch of subjecting English sailors to "very hard and miserable Imprisonment, some of them in Irons," whereas the English are providing for theirs "in all things, according to their several qualities and necessities, putting them under noe further restraynt or imprisonment then was necessary to prevent their escape"; indeed, Council goes on, so light is the captor's touch that some of them do escape. Such issues assume importance in any war, but neither can be said to be central to the larger questions awaiting resolution.

Negotiations continued into the fall with the Council showing little inclination for compromise; but with the resignation of Parliament and the establishment of the Protectorate in December, the English tone changed markedly. Cromwell clearly wanted to end the war; and once he had finally set aside the plan for political union, the other issues proved reconcilable. Among the more difficult was the Dutch insistence that Denmark be included in the peace treaty. The English had grievances to settle with that nation dating back to negotiations broken off in October 1652, after which the Danish king, Frederick III, impounded English merchantmen at Copenhagen, closed the Sound to all English shipping, and declared war in support of his Dutch allies. Cromwell would have preferred to deal with the Danes separately but removed

40. Miller, *John Milton's Writings*, 278–93. Lünig includes five letters exchanged by the two sides in April–May 1653 (nos. 168–71 and 176); but there is no evidence to connect them to Milton (Miller, "Milton's State Letters," 413).

one of the final obstacles to peace by including them in the treaty, although not until Frederick had agreed to reopen the Sound and pay reparations for the impounded ships. A peace treaty was signed on 5 April and ratified by the Lord Protector shortly thereafter.[41] It was a critical accomplishment for Cromwell; and for the balance of his life, he would weigh foreign policy decisions in terms of their effect on that peace.

From all the evidence, Milton was not involved in the negotiations of 1653–54, save perhaps for the two letters proposed by Miller. The question of his participation in the exchanges of January–June 1652 remains at issue, however. The argument against his involvement is supported by the absence of any documents relevant to the negotiations in the seventeenth-century sources, save for the anomalous inclusion of sections of the Demands letter in *Literae*; and certainly consideration must be given to the circumstances of Milton's personal life at the time, the final onset of blindness in March, and the death of his wife and son in May and June 1652, events sufficiently traumatic to cause any man to withdraw into himself.

Concerning the absence of documents, there are in fact only eleven letters to the Dutch in all the early sources, eight to the States General, two to Holland, and one to West Friesland, only one of them earlier than 1655 and five dated in the spring and summer of 1656, when Milton, as the only Latin Secretary available, wrote a number for which he would not otherwise have been responsible. Further, aside from the three dealing with the 1652 Demands, the Piedmont Massacre (W54, P75), and the Swedish war (W75, P109), his letters are all routine petitions and credentials.[42] From all appearances, therefore, Milton was never regularly involved in important correspondence with the United Netherlands; however, the fact that the Demands document is the *only* letter to the Dutch in *Literae* asks for a second look. It is an anomaly in the volume, with a number (43a) which strongly suggests that it was added after type had been set, a conclusion further confirmed by its location at the very end of the section on Parliament's letters, entirely out of chronological order. It is, moreover, a fragment, part of a much longer document which Milton retained in his files.

One must wonder why the document was included in *Literae* at all, since it does not appear in the other two manuscripts, and why it was

41. Parliament, which was not in session at the time, did not officially ratify the treaty until 30 May 1656 (SP 108/280).

42. The other eight are: W66, P92; W69, P99; W70, P98; W80, P110; W104, P138; W105, P141; W106, P140; and W130, P164.

added so haphazardly, seemingly at the last moment. The date of the volume, 1676, is probably significant. For years after the Restoration, England was in a state of constant hostility with the Dutch, the actual war years, 1665–67 and 1672–74, relieved by an all-too-fragile peace. Charles II, unencumbered by any religious or political affinities with the Dutch republic, could focus on the commercial rivalry. The editor of *Literae* may well have concluded that it was impolitic to include any letters reflecting amicable relations with the Dutch, but that this fragment, which catalogues atrocities committed against English merchants, might suit well the temper of the government as well as the intended audience, the English people. Had Milton been responsible for more than these eleven Dutch letters, similar considerations may well have prompted him to exclude all but the most innocuous from the Columbia and Skinner MSS (ten of the letters are in both and, as noted, the Demands letter is in neither). The fact that he had this document in his files lends weight to the argument that he possessed more Dutch letters than the sources reflect, possibly several dealing with the sensitive negotiations in 1652.[43]

Further evidence of Milton's active participation in the negotiations may be deduced from the Order Book entries from 21 January to 15 April 1652 that direct him by name to prepare documents. It does not seem reasonable that Council would have continued to designate him for these tasks had he not been performing them. Concerning the *Scriptum*, Miller is altogether convincing that Milton had a hand here, to which can be added the Council's order that Dugard consult him about the document's publication. And there is a final piece of evidence unearthed by Miller. In the unpublished journal of Leo ab Aitzema, the envoy to England from Hamburg and the Hanse Towns, appears the

---

43. The Public Record Office files contain several from a later period: a letter from Cromwell to Zeeland, dated 16 June 1654 (SP 84/159), and four from Cromwell to the States General, Holland, Rotterdam, and Dort, requesting the resumption of trade for the "Fellowship of Merchant Adventurers" after the signing of the treaty (SP 84/160). Two deserved special attention. When Richard Cromwell became Lord Protector on the death of his father, he wrote letters to the nations of Europe announcing the succession and confirming the incumbent envoys in their posts. Milton included two in the transcripts, those to Louis XIV and Mazarin, both dated 6 September 1658 (W124–25, P159–60). A Latin letter to the States General of the same substance, reappointing George Downing as Resident, *and with the same date*, is in the State Papers Foreign, Holland. It is accompanied by a set of instructions in English to Downing, directing that "in all things which remayne before you or shall occur hereafter, you are untill further Order to act upon ye same Instructions which you had in Our Fathers life tyme received" (SP 84/162/164–65). If Milton wrote such letters to France, it is a reasonable assumption that he was responsible for some of their companions, such as this for the Dutch, to other countries.

following note directly after one dated 9 July 1652: "The Declaration enacted was set into French by Rosin, and into Latin by Milton."[44] It is difficult to avoid the conclusion, therefore, that Milton was closely involved in the 1652 negotiations with the United Netherlands, though available evidence indicates that thereafter he was superseded by another, probably Meadows, in the important correspondence with that nation.[45]

Spain

My sentence is for open war.
(PL 2:51)

During the 1650s Spain and France were in a state of almost constant hostility; and once the Protectorate had been firmly established and the war with the Dutch terminated, Cromwell began to weigh the advantages of allying himself with one or the other of the two powers. In 1655 he determined finally to cast his lot with France. On 26 October, in what was in effect a declaration of war, he issued a statement condemning the Spanish for crimes against the English stretching back to the year of the Armada, and accusing them of treacherously planning to renew the war against England (W169, P84). Cromwell's eye was on a rich prize, the Spanish colonies in the New World; thus the great bulk of the evidence marshaled to justify the declaration consists of accounts, some in garish detail, of "their cruel & unworthy dealings with the English in the West-Indies; enslaving; hanging, drowning, and cruelly torturing to death, Our Countrey-men, spoiling their Ships and Goods, and destroying their Colonies in times of greatest Peace, and that without just cause or provocation at all" (*Works* 13:557).

It is not surprising that England should throw its weight against Spain; what is surprising is that Cromwell was considering an alliance with her ancient adversary in the first place. In fact, however, Anglo-

---

44. Miller's translation. The journal, or *Dagboek*, he notes, is to be found in the Algemeen Rijksarchief, Collectie Aitzema, Invent. nr. 46 ("New Milton Texts" 286).

45. Milton's concern with Anglo-Dutch relations in 1652–53 is confirmed by an intriguing sidelight. He was learning the language! Roger Williams was in England during those years and later gave an account of his frequent meetings with the poet: "The Secretary of the Council, Mr. Milton, for my Dutch I read him, read me many more languages" (Masson 4:531).

Spanish relations were quite cordial during the early years of the Republic. The revolutionary leaders discovered a friend in a most unexpected quarter at a time when there were precious few to be found. Their first overtures to European powers had been anything but promising—Dorislaus assassinated in The Hague, Bradshaw besieged in Hamburg, and Vane forced to flee Lisbon after only three months. The anxiety of the new leaders can be felt in the credentials Milton prepared for Anthony Ascham when he was appointed Agent to the kingdom of Spain in January 1650.

Of Milton's two letters, Patrick identifies the first (W3, P12) as a "safe-conduct" and adds that he probably prepared a similar document for Charles Vane, who was dispatched to Portugal at the same time. This is entirely reasonable. When diplomats of the day were sent on a mission, they carried with them a packet of several documents. Among them were letters of introduction to the various cities and states through which they must travel, such as the five that accompanied William Jephson on his mission to Sweden in 1657 (W94–97, 99; P128–32). Ascham needed only one safe-conduct, since he was traveling by sea; and it was probably intended for his use on the overland voyage from the coast to Madrid, in the hope that a letter to the king would carry sufficient weight to dissuade any threat to his safety in that potentially hostile environment. Each envoy also carried a set of instructions, in English, that outlined the official policy he was to pursue during his embassy. There are a number of these in the public record, and Milton included one in the Columbia MS, the instructions prepared for Richard Bradshaw on his abortive mission to Russia in 1657 (W164, P123).

The most important diplomatic document in the envoy's packet was his "letter of credence" or *creditif*, which officially accredited him as his nation's representative to the host government; and Milton wrote many of these.[46] The texts of a number of them refer to "these Letters," however, indicating that the envoy was asked to deliver more than one (W57, P83; W82, P114; W101, P135); and we have an instance of this practice in the early communication with Hamburg, when Parliament sent two letters to Isaac Lee for presentation to the Senate (W151, P1; P2), the one his *creditif*, the other a companion letter of specific griev-

---

46. To Spain (W4, P11), Hamburg (W151, P1; W11, P14), Denmark (W35, P52), France (W56–57, P82–83; W113–16, P146–49; W145–46, P93–94), Portugal (W82, P114), Russia (W91, P124), and the United Netherlands (W105–6, P140–41). He also wrote a number of routine *recreditifs*, letters releasing foreign envoys to return home: to Oldenburg (W44, P64), Portugal (W65, P67), Sweden (W67, P95; W72, P104), and the United Netherlands (W104, P138).

ances, concerning which Parliament demanded satisfaction. Lee declined the honor of the first, returning it to London, but he did deliver
the second. The sending of two letters where one would do was by no
means a uniform practice, unnecessary when diplomatic relations were
friendly and of long standing, or, as seems to be the case with Ascham,
when reception was uncertain and it would have been impolitic to in-
troduce grievances. It is reasonable to assume that a single secretary
would be assigned the task of preparing the entire packet of documents
intended for a single envoy on a specific mission; hence, if any of "these
Letters" associated with Milton's *creditifs* are located, it is probable
that he wrote them as well. One must be cautious in attributing to him
the sets of instructions usually included in the packet, since they were
prepared in English; but the inclusion of Bradshaw's in the Columbia
MS suggests that he may have been responsible for them on occasion.

The two surviving letters from Ascham's diplomatic packet, both addressed to the king, are subtly different in tone (W3–4, P11–12). His
creditif contains the expected affirmation of "Friendship and the accustom'd Commerce between both Nations" and the request that he may
have "free Liberty of Access to your Majesty." The *creditif* also includes
the customary request that care be "taken of his Safety and his Honour," but the companion safe-conduct shows signs of unease. Parliament, unnerved by the assassination of Dorislaus, was understandably
apprehensive about this venture into diplomatic relations with their traditional enemy. They simply had no idea how Ascham would be received by His Catholic Majesty, Philip IV. The letter asks the king to
"order him a Safe and Honourable Passage to your Royal City"; but it
goes on to request that should Philip be disinclined to receive the envoy,
he inform Ascham "the soonest" and then ensure that "he may be at
Liberty to depart without Molestation." In brief, if the king didn't want
Ascham there, he is asked to send him home, quickly and safely. England's revolutionary leaders, with the help of Milton's stately Latin,
sought to present a bold and confident face to the world; but their
anxiety could not be entirely disguised. As it turned out, their fears were
fully justified.

Spain was in fact the first European country to recognize the Commonwealth, appointing as ambassador Alphonso de Cardenas, a highly
experienced diplomat who had been representing his country in England since 1637; and Philip IV proved to be a useful ally. During the
Republic's undeclared war with Portugal, he opened his ports to the
fleets of Blake and Popham, and closed them to Prince Rupert. Further
evidence of cordiality is to be found in Milton's letter of November
1652 to the Spanish ambassador (W33, P53), a warm note of thanks

for the sanctuary offered by Porto Longone to an English fleet after a brush it had with the Dutch near that Spanish harbor. Again, the Spanish prime minister sent a special ambassador to London in September 1654 to congratulate Cromwell on his assumption of power, and the Lord Protector wrote back effusively acknowledging the "singular affection" shown by the mission and his delight at being "so belov'd and approv'd by your Lordship" (W47, P69).

Prior to Cromwell's decision to seek a French alliance, correspondence between England and Spain was relatively brisk. Aside from the documents associated with the war against Portugal, previously discussed, Milton's letters to Spain focused on two matters that cast light on Cromwell's final choice, for neither of them served to enhance amicable relations between the two nations. The fate of Anthony Ascham was to prove an insurmountable obstacle to any pursuit of the promise of those hopeful beginnings. On 6 June 1650, the day after his arrival in Madrid, the envoy was murdered by royalist sympathizers. Parliament reacted to the news in a moving letter (W13, P17), which "earnestly" requests that the murders be brought to justice and asks that the "breathless Carkass" of their agent be returned so that it may be "Enterr'd in his own Country." The incident continued to rankle; two years later Parliament was still demanding that the "villanous Assassinates [be] . . . brought to deserved Punishment" (W8, P33).

The facts of the incident are fairly clear. Ascham arrived in Madrid on 5 June and on the following night was murdered by six royalists, one of whom escaped while the others sought sanctuary in a nearby church. The Spanish authorities ignored the tradition of the *locus sanctus* and arrested the murderers, whom they subsequently tried, convicted, and were preparing to execute, only to be deterred by the local archbishop who threatened excommunication unless the prisoners were returned to the church. The authorities submitted to *jus ecclesia* and although they mounted a guard at the church door, three of the murderers escaped. One had died in prison and another was recaptured and duly put to death, but four remained at large.

What is not clear is whether there was Spanish collusion in the murder. Just before his final departure from London in 1655, Cardenas had a long, rambling conversation with the Swedish ambassador, Christer Bonde, in which he complained about the unfriendly treatment he was receiving from the English; and he gave Bonde an account of Ascham's death, one from the Spanish point of view at any rate. The ambassador laid the blame on Ascham's carelessness: "It was his own fault to the extent that he ought not to have left his house open for anyone to come and go before announcing his arrival to the secretary of state, in which event proper security for his person could have been provided."[47] There are two letters in SP 94/43, State Papers Foreign, Spain, which give a complete picture of events as seen by George Fisher, Ascham's secretary, and Laurence Sanders, an English merchant living in Madrid; and their version differs in significant detail from that of Cardenas.[48] Sanders reports that Ascham did indeed have a Spanish escort, commanded by a colonel, during his overland voyage from the coast; but upon their arrival in Madrid the guard simply disappeared. Ascham feared for his safety and complained to the colonel that there were no locks or bolts on the doors and windows of his lodgings and that he was left entirely unprotected. The colonel replied that it had been his responsibility to escort the Agent to Madrid and, having done so, his duties were at an end; besides, he said, he was sick and was going home to bed. Fisher and the English merchants promptly found alternate, more secure lodgings, but before they could move Ascham he was dead.

The accounts of the Englishmen in Spain insist that the king was very disturbed when he heard of Ascham's vulnerability and dispatched members of his personal guard to replace the absent escort, only to have them arrive too late. In London it looked suspicious, however: the Spaniards chose Ascham's lodgings for him, the murderers knew where to find him within twenty-four hours after his arrival, they apparently were aware that he would be unguarded, and four of them were allowed to escape. The king, the reports continue to emphasize, was angry over the murder—there was even a rumor that he imprisoned the colonel—but these assurances failed to satisfy the men of the Council of State. They put no store, one can be sure, in explanations involving *locus sanctus* and *jus ecclesia*; in their letter to the king of 30 January 1652 (W7, P24) they demand specifically that he "not suffer [the murderers'] merited Pains to be suspended any longer by any delay or pretence of Religion." The English were inclined to interpret the incident as a reflection of Spain's latent royalist sympathies, and they continued to complain bitterly about dilatory efforts to bring the criminals to justice.

Spain's failure to punish the murderers cast a shadow over the second matter with which Milton's letters are concerned, an abortive effort toward a treaty proposed by the Spaniards. His letters here, save for one, are all addressed to the Spanish ambassador from the Council of State;[49] they are part of a lengthy exchange over the treaty that continued from

---

47. Michael Roberts, *Swedish Diplomats at Cromwell's Court*, 178.

48. SP 94/43/69–84, 35–38.

49. Milton included no letters addressed to the king after that of 30 January 1652 (W7, P24).

December 1651 to just before the establishment of the Protectorate two years later. The negotiations are recorded in welcome detail in a narrative titled "Transactions betweene England and Spayne from the yeare 1650," deposited in the Public Record Office, London.[50] This document offers a full picture of the exchanges between the two nations and helps clarify Milton's role in the affair. The first entry is the account of an audience with Parliament on 2 December 1650, in which the "Letters Credentiall" of Alphonso de Cardenas, as the newly appointed ambassador from Spain, were officially accepted. In a speech he gave on that occasion Cardenas stressed two matters. He observed that Spain was indeed the first European nation to appoint a minister of ambassadorial rank to the Republic as well as the first to acknowledge Parliament as the sovereign power in England; and he conveyed Philip IV's "most lively resentment of the unhappy accident upon Anthony Ascham," as the narrative puts it, and the king's promise that he would not cease efforts until the criminals had been brought to justice. Parliament replied with thanks and also acknowledged their gratitude for "the favour shewed to their admirall and Fleet upon the Coast of Spain by the King & his Officers," but then went on to once again demand punishment for the murderers. Cardenas was also informed that the Council of State would henceforth receive his letters.

For the next year diplomatic relations took their normal course. Milton's letters to Spain include the aforementioned on Ascham (W13, P17), a petition and a letter to the Spanish ambassador (W167H, P27), both of which Council ordered him to translate into Latin,[51] another complaining against injuries to English trade in the Canary Islands (W21, P28), and an answer to a Spanish protest at the seizure of two ships (W32, P54). It was not until an audience with the Council on 19 December 1651 that Cardenas first raised the question of a treaty.

Milton's first two letters on the treaty negotiations, one from Parliament to the king and another from the Council to the ambassador, are

50. The narrative in SP 103/65/191–98, 213–226, State Papers Foreign, Treaty Papers, Spain, has not hitherto been available to Miltonists. It was published in *Original Letters & Negotiations of Sir Richard Fanshaw* (1702), 1:465–510. Fanshawe, appointed ambassador to Spain by Charles II in 1664, was instructed to familiarize himself with former treaties, including "the Transactions betwixt D. Alonso de Cardenas, and the Usurpers here" (1:4). In SP 94/43, State Papers Foreign, Spain, there are a number of letters from Ascham written in March–June 1650, several from George Fisher during the period after the assassination, and others from Alexander Bence and Laurence Sanders. The file contains numerous documents written after August 1655, but they are all royalist in origin.

51. *CSPD* 3:225.

dated 30 January 1652 (W7–8, P24, 33). These certainly appear to be companion letters, although they are dated variously in different editions. Both acknowledge the king's concern over Ascham's death, as reported by his "Embassador," demand again that his "Assassinates" be punished, reject any argument based on religion as a pretense for delay, and warn that future relations between the two nations, and by implication the fate of the proposed treaty, would depend upon Spain's actions. W7, to the king, states darkly that "if Justice be not satisfy'd without delay . . . we see not upon what foundations a sincere and lasting Friendship can subsist." W8, to the ambassador, declares in similar though more forceful terms that "unless Justice be done . . . all the foundations of Humane Society, all the ways of preserving Friendship among Nations, of necessity must be overturn'd and abolish'd."[52]

Milton's next letter, dated 31 March (W23, P40), refers again to the ambassador's audience of 19 December, then to a document of his dated 15 February, and to a subsequent "Conference," which according to the narrative took place two days after its receipt. At the "Conference" Cardenas had asked, very guardedly, whether Parliament did in fact share the king's desire "to beget a nearer union." In Milton's letter Council replies with the complaint that at the meeting, "instead of those things which were expected to have bin propounded," the ambassador had done no more than reintroduce his 15 February letter. They repeat their willingness to treat but also voice their impatience over the vagueness of the Spanish proposals. When the ambassador is ready to "descend to particulars," the letter remarks archly, then the Council can reply in kind.

52. The original manuscripts give no dates. For W7, *Prose* has 21–22 January 1651; *Works* has "Circa July. 1. 1650." For W8, *Prose* has 30 January 1652; *Works* has January 1650/51. *Works'* dates are both too early. In the case of W7, Parliament had already sent a letter concerning Ascham dated 28 June 1650 (W13, P17); there was no need to write another three days later. Further, W7 refers to Cardenas as "Embassador." According to the narrative (SP 103/65), he did not submit his credentials to Parliament until 2 December, and so it is unlikely that he would have been referred to by that rank the previous July. W8 refers specifically to Cardenas's meeting with Council "upon the 19th of December last," that is, the December 1651 audience, and to the "four Writings" he submitted at that time. W8 would have to be dated after the audience; hence, *Prose's* 30 January 1652 is doubtless correct. Patrick's case for the dating of W7 as 21–22 January 1651 is, however, inconclusive. As noted, internal evidence leaves the unmistakable impression that the two are companion letters, one to the king, one to the ambassador, both in response to the Spanish proposal of 19 December. The letter to the ambassador is more specific about his proposals than is the one to the king; but they both say the same thing and, it may be reasonably concluded, were written at the same time. Both, then, may be dated 30 January 1652.

During the first half of 1652, Cardenas was obviously playing a very cautious game. He was understandably uncertain about the Council's readiness to treat, since their effusive assurances of "friendship" and "amity" were invariably accompanied by strongly worded complaints about Ascham, creating doubts about their intentions in the ambassador's mind. It was not until 27 May that Cardenas showed his hand. The Spanish, it appears, were not contemplating anything new; he submitted a "Plenepotency" from the king, proposing that the two nations negotiate on the basis of an earlier treaty, that "betweene the King of Spayne and King Charles the 15/5 Nov. 1630," reworked a bit to reflect "the difference of time, juncture of affairs, and change of government." At his next audience in July, Cardenas pressed the Council, "by word of mouth & writing," for an answer.[53] He received it on 10 August in a long, rather peevish letter (W28, P48) that reviews the progress of the negotiations thus far, citing the Council's reply in March, the ambassador's response of 27 May, and a subsequent audience on 6 August, and complaining that they had as yet no answer to their letter of 30 January, which demanded justice for the murderers of Ascham. Council reaffirms Parliament's desire for a "firm Friendship and good Peace" but again complains that so far they have nothing to work with except a vague reference to an old treaty. With obvious frustration, Council observes that "as soon as your Excellency shall be pleas'd, either out of the Leagues already made, or in any other manner, to frame such conditions" as will achieve that peace, they will be only too happy to respond.

On 2 September, Cardenas finally submitted a draft treaty of twenty-four articles, based largely in wording and particulars on the 1630 document.[54] Some inapplicable articles of the old treaty are omitted and others brought up to date, e.g., in those provisions that require the English to impose sanctions of one kind or another against a third power, Cardenas simply changed the name of the country from "Holland," Spain's old enemy, to "Portugal," its new one. The Spanish strategy did not succeed; the English simply wanted no part of it. As the Council was deliberating over the proposal, they received "a Remonstrance" from English merchants, giving a detailed account of Spain's failure to

53. The narrative refers to an audience on 22 July, W28 to one on 6/16 August. There may well have been two.
54. SP 103/65/193–98, 213–16; Richard Fanshawe, *Original Letters*, 1:469–84. The original 1630 treaty, of thirty-one articles, is in SP 103/65/172–84, where it is dated 17 December. The copy in the narrative has marginal comments entered in English by each article.

observe the 1630 treaty, as well as other examples of perfidious behavior in the interval. Besides, there had been too many unpleasantries since 1630. When Cromwell issued the Spanish Declaration three years later, he cited six separate violations of English merchants and colonists in the West Indies that had taken place between 1650 and 1653 alone, hence fresh in the memories of Council members during the deliberations with Cardenas, one an account of a particularly brutal massacre of the entire population of over a hundred Englishmen on the island of "Sancta Cruce" by Spaniards from Puerto Rico (*Works* 13:545); and the Council wanted to ensure that such atrocities would not be repeated. Consequently, they rejected the Spanish proposals as "not adding anything to ye last peace" and replied with a draft treaty of their own, consisting of thirty-five articles, referring to it pointedly as the only "way into a stricter Amity & Confederation" between the two nations.

At an audience in February 1653 Cardenas complained of the complication and again urged Council to negotiate on the basis of the old treaty. The English were adamant, however, and so "the Ambr. condescended thereunto, and many conferences were held thereupon between him and the Commissrs. of the Counsell." The outcome of these "many conferences" was a copy of the treaty, still of thirty-five articles, which Cardenas returned to the Council on 9 September 1653, laboriously annotated with exceptions and revisions; indeed, he accepted only twelve of its articles without change.[55] Cardenas pressed for an answer the following month, but nothing came of it. In December the Barebones Parliament dissolved itself and Cromwell was appointed Lord Protector. As the narrative concludes rather laconically, "it doth not appeare that they returned any answer, or that the subsequent government made any proceeding therein." Cromwell's vision of a Western Design soon overshadowed all other considerations of peace and war with Spain.

The Order Books of the Council of State refer only once to Milton's involvement in the Spanish negotiations. On 27 March 1652 he was directed "to send a letter to the ambassador of Spain," an obvious allusion to the one of 31 March.[56] Milton, however, remained actively engaged in the Spanish correspondence in the months following the 10 August letter, for among his published papers are five more by his hand in 1652–53. It is a correspondence that gives one the impression of a deteriorating relationship. One on 11 November thanks the Spanish for

55. SP 103/65/216–226; Fanshawe 1:486–510.
56. *CSPD* 3:114.

their aid to an English fleet (W33, P53); but another on the same day
(W32, P54) has a different tone entirely, an unbending rejection of a
Spanish protest at the capture of two of their ships by English men-of-
war. There are two more (W41–42, P57, 56), complaining of the seizure of an English merchant vessel, and a final note of warning to the
Spanish ambassador, admonishing him for allowing English citizens to
attend Mass in his house (W43, P59).[57]

The fact that from January to August of 1652 Milton wrote but three
letters for the Council of State to the Spanish ambassador has led Patrick to conclude that his connection with the negotiations was only
"intermittent."[58] Both the narrative, however, and the internal evidence
of the letters themselves show clearly that those three, of 30 January, 31
March, and 10 August, were the *only ones* that the Council wrote to
the ambassador during that period. Milton, then, was responsible for *all*
of the Council's correspondence with Cardenas in that first year of negotiations, to include as well, we may be sure, the English translations
of the ambassador's replies. The evidence of the State Papers, moreover,
indicates that he was continually engaged in Spanish correspondence
during the period of deliberations over the treaty. Milton's connection
with the negotiations was, therefore, far from "intermittent"; indeed, it
would appear that he was the one to whom Thurloe turned regularly in
matters dealing with Spain.

This practice makes it a near certainty that he was also responsible
for the preparation of the two draft treaties exchanged during the negotiations. The twenty-four articles that Cardenas submitted in September
1652 would have presented little difficulty, for the document was in
most respects a simple revision of the 1630 treaty, which was on file in
government archives; but when the Council replied with their own draft
treaty of thirty-five articles, it had to be submitted to Cardenas in Latin,
as did all their letters. Additional evidence linking Milton with Spanish
correspondence at the time the treaty was under consideration may be
found in the narrative. The copy included carries the date "November
12, 1652"[59] and Milton had prepared at least two letters to Spain
(W32–33, P53–54), both dated *but the day before.*[60] Further, it would

---

57. As the wording indicates, this letter was one of a number sent to foreign envoys in
London at the time (*CSPD* 5:102). If Milton was responsible for one of them, it is probable that he was responsible for them all, as they are not likely to have varied much in
content.

58. *Prose* 5:622.

59. SP 103/65/216.

60. There was yet a third, addressed to the governor of Porto Longone (*CSPD* 4:486),

appear that he kept a copy of the document in his files. In Daniel Skinner's prospectus for the volume of State Papers he intended to publish in 1676, he wrote that it would include "copies of the Spanish, Portuguese, French, and Dutch Treaties," documents which he could have secured only from Milton (Appendix B).[61] Thus, Milton was engaged in the negotiations from the outset and was responsible, again, for all of Council's correspondence with the ambassador; hence if the Latin version of the Council's proposal is found, it may be attributed to him with some assurance.[62]

Indeed, so persuasive is the evidence that the draft treaty of 12 November 1652 was, in part or in whole, Milton's work, that it is included herewith in full with the Council's marginal comments as Appendix C. It has not been available to Miltonists until now and reference to it will clarify some of the features of such documents discussed earlier in conjunction with the Portuguese treaty: their length, their complexity, and the sensitivity of their content. These features help to explain why they were not transcribed in the early manuscripts and why no letters associated with treaty negotiations appear in the Skinner MS. In the case of the Spanish treaty, as noted, there were only three such letters written to Cardenas, those of 30 January, 31 March, and 10 August. Skinner excluded the latter two, which rehearse in laborious detail the dates of meetings and documents exchanged and complain about the vagueness of Cardenas's proposals. Skinner may have intended to print them in the section devoted to the treaty itself, where they might make more sense. He included the first, however, because unlike the others it refers to the negotiations only briefly and is actually one of a series that appears in all the early sources protesting the delay in apprehending "the villanous Assassinates of [the] late Agent, *Anthony Ascham.*"

It is instructive to contrast the wealth of internal evidence in the State Papers Foreign and elsewhere that confirms the attribution of the 1652 Spanish treaty to Milton with the paucity of support for the inclusion

---

a companion to W33; but it has not been discovered. Milton apparently selected only one of these relatively unimportant letters for transcription. *Prose* gives 14 November as the date of W32 (5:638).

61. Although England signed a number of agreements with the other nations during the Interregnum, there was only *one* "Spanish Treaty" prepared and submitted by the Council of State, that of 12 November 1652. Hence, this is clearly the document to which Skinner refers.

62. The English copy in the narrative, as mentioned, has Cardenas's detailed response to each article, written in the margins. The responses are in the third person, i.e., "the Ambassador propounds" or "the Ambassador insists," obviously translated from his Latin reply, hence probably Milton's work as well.

among the State Papers of the Spanish Declaration of 1655, which editors from Thomas Birch to Mabbott and French have printed as his work. Birch published it in 1738 solely on the basis of "the peculiar Elegance of the Stile," and *Works* did so on the basis that it "is included in many editions of Milton's works." *Prose* rejects it, and Patrick chides former editors for accepting it "without a shred of clear evidence."[63] Indeed, an examination of Milton's State Papers persuades one to Patrick's opinion. Cromwell arrived at his decision to cast his lot with France and declare war on Spain only after much debate and presumably a great deal of correspondence. The negotiations were conducted, however, under great secrecy, and few documents survive to record their progress.[64] Milton's role in the deliberations may be deduced from his State Papers, which reflect the fact that he had little role at all. After January 1654 he wrote but one more letter to Spain, and that a routine acknowledgment of the arrival of an ambassador (W47, P69). His French correspondence, other than that associated with the Piedmont Massacre, began in December 1655 with a letter referring to the alliance as an accomplished fact (W61, P85). It is a routine petition from Cromwell to Louis XIV on behalf of English merchants, urging that their appeal be allowed as "the first fruits of our reviv'd Amity and the lately renew'd League between us." In brief, available records indicate that Milton's responsibility for Spanish correspondence came to an end before serious deliberations over an alliance had begun, and that he was not employed in French correspondence until after it had been accomplished. Further, the *Declaration* itself is a compendium of Spanish abuses against the English and the Indians in the New World, a subject that had no apparent impact upon his imagination.[65] Unless one can discover on what basis the eighteenth-century editors attributed the *Declaration* to Milton, it is difficult to justify its inclusion on their word

63. Birch 1:xxxiv; *Works* 18:638; *Prose* 5:712. The *Declaration* is printed in Birch 2:608–17 and *Works* 18:509–63.

64. Peter Gaunt notes that aside from the official Order Books of the Council of State there was also a "private book" used by Council to record "sensitive foreign and diplomatic business" (69). If it is found, we will know much more.

65. Milton's nephew, however, found the issue compelling. In 1656, John Phillips published an English translation of Bartolome de las Casas's *The Tears of the Indians*, a devastating condemnation of Spanish atrocities in America. Estimates of how many Indians died in the years after Cortez's conquest of Mexico vary; Casas's subtitle reads "an historical . . . account of the cruel massacres and slaughter of above twenty-millions of innocent people." I can bring to mind no reference in Milton's poetry or prose to this barbarous destruction of an entire race. Were the Spanish Declaration his work, the passage on the genocide (*Works* 18:514–17) would constitute his sole allusion to it.

alone.[66] On the other hand, there are persuasive reasons to consider the Council's draft of a Spanish treaty in 1652 as his work.

Denmark

His Spear, to equal which the tallest Pine
Hewn on Norwegian hills, to be the Mast
Of some great Ammiral, were but a wand.
                                    (PL 1:292–94)

In the mid-seventeenth century Denmark was considerably larger than it is today. Its monarch, Frederick III, was the "King of *Danemark* and *Norway*"; but of more significance was his rule over both shores of the strategic waterway known as "the Sound." The ships of any nation engaged in trade with ports on the Baltic Sea had to navigate a narrow strait, passing under the brooding battlements of Elsinore, in order to enter those waters. The Danes levied duties on all cargoes passing through the Sound and could with ease deny vessels of hostile nations access to the Baltic. That trade was immensely important to England, for all the ships stores needed to build and maintain the fleet—the tar, pitch, masts, and hemp for rope, indeed everything but oak for the hulls—came from that region; and the new leaders of the Republic were anxious to rebuild a navy sadly neglected during the reign of Charles I and diminished further during the turmoil of the 1640s.[67] It was of equal importance to the Dutch, who dominated Baltic commerce: in 1636 it was estimated that they had as many as six thousand bottoms engaged in trade with that region, far outweighing the merchant fleets of all other nations together, including Denmark and Sweden.[68] They held no territory in the area—the principal power on the Baltic was Sweden, followed in importance by Denmark, Poland, and Brandenburg—but with a highly respected navy and a skillful and industrious merchant fleet, they were the rulers of the sea lanes. Over the years

---

66. Shawcross has proposed to me that its publication was motivated by the campaign to unseat Walpole as chief minister in 1738–41, and that the attribution to Milton lent weight to the case against him.

67. R.K.W. Hinton, *The Eastland Trade*, 87; Michael Roberts, "Cromwell and the Baltic," 414.

68. Gardiner, *History*, 4:198.

Denmark and the United Netherlands had developed a close alliance, manifested in the agreement of February 1651, which gave the Dutch a privileged position in the tariff rates levied on their ships passing through the Sound.

Denmark was one of many nations that hurried envoys to London in the aftermath of the battle of Worcester and the passage of the Navigation Act. In March 1652, Parliament received a letter from King Frederick III in which he took the diplomatic initiative, proposing negotiations for a commercial treaty.[69] The following month Parliament replied with a letter in Milton's Latin (W24, P41). It is characteristic of many of the Republic's first communications with foreign powers: announcing confidently that "it has pleas'd Divine Providence, beholding this Nation with such benign and favorable Aspect, to change for the better the receiv'd Form of the former Government among us"; assuring the Danes of Parliament's desire to preserve "the ancient Friendship, Commerce, and Allyance" between the two nations; and inviting Frederick to send an embassy, which they, "so desirous of your Amity," will "embrace . . . with all Alacrity and Fidelity."

Fortunately, a full account of the embassy appears in a transcript in the Public Record Office, London, one copied at the time by a scribe obviously working under instructions to create for convenient reference a single file of all the papers relating to the negotiations between the two powers. The transcript, titled *A Journall of the Proceedings Upon the Treaty between the Parliament and the Ambassadors of the King of Denmarke with what relates to the detention of the English Ships by the said King in Copenhagen*, is an official record of those negotiations, opening with a chronological account of the meetings and incidents that influenced the outcome from the time of the Danish ambassadors' arrival in May until their departure in November. The bulk of the transcript consists of copies of the important documents bearing on the embassy, two of which appear in the early manuscripts of Milton's State Papers and so have since been published in the various editions (W29, P50; W30, P51).[70] The transcript offers valuable insight into the conduct of the type of negotiations Milton was called upon to assist and

69. According to W24, Frederick's letter (not available) was dated 19 December; but it was not delivered until 12 March, when the king's representative, Henry Rosenwing, presented it at an audience with Parliament (*Prose* 5:604).

70. The transcript, in SP 103/3/239–318, consists of a chronology (239–45) and relevant documents (246–318). The account of the negotiations given here is based largely on this transcript.

makes it possible to place his letters in the chronological sequence of diplomatic exchange, a sequence that strongly suggests that he was responsible for more than just those two.[71]

It was ironically appropriate that on the day after the Danish ambassadors' arrival on 18 May, news reached London of van Tromp's attack on Blake's fleet in the Dover Downs, for the negotiations were to be conducted against a backdrop of the Anglo-Dutch war. The two ambassadors, Erick Rosencrantz and Peter Reetz, were given a courteous audience by Parliament a week later, and at their first meeting with commissioners from the Council of State on 14 June they presented their proposals for a commercial treaty. It is a comprehensive document, consisting of fourteen articles which address points of potential conflict between trading nations of the time, such matters as: the conduct of merchant ships upon meeting men-of-war, assurances of freedom of trade, the form of letters of patent, the assessment of tariffs, the disposition of ships seeking refuge from foul weather, access to courts for owners of shipwrecked and pillaged vessels, and the effect of the proposed treaty on like agreements with other nations. The Council replied on 8 July to each article and quickly raised two troublesome issues. Whereas the Danish treaty proposals stipulate that English ships are to pay taxes and tariffs "customary in places of trade," the Council insists that they "shall not hereafter pay any higher [duties] than the People of the United Provinces" and that English merchants should have the same "freedoms and liberties" extended to those of other countries. England, in brief, was seeking a "most favored nation" status in its commercial dealings with Denmark, the one most favored, of course, being the United Netherlands. Although the Council had further reservations about the treatment of ships pursued by pirates or shipwrecked and the punishment of violators of the treaty, it was the English attitude toward the treaty's fourteenth article that proved most troublesome. The Danes, in order to protect their special relationship with the Dutch, specify that agreements in force with other nations "are to persist safe and entire and nothing shall be understood to be diminished from them by this Confederacy." Council replied curtly that they "cannot consent thereunto."

The negotiations, like those with the Dutch, were conducted through the exchange of two different sets of documents; and, as with the Dutch

---

71. SP 75/16, State Papers Foreign, Denmark, contains no documents relating to the negotiations and only one from 1652, a letter from the ambassadors, dated 18 October, requesting release of the ships on which they intend to return to Denmark (221). SP 108/32, State Papers Foreign, Treaties, contains nothing from the period.

again, yet a third set would later intrude to complicate matters further. In addition to their 8 July response to the fourteen articles of the Danish proposal, the Council presented the ambassadors with another letter setting out six articles of their own. To leave no doubt about their insistance on most favored nation status, the first article specifies that English ships will pass through the "Sound and Belt into the Baltic Sea without search or other molestation and shall pay no fees except those agreed to in the treaty"; and articles 2 and 3 designate what those fees are to be, leaving blank spaces for the sums later to be determined. Article 4 has to do with tariffs on the Elbe River. Article 5 states that England may import "Timber and Firr Trees of any length" from Denmark, a reference to the Norwegian pines, which were the chief source of masts for their ships. Article 6 deals further with the prosecution of pirates.[72]

In the ambassadors' reply to Council's answer on the fourteen articles, delivered on 28 July, they dismiss most of the English changes with the remark that they had not been empowered to treat on the details proposed. They request an explanation for Council's rejection of article 14, protesting that it would be impossible for the king "to remake those Confederacies transactions and Contracts soe solemnly and firmly established with other states heretofore." The Danish answer to the English letter of six articles restates their contention that they are not empowered to treat on such matters as passage through the Sound and the size of timber. They remark offhandedly that tariffs on the Elbe have long since been abolished and insist that Denmark will continue to deal with pirates as they always have, "according to the dictates of the Lawes of nations."

It is apparent from the correspondence thus far that the Council had two goals. The first was the aforementioned most favored nation status. The second is more subtle and must be considered in the context of the widening war with the Dutch. By rejecting the article concerning former treaties, the English sought to demonstrate to the Danes the inconvenience of their friendship with the Dutch and to persuade them, though in a somewhat heavy-handed way, that they would do well to abandon that alliance. It is equally apparent from the Danish replies that they were entertaining no such thoughts. The impasse helps explain not only the content but also the tone of Milton's letters, which are the next in sequence.

The English were slow in replying. Indeed, the Committee for Foreign

72. In SP 103/3, the Danish proposal appears at 250–55, the English response at 255–59, and the English proposal at 259–61.

Affairs did not take up the matter of the ambassadors' 28 July letters until 3 September. Five days later the minutes of the committee record two separate orders: "That ye answere now read to ye paper of ye Danish Ambassadors be reported to Councell to be sent unto them for approval thereof," and "That ye paper now read concerning ye people of this Commonwealth paying . . . be reported to ye Councell to be by them proposed to ye Danish Ambassadors."[73] These are the two letters preserved in the seventeenth-century sources of Milton's State Papers (W29–30, P50–51); they were approved by the Council and delivered to the ambassadors at a meeting on 15 September.[74] By this time the complexity of answer to reply had achieved Byzantine proportions, as illustrated by the titles affixed to Milton's letters in the transcript: "The Answer of the Council of State to the Reply of the Lords Embassadors . . . to the Answer which the Council gave to the Fourteen Demands" and "A Reply of the Council of State to the Answer of the foresaid Lords Embassadors . . . to the Six Articles propounded by the Council aforesaid."[75]

Some measure of the contentious tone of the negotiations may be seen in the controversy over the tariffs on the Elbe River. The English maintained a lively trade with Hamburg, an important city of the Hanseatic League, and enjoyed a sympathetic exchange with its Protestant citizens, earlier tensions having relaxed somewhat. Danish possessions at the time included the city of Glückstadt, which lay on the Elbe and from which they could interdict the river traffic to and from Hamburg. One of the six articles the Council of State insisted be added to the treaty required the Danes to lift the duties they had imposed on river traffic passing Glückstadt. In their reply to the six articles, the ambassadors stated that since such tariffs had in fact been discontinued for some time, the issue need not concern them. In the answer to the reply on the six articles—Milton's letter—the English pointedly insist that the suspension of fees be stipulated in the treaty nonetheless, "lest they should be reimpos'd hereafter." It is abundantly clear that the English do not trust the Danes and equally apparent they they have no reservations about saying so.

73. SP 25/131/24–25.

74. *Works* dates the letters "*After* Oct. 1. 1652" and "*After* Oct. 22. 1652." *Prose* has "October 14 [?], 1652" and "October 22, 1652." According to the transcript all of these dates would place the preparation of the letters after the treaty negotiations had been broken off. They may be safely dated 13 September, two days before they were presented to the ambassadors (*CSPD* 4:400).

75. SP 103/3/265–68.

In the "Answer . . . to the Reply . . . to the Answer" to the Danish
articles, the Council seems conciliatory on some of the minor issues; but
in reference to the effect of the treaty on agreements Denmark has with
other nations, they remark coolly that "it is not proper to give our
Assent to those Leagues and Alliances . . . before it be more clear to us
what they are." In their "Reply . . . to the Answer" of the Danes to the
six articles, Council observes rather haughtily that they have examined
the ambassadors' credentials carefully and find them fully empowered
to "Negotiate all things . . . propounded by this Republick"; hence they
"did not expect the Replies which it has pleas'd the foresaid Lords Ambassadors to give" on the matter, and they request that the Danes "return an Answer" forthwith to the English demands. Further, since the
ambassadors seem to have completely ignored the English insistence on
parity with the Dutch in the payment of customs, Council finds it necessary to add a seventh article, demanding explicitly that English ships
"shall not for the future pay any more Customs, Tribute, Taxes, Duties
or Stipends, or in any other manner, then the people of the *United
Provinces*," and that English citizens shall be extended the same "Freedom, Privileges and Immunities . . . which any other People of Foreign
Nations enjoys . . . throughout the whole Dominions of the King of
Danemark and *Norway*."

> I see all offers made by me how slight
> Thou valuest, because offer'd, and reject'st:
> Nothing will please the difficult and nice,
> Or nothing more than still to contradict.
> (PR 4:156–58)

The Danish reply, of 21 September, reduces the chief points in contention to two. In reference to Denmark's existing treaties, the ambassadors refer to their remarks in the 28 July meeting with the Council, in
which they had sought "to remove all Scruples" the English might have,
assuring them that nothing in the proposed treaty would in any way
infringe upon or be prejudicial to Denmark's standing "Confederacies
and Transactions" with other countries. They repeat that they are not
empowered to treat on such matters as customs and passage of the
Sound; and they ask what the Council proposes to do next. The answer
of the English, dated 5 October in the transcript, is the last in the sequence. It is nothing less than outrageous. On the first point of contention the Council observes that if indeed the proposed treaty does not
conflict with existing Danish agreements, the king will have no objection to supplying the Council "with the particular Treatyes, and confed-

eracies mentioned," so that they may "satisfy themselves" on the validity of the ambassadors' assurances. On the second, since the ambassadors seem to feel they do not have the authority to treat on the issues in conflict, the Council haughtily suggests that they return to their king and secure it. This may cause a regrettable delay, but it is after all their fault. The sting of this dismissal of the embassy was somewhat diminished by the fact that the Danes had already requested an audience with Parliament to seek permission to depart.[76]

> Embassies thou show'st
> From Nations far and nigh; what honor that,
> But tedious waste of time to sit and hear
> So many hollow compliments and lies,
> Outlandish flatteries?
>
> (PR 4:121–24)

One may well wonder about Milton's thoughts as the negotiations came to such a disagreeable close, he who, the previous April, had expressed in eloquent Latin Parliament's fervent resolve to preserve "the ancient Friendship, Commerce, and Allyance" between the two nations. Though such elaborate language was required by the protocol of the time, when hard differences were concealed by extravagant protestations of eternal amity, one would prefer to think that those earlier sentiments had been sincere and that the English attitude toward the Danes was dramatically changed by the outbreak of the Dutch war. It would appear that by September, as Milton was translating the replies to answers, Council had already decided that a treaty with the traditional ally of the Dutch was no longer possible; and buoyed by Blake's victory over de Witt at Kentish Knock on the twenty-eighth, they simply set about to say so. It is worth noting that although the war weighed heavily in the scales during the deliberations, the letters exchanged are silent on the conflict. The two sides maintained the posture of friendly nations working in a mature and responsible manner toward a commercial agreement between trading partners.

It is not that the war went unnoticed. The Danish ambassadors gave two earnest speeches in the name of their king urging peace between the two Protestant powers, one in Parliament on 2 July and another to the

---

76. Ibid. 271–74. Although the letter is dated 5 October, it is appended to a notice of the ambassadors' request for an audience. The summary at the beginning of the transcript indicates that they made this request on 1 October. The sharpness of the English letter may have been prompted by the knowledge that the Danes intended to break off the negotiations anyway.

Council of State on 15 September.[77] The Council of State replied with letters that, arguing on the basis of the Latin employed, Leo Miller concludes were written by Milton. The first, of 8 July, is conciliatory in tone, acknowledging the king's concern and promising copies of the Dutch *Declaration*, in Latin and English, which, Council is confident, will explain everything. The second, of 19 October, is sternly abrupt; the Council, having long since forwarded the *Declaration*, finds "it strange that there should still remayne with those in amitie with this nation . . . the least dissatisfaction concerning the Justice and Candor of the Parlaments proceedings in that affair."[78] The letter ends with a curt dismissal of the subject: "Nothing remaynes needfull to be added" to what has been said. In the negotiations, however, the United Netherlands was mentioned but once, as the most favored nation with whom England demanded parity. Otherwise, the war remained an unlisted agenda item, and the English made their will known by wrangling over such matters as the recovery of shipwrecked goods, the prosecution of pirates, the striking of colors, and the size of logs.

Approval for the departure of the Danish ambassadors was delayed, as it happened, by an incident that occasioned yet another Milton letter (W35, P52). A full account of the incident appears in the transcript, although the letter itself does not, as it was written after the events chronicled in the document. In the summer of 1652, English merchant ships emerging from the Baltic had been instructed not to attempt a crossing of the North Sea alone for fear of interception by Dutch warships. They were told, rather, to rendezvous in the harbor at Copenhagen, there to await a fleet of English men-of-war to escort them to England. A squadron of seventeen ships under Captain Andrew Ball was ordered to that task on 30 August. Ball arrived off the Danish coast on 20 September; but under orders to avoid contact with the Dutch fleet, and apparently mistrustful of the Danes, he had delayed informing them of his mission until after his arrival.[79] Frederick III, quite understandably, took strong exception to the appearance without prior notice of a fleet of warships from a belligerent nation off his neutral shores

---

77. Copies of both speeches may be found in SP 103/3/291–96. The Danes were not the only ones urging peace. On 24 December the Swiss Evangelical Cantons wrote, deploring the conflict. Parliament replied almost a year later with a lengthy justification of their actions, an eloquent letter that ends with praise for the Swiss efforts "to reconcile and pacifie contending Brethren" and the pious prediction that "doubtless will ye obtain the Celestial Reward of Peace-Makers with God" (W40, P63). But the war went on.

78. Miller, *John Milton's Writings*, 276; SP 103/3/293–94, 296–97.

79. This despite the Council's explicit order that "you are to give as timely notice as you can to the King of Denmark" (*CSPD* 4:386).

and in response refused to permit the English merchant ships to leave
the harbor; whereupon Ball, his mission aborted, promptly sailed for
home.

The Council of State received notice of the incident on 13 October,
two weeks after the ambassadors had requested audience with Parliament, and responded by impounding all Danish ships in English harbors, including those commissioned to carry the embassy home. After a
further exchange of letters, the Council directed Richard Bradshaw,
then English Resident at Hamburg, to proceed to Denmark and negotiate the release of the English merchant ships.[80] In Milton's letter of 9
November, Parliament rejects Frederick III's explanation for his actions
and informs him of the appointment of Bradshaw to mediate.

The final outcome of these months of negotiation was no comfort to
the English, as before the year was out Denmark joined the Dutch in the
war and closed the Sound to English shipping. As we have seen, a year
and a half later Cromwell was still negotiating for the release of the
merchant ships and the reopening of the Sound to English trade.

The Council of State's Latin Secretary was involved in the Danish
negotiations from beginning to end, from the first letter in April wel-
coming Frederick III's overtures for a treaty to the one in November
rejecting his account of the events of 20 September and appointing
Bradshaw to mediate. There are several factors which support the view
that Milton's contribution to the exchange of documents was not limited to the four letters that appear in the *Literae* and the Columbia MS.
The first consideration is the sheer amount of work to be done, the bulk
of which fell to John Thurloe, secretary to both the Council of State and
the Committee for Foreign Affairs. He was a busy man, in constant
attendance at meetings of both bodies, from whom he received a steady
stream of tasks, which he then had to perform in the time left him
outside of meetings.[81] Taking into consideration the number of issues
under discussion by the Council in the year 1652, the scope of Thurloe's responsibilities, and the unwieldy, time-consuming procedure required to gain approval for any document, one must wonder whether
he ever slept. The Council was engaged with the Dutch until July, the
Danes arrived in May and the Portuguese in August, whereas negotiations with the Spanish continued throughout the year; and for a period
the English were deliberating over three different treaties at the same
time. These were the same months when they were gearing up for a
war; and Parliament, where most of the Council members sat, was engaged in a heated debate over a constitutional settlement.

80. *CSPD* 4:452.
81. See, e.g., SP 25/131/12, 41, 48, 74, 75, and *CSPD* 4:342, 346, 364, 419.

Along with his other talents, Thurloe was a well-organized man; but he had inherited an inadequate staff of translators, the aged Georg Weckherlin and the blind Milton. Thurloe surely employed others in the voluminous correspondence required of him—Haak to help with the Dutch, Augier and Rosin with the French, and Hartlib in a variety of tasks—but Philip Meadows was not hired to assist in Latin translation until the following summer, leaving Milton as Thurloe's principal assistant in the complex exchange of answer to reply to answer that characterized the Danish exchanges.

In his commentary on Milton's two letters, Patrick observes that "his services as translator were enlisted only when Danish-English relations reached a crisis which required the utmost precision and delicacy in the Latin texts."[82] But the need for "utmost precision and delicacy" is exactly the reason why it is unlikely that a new translator, unfamiliar with what had gone before, would be brought in at that critical stage of the negotiations. It is far more reasonable that the busy Thurloe would have turned his English drafts over to an assistant thoroughly knowledgeable about the issues under dispute and the specific language employed from the outset. He would certainly want to avoid the need to review the whole course of the negotiations with a new translator every time he had an additional set of documents to prepare. Milton was responsible for a letter at the beginning of the negotiations, another at the end, and two prepared at the crucial point where it became a formidable task simply to keep track of all the proposals and counterproposals in the sequence of answer to reply to answer. Both the archival evidence and a realistic assessment of administrative practices in the Council's secretariat strongly suggest that he was responsible as well for the documents leading up to that point and probably those thereafter.[83]

Milton's two letters from the Danish negotiations amply illustrate why similar documents were omitted from the early transcripts. Once isolated from the sequence of which they are a part, they become unsuitable for publication, filled as they are with references to issues introduced in earlier letters not available to the reader. In one of the two, for example, the Council cites their answer to the Danes' original "Fifth, Sixth, Seventh, Eighth, and Ninth Articles" and in the other they express surprise at the Danes' objection to their "First, Second, Third, and Fifth demand," references entirely meaningless to a reader without access to the preceding exchanges. The alternative is to publish them all; and, as we have seen, the *Literae* does include all the Spanish letters of

82. *Prose* 5:632.
83. In the month of October alone the Council of State wrote at least four more to the ambassadors concerning the impounded ships (SP 103/3/271–73, 278, 284, 287).

1652. But in that case there were only three, much fewer than the seven (or nine, if Miller is correct) it would require to provide a complete record of the Danish exchanges. The language, further, is narrowly confined, given necessarily to endless repetition of the same words and phrases throughout, hence of marginal interest to any but the most dedicated of historians. The proposed volume, again, was intended to display Milton's Latin; and if the reader has once seen his rendering of such passages as "any Ship that shall be driven by stress of Weather into Rivers, Ports or Bays belonging to either Party," there is little to be gained in printing it three times over. If it is impossible to include all the letters in a sequence, it is better to include none; hence Milton omitted all documents from the Portuguese, the Dutch,[84] and the Swedish negotiations. Concerning the two Danish letters, one can only conjecture that, since they are the only documents in the early sources that take the form of an article-by-article refutation, they may have been included to illustrate the variety of Milton's service in his office.[85] Were he to choose any from the Danish correspondence, it would be the two letters of 13 September, where the sequence reaches the climax of its complexity and the Latin, if not elegant, is usefully employed. Daniel Skinner, as noted, thought otherwise of their value and, perhaps wisely, omitted such documents from his manuscript, planning perhaps to include them in the missing section, in which according to his prospectus he intended to publish "illustrative documents, German, Danish, and Swedish" (see Appendix B).[86]

The record of the Danish negotiations is revealing in what it tells us of the attitude toward foreign policy of the men whom Milton served. There were surely able statesmen among them; but these "mechanics, soldiers, servants, strong and keen enough, but entirely ignorant of public political affairs," as Milton characterized them, were largely unskilled in political give-and-take or the codes of diplomatic discourse. Whatever the advantages of the Commonwealth form of government, treaty-making was not one of them. The Rump's record is not enviable.

---

84. There is one such document from the Dutch negotiations published in *Literae*, the Demands letter (70). As observed earlier, it is of such a nature as to suggest strongly that it was not a part of the original manuscript.

85. The Rebuttal letter, it will be recalled, was not included in the early sources (W167E, P38).

86. Milton's correspondence with Denmark does not end here; but his later letters are associated with other nations, such as Savoy and Sweden, and will be cited elsewhere. He wrote four more, one a routine petition (W64, P122), one on the Piedmont Massacre (W58, P77), and two concerning the War in the North (W87, P119; W136, P175). He also translated a letter from Frederick III into English (W159, P118).

Of their negotiations with the Dutch, one ended in humiliation and the other in war, as did the deliberations with the Danes. The Portuguese were sent packing and although they returned in August 1652, their cause languished for almost two years. The Spanish also pressed for a treaty for two years but they were no closer to an agreement at the end than at the outset. The contrast with the experience of the Protectorate is striking. Within nine months after his appointment as Lord Protector, Oliver Cromwell, uninhibited by discordant voices in Parliament and advised by a compliant Council, had sealed peace treaties with the United Netherlands, Denmark, and Portugal, and signed commercial agreements with Denmark, Portugal, and Sweden.[87]

The government of the Commonwealth was a noble experiment but its leaders found compromise a difficult art to master, the soldiers accustomed to seeing their enemy clear and the merchants to measuring power as a function of price, none of them comfortable with the subtle play of words that mark unseen shifts of intent and alliance between great nations. Impatient with the veiled speech of ambassadors, it was their nature to take a stand and adhere to it resolutely, a predilection no doubt reinforced by the moral certainties of their religious convictions, which counseled them never to stray from the truth.

Tuscany

Was this your discipline and faith ingag'd,
Your military obedience?

(PL 4:954–55)

Some of Milton's letters quite simply excite the curiosity. Such a one is Parliament's of 14 January 1653, to Ferdinand II, duke of Tuscany (W37, P60), which makes intriguing reference to "the Insolence, as they hear, of Captain *Appleton* in the Port of *Leghorn*," whom the Council of State had relieved of command and ordered back to London for disciplinary action because he had "offer'd Violence to the Sentinel then doing his Duty upon the Mole" and violated a promise "not to fall even upon the *Hollanders* themselves within sight of the *Lanthorn*." Aside from the curious references to the "Mole" and "*Lanthorn*," the letter is

---

87. Masson 4:552–54. In 1654, peace treaties were signed with the Dutch and Danes on 5 April (SP 103/46), and with Portugal on 10 July. Cromwell reached commercial agreements with Sweden on 28 April (SP 108/516, SP 103/69/106–13), Portugal on 10 July (SP 103/57/285–301), and Denmark on 14 September (SP 103/3/131–46).

further intriguing because it is, in effect, an apology. In Milton's letters England's heads of state do a variety of things—they warn, thank, announce, protest, counsel, appeal, exhort, deplore, declare, and congratulate—but this is the only one in the collection in which they apologize.

Before turning to the adventures of Captain Appleton, however, some mention should be made of Milton's first letter to the duke, that of 20 January 1652 (W17, P29). Earlier discussion of this letter has centered on the Council's order of 2 January for its preparation: "That Mr. Milton doe prepare a Letter in Latine of the substance of what was now here read in English to be sent to the Duke of Tuscany,"[88] the wording of which suggests that the Council of State was entrusting Milton, then almost three years in office, with the composition of routine letters such as that to the duke. This is an impression reinforced, it will be recalled, by phrasing in the letter that seems to bear the mark of Milton's personal experience. The Council expresses appreciation to the duke for "the value you have for this nation," as testified by English merchants who trade with Tuscany, but also by "certain of our young Nobility, either Travelling through your Cities, or residing there for the improvements of their Studies," the poet remembering his own journey through Tuscany some thirteen years prior.

The apologetic tone of the letter on Appleton, written a year later, is clarified somewhat by those prepared by Milton during the intervening months. His next to Tuscany is dated 29 July (W27, P46). The war with the Dutch was under way by then and England stood in serious need of a haven for its small Mediterranean fleet, which it appears that the duke was prepared to provide. Tuscany's chief port was Leghorn (the Italian *Livorno*), since over the centuries the Arno had effectively silted in the harbor at Pisa. The Council expresses gratitude for the protection offered English ships anchored there when a Dutch fleet "threatned to Sink, or Burn" them; and they enclose a copy of the Dutch *Declaration* to demonstrate "how unjust and contrary to all the Laws of God and of Nations those People have acted against this Republick." In September the Council, fearful that the earlier letter had gone astray, followed it up with yet another to the duke, "to let your Highness understand once more, how highly they esteem your Justice and singular Constancy in defending their Vessels, and how acceptable they took so great a piece of Service" (W31, P49). English ships, they add, have received strict instructions that "upon their entrance into your Ports, [they are] not to fail of paying the Accustom'd Salutes by Firing their Guns, and to give all other due Honours to your Highness."

88. *CSPD* 4:89.

In a related letter, this one addressed to the Spanish ambassador in London on 11 November, the Council of State asks him to relay their gratitude to the king for the protection given to "Captain *Badiley*, Admiral of the Fleet of this *Republick* in the *Streights*" by the governor of Porto Longone (W33, P53). Captain Richard Badiley was Appleton's immediate superior, and it was his fleet that had benefited from the protection of the duke of Tuscany in July. He had a sharp encounter with the Dutch the following October and sought refuge in the Spanish harbor at Longone, the modern Porto Azzurro, which lies at the eastern end of the Isle of Elba about sixty miles south of Leghorn. The Council asks the ambassador to convey to the king their thanks for "the singular Civility" shown the English fleet on that occasion, which they go on to profess rather grandly as "the copious fruit of the stricter mutual Amity so auspiciously commenc'd," that is, the treaty negotiations under way in London between the two powers.[89]

So anxious was Parliament to stay on amicable terms with Tuscany— and retain access to the harbor—that in November, responding to a request from the duke,[90] they took the extraordinary step of setting aside a judgment by the Court of Admiralty against a "Captain *Cardi* of *Leghorn*" even though the Court had "already pronounc'd Sentence"; and they ordered that Cardi's ship and cargo be restored to him, a gesture intended "to testify how much they value the good Will and Alliance of a Prince so much their Friend" (W34, P55). One can well imagine the distress of Parliament, so dependent upon the duke for the safety of their Mediterranean fleet, when in early December they received an angry letter from him about the English Captain Henry Appleton, who had "offer'd Violence" to his sentinel and done something equally objectionable "within sight of [his] *Lanthorn*."[91] Fortunately, the unhappy adventures of Captain Appleton are fully documented in SP 98/3 and 4, State Papers Foreign, Tuscany; so the tale can be told and curiosity satisfied.[92]

89. In the order of 5 November, the Committee for Foreign Affairs directed Thurloe to prepare a companion to the governor of Porto Longone as well (*CSPD* 4:476). If found, it may reasonably be attributed to Milton.

90. Nalson MS 10:28, dated 29 August.

91. Ibid. 26, dated 27 November.

92. The Appleton affair is among the more fully documented in the public records. The account is based on several letters in SP 98/3/246–69 and SP 98/4/1–65. A number quoted in the text are listed here for reference:

These documents clarify matters. Duke Ferdinand, anxious to maintain an uneasy neutrality in the Anglo-Dutch war and to benefit from the belligerents' purchase of necessary supplies, made provisions for both fleets to use the harbor and roads at Leghorn, but under an explicit agreement that any ships in or near the harbor refrain from hostile action. In compliance, Appleton had written him in August (as presumably had the Dutch admiral), pledging not to "give any disturbance to Flemings in sight of Port or Lanthorn," the latter being a prominent lighthouse in Leghorn. That city has no natural harbor, only one formed by an extensive complex of seawalls or breakwaters, each referred to by the Italians as a "*molo*," hence Milton's "Mole."

The duke's arrangement prevailed until late November, when two encounters between the hostile forces tried his patience. The actual events were to be a matter of some dispute in later months but the essentials can be reconstructed. Milton's letter refers to "the recover'd Ship, *Phoenix* of *Leghorn*," which was an English frigate captured by the Dutch in a battle with Badiley in August. The resourceful Dutch had sailed it into Leghorn harbor, where, it was alleged, they left it at anchor flying English colors as a decoy for unsuspecting merchantmen, which would approach it, only to be boarded and seized by the Dutch crew. The frustrated Badiley, who had to endure the daily sight of his captive ship, conceived a plan to retake it; and on the night of 22 November Captain Owen Cox "surprised ye feinx frigat in that road and carried her away from the enemy," unfortunately within full view of the "*Lanthorn*."

3/246	22 August 1652	Appleton to the duke of Tuscany
3/256v–57	13 December 1652	Longland to the Council of State
3/260	7 December 1652	Longland to the Council of State
3/268–69	8 December 1652	Appleton to the duke of Tuscany
4/1	1 January 1653	Appleton to the Council of State
4/17	2 March 1653	Appleton to the Council of State
4/19	11 March 1653	Appleton to the Council of State
4/38	29 April 1653	Appleton to the Committee of the Navy

SP 18/26–30 contains duplicates of a number of these letters, as well as several not in SP 98. Among the latter are the following, published in vols. 5 and 6 of *CSPD*:

5:31–32	23 November 1652	Appleton to Badiley
5:40	18 December 1652	Appleton to the Council of State
5:195	1 March 1653	Badiley to Appleton
5:214	14 March 1653	Longland to the Committee of the Navy
5:233	25 March 1653	Appleton to the Council of State
5:234	25 March 1653	Appleton to the MP from Hull
5:408	13 June 1653	Longland to Badiley
6:243–49	14 November 1653	Longland to the Council of State

> the Mole immense wrought on
> Over the foaming deep high Archt, a Bridge
> Of length prodigious.
>
> (*PL* 19:300–302)

The second incident, which took place the following day, involved Appleton and Milton's curious "Mole." Puzzling over the word led me on a series of fruitless inquiries, which ended successfully in the Cambridge University Library Map Room, where a learned cartographer produced a large-scale chart of Leghorn, explaining all. It is an artificial port, created by the erection of several seawalls, each identified on the Italian map as a *molo*; and, sure enough, at the tip of one of them jutting into the sea is a lighthouse symbol, the "*Lanthorn*" in question.[93] Appleton's troubles were triggered by a Dutch prisoner he had aboard his ship, the Leopard, one who "having ease to ease himself in the ships-head," as Appleton put it later, seized the opportunity to leap overboard and swim to the nearby *molo*, where he sought sanctuary by placing himself under the protection of a Tuscan sentinel. The captain pursued and demanded custody of the prisoner, only to be confronted by three additional sentinels, who threatened to fire on the English. The prisoner chose that propitious moment to make a dash for freedom, and Appleton had to return empty-handed to his ship. The duke was predictably angry at these violations of his rules of neutrality; and, assuming that Appleton was responsible for both incidents, he sent word by a Tuscan officer summoning the captain to his court in Pisa.[94] Appleton later claimed that he was informed, not by the Tuscan, but by William Longland, the English Resident in Tuscany, whom he accused of conspiring to set him up as a scapegoat in the affair.

---

93. The other documents in the file regularly use "Mold" or "Mould," apparently the usage at the time. Confusion over this word illustrates the advantage of using the contemporary translation. The Latin is "*eum nimirum ab eo vigili dum in molestationem ageret*," which, as noted, Phillips translates correctly as "offer'd Violence to the Sentinel then doing his Duty upon the Mole." In *Prose*, Paul W. Blackford renders the passage, "offered violence to a watchman as he was guarding against molestation" (5:632). In brief, Phillips knew what a "Mole" was, whereas Blackford apparently did not. Miller points out that *Literae* erroneously conflated "mole" and "stationem" although there is a space between them in the Columbia and Skinner MSS; and *Works* printed them as one word, causing Blackford's misunderstanding (Review of *The Miltonic State Papers* 476).

94. There was some dispute over who was responsible. In a letter of 22 November, Appleton describes his role, which was to supply Cox with the boats and some of his men (*CSPD* 4:503). Badiley more than once indicates that he ordered the operation, but claims that he did not know of Appleton's agreement with the duke, which seems unlikely (*CSPD* 5:4, 31, 161–62).

Appleton dutifully proceeded to Pisa, where he was immediately arrested and thrown in prison. Released three days later through Longland's intercession, he returned to his ship without having the opportunity to explain himself to the duke. The Council of State shortly received Ferdinand's indignant letter, demanding satisfaction for the assault upon his sentinel and the seizure of the Phoenix, and holding Appleton responsible for both incidents.[95] Milton's reply informs the duke that the captain has been ordered "to come away without stóp or stay by Land" and answer to his superiors in London for "his unwonted and extraordinary" behavior. In a later defense of his actions, Appleton claims that Longland had misrepresented him to Council, knowing full well, "as God and the World doth, Captain Badily commanded the taking of the Frigot, and . . . that I never touched the Centinel or gave him ill word."[96]

On 1 January, Appleton wrote a long letter to the Council of State in an effort to clear his name. As the record reveals, however, his adventures did not end in January with him setting out for London in obedience to the Council's orders—indeed, they had only begun. His case occupied the attention of the Council for the balance of the year and became a *cause célèbre*, which was eventually fought out in the public press. The chronicle would compel the attention of any student of history, and Milton surely followed the controversy as it evolved.[97] If he wrote any more letters about the unfortunate captain—and there were certainly more written—they were omitted from the early transcripts.

Henry Appleton was a man born under an evil star. His next letter to the Council, dated 2 March, finds him still in Italy; and he is at pains to explain his apparent disregard of his superiors' explicit orders to proceed "without stop or stay by Land" to London. In late January, the English fleet arrived in Leghorn from Porto Longone, where they had spent some weeks because of adverse weather; and Badiley found Appleton still there, dutifully awaiting transport to England. He was, apparently, a highly valued ship's captain, and Badiley was reluctant to lose his services. According to Appleton's letter, a council of war was

95. Nalson MS 10:26, dated 27 November 1652.

96. Henry Appleton, *A Remonstrance*, 7.

97. In 1899, Thomas Alfred Spalding published *A Life of Richard Badiley, Vice Admiral of the Fleet*, the bulk of which is devoted to the events of 1652–53. The book is singularly partisan toward its subject. Appleton is characterized as "a type of degenerate Puritan who was petrified by his profession of religion" (8), and "a halting, hesitant man, not to be relied upon in any crisis which demanded a cool head and a steady hand" (56), opinions not fully warranted by the collection in SP 98/3 and 4, which Spalding did not have available.

called of all the fleet's captains, who arrived at a controversial decision, one which he later cited repeatedly in his defense. As he describes it, his fellow officers "put it to ye vote whether your honours orders might be dispensed withall in this so great necessity tending much to ye honour of ye Parliament and ye whole Nation, namely, fighting ye Dutch." The council of war advised him to seek the duke's permission to stay in Leghorn and pursue his mission. Ferdinand was agreeable, so Appleton decided to "remaine on board Commander of your shipp Leopard" and "resolved to throw myselfe upon ye favorable Censure of your honors for my disobedience."

It is not clear how the Council responded to this blatant disregard of their orders but subsequent events soon rendered the question moot. They very shortly received another letter from their errant captain, one dated but nine days later on 11 March; and they must have been somewhat startled to read the return address: "On Board ye Dutch Vice Admirall Livorno road." Appleton was a prisoner of the Dutch! His letter gives an account of the events that brought about this unhappy condition. On 4 March, two days after he had written to extricate himself from one set of troubles, he played a prominent part in an engagement between the Dutch and English fleets outside Leghorn, which immersed him more deeply in another. In late February the Dutch fleet sailed out of the harbor, and Badiley split his forces, unwisely as it happened, sailing after them with nine ships while leaving Appleton in Leghorn with two men-of-war and four armed merchantmen. The canny Dutch seized the opportunity to double back and blockade the harbor, placing themselves effectively between the two wings of the English fleet. The duke, by now heartily weary of them both, ordered the English to leave Leghorn; and the Dutch positioned their fleet of some twenty-five ships in a hugh crescent, blocking all the entrances to the harbor, and simply waited for Appleton to emerge. The two English captains devised a simple plan to unite their forces. Once they had a good offshore wind, Badiley was to draw the Dutch into an engagement, whereupon Appleton in full sail would speed out of the harbor and join him in the battle.

> As when a spark
> Lights on a heap of nitrous Powder, . . .
> . . . . the Smutty grain
> With sudden blaze diffus'd, inflames the Air.
> (PL 4:814–18)

Appleton's ill luck held. The Dutch pursued Badiley according to plan; but the Leghorn squadron left too soon, before the two fleets became engaged, allowing the Dutch to return quickly and bring the full force of superior numbers to bear against Appleton's six ships. Further, almost immediately a Dutch shell hit the powder magazine of his only other man-of-war and blew it out of the water. He fought on, one against many, until, as he puts it in a later account,

> our stern being beaten in, and Tiller shot to pieces, fourteen guns made unserviceable, the ship every way pitifully torn, almost half our men disabled, and my self, Lieutenant, and many Officers wounded, and the Enemy increased; but most of all, my men being discouraged by their friends forsaking of them, they resolved to fight no longer.

He insists that he wanted to fight on but his men seized him, "putting my shoulder out of joynt" and forced him to surrender. All this while, he complains bitterly in his letter, Badiley failed to come to his aid, but "for what Cause I know not after some short disputes, stood away from me when I could not helpe my selfe"; indeed, according to one account, Badiley ordered a Captain Ellis, who was attempting to support Appleton, to break contact and withdraw. The unfortunate commander lost five of his six ships in the encounter and was taken prisoner along with two of his captains. So he writes on 11 March, pleading for help from a Council of State whose orders he had seen fit to disobey, closing his letter with a plaintive lament: "I now wish with all my hart, that I had not obeyed ye results of ye Counsell of warre." One must conclude that the Council of State received this news with dry eyes, as not entirely sympathetic with the plight of a captain who had disobeyed their express orders and lost a third of their Mediterranean fleet in the bargain.

Longland sought to have him exchanged, while Appleton poured forth further letters, one in March to his MP from Hull and another in April to the Committee of the Navy, pleading with them for help, accusing Badiley of "dessertion," and blaming him again for "standing away with his whole squadron" during the action. On 22 May the three captains were finally set ashore in Tuscany, but under a 12,000 dollar bond to guarantee their appearance "in two months time prisoner in Holland."[98] Longland was there to greet them and for his troubles was

---

98. Appleton 7–16. A "dollar," according to Longland, was worth "6s. 3d." and

roundly abused by one, a Captain Seaman, who, convinced that he had been betrayed by all concerned, had to be forcefully restrained from assaulting the Resident and resorted to hurling rocks at him.[99] Appleton does not record his reaction at the time but his letters clearly indicate that he shared Seaman's sentiments. They reported to Holland and in August were finally exchanged for three Dutch captains in English custody.[100]

Appleton returned to London a very angry man and set out to exonerate himself. In a short tract of some twenty-nine pages, *A Remonstrance of the Fight in Legorn-Road Between the English and the Dutch*, published on 19 September 1653, he gave his version of the encounter, accusing Badiley of various degrees of incompetence, betrayal, and cowardice, calling upon the testimony of three captains and several seamen to substantiate his account. The tract was published by John Field, who was the printer to Parliament, which lent a certain weight to the arguments, so that when Badiley arrived in London he discovered that he was the one on trial, not Appleton. He promptly joined in the pamphlet war, publishing two long tracts, the first attacking the allegations of the three captains and the second excoriating Appleton.[101]

The Council of State was thus confronted with two radically different versions of the recapture of the Phoenix, the incident with the sentinel, and the battle of Leghorn itself, both of which were somewhat suspect; and they resorted to a device characteristic of such bodies by bouncing the issue back and forth among various committees. Council sent it to the Committee for Foreign Affairs, who remanded it to an *ad hoc* body, who decided that it more properly came within the jurisdiction of the Admiralty committee. That body, equally reluctant to confront the issues, shunted it over to the Irish and Scotch committee and it was that improbable body which finally resolved the conflicting accounts of just

---

12,000 dollars, therefore, about £3150 (*CSPD* 5:58, 303). In some letters the bond is referred to as 12,000 "pieces of eight," apparently a comparable sum (*CSPD* 5:362; 6:249).

99. According to Longland's later account, "I found such an encounter from Seaman, that in all my life time I never was halfe so much abused, he call'd me all the base scandalous names he could imagine, took up great stones and flung them at me to have brain'd me, and I am confident if he could have come at me had done me some notable mischiefe, if not to the losse of my life" (Richard Badiley, *Capt. Badiley's Answer*, 72).

100. *CSPD* 6:2.

101. *Capt. Badiley's Reply* and *Capt. Badiley's Answer*. Badiley's case was helped considerably by a letter from Longland to the Council substantiating his account (*CSPD* 6:243–49).

what happened within sight of the Tuscan *"Lanthorn."*[102] There is no record of their deliberations; but in November, a full year after the incident of "the Sentinel . . . upon the Mole," Badiley was promoted to Vice Admiral of the Fleet.[103] At about the same time, Parliament dispatched a letter to the duke, complaining that he had compelled the English ships to leave the harbor in the face of a Dutch fleet of superior numbers; and they awarded Captain Cox £500 for recapturing the Phoenix. The hapless Captain Appleton, on the other hand, was not heard from again, save for a single entry in the Order Books, recording his petition for arrears in pay.[104] In the words of the *Dictionary of National Biography*, he "vanished into the darkness from which he had sprung."

Milton was to hear of some of these captains again. In Badiley's small fleet was the ship, the *Lewis*, commanded by William Ellis (or Ell, as it appears in the pamphlets). He was one of the three captains whose testimony appears in Appleton's *Remonstrance*, the other two being the hot-tempered Seaman, who threw rocks at Longland, and a Captain Marsh. Ellis, like the others, confirmed Appleton's contention that Badiley had withdrawn from the action and left him to face the Dutch alone.[105] Ellis's ship was not a man-of-war but an armed merchantman, and apparently he continued to follow his trade in the Mediterranean after the war.

Five years later Milton prepared two letters referring to this same Captain Ellis, then captain of the ship, the *Little Lewis* (W100, P134; W107, P139). In September 1657 Cromwell wrote the duke complaining that Ellis had been hired by the Turks to carry foodstuffs from Alexandria to Constantinople but had instead sailed off to Leghorn with his cargo, "where he now lives in Possession of his Prey." Cromwell asks the duke to apprehend Ellis and return the cargo to its owners because this "Villanous Act" would expose "the Christian Name to scandal" and English merchants in Turkey "to Violence and Ransack." The duke complied, and in December Cromwell wrote again to thank

102. *CSPD* 5:397; 6:47, 76, 85. It may have been sent to the Irish and Scotch committee because Cromwell was the chairman.

103. Spalding records that Badiley went on to serve with distinction as vice admiral to Blake's fleet in the Mediterranean in 1654 and the campaign against Spain in 1655–56. He died on 7 August 1657.

104. *CSPD* 6:289, 457, 576.

105. Seaman's closing remark is worth noting: "And to conclude, if Captain Badiley had been a Pentioner of the Sates [*sic*] of *Holland*, he could not have done them more service" (15).

him for his prompt action, "finding therein Good will toward us," since "Deeds [more] then Words, Performances then Promises, are . . . marks of cordial Affection." Cromwell had second thoughts about the incident, however, and the letter goes on to request that once arrangements have been made for return of the cargo, Ellis and his ship be released, so that "we may not seem to have had more care perhaps of the *Turks* Interest, then our own Countreymen."

Another name associated with the Leghorn incident came back to haunt the English in later years. It will be recalled that in Milton's letter of November 1652 Parliament announced that, as a show of gratitude to the duke, they had reversed a decision of the Court of Admiralty against a certain "Captain *Cardi* of *Leghorn*." On 6 May 1658 Cromwell wrote the duke asking that "expeditious" action be taken in the case of "the ship Eastland merchant taken by a man of yours called Cardi near Alexandria," and reporting that he is said to have seized yet another English vessel on his homeward voyage. Cromwell followed up on 12 June with another letter confirming that Cardi with two armed ships had indeed "made spoyle of" the merchantman Tripoline "at the entrance of the Thermean or Thessalonean Gulf."[106] He asks that the duke recover the ships, restore the goods, and punish Cardi. Neither of these letters are included in the early sources but Milton seems to have been responsible for correspondence with Tuscany during this period, preparing the two concerning Ellis in September and December of the previous year and two more in April and May of 1658 (W109, P144; W117, P145) and may have written those of May and June about Cardi's depredations as well.

Milton's letter of 14 May 1658 (W117, P145) is of unusual interest in that it provides an ironic epilogue to England's anxious efforts to maintain friendly relations with the duke and secure use of the port of Leghorn. It seems likely that Cromwell's protests about Captain Cardi fell on deaf ears, for when he declared war on Spain in 1655, Mediterranean princes had to reexamine their attitude toward England, and the subtle duke experienced a decided change of heart. In a long letter in Milton's Latin, Cromwell complains bitterly of "how unkindly our Fleet was lately treated at *Leghorn*, how little accommodated with necessary Supplies, [and] in what a Hostile manner twice constrain'd to depart the Harbour," and of how at one point "above Two Hunder'd great shot were made at our Fleet from the Town," all, he observes with

106. SP 98/4/65–66. The seizure was particularly annoying to Longland, who owned the Tripoline.

a touch of scorn, because the king of Spain might be offended by the English presence there; and he advises the duke to consider carefully who his real friends are. As for the English, he warns darkly, "we have learnt to distinguish between Injuries and Acts of Kindness."

3

THE PROTECTORATE

Doth God exact day-labor, light denied?
(Sonnet 19)

Many have considered Milton's public service during the Protectorate
and his political writings in the Anarchy to be closely related. Scholars
propose that there was a decided decline in Milton's participation in
government during the latter half of the Interregnum, and they attribute
this to his growing disenchantment with the policies of the Protectorate,
which they find retrospectively reflected in his works of 1659–60. In
the interest of a clearer understanding of Milton's political thought,
those claims of both decline and disenchantment will be questioned
here. The present chapter addresses the level of Milton's activity in government during the Protectorate, leaving to later pages the interpretation of it.

Arguments for a decline in Milton's activity in office cite two archival
developments; first, a decrease in the number of state letters for which
he was responsible, and second, the virtual disappearance of his name
from the Order Books of the Council of State. On the basis of such
evidence, Christopher Hill has recently noted that "gradually he relin-

quished government [and] was employed from about 1654 only as an occasional translator," and Austin Woolrych that he performed only "a few tasks for the Council of State, but the gaps between the occasional state letters that he composed were often months long, and he withdrew his interests more and more from state affairs." Both historians are perhaps indebted to William Riley Parker, who finds that by the end of 1655 "except for routine labours of translation, Milton's usefulness to his country was apparently at an end"; and having been "relieved of all duties to the Council except occasional bits of translation," he had "closed his mind to all political issues."[1]

Woolrych's reference to the "gaps" between letters, which he elsewhere characterizes as "the silence of the state papers,"[2] implies that Milton was less active in his office than he had been during the Commonwealth. On the evidence of the seventeenth-century sources alone, it would certainly appear that the number of letters attributed to him during the first year and a half of the Protectorate shows a marked decline over earlier years; but those same sources attest to his continued, even more intensive, activity in official correspondence thereafter: thirteen in 1655; thirty-two in 1656, more than in any other single year; twenty-two in 1657; and twenty-two in 1658. It has been a premise of this study that the letters in the early sources represent but a fraction of those for which Milton was responsible, and evidence will be offered below for further attributions; but these figures alone raise serious questions about any notion of a "silence of the state papers." He was quite clearly as active as ever in his office.

The virtual disappearance of Milton's name from the Order Books of the Council of State is another subject entirely. He is mentioned but five times from December 1653 to October 1659, four in reference to his salary and one to his position in Cromwell's funeral, none of which assign him specific duties, as had been the case in earlier orders.[3] The reason for this "silence" in the record is not difficult to determine—he was no longer working for the Council of State. The absence of his name is a consequence of a bureaucratic reorganization, not a decline in activity; and it will be valuable to our understanding of his official status to examine the changes in the secretariat occasioned by the transi-

---

1. Hill, "Milton and the English Revolution," 29; Woolrych, "Milton and Cromwell," 198; Parker 1:464, 468, and 479–81. Hill is restating a position he had taken earlier in *God's Englishman* 149, and *Milton* 191, where he describes the poet as "easing himself out of government service."

2. Woolrych, "Milton and Cromwell," 204.

3. *CSPD* 6:386 and 458, 8:127, 12:131, and 13:256.

tion from Commonwealth to Protectorate, particularly those affecting foreign affairs, Milton's area of responsibility.

With the inauguration of the Protectorate, the status of the Council of State changed markedly. During the Commonwealth it acted as the executive body of the government, and Cromwell sat on it as the first among equals, distinguished from his fellow members by his towering prestige and the fact that he enjoyed the unquestioned loyalty of the army. It was a large body, numbering forty-one, although seldom more than twenty sat at one time. The members were elected annually by Parliament and entrusted with such executive powers as the parent body was willing to delegate. The Protectorate Council was a much smaller body, never numbering more than sixteen; and it had a relatively stable membership, appointed by name in a written constitution, *The Instrument of Government*, hence not dependent upon Parliamentary election for tenure.[4] As many as half were military men who had served Parliament in the wars;[5] and all sat at the pleasure of the Protector, who made few changes, the most notable being the appointment of Nathaniel Fiennes in May 1654 and, in June 1657, the dismissal of John Lambert and the addition of Thurloe. The Protector was empowered to "dispose and order" the military and conduct foreign affairs "with the advice and consent of *the major part* of Council" (emphasis mine), which left him pretty much of a free hand. As Cromwell's powers waxed, the authority of the Council waned; it became known as the "Lord Protector's Council," eventually as his "Privy Council," and directives were issued by "Order of the Lord Protector with the advice of his Council."[6] It met less and less frequently. From March to June 1657, for example, it convened only sixteen times, a sharp decline in activity from earlier four-month periods, such as that of May–August 1654, when it sat ninety-four times. In June 1657, when the Lord Protector was installed under the provisions of a later constitution, *The Humble Petition and Advice*, the powers of Parliament were increased at the expense of the Council, and from that time until the death of Cromwell it averaged no more than ten meetings a month.[7]

This decline in the Council's authority and activity was accompanied

4. Gardiner, *Constitutional Documents*, 413.

5. Gaunt 56–57.

6. *Calendar of State Papers, Colonial*, vol. 3 passim; Gardiner, *Constitutional Documents*, 406, 453.

7. Gardiner, *Constitutional Documents*, 447–59. Peter Gaunt confirms that *The Humble Petition and Advice* withdrew Council's "joint control over the local militias, foreign policy and diplomacy, and the declaration of war and peace" (222). See also Aylmer, *State's Servants*, 49.

by a shift of responsibilities that significantly affected Milton's position in the government, for the Protectorate Council of State was noticeably less influential in foreign affairs than its predecessors. The Council's minutes indicate that its activities focused decidedly on the domestic. It concerned itself with such matters as financial administration, the condition of the clergy, a lengthening list of individual petitions, and the affairs of Scotland and Ireland. Foreign affairs intruded infrequently in the record, and then in the form of allocations of funds to pay the army and provision the navy, the disposition of prize goods, and the occasional approval for the dispatch of ambassadors.

The function of the Council in the Piedmont Massacre is a case in point. On 17 May 1655, that body established a Committee on the Protestants under the Duke of Savoy "to advise what should be done." This committee grew in size and importance until by January 1656 the entire Council and a number of prominent citizens outside the government were included in its membership. Its minutes make it clear that the sole concern of the body was to collect funds domestically for the relief of the victims. One searches the *Calendar* in vain to discover what influence the massacre had on England's foreign policy, although we know from the correspondence between Thurloe and John Pell in Switzerland, for example, that the incident had a decided effect upon Cromwell's plans by delaying the negotiations with France for several months.[8]

This shift in responsibility was but one aspect of the changing nature of the executive branch of England. The designation of Cromwell as Lord Protector in December 1653 was followed by the reintroduction of a number of administrative offices and practices of the monarchy, a trend that culminated in the unsuccessful campaign to persuade him to accept the title of king in 1657. One of the most important of these revived offices was Secretary of State. In the English tradition, these secretaries had served directly under the king in an office quite separate from his Privy Council, the two having distinct functions and spheres of interest. As G. E. Alymer describes the arrangement, "In theory, prerogative matters, that is religion, foreign affairs, and dynastic questions were the sovereign's personal business with the Secretaries of State acting as the Crown's executive agent, while matters involving jurisdiction, arbitration, the raising and spending of extra revenue, and domestic affairs (other than religion) were in the council's sphere."[9] There were exceptions, of course, depending upon the skill and influence of the

---

8. Robert Vaughan, *The Protectorate of Oliver Cromwell and the State of Europe*, 1:192, 206.

9. G. E. Aylmer, *King's Servants*, 18.

individuals involved. During the Protectorate there were some depar-
tures from this general formula of separation of powers, the Council of
State taking a lively interest in religion, for example; but in foreign
affairs this traditional division of labor seems to have prevailed. Shortly
after his investiture, Cromwell reinstituted the office of the Secretary of
State and designated John Thurloe to fill the post, one he held until the
fall of the Protectorate.[10]

As G.M.D. Howat remarks, "From the moment when the 'Rump'
were bidden to 'Go' until his death five and a half years later Oliver
Cromwell dictated the course of English foreign policy."[11] The Protectorate Council, significantly, had no body comparable in authority and
activity to the Committee for Foreign Affairs of the Commonwealth.
Cromwell and a small group of advisers constituted *de facto* such a
body; and it is evident that such ambitious and visionary projects as the
Western Design, the Protestant League, and the Spanish War were all
facets of his world view. It is not clear who were his most intimate
circle of advisers in these affairs, but John Thurloe, Nathaniel Fiennes,
and Henry Lawrence, president of the Council, were certainly among
them.[12] The Protectorate Council, like its Commonwealth counterpart,
was composed largely of men who had never crossed the Channel, although Fiennes and Lawrence, like Milton, had traveled extensively on
the Continent and hence were invaluable advisers in foreign affairs. It
may well be that Fiennes was brought on to the Council in 1654 for this
very reason.

Thurloe, as director of intelligence and Secretary of State, became, to
use Aylmer's phrase, the "executive agent" of the government in its
associations with foreign powers. The scope of his activities is truly
astonishing. He was in constant communication with English envoys
abroad, issuing instructions and keeping them informed of events at
home and in other countries. John Pell in Switzerland, for example, was
noticeably disturbed when he did not receive a weekly letter from the
secretary.[13] In addition, he conducted a clandestine intelligence operation that required we know not what further correspondence. There

10. There is no record of when Thurloe assumed his new position. It may have been
in June 1654, when Cromwell reinstituted the office of the Exchequer (Masson 4:502).
Thurloe was dismissed by the Rump in May 1659, but he was reappointed to the office
the following February (Philip Aubrey, *Mr. Secretary Thurloe*, 185).

11. G.M.D. Howat, 70.

12. *CSPD* 9:ix. Aylmer observes that "high issues of foreign policy were believed to
be settled by the Protector, his Secretary of State, and three or four other intimate confi-
dants" (*State's Servants* 47).

13. Vaughan 1:118.

were agents and ambassadors to be briefed, subtle negotiations to be pursued, wars to be conducted, and always the Protector to be consulted.

The Council was hardly involved. When it was, it acted in a manner characteristic of such deliberative bodies. When the *Spanish Declaration* was brought in on the morning of 26 October 1655, for example, the members instructed Fiennes, who headed the committee, to change the wording, add amendments, and generally revise the document with "Mr. Secretary to assist." The *Declaration*, which represented a major departure in English foreign policy, was most certainly the product of lengthy deliberation within the Protector's inner circle, and Fiennes must have chafed at the delay caused by these instructions to make trivial changes. Cromwell was not present during the morning session, but when he appeared that afternoon, the *Declaration* was speedily passed. One can easily imagine that after the morning's delay Thurloe and Fiennes conferred with the Lord Protector and prevailed upon him to lend the weight of his presence in the afternoon session to head off further needless debate and amendment.

Further research may cast a different light on this relationship, but all available records leave the strong impression of a Lord Protector "going it alone."[14] We do have one quick glimpse of the Council engaged in debate on foreign affairs in the early months of the Protectorate, this in two meetings devoted to whether England should ally herself with Spain or France. The documents, notes made in his own hand by Edward Montague, a member of the Council, were found among the papers of William Clarke and edited by C. H. Firth in the nineteenth century.[15]

> What sit we then projecting peace and war?
> War hath determin'd us.
>
> > (*PL* 2:329–30)

The issue before Council was what to do with the English fleet, "160 ships swimminge," as they put it, now that the Dutch war was over.

---

14. Gaunt's valuable study of the Council of State takes exception to this interpretation. He argues that under *The Instrument of Government* the Council had significant influence in foreign affairs, but that since the deliberations were secret, the minutes of meetings were kept, not in the regular Order Books, but in a " 'private book,' recording sensitive foreign and diplomatic business" (69). Yet, the examples Gaunt cites to illustrate the Council's "influence" are all domestic in nature—the appointment of a Postmaster-General (105–8), the Berwick bridge affair (108–14), and the calling of Parliaments (chaps. 5 and 7).

15. C. H. Firth, ed., *The Clarke Papers*, 3:203–8.

The first account, dated 20 April 1654, is a carefully balanced and clearly reasoned analysis of the advantages and disadvantages of the options open to them: to ally themselves with France or with Spain in the war between them, or to remain at peace. The document is either a summary of the discussion on 18 April or a report prepared for debate on the twenty-first, as the Order Books do not record a Council meeting on the twentieth. Cromwell was absent from both sessions; indeed, he met with his Council only twice in April.[16]

> This place may lie expos'd
> The utmost border of his Kingdom, left
> To their defence who hold it.
>
> (PL 2:360–62)

The second account, much shorter and more hastily written, dated 20 July, is the record of a sharp exchange between General John Lambert and Cromwell over the advisability of dispatching a fleet to the West Indies. Lambert was strongly opposed, arguing that success is "improbable," that England has nothing to gain by expeditions to places so distant, that it will not "advance the Protestant cause," and that the situation in Scotland and Ireland demands their attention. Cromwell replied evenly, according to Montague, that "Wee consider this attempt, because wee thinke God has not brought us hither where wee are but to consider the worke that wee may doe in the world as well as at home. . . . Now Providence seemed to lead us hither, haveing 160 ships swimminge."[17] It was a classic confrontation between a statesman concerned with domestic order and welfare and another convinced that his country's prosperity was dependent upon its position in the community of nations.

Cromwell prevailed in the end, and the expedition sailed under Admiral William Penn and General Robert Venables; but it was every bit the disaster Lambert feared it would be. They set out the following spring and badly bungled an attack on Hispaniola, where a stout Spanish defense and tropical illness combined to repulse the English. They had to settle finally for the occupation of the island of Jamaica, which was only lightly defended at the time; and when they sailed home in September, leaving a portion of their forces behind, Cromwell was so furious that he sent them both to the Tower for returning without permission.[18]

16. CSPD 7:xxxvii.
17. Firth 3:207.
18. Penn and Venables were soon released, however (Masson 5:44–46).

At any rate, as time went on Cromwell grew increasingly reluctant to submit foreign policy plans to the Council, either because he found their vision of "the worke that wee may doe in the world" too limited or because he simply grew weary of confrontations with men like Lambert, whom he may have seen through Milton's eyes as one of those "soldiers, home-grown, strong and bold enough, [but] in public political affairs mostly inexperienced."

The secretariat in the Protectorate government adjusted to the shifting relationship between Council and Protector, emerging a very different body from that which had served the Commonwealth. Thurloe initially remained the General Secretary with his status enhanced by appointment to a seat on the Council, although he did not become a full member until 1657. When he submitted a budget on 3 February 1654, he listed the young Philip Meadows as Latin Secretary, an unnamed Sergeant at arms (still Edward Dendy), Gualter Frost, Jr., as Treasurer, and Mr. Milton without notation of duties or salary (still the same, about £288 a year). There were seven underclerks, including Joseph and John Frost, eleven messengers, nine Sergeant's Deputies, and a number of others. More significant were the additions of William Jessop, who had been engaged the previous October to assist "in despatch of business of foreign affairs," and Henry Scobell, who after a period of service as clerk to Parliament joined the Council's secretariat.[19]

With the establishment of the Protectorate and the reintroduction of the office of Secretary of State the structure of the secretariat changed noticeably. Evidence of the scope of the internal adjustments can be found in Council's order of 17 April 1655, which reflects a restructuring that had apparently been in effect for some time.[20] The government was undergoing a fit of fiscal responsibility of the type that periodically seizes such bodies; and in the general belt-tightening salaries were lowered, positions consolidated, and personnel laid off. This lengthy entry in the Order Books is important for the light it casts on Milton's position in government at the time. Thurloe had become the Secretary of State with a staff of his own, including the Latin Secretary (only Meadows is mentioned) and various clerks and messengers, in an office quite separate from the secretariat of the Council, thus confirming the observation that he was functioning independent of that body. He was no longer clerk to the Council, a position now shared by Henry Scobell and William Jessop, who were assigned their own staff of clerks and

---

19. *CSPD* 6:458; Masson 4:575–79.

20. SP 25/76/31–32; *CSPD* 8:127. Masson gives the entry verbatim from the Draft Order Books (5:177).

awarded healthy increases in salary to reflect their enhanced status. Subsequent references in the *Calendar* fill out the picture somewhat. In May, for example, Scobell was assigned the quarters in Whitehall vacated by a Council member, Philip Skippon;[21] and later in the year he was entrusted with correspondence between the Council and the major-generals.[22] Scobell and Jessop assumed the bulk of the routine duties for a Council of State whose chief interests were domestic; and Thurloe with his staff, which included the Latin Secretaries, constituted a separate office for foreign affairs, responsible directly to Cromwell. There are virtually no references to these Latin Secretaries in the record of the Protectorate Council's proceedings. Although allusions to Scobell and Jessop abound, it is as if Milton, Marvell, Sterry, and Meadows (until his appointment as ambassador to Portugal) did not exist. Further, there are no references in the *Calendar* to the activities of others employed by Thurloe, such figures as Samuel Hartlib, who remained useful in a variety of ways, at one point during Thurloe's illness in the winter of 1658 taking over responsibility for some of his diplomatic correspondence.[23]

The exact position of John Milton in this secretariat is far from clear; but that same order of 17 April 1655 makes it evident that he was working for the office of the Secretary of State, not for the Council. He is not listed in the order as a member of Thurloe's staff, as is Meadows, but is provided for in a separate paragraph: "That the former yearly salary of Mr. John Milton of two hundred eighty eight pounds formerly charged to the Councells Contingencies be reduced to one hundred and fiftie pounds per annum and paid to him during his life out of His [Highness'] Exchequer."[24] The reduction in salary seems a reasonable economy in light of the fact that, according to the early manuscripts at least, he had prepared but one letter since the previous October. This gap in his activity was not to be repeated, however, for the order came on the eve of his intense involvement in Cromwell's response to the Piedmont Massacre, which itself was followed, as we have seen, by three years of accelerated activity in his office.

There is some question whether the reduction in salary ever went into effect, but the stipulation that it was to be "paid to him during his life," has suggested to some that he was awarded a pension and at least semi-

21. *CSPD* 8:160.
22. Ibid. 8:231 and 277; 9:8, 119, and *passim*.
23. Vaughan 2:433–40.
24. SP 25/76/30–31; *CSPD* 8:127.

retired.[25] Several considerations cast doubt on this interpretation. First, the phrase "during his life" does not necessarily indicate that he was put out to pasture; it appears on a number of documents of the period as indicating appointment to an active life post. Henry Scobell's £500 a year, for example, was awarded "for and during the terms of his natural life,"[26] as was the salary of Henry Middleton, Sergeant at arms to the Chancellor,[27] and neither of these men was in any way retired. Further, Milton's name does not appear on any of the documents where pensioners were customarily listed. With one set of such records we are presented with another of those frustrating gaps in Interregnum archives: Official Registers, Entry Books, Debenture Books, and other documents were maintained under the monarchy for the express purpose of accounting for salaries and pensions; some even bear the payee's signature. These records were not kept during the Interregnum.[28] On the other hand, other records were maintained in which, if Milton had been a pensioner, it could be expected that his name would appear. The Letters Patent issued under Cromwell's Great and Privy Seals, for example, include many awards of pensions and salaries to such familiar figures as Scobell, Haak, Hartlib, Du Moulin, and Owen, as well as a host of smaller authorizations of from ten to forty shillings a year.[29] There is a scattering of additional documents about, including two in the Thurloe papers, one for the period 1 November 1656 to 1 November 1657 and another dated 12 April 1658, which contain lists of pen-

25. Parker finds significant the "intention to give Milton a pension for life" in that it implies his superiors regarded "his future usefulness as slight indeed" (1:464).

26. E403/2523/12. The file is calendared in *The Fourth Report of the Deputy Keeper of the Public Records*, App. 2, 189–200.

27. *The Fourth Report of the Deputy Keeper*, App. 2, 196. Middleton has £200 "for and during the term of his natural life." Aylmer gives a longer list of those awarded "life tenure" (*State's Servants* 86).

28. The dates for which there are no records are in parentheses: E403/2415 (1641–60); E403/2417 (1640–69); E403/2444–2511 (1643–60); E403/2180–2258 (1641–61); E403/2590–91 (1640–60); E403/2981 (1643–60); E403/3040–3115 (1640–60); E405/213–21 (1646–60); E405/477–561 (1641–66); E406/45–80 (1643–61); E407/1–2 (1640–60).

29. The dates for which records exist are in parentheses: E403/1756–58 (1654–59); E403/2523 (1654–60); E403/2570–71 (1655–60); E403/2608 (1654–60); E403/2761 (1654–58); E403/2815–18 (1654–58); E404/157–58 (1650–57); E404/238 (1650–59); C82/2246–49 (April–July 1655).

E403/2608 is calendared in *The Fifth Report of the Deputy Keeper of the Public Records*, App. 2, 245–77. This file is especially useful, containing records of payments and pensions to Hartlib, Jessop, Maidstone, Haak, Fleming, Menasseh Ben Israel, Morland, Meadows, Augier, and to the members of the Council, each of whom received £1000 per year.

sioners such as Hall, Hartlib, Peters, Sterry, and Haak; but John Milton is not included in any of these lists.[30]

During the Commonwealth period, when Milton served the Council of State, there are annual entries in the Order Books acknowledging his position and salary. That record is silent on these matters from 1655 to 1659, an indication, as has been noted, not of inactivity but of employment elsewhere. That same order of 17 April 1655 is additionally enlightening in this regard, for it reflects a change in the government's accounting methods. In its revolutionary ardor, the Long Parliament had swept aside many of the crown's institutions and practices, and nowhere are the disadvantages of this policy more evident than in the chaos of the nation's finances during the Commonwealth. It was, for example, through an amorphous fund called the "Council's Contingencies" that the executive disbursed most of the money for the internal operation of the government, including the salaries of the Council members and the secretariat, pensions, gifts, diplomatic expenses (including support for ambassadors), and the like. Apparently, no effort was made to record or audit these expenditures. To put the nation's fiscal house into some kind of order, Cromwell revived the old post of the Exchequer in June 1654 and directed that all funds be disbursed through that office, where at least some measure of accountability could be instituted.[31] The entry of 17 April 1655 reflects this change and gives further evidence of Milton's dissociation from the Council of State. By that order, each office of the executive, the Secretary of State, the Council itself and its secretariat, and the Sergeant at arms, was directed to draw its funds separately from "His Highness' Exchequer." Similarly, the source of Milton's salary was no longer to be the "Council's Contingencies," which continued on a more restricted scale, but again Cromwell's "Exchequer." Unfortunately, the surviving records of that office are fragmentary at best and indicate neither Milton's status nor his salary.[32]

If, however, Milton declined the status of pensioner, where does one look for evidence of his employment? One theory is that the best way to learn where a man is working is to determine who is paying his salary. One would expect to find some record of him among the papers of the office where he was employed, that of the Secretary of State. Again, unfortunately, although there are records to indicate that Frost drew

30. Thurloe 6:593–95; 7:264–65.
31. Masson 4:562.
32. SP 28/1–352, Commonwealth Exchequer Papers, is of no value in this matter.

funds from the Exchequer for the Council's staff and Dendy for his, the files are bare of any authorization of funds to support the Secretary of State.[33] Thurloe was a meticulous and thorough administrator and kept exhaustive records of his expenditures as director of intelligence and Postmaster-General.[34] It must be assumed that he maintained similar records for this more important and expensive office, salaries of ambassadors, secretaries, messengers, and clerks, compensation for overseas travel and entertainment, and the like; but such documents have simply been lost or destroyed and with them any evidence of Milton's financial involvement with that office. There is a glimpse in later years. After the demise of the Protectorate, the Council of State once again assumed responsibility for foreign affairs and resumed the payment of its staff salaries from that old chaotic, fiscal catchall, the "Council's Contingencies." It is from this fund that Milton, on 25 October 1659, was authorized a portion of his annual salary of £200, an entry that suggests, as Masson and Parker propose, that he had not accepted the status of pensioner.[35]

The evidence of the seventeenth-century sources makes it apparent that at the time when Cromwell's international activity was intensifying and the role of the Council in that sphere was of declining importance, Milton continued to perform some of the traditional duties of the Secretary for Foreign Languages. Indeed, there were times when he was the *only* member of the secretariat thus engaged. Philip Meadows so impressed his superiors that he was appointed envoy to Portugal in early 1656, the following year to Denmark, and later to Sweden; and although others were called in from time to time, for a period of some months Milton was left alone in the office of Latin Secretary. It was not

33. Thurloe 7:592. There were two other funds, both assigned to the Protector and apparently absolved from any kind of accountability: "His Highness' Household" account, drawn by John Maidstone, expenditures from which had reached £100,000 a year by 1659, and "His Highness' Privy Purse," apparently administered by William Jessop (Aylmer, *State's Servants*, 236), annual expenditures from which had reached £23,496 by the same date (*Journal of the House of Commons* 7:628). It is possible that some of the expenses of the Secretary of State came from one or the other of these funds.

34. The Public Record Office has over three hundred actual receipts for funds disbursed: SP 18/95/90 (*CSPD* 8:111); SP 18/102/175–279 (*CSPD* 9:83); SP 18/125/202–47 (*CSPD* 9:245); SP 18/154/229–392 (*CSPD* 10:362); SP 18/180/155–234 (*CSPD* 11:354). On 6 May 1657, the Council of State approved Thurloe's expenditure of £25,580 for the four-year period 23 June 1653–1 May 1657, "for the business of intelligence and other services." There are one or two payments to Philip Meadows after he had become ambassador and one to "John Driden" for £50 on 19 October 1657 (SP 18/180/193). For the postmaster account see Rawlinson MS A 64:18.

35. SP 25/107/143; *CSPD* 13:256; Parker 1:464; Masson 5:177–83.

until September 1657 that Nathaniel Sterry was engaged to replace Meadows, only to be succeeded in short order by Andrew Marvell. The record of Milton's activities prior to Sterry's appointment is certainly noteworthy. It shows, for example, seven letters dated on a single day, 20 August 1657, six of which dealt with a single matter, the embassy of William Jephson.[36] Equally suggestive is the relatively intense period of activity of the following spring, when in the six weeks from 14 May to 1 July, Milton was responsible for the preparation of thirteen letters.

As has been noted, Woolrych observes of these years that "the gaps between the occasional state letters he composed were often months long," from which he concludes that Milton withdrew "his interests more and more from state affairs."[37] One would be equally justified, on the other hand, in assuming that 20 August was not the only day in 1657 that England's Secretary for Foreign Languages was so very busy, nor was William Jephson the only diplomat for whom he prepared a set of credentials, nor was 14 May–1 July 1658 an isolated period of activity. Given the scope of Thurloe's duties, Milton's position within a sometimes woefully understaffed secretariat, and the intense diplomatic activity of the period, it is certainly as reasonable to assume that the "gaps" lie not so much in Milton's activities as in the surviving record of them. There are, in brief, too many alternative explanations for the "gaps" to justify citing them as evidence of his voluntary withdrawal "from state affairs," particularly in light of the fact that the number of letters in the early manuscripts reflects only the barest minimum level of his activity during these years.[38]

The modern scholar who seeks further evidence of Milton's services for the Secretary of State is disappointed by the paucity of surviving diplomatic correspondence from that office. Among the State Papers Foreign in the Public Records Office, for example, the file for Spain

---

36. W92, 94–99; P127–33. The other concerns Meadows.

37. Woolrych, "Milton and Cromwell," 198.

38. Milton's reply to Peter Heimbach on 18 December 1657 is occasionally cited as evidence of his isolation from public affairs (Parker 1:507). Heimbach had written seeking Milton's aid in securing a position as secretary to the new minister to Holland, George Downing. Milton replied that he was unable to provide such help, pleading that his "influential friends were few" and that he was "nearly always at home." It cannot escape notice, however, that Milton was singularly well informed about the embassy for one supposedly so cut off from events. He knew that the position had already been filled and was even able to give accurate information concerning the schedule of the party. Indeed, he had prepared Downing's credentials, dated only the day before (W106, P140). French suggests that pleading a lack of influence was probably a polite way of putting the young man off (4:189).

contains no records whatsoever for 1653–59,[39] that for Portugal contains papers dealing with one isolated incident,[40] and that for Switzerland three documents for the entire period 1641–60.[41] The files for France,[42] Holland,[43] and Sweden[44] are more rewarding but still obviously incomplete. There is a scattering of interesting documents in other files, such as State Papers Foreign, Treaties,[45] and Treaty Papers,[46] but when compared to the sheer bulk of the same files for the reigns of Charles I and Charles II, it is evident that these collections are also fragmentary. There are, of course, other important collections, the Rawlinson and Tanner MSS in the Bodleian Library, to name but two, as well as a number of private holdings. The Rawlinson MS might be expected to help somewhat, since it includes the papers of John Thurloe, for whom Milton worked, when he worked; but even a cursory glance at these documents tells why Milton's name is not likely to appear in the collection. These papers, which Thurloe kept from the authorities by hiding them in the false ceiling of his office at Lincoln's Inn, consist largely of correspondence between other figures, letters Thurloe intercepted and kept or had transcribed, as well as communications on foreign intelligence from ambassadors and agents, reports on interrogations, and letters addressed to himself. The type of document that is noticeable by its infrequency is a letter *from* Thurloe;[47] and almost totally lacking are letters from Cromwell and the Council of State—precisely the type of

39. SP 94/43 (1649–59).

40. SP 89/4 (1634–60); Blake's seizure of British ships in Lisbon Harbor on 20 May 1650.

41. SP 96/6, one of which is Milton's State Letter of 7 June 1655 to the magistrates of Geneva. The correspondence with the Evangelical cantons concerning the Piedmont Massacre is well represented, including two more of Milton's letters; it can be found in SP 92/24/291–358.

42. SP 78/113–14. Many of the letters between Thurloe and Lockhart are in *Thurloe*. One, SP 78/114/113, is a letter from Andrew Marvell citing the secretary's illness as reason for his not writing.

43. SP 84/159–62. The collection includes many royalist letters. There are no papers relating to the Dutch negotiations of 1652.

44. SP 95/5A and 5B.

45. SP 108. There are no papers for Spain, Germany, or Denmark; nations represented are Holland (2), Sweden (1), Portugal (1), and France (4).

46. SP 103. This collection is more rewarding. SP 103/24, for the German States, for example, includes two copies of the count of Oldenburg's petition to Parliament of 1651, three copies of the Safeguard itself, and one of Mylius's thanks to Parliament in Latin with the English translation.

47. The long correspondence between Thurloe and Henry Cromwell was not a part of the original Thurloe papers. These letters were contributed later by the Earl of Shelburne and Joseph Jekyll, Esq. (Thurloe 1:vii).

document Milton would have been engaged to write. Indeed, the collection in the Rawlinson MS appears to be a highly confidential file rather than an official archive, one Thurloe would have been more likely to compile in performance of his intelligence duties than as Secretary of State, which probably explains his reluctance to surrender it to Charles II.

In all of these collections, one is faced with the frustrating infrequency of documents dispatched by Cromwell or his Secretary of State in the normal day-to-day conduct of relations with foreign governments and the even fewer papers dealing with the crucial issues of their tenure—the negotiations with France in 1655, for example, which dragged on for months. The meticulous Thurloe surely kept such documents—working papers, instructions to envoys, drafts of important agreements, correspondence from ambassadors—for it appears that he kept *everything*. Documents of this nature would tell us much about Milton's role in government during the Protectorate one way or the other, but we are denied such evidence.[48]

The Protectorate years were a period of English ascendency. Antonia Fraser observes that in 1672 Charles II complained to the French ambassador that England was not as respected abroad as she had been under the Protectorate, to which the envoy reportedly replied, "Ha, Sire, that was another matter: Cromwell was a great man and made himself feared by land and by sea."[49] The story may be apocryphal—it seems an undiplomatically candid thing to say to a monarch—but it makes the point. Cromwell rebuilt the English fleet into a formidable force and maintained a sizable standing army with an enviable reputation—it had never lost a battle—thus gaining the respect of Continental powers. His ambitions somewhat exceeded his resources, however. The Western Design, which envisioned England as a rival to Spain in the New World, ended in disappointment. The hopelessly mismanaged Penn-Venables expedition to the Caribbean acquired a single new possession, the island of Jamaica; and English depredations on the Spanish silver fleet failed to balance the Protectorate budget, as had been hoped. The only tangible fruit of the French alliance was the acquisition of the ports of Dunkirk and Mardyke in 1658, after the defeat of the Spanish in Flanders.

Cromwell's deep religious convictions had a decided influence on his foreign policy. He envisioned an alliance of Protestant powers ranged

48. SP 104, as a further example, contains official letters books and registers, copies of outgoing letters, and so on, but only Sweden is represented for the period.
49. Antonia Fraser, *Cromwell: The Lord General*, 551.

against the Catholic nations of Europe, a prospect those powers, with fresh memories of the devastation of the Thirty Years War, from which England was spared, were evidently reluctant to embrace. Cromwell seized upon the Piedmont Massacre as a means to incite indignation over Catholic barbarities and wrote letters to most of the Protestant nations of Europe, suggesting "consultations" with them on measures to be taken. It seems, however, that his potential allies were much too engrossed in their own national interests to undertake such a cause. France was pushing her borders north, the Dutch continued to expand their commercial empire, the thoughts of Frederick William of Brandenburg turned east rather than south, Denmark was intent upon maintaining her strategic position in Scandinavian trade, and Sweden had her eye on the Baltic.

During his reign, Cromwell's attention was continually drawn to the north, where the young king of Sweden, Charles X, undertook a series of brilliant military campaigns whose purpose it was to turn the Baltic Sea into a Swedish lake. His ambitions brought him in conflict with other Protestant powers, darkening Cromwell's vision of a great league against the Catholic Antichrist; and the Lord Protector wrote a steady stream of letters in an effort to mediate Charles's clashes with his neighbors. England's close friendship with Sweden created a dilemma for Cromwell, for the Dutch, whom he had vowed never again to fight, were opposed to Charles's ambitions in the Baltic, forcing the Lord Protector to walk a narrow diplomatic path between the two powers.

This, then, was the stage on which Milton played his small role during the second half of his government career. It is apparent that, as in his early years, he was used quite selectively in correspondence, for fully 70 percent of the letters he prepared from 1655 to 1659 were occasioned by only three concerns: relations with France, the Piedmont Massacre, and England's efforts to mediate Sweden's wars. During several months in 1656, when he appears to have been alone in his office, he was responsible for correspondence with other nations as well; and if those letters are discounted, his preoccupation with these three matters is even more evident.[50]

> Servant of God, well done, well hast thou fought
> The better fight.
>
> (PL 6:29–30)

---

50. From April to October 1656, he wrote ten letters to Algiers, Portugal, and Hamburg.

Milton continued to live in his house on Birdcage Walk, a short stroll from the corridors of Whitehall, and to perform the duties of his office. He remarried in 1656 and lived contentedly with his second wife, Katherine Woodcock, for some fifteen months, only to lose her from complications associated with childbirth, as he had his first. He resumed his role as the English republic's international advocate with the *Second Defence* in 1654, and as his own advocate with the *Defence of Himself* the following year. The appearance of the *Second Defence* in May 1654 may well have influenced his superiors to reevaluate their concept of his usefulness to the Republic.[51] The early manuscripts show a marked decline in translations up to that time, only two letters during the fifteen-month period from February 1653 to June 1654. This hiatus then came to an end, with eight for the balance of 1654, followed by the sudden spurt of activity precipitated by the Piedmont Massacre the next year, and the far heavier involvement thereafter. The *Second Defence* may have persuaded Cromwell and Thurloe that this blind Latin Secretary was an asset despite his affliction, for in May 1655 it was to him that they turned to compose some of the soaring Latin letters with which Cromwell hoped to rally the Protestant powers of Europe. The lengthy *Defence*, his first extended effort since the failure of his eyesight, reassured Milton that he could compose on a sustained basis, and paved the way for his later achievements.[52]

Savoy

so violence
Proceeded, and Oppression, and Sword-Law
Through all the Plain, and refuge none was found.
(PL 11:671–73)

Among the best known of Milton's State Papers are those dealing with an event that aroused the ire of Oliver Cromwell and the indignation of

---

51. There is no record of Council officially ordering Milton to write the *Second Defence*, as they had the first (*CSPD* 1:474). We have only his assurance in the *Defence of Himself*: "You ask why I should reply to the author of *Cry*? Because I was so ordered, I say, publicly by those whose authority ought to have weight with me; otherwise I would hardly have put my hand to the task" (*Prose* 4:767). Again, since the Latin secretaries were under Thurloe's supervision, the order would have probably come from him, not from the Council, hence would not have appeared in that body's minutes.

52. As observed by Parker (1:450).

the English people—the Piedmont Massacre. In April 1655, Carlo Immanuel II, the duke of Savoy, for reasons not fully understood,[53] ordered his army to root out and destroy a community of Reformed Protestants who for centuries had lived peacefully in the mountainous sector of his country southwest of Turin and whose chief offense, it seems, was that they worshiped God in a manner contrary to the practice and doctrine of Rome. These people were referred to as Waldensians because of their adherence to the teaching of Peter Waldes, a twelfth-century ascetic, or as Vaudois after the geographical area where they lived. The use of the word "massacre" to characterize their expulsion from their ancestral lands was most apt, for the operation was carried out with a brutality that was shocking even to an age grown accustomed to the savagery of religious wars.

Over many years the industrious Vaudois had gradually extended their holdings from their original Alpine homeland into towns and villages in the plains below. In January 1655 the duke of Savoy issued the Edict of Gastaldo, which ordered the Vaudois to evacuate the towns at the foot of the mountains and return to the upper valleys from which they had come, unless within twenty days they could give evidence that they had converted to the Catholic faith. The Vaudois petitioned the duke for a peaceful resolution of differences but he apparently grew impatient. On 17 April elements of the Savoyard army under the marquess of Pianezza moved into the area and on the twenty-first the carnage began. Word reached the Evangelical Cantons of Switzerland on the twenty-ninth and was passed on the following day to the States General of the United Netherlands.[54] The news reached Cromwell shortly thereafter but he took no action for several days apparently awaiting more detailed information about the brutalities. Finally persuaded that the accounts were accurate and every bit as horrible as the first reports had indicated, he acted with characteristic swiftness and resolve. On 17 May, the Council of State was officially informed and a committee appointed to determine what should be done. On 23 May, Cromwell designated Samuel Morland ambassador extraordinary and alerted him for a mission to Savoy. Two days later the Council proclaimed "a day of solemn fasting and humiliation" for all of England.[55] Parishes were directed to take up a special collection to assist the sur-

---

53. Both Morland (288–90) and Jean Baptiste Stouppe (*A Collection of Several Papers* 39–41) discuss the duke's motives at some length, but inconclusively. Both suggest that his mother was the real force behind the massacre.

54. Morland 543–45.

55. *CSPD* 8:165; Morland 563; SP 18/97/165–66.

vivors, a fund which eventually mounted to over £38,000, £2000 of which Cromwell contributed personally.[56] Seeking to rally the indignation of Europe, he dispatched letters to at least nine heads of state, urging them to condemn the massacre; and he interrupted for four full months the then-secret and delicate negotiations for a treaty of alliance with France because he learned that French regiments had been on the scene at the time.[57]

Of these nine letters, five are markedly similar in style, content, and organization (see Appendix A). The other four had to be individualized, as each carried a specific, and different, message. The letter to the duke of Savoy (W51, P73) was to be delivered to him by Morland at the close of a speech prepared for presentation at the audience; the two, therefore, were composed to complement each other. The speech contains a long list of horrifying details of the massacre and asks the duke to show mercy to his suffering subjects. The language of the letter is more general; it is a long, rambling epistle, filled with vague and pious statements about "Duty to God," "Brotherly Charity," and "Clemency and Benignity." In the midst of all the verbiage, however, lies the kernel of Cromwell's demands. The duke is urged to abrogate the decree that deprived the Vaudois of their homes and triggered the massacre, to newly ratify their traditional liberties, to "command their Losses to be repai'd," and to put an end "to their Oppressions." No threats are made, or implied; but the letter leaves unmistakable the course the duke must take to maintain the "Alliance and Friendship between this Republick and your Dominions."

Writing to Louis XIV was a delicate matter indeed, since negotiations for a treaty between the two countries were well advanced and Cromwell had little desire to upset them. But the evidence was overwhelming that French troops had participated in the massacre, and their atrocities could no more be ignored than those of the Savoyards. The letter is carefully worded to allow the king deniability, however (W139, P78). French participation has been reported, it suggests, "but how truly, as yet we know not"; and "we have been very loath to give any belief to these things" since the king's ancestors had been models of tolerance toward their Protestant subjects and he has given every indication that he would follow in that tradition. (Letters to Louis regularly refer to his ancestors; it was considered that such an appeal would carry weight with the young king.) Having mentioned the incriminating evidence, the letter then adroitly sidesteps the issue. The king is simply asked to use

56. Morland 589.
57. Gardiner, *History*, 4:86–87.

his "Interest and Authority with the Duke of *Savoy*" to right the wrong done the Vaudois, so that "Peace may very easily be procured for those poor people, with a return into their native country, and to their former liberty."

The companion to Mazarin stands in sharp contrast (W112, P79). It is a cover letter, enclosing the one to the king, but it has a message of its own. Cromwell minces no words; raising the question of the treaty, he assumes, will catch the cardinal's attention. It was the traditional tolerance of France, the "Liberty and . . . Privilege" allowed Protestants in the kingdom, the letter hints broadly, that prompted England in the first place to desire "the Friendship and Alliance of the *French* people." The cardinal is advised to add the weight of his counsel to the English "Intercessions" with the king on behalf of the Vaudois; or else, it is implied, that alliance, "the setling of which we are now treating with the King's Embassador" and which is "almost brought to conclusion," might well be in jeopardy.

The last of these letters written in the immediate aftermath of the massacre, that of 7 June, is addressed to the "Consuls and Senators of the City of Geneva" (W59, P81). It differs from the others in the candor of its language and in its personal tone. It is in essence a letter of credit, in which Cromwell transfers £2000 of his personal funds to the Geneva Senate to be used by them for the relief of the Vaudois, and promises that more funds will be forthcoming as a result of "a gathering of Alms to be made throughout this whole Republick." According to the terms of the letter, he gives the money outright to the city, apologizing for "the trouble impos'd upon ye" but having "no scruple to commit the Paying and Distributing [of] this Sum of Money to your Care . . . to the end that though the Sum be small, yet there may be something to Refresh and Revive the most Poor and Needy, till we can afford 'em a more plentiful Supply." This tone of compassion is matched by one more militant, however, an angry prayer that God will "stir up the hearts of all his People Professing the Orthodox Religion, to resolve upon the common Defence of themselves, and the mutual Assistance of each other against their imbitter'd and most implacable Enemies." It is tempting to consider these Milton's words; but in truth they are more likely to have been Cromwell's. This is a direct and personal letter, containing none of the subtle conceits of diplomatic posturing. Although Cromwell was certainly not adverse to making use of the massacre as a rallying point for Protestant unity, his words leave the undeniable impression that the suffering of these oppressed brethren deeply moved him. He was, after all, forwarding his own money and may well have composed the letter to accompany the funds, reflecting what was obviously a sincere personal commitment.

According to his own account, Morland left London on 26 May, carrying with him two letters from Cromwell, those to Louis XIV and the duke of Savoy.[58] He also carried a carefully prepared speech, "an earnest Intercession by word of mouth in his Highness Name," as he later called it, which he was directed to address personally to the duke, informing him of the displeasure of the Lord Protector. Morland was politely, if coolly, received in Savoy and did, as instructed, address the duke at his court in Rivale on 24 June.[59]

Morland's speech has been the subject of some controversy. The document appears in *Works* (W153) but is not so much as mentioned in *Prose*; newly discovered archival evidence and historical sources, however, would seem to indicate that the Columbia editors were the more correct. There is no question that Milton was intimately involved in Cromwell's initiative. The Lord Protector's letters to European heads of state, including those that Morland carried with him, are all part of Milton's State Papers; and the evidence indicates that he was well informed about the details of the massacre.

In addition to his letters, Cromwell undertook a concerted effort to rally support through the press. In June there appeared a short pamphlet entitled *A Collection of Several Papers Sent to his Highness the Lord Protector . . . Concerning the Bloody and Barbarous Massacres*. It was prepared by Jean Baptiste Stouppe "by Command of his Highness," as the title page attests, and published obviously to inform the English people of the event. Later in the month the Council of State authorized Benjamin Master to publish an account in Latin, *Sabaudiensis in Reformatam Religionem Persecutionis Brevis Narratio*, designed apparently to enlist international support.[60] At the same time John Thurloe was encouraging Morland to chronicle the event in full, resulting in his compendious *History of the Evangelical Churches of the Valley of Piemont*, which was finally published in 1658.

> O what are these,
> Death's Ministers, not Men, who thus deal Death
> Inhumanely to men, and multiply
> Ten thousandfold the sin of him who slew

---

58. Morland makes no mention of yet a third letter he carried with him, that to Cardinal Mazarin, also Milton's (W112, P79). Louis XIV, still in his minority, had not yet taken over the reins of government, then firmly in the cardinal's hands. Every letter to the king required a companion to Mazarin.

59. Morland a2, 567.

60. *CSPD* 8:222, 607.

His Brother; for of whom such massacre
Make they but of thir Brethren, men of men?
(PL 11:675–79)

It is in Stouppe's *Collection* that we find letters of the kind that
prompted Cromwell to undertake his extraordinary campaign and inspired Milton to write of those "Slain by the bloody Piemontese, that
rolled / Mother with infant down the rocks." One, apparently an eye-
witness account "written from the Vale of Perouse the 17 of April
1655," describes how the soldiers "tormented one hundred and fifthty
women and small children, and having cut off their heads, they dashed
others against the Rocks." Another letter, dated 8 May, gives an account of how the Savoyards took from a mother "her little child in
swadling Bands, and threw him from a precipice with many others" and
of "Women with Child, of whom many miscarried, and lay dead near
their children."[61] Anna Nardo observes that Milton's image of the victims' "moans" that the "Vales redoubl'd to the Hills" may have been
suggested by that same letter of 8 May, which describes the "fearful
scriechings, made yet more pitiful by the multitude of Eccho's, which
are in those Mountains and Rocks."[62]

Thus Milton drew on the accounts received in London for the imagery of his poem. But more to the purpose of the present study are the
suggestive parallels between the sonnet and the speech to the duke, both
composed at about the same time. The poetic image of "Mother with
infant" rolling "down the rocks" appears in the speech as "Some infants have been dashed against the Rocks." Again, in Milton's sonnet
those same "moans" of the victims are further echoed "To Heaven"
and in the speech "Heaven it self seems astonished with the cries of
dying men." The tone of the sonnet is somewhat ambivalent in that it

61. Stouppe 29, 34, 35. One particularly shocking incident from the *Collection* is
recorded in Morland's speech. The 8 May letter reports that "After they had abused
severall women, they thrust many stones in their privy parts, and walked them in this
posture till they died" (35). Masson found the Latin of the speech, "*injectis in ventrem vi
lapillis*," far too indelicate for translation, rendering it "hideously abused." Morland, who
was striving for effect, had no such reservations. He changed the Latin to "*lapillis ac
ruderibus utero*" and translated the passage, "Virgins being ravished, have afterwards had
their wombs stuffed up with gravel and Rubbish, and in that miserable manner breathed
their last" (*Works* 480–85).

62. Nardo, *Milton's Sonnets and the Ideal Community*, 132–33. Morland's reference
to cries and echoes is yet more graphic, although since it was composed later, it did not
influence Milton's imagery. He writes of soldiers "taking their young Infants (whose wo-
full Cries made such a lamentable Echo among the Rocks, as they were hurl'd in the air
from off the Enemies Pikes and Halberds, that it would have melted the Heart of any
Christian Soul to have heard it) and dashed their Brains against the Rocks" (523).

opens with the militant "Avenge, O Lord," but ends on a different note
entirely. The "martyred blood and ashes" sown "O'er all the Italian
fields" will "grow / a hundredfold"; but that righteous harvest will not
be the armed men which the Cadmus myth and the octave of the poem
might lead the reader to expect. This will be no Army of Saints rising up
to wreak vengeance "on the bloody *Piemontese*"; rather, they will be
wise and prudent Christians who, having learned God's ways from the
massacre, will know to flee "the Babylonian woe." This pacific turn in
the sonnet is reflected in the words of the speech, which asks that God
not be vengeful: "do not thou take that which is due to so great wicked-
nesse and horrible villanies! Let thy bloud, O Christ, wash away this
bloud!"[63]

There is no direct evidence of who was responsible for the wording of
the speech but there are suggestive parallels between it and Milton's
letters. Each of those written to heads of state includes a graphic description of the suffering of the Vaudois (Appendix A). That to the
Dutch (W54, P75), for example, reads in part as follows:

> You have already bin inform'd of the Duke of *Savoy's* Edict, set
> forth against his Subjects Inhabiting the Valleys at the feet of
> the *Alps*, Ancient Professors of the Orthodox Faith; by which
> Edict they are commanded to abandon their Native Habita-
> tions, . . . and with what Cruelty the Authority of this Edict has
> rag'd against a needy and harmless People, many being slain by
> the Soldiers, the rest Plunder'd and driven from their Houses
> together with their Wives and Children, to combat Cold and
> Hunger among desert Mountains, and perpetual Snow.

A similar passage appears in the speech (W153):[64]

> I mean those, who inhabiting beneath the Alps, and certain
> Valleys under your Dominion, are Professors of the Protestant
> Religion. For he [Cromwell] hath been informed . . . that part
> of those most miserable people, have been cruelly massacred by
> your forces, part driven out by violence, and forced to leave

---

63. Nardo is untroubled by this turn. She observes, "The sonnet may end in a vision
of triumph wrested from defeat, but it begins as a cry for vengeance" (134). This ambivalence presents no problem for her, however; the poem "moves from present sorrow and
defeat to future joy and victory" (133).

64. The passage is quoted from Morland's translation of the speech as he delivered it
(lines 11–19), but the Latin is unchanged from the draft, which, as I argue below, is
Milton's (lines 16–24). The contemporary English reflects the sentiments more accurately
than does Masson's sanitized translation (see note 61 above). See *Works* for the original
Latin (478–82), Masson's translation (477–83), Morland's revised Latin (482–88), and
his translation of it (483–89, also in Morland 568–71).

their native habitations, and so without house or shelter, and
destitute of all relief, do wander up and down with their wives
and children, in craggy and uninhabited places, and Mountains
covered with snow.

These textual parallels between the sonnet, the speech, and the letters
are reinforced by archival evidence that links the speech and the letters
even more closely. In the Public Record Office, London, is a file of
documents, once again only very recently to have come to the attention
of Miltonists, which has unique features lending support to the position
that the poet was in whole or in part responsible for the speech.[65] The
file contains transcripts of documents, some thirty in number, dated
from March through August 1655, dealing with the Piedmont Massacre. The more important of the documents are known, having been
published in Morland's *History*; it is their order in the archive that is so
instructive.[66]

The collection is chronologically arranged; but the documents have
distinguishing features which imply that originally two different groups
of letters were combined to form the file, those dated during the six
weeks from 30 April to 12 June 1655, and those dated before and after
that period. The two groups are distinctly different: Those dated before
and after that six-week period are in French, were transcribed by several hands, and consist largely of letters between the Swiss and the duke
of Savoy and Morland's correspondence with various figures. Those
dated during the critical weeks when Cromwell was first informed of
and reacted to the massacre, are for the most part in Latin, the exceptions being three French letters inserted to maintain chronology. Significantly, the eleven Latin documents in this group are all transcribed in
the same hand, one unlike any other in the file from those weeks; and
they are for the most part letters addressed to and from Cromwell.[67]

65. Fallon, "Miltonic Documents," 82–83.
66. The documents are scattered in the records, appearing at various locations in SP
92/24, State Papers Foreign, Savoy, and SP 96/6, State Papers Foreign, Switzerland.
67. The letters in this group are listed below in chronological order, citing the present
folio numbers in SP 92/24 (the two from SP 96/6 are so indicated) and where appropriate
the page from Morland's *History* where they first appeared, e.g., M544. Milton's letters
are identified by their numbers in *Works* and *Prose*:

30	April	Swiss Cantons to the States General, f. 298, M544.
14	May	Swiss Cantons to the States General, f. 302.
25	May	Cromwell to the States General, ff. 304–5, M558, W54, P75.
25	May	Cromwell to the king of Sweden, ff. 306–7, M554, W53, P74.

The collection was thus assembled from various sources by various hands, but the eleven Latin documents give every appearance of having been transcribed from a single file. They have been moved about by successive Keepers of the Public Record Office so that they are to be found today in four different locations in two separate files. Of the various folio numbers in their margins, however, there are two se-quences—and those the only ones in ink, hence the earliest—which show the papers in consecutive order from ff. 11 to 36 and 19 to 68. Hamilton appears to have discovered the Savoy transcript before it was scattered throughout the files; and he published the speech because it was "written *in the same hand as the other official copies of Milton's letters*, and in a style which proves its identity of source" (italics mine). Thus, the archival evidence clearly indicates that these eleven docu-ments were deposited initially as a single bundle and, it may be safely assumed, at the same time.[68]

---

25 May	Cromwell to Louis XIV, ff. 308–9, M564, W139, P78.
25 May	Cromwell to the Swiss Cantons, ff. 310–11, M561, W55, P76.
25 May	Cromwell to the duke of Savoy, ff. 312–13, M572, W51, P73.
7 June	Cromwell to Geneva, SP 96/6, ff. 121–22, W59, P81.
7 June	States General to the Swiss Cantons, SP 96/6, ff. 123–24.
12 June	States General to Cromwell, f. 318, M601.
n.d.	Morland's Speech, ff. 358–59, M568, W153.

There is one additional letter in SP 92/24 *in this hand*, dated 24 August, the Vaudois to the Swiss Cantons, ff. 338–41. It is in Italian.

Three of Milton's letters, written at about the same time, do not appear in this file:

25 May	Cromwell to the king of Denmark, M556, W58, P77.
25 May	Cromwell to Cardinal Mazarin, W112, P79.
31 May	Cromwell to the prince of Transylvania, W52, P80.

Thus, in his *History*, Morland published Milton's letter of 25 May to the king of Den-mark, which is not in the transcript, but for some reason omitted the one of 7 June to the city of Geneva, which is. He also published (609–11) Milton's letter of 31 July, Cromwell to Louis XIV (W56, P82) but not its companion to Mazarin (W57, P83). Neither of these later two is in the transcript.

68. Hamilton 18. The documents are listed below in the sequence of their early folio numbers. Again, the Latin letters are in the same hand, the French in several.

Early folio nos.		Present folio nos.	Date	Language
A	B			
11–12	19–20	298	30 April	Latin
13–14	21–24	316–17	? May	French
15–16	25–28	300–301	4 May	French
17–18	29–32	302	14 May	Latin
19–20	33–36	304–5	25 May	Latin
21–22	37–40	306–7	25 May	Latin
23–24	41–44	308–9	25 May	Latin

The contents of the eleven Latin documents give every indication that they were transcribed from a file in Milton's possession.[69] Six are letters from Cromwell to foreign heads of state—and all six are Milton's. Of the others, one is addressed to Cromwell and three are communications between foreign states, the type of correspondence Milton was called upon to translate into English. This group, then, contains six letters which he retained in his files and had transcribed later in life, and four which he would have retained as a necessary part of the record but would not have had transcribed because the Latin was not his. The eleventh document is the speech itself, whose Latin, I propose, is very much his.

The archival evidence offers further confirmation. The early folio numbers position Morland's speech (27–27 bis, 49–52) between Cromwell's letter to the Swiss (25–26, 45–48) and that to the duke of Savoy (28–29, 53–56), indicating clearly that it was an integral part of the file of letters written by Milton and dated 25 May. The speech is separated from the letters in the present file but there can be no doubt about its original location, immediately preceding the letter to the duke. Indeed the text of the speech refers specifically to the letter, indicating that it is to be presented to the duke at the close of Morland's address. Again, these six letters are *all from* Cromwell, *as is the speech*; as has been noted, Morland refers to it as "an earnest Intercession by word of mouth in His Highness Name."

Morland did make changes in the speech before delivering it, one of which reflects the position assumed by the English government concerning the culpability of the duke. It will be recalled that in Cromwell's letter to Louis XIV he expresses himself "loath to believe" the reports of French complicity in the massacre. The speech takes this posture one step further to assume that the duke himself is not to blame: "No man

25–26	45–48	310–11	25 May	Latin
27–27bis	49–52	358–59	1655	Latin
28–29	53–56	312–13	25 May	Latin
30–31	57–58	314–15	3 June	French
32–33	59–61	121–22 (SP 96/6)	7 June	Latin
34–35	63–66	123–24 (SP 96/6)	7 June	Latin
36	67–68	318	12 June	Latin

Those numbered before and after this sequence are in French.

69. The transcript appears to be one that Thurloe had prepared from files in London and sent to Morland to assist him in his project. In his *History* Morland published many of the letters associated with the massacre, affixing to a number of them, including Milton's six, a headnote reading, "An authentick Copy of the true Original whereof was communicated to the Author, by the right Honorable Mr. Secretary Thurloe." Eight of the group of eleven Latin documents appear in the *History*.

can say [the massacre] was done by the will of your H." Morland was obviously uneasy about the reception the speech would receive, for at a point where the text grows particularly vehement, declaring that "all the Neros of all time and ages" would have found themselves outdone by the savagery, he nervously added, "which I would have spoken without offence to your Highness, seeing we believe none of these things were done through any default of yours." His mission completed, Morland left Turin on 19 July and returned to Geneva, where he remained for over a year, charged with the distribution of funds collected for the relief of the Vaudois.

It is not surprising that the speech was omitted from the original manuscript sources. Those early collections are almost exclusively letters, and the speech is not a letter. It is one of a group of documents, including the Oldenburg Safeguard, the Dutch Declaration, and the Swedish treaty, that editors of the State Papers have included as Milton's on the basis of historical evidence rather than the manuscript sources. These documents are either international treaties, official state proclamations, or in the case of Morland's speech a personal communication from one head of state to another. Although Milton appears to have retained copies of these documents, he decided not to have them transcribed because he would have been aware that it was inappropriate, and probably illegal, for a private person to publish such papers.

In conclusion, if Milton wrote the letters, it can be reasonably assumed that he wrote the speech and that it can safely be dated 25 May, as are the letters. In addition to the revealing textual parallels, the archival evidence confirms the close association between the speech and Milton's letters. The historical evidence is all but conclusive. It will be recalled that, according to his own account, Morland was informed of his mission on 23 May and left England three days later, carrying with him three documents, the letter to Louis XIV, the letter to the duke, and the speech in Latin draft. The speech, therefore, was composed prior to 26 May.

It has been suggested that Morland wrote it himself, but this does not seem likely.[70] He was a relatively young man, thirty years old at the time, and inexperienced in such duties. He had served previously on only one diplomatic mission, as a relatively obscure member of Whitelocke's embassy to the queen of Sweden in 1653, and was engaged as an assistant to Thurloe the following year. It is improbable that a young man of no literary accomplishment and but three days to prepare for his

---

70. Masson raises and quickly dismisses the possibility, although on different grounds than I propose here (5:188n).

first independent diplomatic mission would have had time to undertake such a task, nor is it likely that a man of such relative inexperience would have been given responsibility for preparing a speech that was to be represented as the words of the Lord Protector himself. In his *History*, Morland is not overly modest about his mission but, as Masson notes, he nowhere claims credit for composing the speech. Indeed, it was probably prepared beforehand precisely because of Morland's inexperience. It was the English practice to provide envoys with a lengthy list of "Instructions," such as those Richard Bradshaw carried with him on his abortive mission to Russia in 1657 (W164, P123), and to depend upon their rhetorical skills to prepare the address itself; however, because of Cromwell's intense personal interest in the mission and Morland's inexperience, it was probably decided that it would be advisable to compose the speech for him.

And who was to do it? Milton was by then an international figure, widely admired for his Latin *Defences* and acknowledged as a master of the ancient tongue. He had been employed for days in preparing letters addressed to several foreign governments, each deploring the duke's actions; he was as well informed as anyone in the government about the details of the Savoyard's barbaric cruelty; and he fully shared Cromwell's distress over the accounts of the massacre. Under the circumstances, one must wonder at the suggestion that the Lord Protector would turn to anyone other than John Milton to prepare such a document.

Louis XIV replied to Cromwell's letter in June and by the end of July the Lord Protector could declare himself satisfied with the answer (W56, P82). It is clear, he writes, that the French troops had acted without the king's "Orders and Commands," and he is to be commended for expressing his displeasure to his "Collonels and Officers." Cromwell presses the issue, however; if Louis wants to persuade "Foreign Princes, that the Advice or Intentions of your Majesty were no way contributing to this prodigious Violence," he must "inflict deserved punishment upon those Captains and Ministers" responsible. The king is praised, also, for his efforts to intercede with the duke; but, since those efforts seem to have availed little, he is encouraged to apply his "Authority and Assistance once again" on behalf of the Vaudois.[71]

Thanks, indeed, to French pressure, the duke was forced to relent and in August at the Treaty of Pignerol, to retract his Edict and restore the Vaudois to their former liberties. The treaty, however, proved porous

---

71. There is a companion to Mazarin (W57, P83), but it is only a brief cover letter, enclosing a copy of the king's.

and the duke continued to persecute his Protestant subjects. Three years later, in May 1658, Cromwell was again writing letters protesting Savoyard oppression, two of which, those to Louis XIV (W110, P151) and the Swiss Protestant Cantons (W111, P152), Milton had transcribed. In a long, highly charged letter to Louis, Cromwell reports of the treaty that "by false Construction, and various Evasions, the Assurances of all [its] Articles are eluded and violated"; and, citing again the young king's reputation, the example of his magnanimous ancestors, and the force of the alliance between the two nations, he requests that France offer safe asylum to the Vaudois fleeing persecution. To the Swiss, in equally inflammatory language, he condemns the Savoyard oppression which "will certainly prove the utter extirpation of the whole race," and exhorts them, so close are they to the scene "as to behold the Butcheries, and hear the Outcries and Shrieks of the Distressed," to come to their aid. The English, he assures the Swiss, though "so far remote" from the area, are doing what they can to succor the victims, an obvious reference to the flow of funds that had continued over the intervening years; and fellow Protestants are asked to "Consult your Prudence, your Pity, and your Fortitude" to do what they can for their "Neighbors and Brethren, who must else undoubtedly and speedily perish."

France

Today deep thoughts resolve with me to drench
In mirth, that after no repenting draws;
Let Euclid *rest and* Archimedes *pause,*
And what the Swede *intend, and what the* French.
                                                        (Sonnet 20)

The letters on the Piedmont Massacre that Milton addressed to Louis XIV and Cardinal Mazarin on 25 May 1655 were his first to France (W112, P79; W139, P78).[72] This "beginning late" in Anglo-French correspondence would seem to indicate, as has been noted, that he was little involved in the negotiations that led up to the alliance between the two nations, finally consummated in 1655; but once he did begin, he remained busily engaged. Of the hundred or so he wrote during the last

---

72. These letters and a later one to Louis XIV on the massacre (W110, P151) are discussed in the section on Savoy.

four years of the Protectorate, 1655–59, thirty were to that country, twice as many as to Sweden, the one next most frequently addressed. It is probable that Milton assumed these duties as a replacement for René Augier, who passed out of government service early in 1655. Augier, who had been assisting Thurloe with French affairs, was among those cut from the payroll on 17 April, and his duties were distributed among the surviving members of the secretariat. It may well be that what responsibilities he had for correspondence with France then fell to Milton.[73]

Of the thirty letters in the early manuscripts addressed to France, sixteen are written in pairs, that is companion letters of the same substance, presumably composed at the same time, a practice made necessary by the unusual situation prevailing within the French monarchy.[74] During the 1650s, Louis XIV, although king of France, was still a minor; the queen mother, Anne of Austria, acted as regent; and the reins of government were firmly in the hands of her very able chief minister, Cardinal Jules Mazarin. As a consequence, the protocol of the time required that any letter written to the king be accompanied by another to the cardinal, who would probably act on the matter in any event. Those addressed to Mazarin are on occasion but brief cover letters enclosing a copy of the one to Louis (W57, P83) but more frequently they are lengthy companions to the king's letters, of the same substance but, of course, with different wording.

Here was a challenge indeed, to engage in the art of elaborate compliment in companion letters to a young, ambitious king, eager to assume the power to which he was heir, and an aging cardinal, who held that power firmly in his hands, especially as there was a distinct possibility that they read each other's mail. The writer had to praise one without diminishing the other. Those to Louis, then still in his teens, stress his honor, his reputation, his dignity as king, his military prowess, and the grandeur of his court. In a petition concerning the illegal seizure of an English ship by French privateers, for example, Cromwell insists that the king's "Honour" is at stake and that those who presume "to violate the League and most Sacred Oath of their Sovereign, should suffer the Punishment due to so much Perfidiousness and daring Insolence" (W73, P111); and in another letter of similar substance Louis is advised that

73. *CSPD* 8:127–28. In May 1649 Milton was ordered to translate some letters received in French (*CSPD* 1:147), but this was before Augier had returned from France.
74. The pairs are: W112, 139, P79, 78; W56–57, P82–83; W145–46, P93–94; W73–74, P111, 113; W113–14, P146–47; W115–16, P149, 148; W118–19, P154–55; W124–25, P159–60; W143–44, P156–57.

"your Authority it self, and the Veneration due your Royal Name, are chiefly in dispute" (W86, P120). It was thought that such appeals would carry weight with the young king, whereas a different approach was called for with the seasoned cardinal. He is praised for the qualities that equip him to run the kingdom. He is "the sole and onely person, whose singular Prudence Governs the most important Interests of the *French* Nation, and the most weighty Affairs of the Kingdom with Fidelity, Council, and Vigilance" (W74, P113); he is the one "upon whose care the Prosperity of *France* depends" (W125, P160). Honor, authority, and preservation of the "Royal Name," then, were considered the young king's concerns; prudence, vigilance, and fidelity the cardinal's.

> . . . no mean recompense it brings
> To your behoof, if I that region lost,
> All usurpation thence expell'd, reduce
> To her original darkness and your sway
> (Which is my present journey) and once more
> Erect the Standard there of *ancient Night*.
> (*PL* 2:981–86)

Although most of Milton's letters to France are routine in substance—petitions and credentials—a number are associated with an important event in the history of the Republic, the acquisition of the city of Dunkirk in the spring of 1658. It was one of Cromwell's fondest objectives to secure a "footing on the continent," an advantage England had lost when Mary Tudor surrendered Calais in 1558.[75] The alliance between England and France, achieved in the commercial agreement of 1655, was strengthened two years later by a military treaty, in which Cromwell engaged to commit the English navy and an army of six thousand soldiers to help the French expel the Spanish from Flanders. In return England was to acquire the Channel ports of Dunkirk and Mardyke. An Anglo-French army under Turenne managed to corner Spanish forces on the coast in the spring of 1658 and at the "Battle of the Dunes" to defeat them soundly. Dunkirk surrendered on 14 June and in compliance with the treaty was immediately handed over to the English. Ironically, one of Charles II's first acts after the Restoration was to sell the port back to the French.

---

75. Cromwell's efforts to secure a Continental base were not restricted to the Channel coast. He also attempted to gain possession of the Duchy of Bremen, the city of Stade on the Elbe, and Landskrona on the Sound.

Eight of Milton's letters to Louis XIV and Mazarin, in four pairs, are associated with the event. The first two are innocent enough, letters of introduction for Viscount Fauconberg, Cromwell's son-in-law, who was planning a trip to Paris (W113–14, P146–47). Before he could deliver them, however, it was discovered that both the king and the cardinal had joined the French army besieging Dunkirk in order to be present for what promised to be a signal victory; and so Milton had to write two more for Fauconberg, who was ordered to follow Louis to Flanders, where his presence would ensure that the agreement would remain fresh in the young king's mind (W115–116; P149, 148).[76] There is a distinguishable contrast between the latter two letters. The high-spirited Louis, at the head of his armies, is encouraged to capture "*Dunkirk*, that infamous nest of Pyrates, and Place of Refuge for Sea-Robbers" so that the seas will be "less infested by those plundering Rovers"; he is urged "by your Military Prowess [to] take speedy Vengeance of the *Spanish* Frauds." Its companion to Mazarin repeats the theme but in less inflammatory terms: against "our common enemy the *Spaniard.* . . . Armed Courage now will soon exact a rigorous account of all his Frauds and Treacheries." On a much more subdued note, Cromwell wishes the aging cardinal "long Life and Health in our Name" and gives thanks that his "Fidelity, Prudence, and Vigilance" have carried the enterprise to the verge of success.

It would seem that neither letter was delivered. *Prose* publishes what appears to be the final version of the one to Mazarin (P150), to be found in the *Archives du Ministère des Affaires Étrangères* in Paris; and Patrick suggests that the one to the king is also a draft.[77] If such is the case, Cromwell had second thoughts about the situation in Flanders, for the final letter to Mazarin is markedly different from the earlier version. Gone is the elaborate compliment to Mazarin's "Fidelity, Prudence, and Vigilence"; gone is any reference to "our common enemy the *Spaniard*"; and conspicuously absent is any allusion to "Armed Courage" and the commitment of English "Forces." As revised, it is bland and cautious in tone, promising only vaguely "to promote the public weal of France or the private affairs of Your Eminence." If the companion to the king (W116, P148) is also a rejected draft, and if its final version

76. Cromwell's instructions to Fauconberg are printed in Abbott 4:809–10. Since Milton prepared the letters, he may well have been involved in writing the instructions, as he was in those for Richard Bradshaw on his mission to Russia the year before (W164, P123).

77. *Prose* 5:829. A copy is in PRO 31/3/102/201.

can be found, it would be of interest to determine whether it is equally as subdued.

Several factors may have tempered English enthusiasm. There had been some discontent about the deployment and support of the English army in Flanders, and Cromwell may have had reservations about the continued commitment of English troops under French command.[78] Further, as we shall see, there was some anxiety about French willingness to honor the agreement to turn over Dunkirk to the English. At any rate, caution prevailed, and it was decided to dampen the rhetoric until the victory was assured. In Cromwell's letters following the capitulation (W118–19, P154–55) and prompt transfer (W143–44, P156–57) of the town, he allowed himself an exuberance matching that of the earlier, rejected draft.

Once the city had fallen, the French sent news of the victory to London by way of an embassy headed by Louis's representative, the duke of Crequi, and Mazarin's nephew, M. Mancini—they seemed to do everything in pairs. Cromwell replied immediately, thanking both king and cardinal for their courtesy (W118–19, P154–55); but a note of anxiety can be detected in the letter to Louis, as if there is some question in Cromwell's mind that the young king, in the heady moment of victory, might forget his obligations under the treaty. There is reference to "Reputation and Dignity" and the letter pointedly reminds Louis of the English contribution: "Our People in that Battel were not wanting to your Assistance, nor the Military Glory of their Ancestors, nor their own Pristine Fortitude." It continues: "As to your Promise, That you will take care of our Interests, we mistrust it not in the least, upon the Word of a most Excellent King and our most assured Friend." The companion to Mazarin conveys no such uneasiness; it sounds rather like a letter to an old and trusted friend, though it is perhaps somewhat more effusive than customary in its praise, packing references to the cardinal's "Civility, Candour, and Friendship," his "Prudence and Vertue," and his "Renown to Govern Kingdoms" into a very few lines.

In the end the French were true to their word and promptly handed the city over. If Cromwell had any doubts about French intentions, in his letters acknowledging the transfer he takes pains to ensure that they will have no doubt about his (W143–44, P156–57). To Louis he writes "that there shall be no lack of care or integrity on our part in performing all that remains of our agreement with the same faith and diligence

78. Masson 5:310–11; Aubrey 165–66.

as heretofore"; and to Mazarin, "What pertains to my promises, since
nothing is more sacred and customary with me than to keep a pact
faithfully . . . I shall care alike for my own good faith and [your] reputation."[79] Cromwell presses the point with Mazarin—the Latin *fide* appears three times in the sentence.

It was a memorable occasion, for although the English navy had
scored signal victories, this was the only one for the army abroad during the Interregnum (to dismiss the hopelessly mismanaged occupation
of Jamaica). Milton had all eight letters transcribed, including the first
pair of Fauconberg's credentials, perhaps because he wished it to be
remembered that he had participated in the victory, continuing to act in
the role he had defined for himself in the *Second Defence*: "I concluded
that if God wished those men to achieve such noble deeds, he also
wished that there be other men by whom these deeds, once done, might
be worthily praised and extolled."[80] Then, too, the Latin is to be admired. The English words may have been Thurloe's, although at this
stage of the game one might assume that the Secretary of State would
have given his seasoned Latin Secretary full rein to compose; but the
Latin had to catch the nuances reflecting the delicate balance between
the king and the cardinal, to praise each at his worth. If Milton had to
choose from among his letters to France, these were admirably suited to
display his mastery of the language, far more interesting certainly than
some of those whose companions he chose to exclude, such as that for
the duchess of Richmond (W132, P167), or the petition of Peter Pet
(W134, P168).

The fact that these letters were dispatched in pairs is a further indication that Milton was responsible for many more than appear in the
seventeenth-century sources of his State Papers, for among those to
France are seven, written over the same period, 1655 to 1659, addressed to Louis XIV and signed by Oliver, and after his death Richard,
Cromwell for which there are no companion letters to Cardinal
Mazarin. And two of those addressed to the cardinal are without companions to the king.[81] It could be argued, of course, that they were not

---

79. It is a curious feature of these letters that Edward Phillips cannot bring himself to
use the first person singular, although the Latin clearly calls for it. He prefers rather the
royal "we" and "our," relenting only in the last two, where Cromwell is obviously making a personal pledge.

80. *Prose* 4:553. For a discussion of the influence of the campaign in Flanders, and in
particular the acquisition of Dunkirk, on *Paradise Lost*, see Fallon, *Captain or Colonel*,
139–49.

81. The letters without companions to Mazarin are: W61, P85; W68, P97; W81,
P112; W86, P120; W110, P151; W131, P166; W140, P88. Those without companions to

in fact written, since most of them deal with less than earth-shattering issues, grievances against French privateers and opportunists concerning whose sharp practices the Lord Protector had been persuaded by English merchants and shipowners to complain to the king of France. But even such routine petitions called for companion letters to Mazarin, such as, for example, Richard Baker's appeal against "one *Giles* a *French-man*, a petty Admiral of Four Ships" (W73–74; P111, 113). Again, it might be assumed that the protocol of paired letters would have been abandoned eventually but this does not seem to have been the case. The last letters of Oliver's reign (W143–44, P156–57) and the first of Richard's (W124–25, P159–60), written when Louis, still only twenty, had yet to assume his full powers, observed the practice. Further, two of these letters, conspicuously without companions, address religious issues close to the concern of England's leaders, the Piedmont Massacre (W110, P151) and a report of discrimination against French Protestants (W131, P166), either of which would have justified the English bringing to bear the full weight of Milton's rhetoric to move both king and cardinal.

Hence, all the evidence indicates that the companion letters to the nine lacking them were indeed composed and dispatched. Further, given the protocol, it must be assumed that if Milton was responsible for one, he was responsible for both.[82] John Thurloe, an eminently practical man, would certainly not have had two different secretaries, at opposite ends of Westminster, write separate letters on the same subject to co-rulers of a nation, particularly if he had a John Milton hard by, one who had been observing the protocol for years.

In addition to these incomplete pairs, one can turn to the French holdings in the Public Record Office for documentary confirmation of the somewhat self-evident observation that the governments of the Republic dispatched many more letters to foreign heads of state than are

---

Louis XIV are W132, P167, and W134, P168. Two other letters, addressed to the French ambassador and signed by the president of the Council, would not have required companions (W93, P126; W102, P136).

82. Although *Prose* rejects it (710), one of these most certainly must be listed as Milton's, that dated 31 July 1655, Cromwell to Mazarin, *Cum E Re Visum*. A copy appears in PRO 31/3/98/85, and therefore is certainly the version finally delivered. A letter of the same date, addressee, and substance is included in all three seventeenth-century sources, and therefore in both modern editions (W57, P83), as *Cum Nobilem Hunc*. In both Cromwell introduces his envoy, George Downing, to Mazarin. The only difference between *Cum Nobilem Hunc* and *Cum E Re Visum* is that the former refers to Downing only as "*nobilem hunc virum*," whereas the latter cites him by name. Shawcross attributes it to Milton (*Bibliography* 58).

to be found in the seventeenth-century sources of Milton's State Papers. The correspondence with France is one of the most complete collections of letters to and from foreign states in English archives; and nowhere else does one find more persuasive evidence that Milton was responsible for more letters, in both Latin and English, than those early sources document.

In the late nineteenth century the French archivist, Armand Baschet, undertook the task to assemble, from the *Bibliothèque Nationale*, the *Archives Nationale*, and the *Archives Ministère des Affaires Étrangères*, where they lay scattered, documents from the early diplomatic correspondence between the two nations. He deposited a transcript of these documents in the Public Record Office, one entitled "Lists of Despatches of Ambassadors from France to England; Henry VIII.—George I.; 1509–1714."[83] A catalogue of the transcript was published in 1878 in *The Thirty-ninth Annual Report of the Deputy Keeper of the Public Records*; but it is unreliable, listing some documents not in the transcript and failing to list some that are.[84] Aside from the "Despatches of Ambassadors" there are included, as "*Pieces Diverses*," a number of letters exchanged between the heads of state of the two governments. Of those from the period of the English Republic the transcript includes thirteen from Cromwell to Mazarin and Louis XIV, seven of which are Milton's.[85] There are eight additional such letters, listed in the catalogue

83. PRO 31/3/1–203. Those for the period of the Republic are in 31/3/89–106.

84. Appendix 8:573–826 (Interregnum records at 705–16). A corrected copy of the catalogue is available in the PRO Round Room reference shelves, no. 19/42. Baschet's preliminary reports are in *The Thirty-sixth Annual Report* (1875), App. 1, No. 5:230–58, and *The Thirty-seventh Annual Report* (1876), App. 1, No. 3:180–194.

85. Cromwell's letters are as follows, cited by piece and folio numbers in PRO 31/3. Items 90/630 and 95/13 are in French; 90/586 is in English. The rest are in Latin. Milton's letters are identified.

90/630	after 31 March 1653	Cromwell to Mazarin	
95/13	9 June 1653	Cromwell to Mazarin	
90/586	26 January 1654*	Cromwell to Mazarin	
98/15–16	25 May 1655	Cromwell to Louis XIV	W139, P78
98/17–18	25 May 1655	Cromwell to Mazarin	W112, P79
98/82–84	31 July 1655	Cromwell to Louis XIV	W56, P82
98/85	31 July 1655	Cromwell to Mazarin	W57, P83
98/182–83	4 December 1655	Cromwell to Louis XIV	
98/184–85	4 December 1655	Cromwell to Mazarin	
98/188–89	12 December 1655	Cromwell to Mazarin	
99/8	4 April 1656	Cromwell to Mazarin	W146, P94

*Incorrectly filed with 1653 letters. The date is obviously old style, as it is signed "Oliver P." In letters prior to December 1653 the signature is "O. Cromwell."

but absent from the transcript, two of which bear the same dates as Milton's letters.[86] Thus the Paris archives hold at least twenty-one letters from the Cromwells to Louis XIV and Mazarin, dated during the years when Milton was responsible for French correspondence; but at the most only nine of them are included in the early manuscripts. Surely, not all of the others are Milton's work; but just as surely, *some* of them are.

The French, of course, replied meticulously to each letter they received; and the transcript also contains twenty-five *from* the French rulers *to* the Cromwells, nine of which are of particular interest because they were sent during those months in 1658 when Milton was engaged in correspondence relating to the siege and capture of Dunkirk and the transition of power after Oliver's death.[87] Further, of these twenty-five, six were written in answer to letters Milton wrote.[88] It can be reasonably assumed that he was responsible for translating into English, if not all, at least the majority of these letters from France.

In summary, the correspondence with France was voluminous during the period when Milton was regularly employed in translating or com-

---

| 100/57–58 | 25 September 1656 | Cromwell to Mazarin | W74, P113 |
| 102/201 | 20 May 1658 | Cromwell to Mazarin | P150 |

86. These eight, all addressed by Oliver and Richard Cromwell to Mazarin, are listed in the catalogue but are not in the transcript. They bear the following dates: 29 June 1654, 4 April 1655, 25 September 1655, 29 March 1658, 1 April 1658, 1 July 1658, 6 September 1658, 15 November 1658. Of Milton's letters, W144, P157 is dated 1 July 1658, and W125, P160, 6 September 1658.

87. The letters, all dated 1658, are identified by folio pages in PRO 31/3/102:

126–27	6 April	Mazarin to Cromwell
148	12 April	Mazarin to Cromwell
240–41	12 June	Mazarin to Cromwell
242–43	20 June	Louis XIV to Cromwell
267	20 June	Mazarin to Cromwell
268–69	? June	Louis XIV to Cromwell
273–74	25 June	Mazarin to Cromwell
450–51	25 September	Mazarin to R. Cromwell
498	24 October	Mazarin to R. Cromwell

88. The answers are cited, again, by piece and folio number in PRO 31/3. They are all in French:

98/40–42	12 June 1655	Louis XIV to Cromwell	(to W139, P78)
98/43	13 June 1655	Mazarin to Cromwell	(to W112, P79)
98/107	1 September 1655	Mazarin to Cromwell	(to W57, P83)
102/268–69	? June 1658	Louis XIV to Cromwell	(to W116, P148)
102/273–74	25 June 1658	Mazarin to Cromwell	(to W119, P155)
102/450–51	25 September 1658	Mazarin to R. Cromwell	(to W125, P160)

posing the exchanges between the two nations.[89] This is not to suggest
that he was responsible for all of the correspondence that passed between them, but there is evidence that permits us to add substantially to
the number included in the seventeenth-century sources: Nine of the
letters attributed to him, customarily written in pairs, are wanting the
companion which the protocol of the correspondence demands. Further, those dealing with any single issue, such as the employment of
English forces in France during 1658, can be attributed to him with a
high degree of probability. And one can say, with assurance, that he
was called upon to translate into English the replies to letters whose
Latin he had composed. It is not clear that he kept copies of all he
wrote, but among the copies of those he did keep he excluded for one
reason or another a number from the group he chose to have transcribed.

Sweden: The War in the North

War therefore, open or conceal'd, alike
My voice dissuades.

(PL 2:187–88)

Milton's letters to Sweden brought to his attention one of the most
dynamic figures of the mid-seventeenth century—Charles X. Until 1654
the ruler of Sweden was Christina, for whom Milton had a special affection because of her praise for his first *Defence*; but in a sudden turn
of events she secretly converted to Roman Catholicism, abdicated her
throne in favor of her cousin, and retired to Rome to live out her years.
Soon after mounting the throne Charles X launched a series of military
campaigns whose objective was to turn the Baltic Sea into a Swedish
lake, and in doing so he incurred the hostility of almost every major
power in the area. He was at one time or another opposed by Poland,
Brandenburg, Russia, the United Netherlands, Denmark, and the Duchy
of Bremen. Although Milton's letters on occasion congratulate Charles
on his victories, with far more frequency and passion, they urge peace

89. SP 78/113 and 114, State Papers Foreign, France, contains only one item of interest. Milton prepared the credential letters for William Lockhart when he was designated
English envoy to France in April 1656 (W145–46, P93–94). SP 78/113/84–89 is a copy
of Cromwell's instructions to Lockhart on that occasion. SP 108/54–56 contains the ratification documents for French treaties, dated 3 March 1657, 18 March 1658, and 21
January 1659.

and praise the treaties that promise it. Sweden's wars were actually quite disturbing to Cromwell, for they clouded his grand vision of a powerful league of Protestant nations of northern Europe against the Catholic south. His letters to the king are filled with ardent pleas for reconciliation with his neighbors, reminding Charles time and again of the sacred obligation they share to protect the reformed religion against the oppression of the papists.

Cromwell's relations with the Protestant nations of northern Europe were complicated by a tangled web of conflicting allegiances and ambitions. Insofar as those powers stood in the way of his efforts to enhance England's position as a naval power, they were rivals, even on occasion wartime enemies. Insofar as they were Protestant, they were potent allies in the crusade against the agents of the Antichrist, chiefly the Hapsburgs of Austria and Spain. In charting a policy toward the United Provinces, Cromwell had to perform a precarious balancing act, for the Dutch were the dominant commercial power of Europe. Their ships, according to various estimates, carried as much as three-quarters of the European trade; and the great bulk of it was in the Baltic, where the Dutch enjoyed a virtual monopoly over commerce.[90] On the other hand, they were much admired for their religious toleration and their sturdy resistance to Catholic Spain. Cromwell's religious convictions seemed in this instance to outweigh other considerations, for soon after assuming the Protectorate he brought the Anglo-Dutch war to an end; and for the balance of his reign he sought to avoid any alliances, commercial or military, that would adversely affect England's amity with the United Provinces.[91]

The English Republic's relations with Sweden were congenial from the outset. Queen Christina proved sympathetic, and the two nations signed the Treaty of Uppsala in April 1654, a commercial agreement the details of which were to be worked out during the embassy of Christer Bonde the following year.[92] Once Charles X assumed the throne in 1654 the two nations grew even closer, although their friendship was not without its ambivalences. When Charles's campaigns added to the discomfort of Catholic powers and promised favorable conditions for English shipping in the Baltic, Cromwell offered enthusiastic support. When, however, Sweden became embroiled in conflicts with other Protestant nations, he was deeply distressed. Charles persistently requested military assistance from the English, something Cromwell was very re-

90. See Chapter 2 herein for a discussion of Dutch predominance in European trade.
91. Roberts, *Swedish Diplomats*, 26.
92. A copy of the treaty is in SP 103/69/106–13.

luctant to provide because, once again, to do so would jeopardize amity with the Dutch, who opposed Sweden's effort to supplant them as the dominant commercial power in the Baltic.

Relations with Denmark were never entirely amicable, although that nation was solidly Protestant and a close ally of the Dutch. Denmark was critical to English interests, however, because of its control of the Sound, with its narrow entry to the Baltic Sea.[93] After the abortive Anglo-Danish negotiations of 1652, in which, as we have seen, Milton played a part, the Danes allied themselves with the Dutch in the war and closed the Sound entirely to English shipping. Relations improved after the war, once Denmark had reopened the Sound; but the English had to consider that it could be closed again, at any time convenient to the Danes.

Cromwell's relations with the Protestant states and cities of northern Germany are not central to our study, for after 1654 Milton's correspondence with them was limited almost exclusively to matters relevant to the War in the North—but they are certainly interesting.[94] Soon after the establishment of the Protectorate, England renewed Oldenburg's safeguard, and commerce with Hamburg proceeded on a relatively amicable basis with little evidence of Richard Bradshaw's early troubles. Cromwell's attitude toward Bremen, however, is revealing. From the beginning of his campaigns Charles made repeated efforts to pressure England into a military alliance, specifically requesting a substantial loan and the assistance of English warships to support his navy. Cromwell resisted all such overtures until Denmark declared war on Sweden in 1657, whereupon he declared himself agreeable provided Charles would cede the Duchy of Bremen to England. The price was too high for Charles but Bremen remained a bargaining chip in Anglo-Swedish relations for the next two years.[95]

Clearly, Brandenburg was the most important of the north German states, and Cromwell's policy toward Frederick William, the "Great Elector," focused on keeping him firmly in the Protestant camp. In this effort he was unavailing, for in Germany political and commercial considerations overshadowed religious alignments. When Charles invaded

93. See Chapter 2 herein for a discussion of the importance of the Sound.

94. Milton included Cromwell's letter of March 1657 to the landgrave of Hesse, a plea for unity among Protestant churches and praise for "our Agent [John] *Dury*, for many years in vain endeavoring the same Reconciliation" (W88, P121).

95. Roberts suggests that Cromwell deliberately made the price so high that Charles could not agree (*Swedish Diplomats* 41). But Cromwell had long desired "a footing on the Continent" and indeed secured one the following year when he acquired the port of Dunkirk.

Poland in 1655, Frederick William initially opposed him but was soon forced to abandon the Poles and join forces with the Swedes. Two years later, when Charles had to withdraw from Poland and concentrate his armies against Denmark, Frederick William switched sides again and renewed his alliance with the Catholic Poles.

This, then, was the maze of conflicting interests, secular and religious, that occupied Milton's attention from the moment when, as it would appear, he assumed responsibility for England's correspondence with Sweden.[96] His first letter to Charles, in August 1654, congratulates him on his accession to the throne (W46, P68). It is a carefully worded message that, perhaps quite deliberately, makes no mention of military prowess, except for a brief phrase praising Christina as "the Daughter of Gustavus." Barely two months later, however, Cromwell wrote another (W48, P70), the theme and tone of which Milton was to repeat in letter after letter in the years to come. In 1648 the signers of the Treaty of Westphalia, which ended the Thirty Years War, had ceded the Duchy of Bremen to Sweden. The burghers of the city rose in revolt against Christina, and when Charles inherited the rebellion he took steps to quell it. Cromwell writes to urge peace, lamenting the "bloody Conflicts and mutual Slaughters of the Bremeners and Swedes," particularly at a time when there is such a pressing need for a "common Peace of the Protestants" who should more properly be united against the "Papists [who] are said to Persecute the Reformed all over *Germany*." He hears that the two sides have agreed on an armistice and hopes that it will lead to a "most firm peace."[97] There is a companion to Bremen (W49, P71) in which the Lord Protector reaffirms his desire that "the whole Protestant Name would knit and grow together in Brotherly Unity and Accord" and informs the city's senate that he has written to Charles in an effort to mediate. He urges them to "bear an equal Mind" and remain open to reconciliation.[98]

---

96. Milton was responsible for only one letter to Sweden during the Commonwealth period (W19, P36). In December 1651 Queen Christina sent Peter Spiering, Lord Silvercrone, as an envoy to England, but without supplying him with the necessary credentials. After waiting for almost two months for an audience, he died (Miller, *Oldenburg*, 170). In March 1652 Parliament wrote to Christina, piously attributing the death to "the Supreme Moderator and Governour of all things" and expressing regret that they had not had the opportunity to hear what he had to say.

97. For the peace terms, signed 10 July 1654, see SP 103/69/114–21.

98. The Columbia MS includes an English copy of the Bremen letter (W154, P71), which is identical to the final document save for the lack of two brief passages. In the MS it is crossed out (85), which suggests to the editors of *Works* that its attribution to Milton is questionable (13:634). This was done, however, because it was a duplicate of one

Cromwell, of course, was not opposed to all of Charles's wars. Sweden invaded Poland in July 1655, and Charles entered Warsaw but a month later, after a dazzlingly swift campaign. Brandenburg opposed him initially but was quickly brought to heel. Cromwell was delighted and in February 1656 wrote the king, applauding his rescue of "the Kingdom of Poland from Papal Subjection" and praising him for making peace with Brandenburg, which will be "most highly conducing to the Tranquility and Advantage of the Church" (W63, P89). Charles's conquests predictably earned him the hostility of other interested powers, however. His siege of Danzig in the summer of 1656 brought a large Dutch fleet into the Baltic, supported by a Danish squadron, under orders to relieve that city.[99] This confrontation between the United Provinces and Sweden was particularly alarming to Cromwell, and the impassioned rhetoric of his letters to both nations in August reflects a level of concern matched only by his response to the Piedmont Massacre. In one of Milton's longer letters (W79, P108), the Lord Protector expresses to Charles his concern that the confrontation in the Baltic "seems to bode an unhappy rupture." He pleads that the reformed religion is being persecuted throughout Europe, naming Austria, Switzerland, and the Piedmont,[100] and warns dramatically that when there is "Dissention among Protestant Brethren, more especially between Two Potent States, upon whose Courage, Wealth, and Fortitude . . . the Support and Hopes of all the Reformed Churches depend, of necessity the Protestant Religion must be in great jeopardy, if not upon the brink of destruction." In another, even longer (W75, P109), Cromwell pleads with the Dutch as well, citing the same persecutions and cautioning them not to abet the designs of Spain, whom he describes as the secret instigator of dissension among the Protestant nations. It is a fervent plea in which Cromwell at one point chides the Dutch bitterly for letting themselves fall under Spanish influence and begs them not "to forsake

---

already transcribed (59). It is doubtless an early English draft, which Milton used in preparing the official Latin document and its presence in the MS suggests that he composed the English as well.

99. Roberts, *Swedish Diplomats*, 307n.

100. Switzerland at the time was sharply divided into militant Protestant and Catholic sectors, and Cromwell was alarmed at the increase in persecution of Protestants in the Catholic cantons. In January he had written the Swiss Protestants, encouraging them to remain "Magnanimous and Resolute; [and] suffer not your Privileges, your Confederacies, the Liberty of your Consciences, your Religion it self to be trampled under foot by the Worshippers of Idols," the chief offender being the Catholic "Canton of *Schwits*." He urged them, further, to continue their aid to "those most deplorable *Piedmontois*" (W62, P87).

your Ancient and most Faithful Friends the *English, French* and *Danes*"; he goes so far as to scold them for seeming to "enter into a strict Confederacy with your old Enemy, and once your domineering Tyrant, now seemingly atton'd."[101]

Meanwhile, the king of Denmark grew uneasy. As early as February 1656, Frederick III had reacted to Charles's invasion of Poland with a letter to Cromwell, an English translation of which Milton kept on file (W159, P118). The king warns that "the present danger is so spreading, that it seems likely to reach round" to other nations; and he asks the Lord Protector to intercede, since "his Majestie of Sweden is so considerate, as he will not easily be induc'd to oppose the precedence of so great a friend." Frederick is particularly concerned that Charles "might hinder or retard the course of commerce." In August, when the combined Dutch and Danish fleets confronted Charles's forces at Danzig, Cromwell promised Christer Bonde, the Swedish ambassador in London, that he would write those two powers in an effort to head off open hostilities.[102] As we have seen, he did dispatch long, impassioned letters to both Sweden and the United Provinces; but for some reason he failed to send a companion letter to Denmark at the same time.

Hostilities were avoided, as it happened, and in September Sweden and the United Provinces signed the Treaty of Elbing, temporarily patching up their differences.[103] Apparently, the Danes took exception to the treaty, for in November the Council proposed that a letter be sent to Frederick III protesting his efforts to obstruct its ratification.[104] It was decided to put the letter to a larger purpose, however, for it makes only brief reference to Danish opposition to Charles "in his contracting those Alliances which he seeks," and this without a word of protest. The letter (W87, P119) is, first, an answer to Frederick's earlier one of February, to which it refers in the opening sentence. It is, further, the letter of mediation Cromwell had promised Bonde he would write in August. He refers to those sent at that time to the States General and Charles and repeats the same warnings to be found in them concerning Catholic oppression in Austria, Switzerland, and the Piedmont, as well as his conviction that it is "the Artifices and Machinations of the *Spanish*" that lie behind all the difficulties. Bringing matters up to date, Cromwell

---

101. Spanish collusion was suggested to Cromwell by the Swedish ambassador, Christer Bonde, who played upon the theme in pressing for a military alliance between the two nations (Roberts, *Swedish Diplomats*, 323).

102. Ibid., 327.

103. A copy is in SP 103/69/122–39.

104. *CSPD* 10:160.

takes the occasion to attempt a resolution of the "Suspicions" and "sparkes of jealousy" he has observed growing between the two monarchs of late. In language similar to that of the two earlier letters, he warns that their nations compose "the chiefest part of our strength"; and if "two such Potent monarchs" were to have a falling out, then "most certainly the interests of the Protestants must go to ruine, and suffer a total and irrecoverable Eclipse."

Frederick's fears that Charles's Polish campaign was "likely to reach round" and involve other nations proved prophetic, for in June 1656 Russia, alarmed by Swedish successes, entered the war against Charles, whereupon Cromwell found it necessary to undertake mediation of that conflict as well. In April 1657 he ordered Richard Bradshaw to Moscow with a letter to the czar referring broadly to matters "which may conduce to the Good of *Christiandome* and your own Interests" (W91, P124). What those matters were is revealed in the "Instructions for the Agent of the Great Duke of Moscovy," which Milton apparently had a hand in drawing up, for the Columbia MS contains a copy among its English letters (W164, P123). Bradshaw is directed to urge the czar to make peace with Charles, and, in a gesture so transparent as to appear almost naive, to distract him from his territorial ambitions in the Baltic with an exhortation to undertake "a glorious expedition against the Turk, & thereby win him selfe honour throughout Europe as cheif defender of Christendome." As it turned out, Bradshaw was unable to carry out the instructions, or even to deliver Cromwell's letter, for the czar, an adamant enemy of the Commonwealth, refused him permission to enter the country.[105]

English efforts to draw together the Protestant nations of the north in a common cause were to no avail, for in June 1657 Denmark finally declared war on Sweden and invaded the Duchy of Bremen. Cromwell found himself once again in the position of mediator between the Swedish king and one of his neighbors. Charles was forced to withdraw his army from the ravaged fields of Poland and march toward the Danish border, and Cromwell launched a concerted diplomatic effort to contain the damage. He dispatched William Jephson as "Envoy Extraordinary" to Sweden and Philip Meadows to Denmark to prevail upon the two monarchs. In Jephson's letter of credential Cromwell informs Charles of the "disturbance and grief of Mind" with which he "receiv'd

105. The letter appears to have reached the czar, however, for Shawcross lists the Latin original in the Moscow archives (*Bibliography* 65). In March 1658, Milton prepared a letter to the duke of Curland, thanking him for the hospitality shown Bradshaw en route (W89, P142).

the News of the fatal War broke out between your Majesty and the King of *Danemark*" and warns him of the "Mischief" and "Calamities" which it "will bring upon the Common Cause of Religion" (W92, P127).

A sizable diplomatic packet accompanied Jephson. Aside from his credential letter, he carried with him five others, all dated 20 August 1657, addressed to states he would visit on the way: Brandenburg, Hamburg, Bremen, Holstein, and his final destination, Lübeck, where the Swedish army, "encamping not far from" that city, was preparing to launch its invasion of Denmark (W94–97, 99; P128–32). He had also a set of "Secret Instructions," which direct him to propose that, in return for a substantial loan and the commitment of an English fleet in support of Charles, the king would cede the Duchy of Bremen to England.[106] A comparable packet was prepared for Philip Meadows, including his credential letter to Frederick III, which is on file in the Copenhagen *Rigsarkivet*, and similar letters of introduction, though only the one to Hamburg is included in the early manuscripts of the State Papers (W98, P133).[107] Like Jephson, he had a set of instructions, directing him, as he later put it, "to remonstrate how unwelcome it was to them in *England* to understand of the Rupture betwixt the two Crowns," and to warn that "the continuation of that war in so perilous a juncture considerably endangers the whole Protestant Cause."[108]

---

106. BL, Add MS 4157, 201–4; printed in Abbott 4:603–5. The transfer of Bremen was a sensitive issue, and Cromwell had to tread very lightly. Over half of Jephson's instructions advise him on how to address it. He is not to broach the subject himself but is to discuss it only if Charles "shall take notice of" it. The caution is later repeated: "You shall not make any mention of this of Bremen unlesse his majestie shall administer the occasion thereof." Then he is to argue that an English fleet in Danish waters will have need of a base of operations, "some place of strength and securitie to have recourse to." Indeed, Jephson, a military man, is instructed to examine port facilities in the duchy for possible use. He is to propose further that the transfer need only be temporary; once the loan is repaid (an unlikely event), Bremen is to be returned.

107. Shawcross lists Meadows's credentials in the *Rigsarkivet*, T.K.U.A., A.II.16., dated as the others on 20 August. The file also contains a letter from Cromwell to Frederick III concerning Jephson, dated 19 October (*Bibliography* 64).

108. Philip Meadows, *A Narrative*, 18–19. Frederick replied on 25 September and Charles on 19 October, both expressing themselves agreeable to peace, once certain conditions are met, of course.

A number of these sets of instructions from English archives are cited in the text, several of which are printed in Abbott:

    To Jephson, 22 August 1657 (BL MS 4157, ff. 201–4; Abbott 4:603–5)
    To Meadows, August 1657 (SP 75/16/240–44; Abbott 4:605–7)
    To Meadows, 9 April 1658 (SP 95/5A/72–75; Abbott 4:779–81)
    To Viscount Fauconberg, May 1658 (Abbott 4:809–10)

Jephson's five-city tour of northern Germany was intended to enlist aid for the English peace effort; but before he could reach Berlin, Cromwell apparently learned that Brandenburg was growing restive. He hurried off a follow-up letter to Frederick William in September (W101, P135), designed to reinforce Jephson's presentation to the Great Elector. Cromwell praises him grandly for his "Faith and Conscience," which have been, "by all manner of Artifices Tempted and Assail'd, by all manner of Arts and Devices Solicited," presumably by the Spaniards, but which, he continues confidently, "cannot be shaken, or by any Violence be rent from your Friendship and Alliance" with the king of Sweden, from which Cromwell concludes that Frederick William, like any enlightened ruler, "rather consults the common Cause of the Reformed Religion, then your own Advantage." Ironically, even as these high sentiments were being composed, the Great Elector was in the act of abrogating his treaty with Charles and allying himself with Poland against Sweden.

Charles's 1657–58 campaign against Denmark is one of the most daring recorded in the military annals of the age. He marched his army north into Jutland and then across the frozen waters of the Great Belt, advancing precariously from island to island, and finally appeared, to the surprise of the Danes, before the gates of Copenhagen. Frederick III sued for peace in February, and the following month Cromwell could once again applaud a Swedish victory (W108, P143), rejoicing that after their successes, the king of Denmark has finally "judged peace . . . more advantageous to him than the war undertaken against you." On a conciliatory note he raises the specter of Spain once more, suggesting that Frederick may not have declared war "by his own will and interests" but that the conflict was instigated "by the arts of common foes," the insidious "enemies of Religion" who were the true "kindlers of this war."

The Treaty of Roskilde, brokered by Philip Meadows, was signed by the two nations on 26 February 1658.[109] It was highly advantageous to England in that the Danish provinces on the eastern shore of the Sound were ceded to Sweden, in effect dividing control of that narrow passage

---

To Adm. Goodson, 12 November 1658 (SP 95/5A/61–65)
To Meadows, 12 November 1658 (SP 95/5A/66–68)
To Meadows, 9 December 1658 (SP 95/5A/69–71)
To Meadows, 18 March 1659 (SP 95/5A/95–96)
To Adm. Montague, 18 March 1659 (SP 95/5A/97–105)
To Adm. Montague, 2 July 1659 (SP 75/16/262–68).
109. A copy is in SP 103/3/71–90.

between the two powers. The Danes could not again unilaterally deny English fleets access to the trade of the Baltic, as they had in 1653–54. The treaty did not hold, however, falling victim to Charles's unsatisfied ambitions. Hostilities resumed in August, and Swedish forces were soon again besieging Copenhagen.

To appreciate the significance of Milton's next four letters to Sweden and Denmark, it will be helpful to scan briefly the rapid evolution of events in both England and the Sound during the years 1658–59. On 3 September 1658 Cromwell died and was succeeded by his son, Richard, who immediately dispatched letters to foreign powers, assuring them of an untroubled transition and the continuation of the dead Protector's policies. Milton had two of these transcribed, those to Louis XIV (W124, P159) and Mazarin (W125, P160), and it is most probable that he was responsible for a number more.[110] In a letter to Charles, written in October, Richard cautiously confirms his "Resolution to continue the League concluded by our Father with your Majesty" and offers the wish that God will "long preserve your Majesty to his Glory, and the Defence and Safeguard of his Orthodox Church" (W126, P161).[111] Even as Milton was preparing the Latin letter, however, the situation in the Sound was changing radically. The United Netherlands found that it could no longer remain neutral. In October a powerful Dutch fleet under Admiral Opdam, with a sizable army aboard, arrived on the scene while the armies of Brandenburg and Poland occupied Jutland. The following month Opdam forced his way into the Sound, scattering the Swedish navy and relieving Copenhagen. Charles, although he still commanded a powerful army before the gates of the city, was effectively isolated; and the English, whose interests would certainly not be advanced by a Swedish defeat, decided to take action. On 13 November Richard wrote again, informing Charles that in keeping with the "League" between them, he has ordered "a Fleet into the *Baltic* Sea," concerning whose mission Philip Meadows, by then ambassador to Sweden, will fully inform him (W127, P163).

The admiral of the English fleet, William Goodson, was instructed to assist Meadows in securing a treaty between Sweden and Denmark; but should that effort fail, he was "to give assistance to the Kinge of

110. Both are dated 6 September 1658. Another, from Richard Cromwell to the States General, with the same date, is in SP 84/162/164–65.

111. This letter is almost certainly not Richard's first to Charles. It is a reply "to some particulars, which your Embassadours have propos'd," not an announcement of the succession. Richard doubtless sent a letter to Sweden of the same substance as those to Louis XIV, Mazarin, and the Dutch States General, and probably on the same day, 6 September.

Sweden for his defence against such as shall assault him," once Meadows had arrived at agreeable terms with Charles. Goodson's fleet never reached the Sound, prevented by adverse weather, and it was not until April 1659 that English warships under Admiral Edward Montague arrived in Danish waters. By that time the situation had changed yet again, and to the further discomfort of Charles X. He had launched an unsuccessful ground assault on Copenhagen in February and the following month the Dutch had reinforced their fleet to a total of eighty men-of-war, commanded by the able Admiral de Ruyter. Thus, Cromwell's dream of a great Protestant League died with him, for within months after his funeral an Anglo-Swedish fleet stood opposing the combined navies of Denmark and the United Netherlands in the Sound, the four most powerful Protestant nations facing each other in hostile confrontation.

Montague sailed under a much more elaborate set of instructions, since he was not only the admiral of the fleet but also a highly influential member of the Council of State; and it is apparent from his orders that he was to assume responsibility for the mediation effort.[112] He was, first, to inform both kings that he had "brought the Fleet to those parts by our command as a Common friend of them both" and to urge them to restore peace on the basis of the Treaty of Roskilde. Should Denmark refuse, he was "to give assistance to the King of Sweden as our friend and alleye," but to "mannage it that before you engage the Fleet in action the King of Sweden doe agree and authentiquely ratify" a treaty between them. Should Charles refuse, Montague was to inform him that "We shall be obliged to provide for our owne interest." Years later, Philip Meadows wrote an account of these events in which he disclosed the terms of the treaty. The English had failed to persuade Charles to cede the Duchy of Bremen to them; but still ambitious for additional Continental holdings, they asked that he provide them with "*Stade* upon the *Elb*, and *Landscroon* in the *Sound*" in return for their assistance.[113] Apparently, the king was no more enthusiastic about this proposal than he had been the earlier one.

For a time developments had to wait on events in London. On 23 April, Richard dissolved the Protectorate Parliament; but three weeks later he was himself dismissed and the Rump recalled to constitute the government of England. It was for this body that Milton wrote com-

---

112. SP 95/5A/97–105. Montague carried a set of instructions for Meadows as well but it is a relatively short document (SP 95/5A/95–96).

113. Meadows 120. Stade, in the Duchy of Bremen, is just down the Elbe from Hamburg. Landscroon is modern Landskrona, a Swedish port on the Sound.

panion letters to Denmark and Sweden, the last recorded of his public career (W135–36, P174–75). In both, dated 15 May, Parliament announces their restoration, by the hand of "the most merciful and omnipotent God," and reaffirms their "Zeal" to promote peace between the two monarchs, offering Philip Meadows again as mediator. The letter to Frederick contains a somewhat suspect note of sympathy, of "how much we lay to Heart your ill success," but it was doubtless sincere in its desire for reconciliation.[114]

The legacy of Oliver Cromwell's pacific policy toward the Dutch continued to serve as a restraint on English actions and there were no hostile encounters between the two fleets during the months to follow. Indeed, even as they faced each other in Danish waters, envoys of the two nations, in concert with France, were meeting in Holland in an effort to end the war. On 11 May, the three signed the Treaty of The Hague, dictating the terms of peace between Denmark and Sweden.[115] It provided for a reaffirmation of Roskilde, making permanent the divided control over the Sound, an arrangement advantageous to all three signatories. In July, Montague received a new set of instructions, directing him to pressure both kings to end the war on the basis of the treaties of Roskilde and The Hague. Should they refuse, he is to open negotiations with the Dutch, contacting "the Publique Minister of the States General" in an effort to defuse the situation. If the Dutch, he is instructed, "shall agree to withdraw ye assistance of the United Provinces from ye King of Denmark . . . they you shall also agree to withdraw ye Assistance of this Common Wealth from ye King of Sweden."[116] Little came of the initiative, and Montague sailed home at the end of August after five months "without doing anything," as Meadows put it.[117] In November, de Ruyter soundly defeated the Swedes, thus ending Charles's dream of a Swedish lake; and within months, the king was dead.

Thus Milton was deeply involved in the correspondence with and about Sweden from 1654 through 1659. Aside from the nineteen docu-

---

114. Frederick III's reply, dated 10 June, is in SP 75/16/255.

115. The treaty had to be signed again on 2 July because of the change of government in England.

116. SP 75/16/162–68. Still angling for Continental bases, the Council directed him to "endeavor to procure such fitt place or places to be delivered into ye hands of ye Parliament of the Commonwealth."

117. Meadows 121. There is some suggestion that Montague hurried home to support Booth's uprising in August (Masson 5:478). He was not a commonwealthsman and showed decided royalist leanings during the troubles that followed. It was he who escorted Charles home to England, for which he was rewarded with a knighthood, named earl of Sandwich, and made Master of the Wardrobe (Masson 6:17–18).

ments addressed to that country during those years (including the treaty), an additional sixteen were occasioned in one way or another by Charles's campaigns, three to and one from Denmark, two each to Hamburg, Russia, and Brandenburg, and one each to the United Netherlands, Holstein, Lübeck, Bremen, Danzig, and Courland, amounting to over one-third of all the papers in the early manuscripts for that period.[118] And there were certainly more, as Cromwell bent every effort to bring peace to Scandinavia and repair the damage done to his dreams of a Protestant League by Charles's ambitions.[119] One of the more promising sources for additional attributions is the diplomatic packet of Philip Meadows. It seems reasonable to assume that his documents and those for Jephson were prepared by the same secretary, hence that the letters of credential to the two kings may be considered companions. Further, Milton prepared five letters of introduction for Jephson; and although only one for Meadows was transcribed, that to Hamburg, there were doubtless others, for his route would have taken him at least through the territories of the duke of Holstein. All of the extant letters, including Cromwell's addressed to Frederick III in the Copenhagen archives, are dated the same day, 20 August 1657. Thus the evidence strongly favors the conclusion that Milton was responsible for both diplomatic packets, but that, although he may have had both sets of documents on file, he considered it unnecessarily repetitious to include two such similar groups of letters in the transcript. There is also the question of the set of "Secret Instructions" that each carried as part of his diplomatic packet, both of which are available in the Public Record Office. Although such documents are in English, Milton included the one for Richard Bradshaw's abortive mission to Russia in the Columbia MS,

---

118. Those letters not mentioned in the text are W64, P122; W67, P95; W72, P104; W83, P117; W90, P125; W120, P153; W128, P162; W129, P165; W142, P102; and W150, P173. W142 is of particular interest. On 13 June 1656 Cromwell issued a safe-conduct to Peter George Romswinckel, instructing all English officials to permit him "to travel unharmed and free by sea and land, without interference, or inspection of his baggage" (W141, P101). W142 is a companion letter addressed to the king of Sweden on the same date, introducing Romswinckel and asking "easy access and kindly audience, together with timely help and protection." Patrick notes that "there are almost identical letters in the archives of The Hague, Amsterdam, and Brandenburg, differently addressed" (5:744). Milton certainly prepared these three and any others of the same date and substance.

119. Abbott, for example, lists four additional letters from Cromwell to Denmark, dated 23 November 1655 (2), 17 May 1657, and 26 March 1658, and eight to Sweden, dated August 1657, 29 October 1657, 1 March 1658, 2 April 1658, 9 April 1658 (3), and 16 July 1658 (4:925–43).

and may well have had a hand in preparing those which Jephson carried to Lübeck and Meadows to Copenhagen.

> . . . and in my ear
> Vented much policy, and projects deep
> Of enemies, of aids, battles and leagues.
> (PR 3:391–93)

The case for attribution of these documents is further strengthened by the fact that there were extended intervals when Milton was the only Latin Secretary available to Cromwell. One of these periods comes to light in the records of the embassy of Christer Bonde, who was in London from July 1655 to August 1656 to negotiate a treaty with England. Bonde actually had two missions, the first to settle details left unresolved by the Treaty of Uppsala in 1654, and the second, of even more importance to Charles, to persuade Cromwell to join Sweden in a military alliance. In the latter effort Bonde was entirely unsuccessful, largely because the two parties had radically different attitudes toward the objective of such an alliance, differences that arose from Sweden's insistence upon the inclusion of a Latin phrase in the draft treaty. Charles was intent upon a defensive alliance *"contra quoscunque,"* that is, against any and all enemies of Sweden, whereas Cromwell preferred that it be directed specifically against the House of Hapsburg and Spain.[120] The king, whose eye was on the Baltic, was unwilling to commit himself to a Protestant crusade to the south. He wanted, rather, an active partner in his wars, specifically requesting that England commit twenty men-of-war to help him police the Baltic, something Cromwell, who feared offending the Dutch, was equally unwilling to do.

Agreement on a commercial treaty showed more promise, and the negotiations that led to its signing are of interest to Miltonists for two reasons. The first is the revealing detail about the poet's status on the secretariat, discussed above; and the second, of equal concern, is the question of his responsibility for the final document. There were serious differences left unresolved by Uppsala. Bonde reports that on 21 April 1656 he delivered to the Council of State's commissioners "a draft, with the text as they had drawn it on one side of the sheet, and on the other the text as I would have it." The English response was slow because, as Bonde complains, "it is a scandal that now that Mr Meadowe has gone to Portugal they have no one who can write a decent line of Latin, but

---

120. Roberts, *Swedish Diplomats*, 36–37, 254n, 281, and 309.

the blind Miltonius must translate anything they want done from English to Latin, and one can easily imagine how it goes."[121] Philip Meadows had departed on his mission in March; and the Council simply neglected to appoint a replacement in his absence. Bulstrode Whitelocke, one of the Council's commissioners, records Bonde's complaint in his *Memorials of the English Affairs*;[122] and on the basis of that report Milton's editors since Hamilton have attributed the Latin of the treaty to him. *Works* includes it (W170), but *Prose* does not (P96). Citing Whitelocke's account, Patrick concludes "that Milton was asked only to put a few articles of the treaty into Latin," hence that he was responsible for only an unspecified part of the text and that the *Works* editors erred in publishing the entire document. Bonde's dispatches, which Patrick did not have available, make it clear that there was disagreement over much more than just "a few articles" and that Milton worked on the 21 April draft of the *entire* treaty.[123] There were further exchanges of documents during the following months. In May Bonde submitted "a new draft of the whole treaty," and in mid-June "the treaty re-drafted for the second time," which presumably had to be translated once again; and on the eve of the final signing he was still revising the preamble and conclusion.[124]

If, as Bonde reports, "the blind Miltonius must translate anything they want done from English to Latin," then the poet must have been regularly employed to prepare the various proposals and counterproposals exchanged during those months; and when final agreement was reached in July, and the treaty had to be cast into Latin, no one had

121. Ibid., 282.

122. Whitelocke describes the incident also: "The Swedes Ambassador again complained of the delays in his business, and that when he had desired to have the Articles of his Treaty put into *Latine*, according to the custom in Treaties, that it was 14 dayes they had made him stay for that Translation; and sent it to Mr. *Milton*, a blind man to put them into *Latine*. . . . The Imployment of Mr. *Milton* was excused to him, because several other Servants of the Council fit for that Imployment were then absent" (4:257).

123. In his dispatches Bonde specifically records the controversy and compromise associated with the first seven of the eleven articles in the treaty, each of which required extensive revision (see esp. Roberts, *Swedish Diplomats*, 312–13). The chief cause of delay was Article 2, which spelled out items to be classified as "contraband," hence subject to seizure. England insisted the naval stores be included; Sweden objected. Bonde finally agreed that Sweden would not "carry pitch, tar, hemp, cables, sail-cloth, or masts" to Spain (*Works* 13:591), but only if this detail was omitted from the text and hidden in a secret protocol.

124. Roberts, *Swedish Diplomats*, 292, 305, and 318. The text of the treaty is in SP 103/69/122–31. It was signed by Cromwell on 15 July, Bonde on 17 July, and Charles on 14 November.

as yet been appointed to replace Meadows. If at all possible, Thurloe would certainly have chosen to employ the same translator throughout, one already familiar with the issues under debate and able to reflect in appropriate language the subtle compromises arrived at.[125] Again, Milton was available—apparently the only one available—he was on the payroll, he was familiar with the issues, and he was a superb Latinist. Why use anyone else?

It is not certain how long Milton remained alone in the office of Latin Secretary. Meadows left on his mission to Portugal in early March 1656 and returned in July, but he was still recovering from a wound suffered in the attempt on his life in Lisbon the previous May. In February 1657 he was appointed envoy to Denmark; and although he did not actually leave until early September, one must wonder just how regularly he became engaged in the work-a-day activities of that office once he had attained the status of diplomat. It was not until after his departure that Nathaniel Sterry was appointed to succeed him.

It is clear, at any rate, that John Thurloe turned consistently to Milton for assistance in preparing documents occasioned by Sweden's wars; whoever else may have been available, there was no need to change that practice in dealing with whatever additional correspondence was required by Cromwell's long and ardent effort to secure peace in the north.[126] In that correspondence a few themes reappear time and time again: a rallying-cry to the cause of the "Reformed Religion," the threat of Protestant dissension to that cause, Catholic oppression in Austria, Switzerland, and the Piedmont, and the allegation that Spain was the secret instigator of all their troubles. This repetition suggests that once the substance of the first of these letters had been determined, Milton was given a free hand in similar passages of those that followed, where the same themes are trumpeted in prose approaching the prophetic in tone.

Historians are divided in their judgment of the motivation behind and the effectiveness of Cromwell's foreign policy. Some consider his cru-

---

125. Although Bonde was fluent in English, he insisted that Latin be used in the deliberations. He complained bitterly when the Council of State submitted their first set of proposals to him *in English*, protesting that "in negotiations much importance might attach to a single word," as was certainly the case with *quoscunque* (Roberts, *Swedish Diplomats*, 245).

126. SP 95/5A and 5B are singularly empty of letters addressed to or from the English head of state. SP 103/69 includes a number of documents relating to the Anglo-Swedish negotiations of 20 January–6 October, 1653, which led to the Treaty of Uppsala, signed on 11 April 1654, as well as several other treaties. SP 108/516 contains only Cromwell's ratification of Uppsala, 31 July 1654.

sading fervor for Protestant unity the motor that drove all his efforts, others find it but propaganda for thinly disguised imperialistic ambitions. Some conclude that his religious convictions blinded him to England's true interests, others that he achieved lasting benefits for his country. His vision of a Protestant League, it is said, caused him to ally himself with a resurgent France rather than a declining Spain, thereby upsetting the precarious European balance of power, and his obsessive reluctance to offend the Dutch prevented him from confronting their commercial power, the chief obstacle to English prosperity.[127] The conflict within him between religious and secular concerns, especially in the dilemma posed by the need to choose between the interests of the Swedes and the Dutch, at times left him "forced into circumspection, almost passivity," as Derek Hirst puts it, though that posture achieved some successes, such as the division of the Sound between Denmark and Sweden.[128] Michael Roberts concludes that he charted a realistic and generally effective course between the two concerns: "Cromwell's Baltic policy, then, does not represent the sacrifice of trade to religion, nor the subordination of the interests of England to the dream of a Protestant Front."[129]

A reading of Milton's letters can add to the debate in the indelible impression they leave of a Cromwell passionately committed to Protestant unity, urging it repeatedly as a holy cause and deploring the divisions, which he predicts will ruin it. Of course, any judgment to this effect must be tempered by an uncertainty as to how much of the ardor of the letters can be attributed to Cromwell and how much to Milton, since we have no way of knowing how much latitude the poet was given in writing them. But it must be said that the apocalyptic passages in the documents certainly have a familiar ring to them.

---

127. See Roberts, "Cromwell and the Baltic," 138–40, for a comprehensive survey of conflicting views on the issue.

128. Derek Hirst, "The Lord Protector," 147. Cromwell's ambivalence or "passivity" is illustrated by his procrastination in sending an envoy to Denmark in 1657. Warned perhaps by the tone of Frederick III's letter to the Protector (W159, P118), the Council advised sending Philip Meadows on the mission as early as 24 February and reminded him again on 19 March. On 4 August, after Denmark had declared war on Sweden, they "advised" him once again. Meadows did not leave until early September (CSPD 10:291, 317; 11:52). It was not until after Oliver's death that his son finally ordered an English fleet to the Baltic, although it did not arrive until April 1659.

129. Roberts, "Cromwell and the Baltic," 173.

4

MILTON ON GOVERNMENT

Yet sometimes Nations will decline so low
From virtue, which is reason, that no wrong,
But Justice, and some fatal curse annext
Deprives them of thir outward liberty,
Thir inward lost.

(PL 12:97–101)

As observed at the outset of our study, reflection on what influence Milton's decade of public service had on his poetic imagination must await another day. Something may be said, however, about its influence on his political thought, since during the months prior to the Restoration, he felt obliged to address his countrymen on the most compelling issue before them—their choice of government. After a four-year silence, he took up his pen once more to comment on his times, interrupting work on *Christian Doctrine*, which, it is generally agreed, was well advanced by 1659, and perhaps on the early books of *Paradise Lost*.[1]

---

1. Milton published the *Defence of Himself* in 1655. In the interim he also published an edition of *The Cabinet-Council*, said to be the work by Sir Walter Ralegh, and a revised edition of the first *Defence* with a brief postscript. William B. Hunter, Jr., has suggested that *Considerations Touching the Likeliest Means* may have been written in 1653 and revised for publication later (*Prose* 7:230). Shawcross states unequivocally that *The Cabinet-Council* is not Ralegh's ("Survey of Milton's Prose Works" 331).

He continued in his official position for most of that year, though there
was precious little to do. So engrossed was the nation in domestic up-
heavals that its leaders had little time or energy to concern themselves
with foreign affairs and the Latin Secretaries were seldom employed.
The last important diplomatic initiative of the English Republic was the
Treaty of The Hague, signed in May by England, France, and the
United Netherlands and renegotiated in July.[2] Military activity abroad
ended with the return of Montague's fleet from the Sound in September.
Milton wrote two letters for the restored Rump Parliament in May, the
last to be included in the early manuscripts (W135–36, P174–75); and
although his office was once more responsible to the Council of State,
the only mention of his name in the Order Books is a notation on 25
October that he is to receive the balance of his annual salary of £200.[3]

Some measure of the turbulence of those months may be seen in the
succession of ruling bodies that assumed the helm of government, some
by force, others by default. From April 1659 to April 1660, four different Parliaments sat at Westminster—Richard Cromwell's Protectorate,
the restored Rump, the Rump plus the excluded members, and the Convention—the first three of which were dissolved under pressure from
the military. A procession of smaller executive bodies, of constantly
changing numbers and membership, presided over affairs, two of them
at one point sitting simultaneously, both claiming legitimacy. Political
stability was further undermined by a royalist uprising and a split in the
army, which resulted in two hostile elements of that once proudly
united force facing one another across a northern river. And beneath
the discord, like an insistent bass theme, subdued at first but slowly
rising under the dissonance of conflicting voices until it finally overwhelmed them, was the cry to restore the king. During the final months
royalists pressed their case with impunity in the streets and the press
until the distracted republicans, whose cause had disintegrated into
wrangling factions, finally gave up in despair. The period is aptly called
the "Anarchy."

God from the Mount of *Sinai* . . .
. . . .
Ordain[ed] them Laws; part such as pertain

2. The English exercised "no influence at all," according to Godfrey Davies, on the
Treaty of the Pyranees signed by France and Spain on 28 October (*The Restoration of
Charles II* 208). I am indebted to Davies for the bulk of the historical narrative.
3. *CSPD* 13:256.

> To civil Justice, part religious Rites
> Of Sacrifice.
>
> (*PL* 12:227–32)

Milton's first two tracts of the period contain a plea for a principle that underlies all of his political thought—the separation of church and state. He viewed governments as one of the unhappy consequences of the Fall, their function to provide political and judicial order so that men, with the aid of Scripture, could wrestle with their fallen nature and find their own way to salvation. This they could never do, he believed, so long as these governments insisted on controlling their religious lives as well. From the first to the last of his public statements, during all of the shifting allegiances of his turbulent time, Milton never wavered in the conviction that political freedom can be attained only by those who enjoy "liberty of conscience." In one of his first ventures into public print he proposed that "the property of Truth is, where she is publickly taught, to unyoke & set free the minds and spirits of a Nation first from the thraldom of sin and superstition, after which all honest and legal freedom of civil life cannot be long absent." In the summer of 1659, he again put this relationship between spiritual and political freedom clearly in perspective: until "religion [is] set free from the monopolie of hirelings, I dare affirme, that no modell whatsoever of a commonwealth will prove successful or undisturbd." In *The Readie and Easie Way* he reaffirmed his conviction about which must come first, "who can enjoy anything in this world with contentment, who hath not libertie to serve God and save his own soul." The message is clear: until Man is free spiritually he cannot be free politically (1:853; 7:275, 379).

> Then shall they seek to avail themselves of names,
> Places and titles, and with these to join
> Secular power, though feigning still to act
> By spiritual.
>
> (*PL* 12:515–18)

Thus, in his eyes the greatest enemy of spiritual freedom was ever the established church with its hierarchy of ministers, whether "New Presbyter" or "Old Priest," its onerous system of tithes, and its oppressive ritual. He blasted the bishops, excoriated the Presbyterians of the Westminster Assembly, and exhorted Cromwell, his campaigns behind him, to reap the fruits of his victories: "Help us to save free Conscience from the paw / Of hireling wolves whose Gospel is their maw." All of Milton's political allegiances were directed to this end; he supported those policies, leaders, and institutions that showed promise of limiting the secular power of the church, and he opposed those who sought to augment its authority over the spiritual lives of men.

When the last Protectorate Parliament convened on 27 January 1659, Milton sensed a new opportunity to press once again for realization of his most cherished dream, the abolition of state support for the ministry of the church. Oliver Cromwell had disappointed him in this regard, as had the Commonwealth government before him; but here was a new Protector and a new Parliament, who might be swayed to make the dramatic change that to his mind was the ultimate purpose of the English Revolution, the civil wars, Pride's Purge, the Republic, indeed everything that had happened in those two decades of astonishing upheaval. If he sadly misjudged the tenor of that body, nothing can detract from the passion of his commitment.

Milton addresses *A Treatise of Civil Power in Ecclesiastical Causes* to Parliament, greeting them as the "supream Councel" of the land and informing them that the work has been in preparation "against the much expected time of your sitting." It is, he goes on, but the first of a two-part tract, the theme of which is the "mischief" worked by political control of the church, which results in "force on the one side restraining and hire on the other side corrupting" the clergy (7:239–41). Before he could complete the "hire on the other side corrupting" part, however, events overtook him, as they did so frequently in that final year. The Protectorate Parliament proved unexpectedly troublesome, its members declaring themselves openly hostile to the army. In religious matters, its tone was alarming; in April the House ordered all ministers to subscribe to the Westminster Assembly's *Confession of Faith*, a clear indication that they intended to tighten state control of the church. The imposition of the Presbyterian-sponsored *Confession* had been one of the causes for the militant reaction against Parliament by the more radical Independents of the army in 1648, and eleven years later they were no less disturbed. After the death of Cromwell the most highly respected military leader in the country was his son-in-law, General Charles Fleetwood. In April some five hundred officers of the army met under his leadership to oppose Parliament's policies. This Wallingford House Party, as it was called (after Fleetwood's residence), forced Richard to dissolve his Parliament on 22 April. Rising pressure from the more radical junior officers and from the rank and file of the army persuaded Fleetwood, two weeks later, to restore the old Rump Parliament, which had been dismissed by Cromwell in April 1653. That body's first meeting on 7 May marked the end of the Protectorate.

The members of the Rump, with memories of 1653 still fresh, set about conscientiously to pull the teeth of the army, which they considered a continuing threat to their existence. In the months to follow they instituted measures to restrict the powers of Fleetwood, the commander-in-chief, and to weed out officers identified as closely associated with the Cromwellian regime. By October more than 160 officers had been cashiered. More probably would have been, had not events forced Parliament to call upon the army for protection.[4] On 1 August Sir George Booth led an ill-timed and poorly organized royalist uprising, which within weeks was put down with ease by General John Lambert at Winnington Bridge.

From Milton's point of view the restoration of the Rump was a truly promising development. The Protectorate Parliament had turned a deaf ear to his proposals; but the old champions of the revolution, seated once again, might be persuaded anew to separate church from state. It is to them that he addresses the second half of his argument, *Considerations Touching the Likeliest Means to Remove Hirelings Out of the Church*, greeting them as "supream Senat." The republicans of that body, to his further disappointment, were no more inclined to take that revolutionary step than they had been six years earlier; and they were soon embroiled in a constitutional crisis that turned their attention, and Milton's, away from such fundamental matters to a more immediate concern for their political survival.

As observed earlier, modern scholars seem intent upon disassociating Milton from the Protectorate regime of Oliver Cromwell.[5] It is a theme that pervades commentary on the level of his activity in office over those six years, conjecture which, as we have seen, is based chiefly on the absence of his name from the Order Books of the Council, for whom he was not working, and the loss of records from the office of the Secretary of State, for whom he was. Again as we have seen, he was not indeed "easing himself out of government service" or withdrawing "his interests more and more from state affairs," as has been proposed;[6] he was, rather, heavily engaged in such duties as his blindness permitted. Much of this commentary goes on to conjecture that his supposed withdrawal from public affairs was quite purposeful, motivated by a

---

4. Davies 108.

5. See, for example, Hill, *Milton and the English Revolution*, 197; Wolfe 290; Merritt Hughes, *Ten Perspectives on Milton*, 267–68; and Emile Saillens, *John Milton*, 200. Michael Fixler is less disposed to this view, finding the poet content with a "temporary dictatorship . . . till matters were set in order, as in a free Commonwealth" (*Milton and the Kingdoms of God* 193).

6. Hill, *God's Englishman*, 191; Woolrych, "Milton and Cromwell," 198.

growing distaste for the Cromwell regime. This theme pervades analysis of Milton's works during the Anarchy, in which scholars have discovered in several of his words and phrases evidence of a retrospective rejection of the Protectorate years.

Joseph Summers has observed that "it is a rare critic who can resist the tendency to reduce an admired figure to his own image";[7] and something of this order may help explain the persistence of this opinion, especially since it is based on such tenuous evidence. The Protectorate was a military regime, supported by a formidable standing army whose officers held important posts in government, close to Cromwell, who frequently sought their counsel. He himself was known in his own time, as he is today, as a consummate soldier, the Lord General; and it was in this capacity that he dismissed the Rump in April 1653. The following December he assumed the position of Lord Protector under a written constitution whose chief architect was another general officer, John Lambert. In October 1655 Cromwell inaugurated the distasteful rule of the major-generals; and though this experiment proved so unpopular that it had to be terminated, the experience left little doubt as to who held power in the state.

It is not too much to say that present-day academics distrust authoritarian governments of any description, but especially military regimes, which have an unenviable record of brutality in this century. It may well be that Miltonists have an instinctive desire to rescue the poet from any taint that might result from his service to such a regime, and that this helps explain the frequent claims that he was deliberately withdrawing from participation in a government because of a growing disillusionment with its practices. It is certainly the sort of thing any self-respecting liberal intellectual might be expected to do today, at any rate. This reading has the satisfying effect of drawing the poet comfortably in line with certain twentieth-century political sensibilities; but it may not reflect accurately the allegiances of a citizen of the seventeenth-century English Republic, however devoutly one may wish it so. What is disturbing is the largely unstated implication of this rescue operation, the assumption that his public service during the Protectorate taints not only the poet but somehow his poetry as well, for that is the ultimate intent, to shield *Paradise Lost* from the stain of Milton's association with Oliver Cromwell. Certainly, every age must come to terms with great works of literature in its own lights, but it does not aid our under-

---

7. Summers, "Milton and the Cult of Conformity," 30. E.M.W. Tillyard remarks of another group of scholars, "People are so fond of Shakespeare that they are desperately anxious to have him of their own way of thinking" (*Shakespeare's History Plays* 204).

standing of a great artist three hundred years dead to impose upon him, intentionally or unintentionally, the values of these later times.

Such seems to be the practice, at any rate, with readings of isolated words and phrases in Milton's religious tracts of 1659. Austin Woolrych, for example, suggests that in addressing Richard's Parliament in *A Treatise of Civil Power* as "The Parlament of the Commonwealth of England" and "supream Councel," Milton is by implication questioning the authority of the Protector.[8] Woolrych disregards the fact that he addresses the Rump by the same title six months later in *Considerations Touching The Likeliest Means*, when the authority of the Protector was no longer at issue. "The Parlament of the Commonwealth of England" was a title adopted by the House in 1650 and subsequently used to identify all the Parliaments of the Republic.[9] Milton is not making distinctions between institutions of the Commonwealth and the Protectorate, but is referring to both as continuations of the Long Parliament. In the opening sentence of *Considerations*, for example, he thanks the Rump as "supream Senat" for protecting "this libertie of writing which I have us'd these 18 years" in the cause of freedom, that is, for the entire tenure of the Long Parliament (7:275).

A somewhat more controversial phrase appears in the introductory paragraph of *Considerations*, where Milton praises the restored Rump in somewhat extravagant terms: "The care and tuition of [England's] peace and safety, after a short but scandalous night of interruption, is now again by a new dawning of Gods miraculous providence among us, revolvd upon your shoulders" (7:274). Scholars disagree concerning just what "night of interruption" he is referring to and just how long or "short" it was. William B. Hunter, Jr., proposes eight months, the period of Richard's rule as Protector, and suggests that Milton is questioning the legitimacy of his succession. Austin Woolrych, in a long and closely argued study, rejects Hunter's proposal and offers his own, the entire six years of the Protectorate, a judgment in which he is joined by a number of other scholars.[10] Woolrych's reply is persuasive but, as will

8. Woolrych, "Milton and Cromwell," 199. Woolrych later contributed the valuable introduction to vol. 7 of *Prose*, although he repeats there many of his views on Milton's sentiments. He appears to hedge a bit on the present point, however, in both works. The reference, he says, "may or may not" imply criticism of the Protectorate ("Milton and Cromwell" 199), and adds "It would be rash to read" such an interpretation into the phrase (Introduction 47). But he then proceeds to do just that, leaving little doubt concerning his mind on the subject.

9. See, for example, the opening sentence of the constitutional bill of the first Protectorate Parliament (Gardiner, *Constitutional Documents*, 427).

10. William B. Hunter, "Milton and Richard Cromwell," 253; Woolrych, "Milton and

appear, I think both men miss the mark.[11] Masson, having considered a similar suggestion, rejected it quite emphatically on the reasonable grounds that such a period could hardly be considered "short" since it "exceeded in length the whole duration of the Commonwealth it had interrupted," that is, the four years from February 1649 to April 1653. He suggests that the phrase refers to the "fortnight or so of the Wallingford-House usurpation," that is, 22 April to 7 May 1659, the interval between the dismissal of Richard's Parliament and the restoration of the Rump.[12]

Masson's judgment deserves further consideration, quite aside from the obvious fact that the word "short" better defines a two-week period than it does one of six years. It is certainly true that the Protectorate Parliament of April was composed of a very different group of men than was the Rump of May; but the obvious differences in size, sentiment, and composition may cause one to overlook an important similarity between the two—the identity of the republicans in their number. An examination of the records reveals that of the 122 men who sat from time to time in the restored Rump, 59 had been members of Richard's Parliament; and, again, of the 31 men who made up the Rump's Council of State, 25 had been members of that deposed body.[13] Milton had addressed A Treatise of Civil Power to a "supream Councel" in which the republicans upon whom he pinned his hopes had been but a vocal minority; he addressed his Considerations to a "supream Senat" in which they constituted the majority of a much diminished body, now largely purged of Presbyterian and Cromwellian influence. The minority may have become a majority but the composition of that faction had changed but little. Milton was surely aware that he was writing to a body of men, most of whom had been turned out of Westminster in April and had returned to resume their seats in May, men for whom the

---

Cromwell," 202. Woolrych is joined in this opinion by, among others, Wolfe 289–90; Barbara Lewalski, "Milton," 192; H.J.C. Grierson, Milton and Wordsworth, 68; and Paul P. Morand, The Effects of His Political Life on John Milton, 106–8. James S. Smart is particularly emphatic: "This is no art of interpretation which can reconcile these words with his approval of the expulsion of the same Parliament six years before" (The Sonnets of Milton 80). In Milton and the English Revolution, Christopher Hill is content to call the phrase ambiguous, but the remark caps a paragraph demonstrating Milton's rejection of the Protectorate (217). Hill's sentiments are quite clear.

11. This is certainly not to dismiss Hunter's scholarly and interesting study. My argument is with those who suggest that Milton is repudiating Cromwell. Hunter and I agree that he is not.

12. Masson 5:607.

13. Ibid. 453–56.

"interruption" had indeed been "short." Such labels as "Protectorate," "Commonwealth," "Rump," and "Republican," while necessary to our discussion of that distant time, have a way of clouding the vision. Masson is remarkably clear-sighted in perceiving that it was the sitting *of Parliament,* that is, the "old famous" legislative body of England, that had been interrupted. So at least it must have seemed to those men to whom Milton was addressing his pleas for religious freedom.

There may be a question of how short or long the interruption was but there can be no doubt that Milton considered it "scandalous," which brings us to another of the army's actions that Milton later characterized with the same word. In order to counter Booth's uprising in August, Parliament had mobilized the New Model Army; and one of the ominous consequences of the incident was that once the rebellion had been quelled, a substantial army remained in the field under the command of its officers. Parliament was initially lavish in its praise but reacted violently when presented with an address, *The Humble Representation and Petition of the Officers of the Army,* which contained two provisions, among others, that were particularly alarming. The first was a proposal for the establishment of a permanent senate, which would act as a balance to the power of the House; the second was a demand that no member of the army could be dismissed except by order of a court-martial, that is, by the army itself. These were, in fact, only restatements of proposals that the Wallingford House Party had presented to the Rump the previous May, only to have them ignored. The army, smarting from the wholesale dismissal of officers during the summer, was obviously trying to protect itself from further deterioration of its command structure; but the members of the Rump saw these provisions as an outrageous challenge to their authority. The lines of conflict between the two bodies were now clearly drawn, and Parliament responded by summarily dismissing nine of the chief officers of the army. In retaliation, on 13 October General John Lambert rallied his forces in St. James's Park, marched them to Westminster Hall, and locked out the Rump, precipitating a constitutional crisis that occupied the attention of John Milton for the next six months.

The army set up a Committee of Safety to preside over affairs, even as the Rump's Council of State continued to sit for a time, although ineffectively at best. The army's Committee soon proved unacceptable to the people, and there was strong agitation in the streets of London for the restoration of the Rump. More ominous for the military was the split in their own ranks, with General George Monk in Scotland, the forces in Ireland, and the Fleet urging strongly that Parliament be reseated, which units loyal to Fleetwood and Lambert opposed. When

Monk moved his forces to Coldstream on the Tweed, threatening to march to the aid of the Rump, Lambert marched north to confront him across that northern river. In the end the public agitation proved too powerful, Lambert's army literally melted away as his troopers refused to enter combat with their comrades, and on 26 December the Committee of Safety was compelled to readmit the Rump.

This bare outline of events cannot begin to convey the complexity of the issues involved, but it does highlight the division that posed the most dangerous threat to the life of the Republic—the antagonism between the army and Parliament. Milton's attitude toward these two bodies is well documented. Throughout his public career he trusted, praised, and admired the Army of Saints that had brought about the Puritan Revolution. Its psalm-singing, prayer-meeting ranks were the very embodiment of the "liberty of conscience" in which he so fervently believed.[14] Its leaders—Cromwell, Ireton, Lambert, Fleetwood—created the English Republic; and although their ardor for reform may have slackened somewhat once they reached high office, Milton knew that his dream of disestablishment could not be realized unless the army espoused the cause. On the other hand, he mistrusted elected legislatures. During his career, he supported those bodies which showed promise of effecting disestablishment and applauded their dissolution when they demonstrated an unwillingness or inability to do so. He approved of Pride's Purge because in his eyes it left a Parliament stripped of a Presbyterian majority and capable of ridding England of its king. He praised Cromwell's dismissal of the Rump in 1653 when that body became so preoccupied with its own perpetuation that it neglected its obligations. The *Second Defence* issues no stirring call for a new Parliament, for as he says, who would "think his own liberty enlarged one iota by such caretakers of the state?" He simply advised Cromwell to surround himself with the "comrades in your toils and dangers," and proceed with the great work (4:683, 674). He scorned the Barebones— "The elected members came together. They did nothing" (4:671)—and although we have no record of his attitude toward the Lord Protector's two Parliaments, we can hardly expect him to have had much sympathy for bodies that wanted to crown Cromwell. Nor can he have looked with approval on the Protectorate Parliament dissolved in April 1659, which had moved to establish the Presbyterian *Confession of Faith* as the law of the land.

John Milton was in many ways a political realist, *The Readie and*

14. For a discussion of Milton's allegiance to the New Model Army, see Fallon, *Captain or Colonel*, 83–91.

Easie Way notwithstanding; and the realities of the English Republic were these: it could not stand without the support of the New Model Army, and it could not prevail without the constitutional legitimacy that only an English Parliament could provide. Further, although a lasting and legitimate disestablishment of the church could be achieved only by Parliamentary act, it was evident to him that no freely elected body of Englishmen would ever carry out such a program. Only a select Parliament of like-minded republican statesmen would be so disposed; but no such body could come together without the support of the English army. The realization of his long-cherished hope depended ultimately on one factor alone, the close cooperation of these two institutions; and his distress during the closing months of the Republic was caused chiefly by the spectacle of the two bodies locked in a power struggle that promised to bring the whole fragile constitutional structure down about their ears.[15]

Milton's reaction to the crisis precipitated by Lambert's coup is recorded in six documents: *A Letter to a Friend*, dated 20 October 1659, written after a visit from an unnamed acquaintance, who had given him an account of the dismissal of the Rump; *Proposalls of Certaine Expedients for the Preventing of Civill War*, written sometime between that date and the reseating of the Rump in late December; *The Readie and Easie Way to Establish a Free Commonwealth*, which appeared in two editions, the first in February, the second in April, 1660; *The Present Means, and Brief Delineation of a Free Commonwealth*, a private letter addressed to General Monk in March; and *Brief Notes upon a Late Sermon*, a reply to Dr. Matthew Griffith, published in April.

No reader of these tracts will come away with the impression that Milton was particularly original in his political thought.[16] He was perhaps too much of a single-issue man in the political sphere, persisting in

15. Not all were so clear-sighted, according to Godfrey Davies. Milton's perspective was very close to that of Sir Henry Vane, however, who was convinced that "to insure the continuance of the present regime, an alliance between the army and Rump was essential" (109). This congruence of opinion adds substance to the arguments of Masson (5:618) and Barker (260) that the "Friend" who informed Milton of Lambert's coup was Vane.

16. This is not to say, however, that he has been without influence. In *That Grand Whig Milton* George F. Sensabaugh has shown how often Milton was quoted, paraphrased, and copied in the controversies over liberty of conscience and the power of kingship that led to the constitutional settlement of 1689; but he was admired for the persuasive power of his eloquence and the force of his logic rather than for any original contribution to thought on the issues. Further, it appears that after the initial royalist reaction of 1660 his political works of that winter and spring were virtually ignored. It was his earlier tracts, *Areopagitica* and the publications of 1649–51, that received the attention, not his design for a free Commonwealth.

his conviction that not until liberty of conscience had been achieved was any kind of political freedom possible. The need to evolve a political settlement was thrust upon him by the dangers of the moment, and he was forced by events to turn from the contemplation of religious freedom, which had occupied his thoughts earlier in 1659, to the less congenial sphere of political theory. In the letters and tracts composed after Lambert's coup he is clearly improvising as he goes along, and it would appear that he is more indebted to the experience of ten years of public service than to any carefully constructed corpus of political thought. In *A Letter to a Friend* of October 1659, for example, he has not yet made up his mind about the nature of his legislature, "whether the civill government be an annuall democracy or a perpetual Aristocracy" (7:331). By the following February he has settled on a perpetual senate, in many ways but an expanded replica of the Protectorate Council of State. The chaos of the intervening months had persuaded him that the English people were not sufficiently advanced in spiritual maturity to be worthy of the political freedom implicit in the practice of annual elections.

In any event, although Milton was surely drawing on the experience of his decade of public service, his adherence or nonadherence to the Protectorate was largely irrelevant to his works during the Anarchy. He was writing in immediate response to swiftly moving events, not in retired contemplation of a long-dead regime.[17] One theme prevails throughout these works—his apprehension that the domestic broils will expose the Republic to the danger of a returning monarchy. His message to the army and to Parliament is a plea for reconciliation, and he looks to the officers to heal the political wounds of the nation, "since they only now have the power" (7:329).

Milton surely did not approve of the Wallingford House coup of April 1659, though he makes only two explicit references to that event in his tracts. In *Considerations* he calls it "scandalous," a word that expresses his opinion of military coups *in 1659*, not of Cromwell's action some six years earlier, as Woolrych and others suggest. The second reference to the April coup appears in *A Letter to a Friend*, but in words of praise rather than censure:

> I was overjoyed, when I heard that the Army under the working of Gods holy spiritt, as I thought & still hope well, had bin so far wrought to Christian humility & and self-denyall, as to confesse in publick their backsliding from the good old cause,

17. As Barbara Lewalski puts it, "Milton the practical politician, close to affairs" was concerned throughout with rescuing the Puritan cause (195–97). See also Barker 260.

> & to shew the fruits of their repentance in the righteousnesse of
> their restoring the old famous parlament, which they had with-
> out just autority dissolved.[18] (7:324)

The advice is meant for the army leaders, and their exemplary conduct
in the spring is held up as a model for their actions in October. The
Wallingford House Party had dismissed and quickly recalled Parliament
on that earlier occasion; and the officers of the Committee of Safety,
many of them the same men, are enjoined to follow their own good
example, repent, and restore Parliament yet again.

Milton's judgment on Lambert's coup is couched in stronger language. In *A Letter to a Friend* he uses the same word, "scandalous," to
criticize the army's actions in October; and the discussion that follows
indicates clearly that he uses the word in its primary sense, that is,
"causing scandal." His chief concern about Lambert's coup, and we
may assume Fleetwood's, is that it damages the reputation of the army:
"This I say other nacions will judg to the sad dishonour of that army
lately so renowned for the civilest & best ordered in the world, & by us
here at home, for the most conscientious." But it is apparent that he has
very mixed feelings about the account given him. Indeed, it is almost as
if he cannot believe what he has heard, or doesn't want to, for each
time that he condemns the action he takes pains to hedge his criticism,
softening its effect with qualifications. The news "amazes" him, he says,
but "I presume not to give my censure upon this action, not knowing,
as I doe not, the bottome of it. I speak only what it appeares to us
without doors, till better cause be declared." He remains convinced that
some reasonable explanation will be forthcoming, for, he continues,
"neither do I speak this in reproach to the Army, but as Jealous of their
honour, inciting them to manifest & publish with all speed some better
cause of these their late acions, then hath hitherto appeared" (7:326–
28). He cannot bring himself to out-and-out denounce that Army of
Saints, which for a decade and a half had been the embodiment of his
fondest hopes for religious freedom. Even later in *The Readie and Easie
Way*, when he cites "the frequent disturbances, interruptions and disso-
lutions which the Parlament hath had partly from the impatient or dis-

---

18. It is fruitless to speculate about what Milton meant by "the good old cause." It was
a phrase much bandied about at the time and, as Godfrey Davies observes, "Who could
define it, when Levellers, Fifth Monarchy men, grandees, and subordinate officers to
name a few of the groups within the Republican fold, all had different notions?" (154). I
would suggest only that he saw the "cause" as religious freedom; and if the phrase has
any political implications, they concern the rejection of the monarchy, as in his *vale* ending *The Readie and Easie Way* (7:462–63).

affected people, partly from som ambitious leaders in the Armie," he quickly qualifies the criticism, "much contrarie, I beleeve, to the mind and approbation of the Armie it self and thir other Commanders, once undeceivd, or in thir own power" (7:430).

Whatever the qualifications, he found these actions ill-advised, dangerous, and "scandalous." It has been suggested that in this judgment Milton demonstrates a certain inconsistency in his political thought, by disapproving of Fleetwood and Lambert, but praising Cromwell's dissolution of the Rump in 1653 and urging Monk to a similar assumption of power in March 1660. Milton's consistency lies in his conviction that true freedom would follow only when the English government took steps to assure its citizens liberty of conscience. If he changed, it was only in his perception of the means necessary and available to achieve that end. When Cromwell dissolved the Rump, that body had demonstrated itself either unwilling or unable to address itself to the problems of the nation. He dismissed the members when they insisted on perpetuating themselves in power, and in the *Second Defence* Milton fully justifies the act. Each of its members, he writes, had been "more attentive to his private interest than to that of the state," and the English people "had been deluded of their hopes," a reference probably to the Rump's duplicity or impotence on the church question (4:671). Cromwell, backed by an Army of Saints, he hoped might work the miracle. Milton could applaud the act, therefore, as necessary to the cause of liberty.

Actually, when viewed from a historical perspective, Cromwell's conduct was not without precedent. He had peremptorily assumed the mantle of the executive figure in the English constitutional system and in that capacity had acted in much the same manner as a line of rulers before him, simply emphasizing his assumption of authority by the presence of "two files of musketeers."[19] In 1659, however, circumstances were much altered and the acts of the army of a very different order. A peaceful resolution depended entirely upon some kind of accommodation between the army and Parliament. Milton "can have felt no regret," as Woolrych puts it,[20] when the Wallingford House group dismissed the Presbyterian-leaning Protectorate Parliament, but it was the manner of that dissolution that was so shocking and fraught with peril. There is a great deal of difference between a Cromwell suddenly donning the cloak of executive authority to dismiss the Rump with a few

19. As reported by Edmund Ludlow, *Memoirs*, 1:357. Charles I, for example, had appeared in the House accompanied by "a guard of soldiers" to arrest the five members in January 1642.

20. Woolrych, "Milton and Cromwell," 200.

soldiers and a Fleetwood intimidating Parliament by marshaling a body of five hundred officers and several thousand troops in St. James's Park, perhaps so close to Milton's home in Petty France that he could hear the shouts of command and the clank of armor that ushered in the "night of interruption." This was a naked and "scandalous" act of war, without even the thin veil of constitutional precedent to blur its harsh outlines. When Lambert repeated the performance in October, marching his troops once more into St. James's, there was no one of Cromwell's stature on the scene upon whom to pin one's hopes. The Republic was in jeopardy.

A *Letter to a Friend* is dated 20 October, a week after Lambert's coup. Milton wrote it at the request of an unnamed acquaintance who visited him, apparently the night before, to inform him of the events of that week. Milton's thought, as has been mentioned, was not very profound; it was, however, prophetic. Lambert's coup, he sees with utter clarity, opens the way for the restoration of the monarchy. The animosity between the army and Parliament, which had its origins in 1647, had resurfaced, and threatened the life of the Republic. Milton scolds the officers soundly, attributing their actions to "that Achan among them" plotting "to bring in again the Common enemie, & with him the destruction of true religion & civill liberty." If they will not accept his proposal for a resolution, "be confident there is a single person working underneath" (7:328–31). The suggestion that this "single person" is Lambert is wide of the mark.[21] He was an ardent commonwealthsman whose last thought would be "to bring in again the Common enemie," and marching five thousand men into St. James's Park can hardly be considered "working underneath." The "single person" is the king, as it is always with Milton. In the later *Proposalls* he repeats the warning that the disorders place the nation in danger from "the common enemy at home" and "Spain & France" abroad, a reference to the rumors that Charles II was gathering an army for "a speedy invasion of this Iland"; and he closes with the prophecy that if they "fall into evills & discords incurable, the speedy end whereof wilbe utter ruine" (7:336, 339).

The solution Milton proposes in A *Letter to a Friend* is quite simple. Since each of the contending bodies fears the power of the other, members of both should be confirmed in their positions for life. The legislature should be composed of "the parlament readmitted to sitt"; or, alternately, if the Rump "be thought well dissolv'd, as not complyeing fully to grant liberty of conscience [and] The Removall of a forc't main-

21. Parker 1:536. Others have suggested that Milton was referring to Richard Cromwell, but this hardly deserves consideration.

tenance from Ministers," then the army must form a "councell of State"
that would so comply. All must agree, he repeats again and again, to
"Full liberty of conscience, & the abjuracion of Monarchy proposed."
If things are not settled "one way or the other," he warns, "we instantly
ruine; or at best become the servants of one or other single person, the
secret author & fomenter of all these disturbances" (7:329–32). Milton
may be justly accused of seeing a royalist under every bush; but with
the August uprising of fresh memory and rumors of an invasion by
Charles widespread, he may be forgiven for supposing that some agent
of the king was the "secret author & fomenter" of the troubles. His
language here echoes that of Cromwell's letters to Denmark, Sweden,
and the United Netherlands during the War in the North, wherein he
warned them constantly that Rome and the Spanish, "the enemies of
Religion," are the secret "kindlers of this war" (W108, P143), and that
unless their "Artifices and Machinations" are resisted, "the Interests of
Protestants must go to ruine, and suffer a total and irrecoverable
Eclipse" (W87, P119).[22]

Six weeks later, the situation was even more grave, confirming Milton's worst fears. The Committee of Safety had come under unrelenting
attack, and the military was split into hostile factions, with elements of
the army facing one another in armed confrontation across the Tweed.
Milton's *Proposalls* are appropriately, "expedients for the preventing of
a civill war now feard." So intense was the agitation to reseat the Rump
that he no longer suggests that they may have been "well dissolv'd,"
proposing rather that they be "treated with to sitt," but only under
certain conditions, ten in all. The differences between the two bodies
are to be resolved by an Act of Oblivion and members of both are again
to be confirmed in "their places during life." The legislature, no longer
to be addressed by its ancient title of "parlament," is renamed the
"Grand or Supreme Counsell," and its members are to be nominated,
either by the Council itself or the "well affected people." All, of course,
will subscribe to the two key provisions, a commitment in favor of
"Liberty of conscience [and] against a single person & house of Lords"
(7:336–39).

Milton doubtless engaged in conversations about his design with
more than one "Friend," and they seem to have conveyed to him a
concern that a legislative body with members appointed "during life"

---

22. In another of Milton's letters Cromwell warns in equally apocalyptic terms that if
the dissension between Sweden and Denmark continues, two nations upon which "the
Support and Hopes of all the Reformed Churches depend, of necessity the Protestant
Religion must be in great jeopardy, if not upon the brink of destruction" (W79, P108).

may wax too powerful. Whatever the origins of the concern, in *Proposalls* he significantly limits the reach of his Council. They will "deale as little as may be with the execution of lawes," relinquishing responsibility for "the administration of Civill Justice [to] the City or cheif towne of every county without appeal." The Grand Council, of course, will leave "both maintenance of Ministers & all matters Ecclesiasticall to the church in her severall congregations." Such limitations, he argues "wilbe an undoubted cause of great peace and quietness among us & of great ease & health" to the members, who will have "many dayes of leasure & intermission from the toile of their constant sitting" (7:336–39). It is tempting to read irony into these lines, which seem to but thinly disguise Milton's disdain for legislative bodies burdened with "the toile of their constant sitting"; but one must credit him with a serious intent in the crisis he is laboring to resolve. Although painfully impractical when viewed from the advantaged perspective of hindsight, Milton's proposals represent a valiant effort to grapple with intractable forces that would, and indeed did, reduce lesser men to despair. In later works he would expand, however vaguely, on the limitations to be imposed on the powers of his "Grand or Supreme Counsell."

Neither of these tracts was published; and by the time Milton was prepared to make his thought public, the political situation had deteriorated further, requiring him to give his work a different tone entirely. One of the puzzling aspects of this period was the inability of the military, which had stood in sturdy support of the Republic for so many years, to prevent the return of the king. A part of the reason for this inaction lies in the divisions within their ranks caused by the dismissal of the Rump. Another factor is the measures taken by Parliament once the Committee of Safety had submitted to popular pressure and allowed the members to resume their seats on 26 December. The Rump resumed the "remodeling" of the army with a vengeance, and by the end of January over half of its officers had been either dismissed or transferred with their units to remote parts.[23] General George Monk, in distant Scotland, was able to avoid the worst effects of the remodeling and retain a cohesive force of some ten thousand men loyal to him. On 1 January he began a slow, deliberate march south with half of this force, stopping here and there along the way to confer with the country gentry. On 3 February he paraded into Westminster to be greeted as a liberator by Parliament. By that time the Rump, because of its resistance to growing demands to declare new elections and dissolve itself, had

23. As Godfrey Davies remarks of the army, "No wonder cohesion was lacking during the winter and spring of 1660" (261).

become thoroughly discredited in the eyes of the people; and, since the rest of the army was powerless, Monk marched his small force into a political vacuum, where it constituted the only credible power base in the nation.

> To whom these most adhere,
> Hee rules a moment; *Chaos* Umpire sits,
> And by decision more imbroils the fray
> By which he Reigns: next him high Arbiter
> *Chance* governs all.
>   (*PL* 2:906–10)

Scholars differ on when Monk determined to work the return of the monarchy, for during those months he kept his purposes close, issuing numerous declarations of his continued loyalty to the Commonwealth while corresponding secretly with the king. The night of 11 February seems to have been a watershed, however. Parliament's differences with London had reached an impasse, and they directed Monk to occupy the city and assert their authority over the magistrates and people. He obeyed; but when he found the citizens so incensed against the Rump's apparent design to perpetuate itself, he addressed a letter to the members, demanding among other things that they declare their intention to dissolve. When the news of his stand reached the streets of the city, it set off a wild celebration with bonfires in the streets over which the people roasted symbolic "rumps." What may have been even more persuasive for Monk were the frequent open expressions of sentiment for the return of the king. At any rate, from that night forward, it seems, he set about with deliberate speed on a course of action that led inevitably to the Restoration.

It would have been pointless for Monk to dismiss the Rump yet again, a move bound to be opposed by the rank and file of his army, where devotion to the Commonwealth was still strong. Besides, it had been tried before with devastating results. Monk found, therefore, an alternate method to circumvent Parliament's adamant republicans. Ten days after that night of the "Roasting of the Rump" he gathered together a number of the members who had been excluded from Parliament by Pride's Purge and forced the House to reseat them. The admission of these men, who had been denied their seats in 1648 because of their opposition to the prosecution of Charles I, tipped the balance against the commonwealthsmen of the Rump, creating a body that suited well Monk's hidden purposes. As a condition for his support, he had extracted agreement from the excluded members on a number of provisions, and in response to his further pressure they issued writs for a new election and dissolved themselves. The Convention Parliament met on 25 April and two weeks later declared Charles Stuart the king of England.

By February 1660, the Rump had become so thoroughly discredited and the army demoralized by the remodeling that the conflict between them was of less import than it had been the previous fall. As Milton had feared, the struggle for political power between the two institutions had weakened the Republic to the point of dissolution. Milton had to shift the focus of his thought to deal with the real prospect of a restored monarchy. He finished the first edition of *The Readie & Easie Way to Establish a Free Commonwealth* some time after the admission of the excluded members on 21 February, for that event is mentioned in its opening lines. He completed the second edition some time after the dissolution of Parliament on 16 March, since Milton observes that "writs for new elections have bin recall'd" (7:407). The latter, a revision of the earlier edition and almost twice its length, represents Milton's final thought on the subject, hence will be more rewarding of study, although it will be of interest to note on occasion how Milton's ideas evolved in the short interval between the two. Even a cursory reading of the work will disclose that it fails to fulfill the promise of its title, for there is precious little in it about a *Free Commonwealth*. It is instructive to examine the elements of Milton's argument, which break down approximately as follows (citing the pages of the second edition):

> 3–18—an account of the rebellion against the king.
> 18–40—the evils of kingship, as compared to a commonwealth.
> 40–67—an argument for a permanent Grand Council.
> 67–93—the evils of kingship, if it returns.
> 93–102—the settling of a free commonwealth.
> 102–8—peroration.

This summary is admittedly rough but it makes clear Milton's focus on two matters. Almost two-thirds of the work are devoted to a denunciation of monarchy, to include the king's duplicity during the civil wars, the evils of kingship in general, and the dangers for England in particular should he return. Perhaps a third of the work argues the advantages of establishing a permanent senate as the ruling body of the Commonwealth; and the bulk of these sections develop a theme first introduced in *Proposalls*—the people need have no fear that such a body will be powerful enough to threaten their freedom. Such detail as Milton offers on constitutional structure is limited to ten pages, and the

settlement he outlines is but one of several elements of his argument
that none need fear the powers of a Grand Council. The political structure outlined in these ten pages shows little evidence of extensive
thought on the subject; its hastily collected provisions were designed
rather to meet the most immediate threat to the Republic.[24] The Council, by its very permanence, will be insulated from the shrill cries in the
streets, hence better constituted to resist the return of the king. Milton's
task was to convince his readers that such a body could never place
their liberties in jeopardy; and to that effect he clipped the wings of its
authority over their lives.

> . . . thir summons call'd
> From every Band and squared Regiment
> By place or choice the worthiest.
> (*PL* 1:757–59)

Any constitutional design must address several issues: the character
of the legislative, judicial, and executive branches and the division of
powers among them; the manner of selecting members of each, whether
by appointment or election; the relationship between local and central
government; and two matters of particular concern in Milton's time,
the questions of church and state and control of the military. At the
heart of Milton's vision was the "grand councel of ablest men, chosen
by the people to consult of public affairs from time to time for the
common good"; and again this body, "being well chosen, should be
perpetual" (7:432–33). He is not specific how members are to be "well
chosen," however. In *Proposalls* he favored a tightly controlled process
whereby they are either "nominated by the grand Councell, & elected
by the well affected people, or nominated by those of the people &
elected by the grand Councell" (7:337–38), a design similar in many
respects to that employed in the selection of members for the Barebones
Parliament, which was designated at its sitting as the "Nominated Assembly." At the time of the writing of *The Readie and Easie Way*, however, events had preempted the choice: "Writs are sent out for elections" already and he can only hope that the people "will elect thir
Knights and Burgesses able men" (7:430–31). Milton does not abandon
his preferred method of choosing members in the face of this new devel-

---

24. Parker agrees that it "was not a statement of reasoned political theory . . . but a
hurried mixture of really desperate expediency and the minimum of principles that could
not, must not, be sacrificed" (1:543).

opment; he adjusts his design to the changing political scene by proposing that the vacancies which will occur in the body from time to time be filled through an elaborate system of nominations by those "who are rightly qualifi'd" and "of better breeding" (7:442–43).

Members, then, will sit permanently in a permanently sitting body, its sessions uninterrupted by peremptory dismissals; and Milton expands somewhat on the restrictions he had outlined in *Proposalls*, those designed to guard against the possibility "that long continuance of power may corrupt sincerest men" (7:434). The guiding principle of his government structure is the decentralization of political power. His is essentially a federal system in which the authority of the ruling body is balanced by strong local governments, so that "every countie in the land were made a kinde of subordinate Commonaltie or Commonwealth." The Grand Council, although "both foundation and main pillar of the whole State" (7:434), will be seriously limited in its jurisdiction. It will not, of course, meddle in the religious life of the people. Local governments, moreover, "shall have justice in thir own hands [with] laws executed fully and finally in thir own counties and precincts," and there will be a minimum number of national laws to administer. Lower courts will rule "without appeal" in disputes that arise "between man and man," whereas higher courts will be restricted to litigation in cases "between men of several counties." Shires and cities will be responsible for educating the young and directing the militia. The relationship between the local assemblies and the central government is only vaguely defined. Should the Grand Council pass laws "of any great concernment to public libertie," the legislation will have to be ratified by local assemblies, who will vote "thir assent or dissent" and elect deputies to convey their decision to the Council. Such laws will become effective only when approved by a majority of the counties, whereupon they will be enforced for all, none reserving "any exemption of themselves, or refusal of agreement with the rest" (7:458–60). A Council of State will be needed "for the carrying on som particular affairs with more secrecie and expedition," one that can readily manage affairs during the larger body's "intermissions or vacations." It will be, however, an elected body of members chosen by the Grand Council "out of thir own number and others," as it had been under the Commonwealth (7:433). With such a settlement, Milton is confident, the people "shall not then need to be much mistrustfull of thir chosen Patriots," especially since "the most of thir business will be in forein affairs" (7:443).

Provisions made for the control of the military are a critical element of any such settlement. This was an issue that had divided the nation's leaders for over a year, and the failure to resolve it had eventually brought the Republic to the edge of extinction. Although it might seem an issue that Milton would be compelled to address in his constitutional settlement, he managed adroitly to avoid doing so. It may have been that he considered the subject too volatile to discuss, given the heated divisions of the day, or so intractable that he did not have time to resolve the matter to his own satisfaction. Whichever the case, his position on the control of the military is frustratingly unclear.

Under the Commonwealth, the military had fallen under the jurisdiction of Parliament, as had all of the institutions of government, and it operated under orders from the Council of State, to whom a degree of executive authority had been delegated. Cromwell, as Lord General, was the commander of the army; but he sat as only one member of the Council. To be sure, because of his soaring prestige, he sat as the first among equals; but until April 1653 he acted only at the direction of that body. Under the Protectorate the offices of commander-in-chief of the armed forces and the head of state were united in one man, the Lord Protector.[25] The army operated essentially as a separate entity in the state responsive to the will of the Protector, although it made its presence felt through individual officers, who held important positions in the government structure. These men were highly influential in that they had the ear of the Protector, a privileged position that enabled them to obstruct Parliament's pressure to make Cromwell king but not of sufficient weight, apparently, to press on him the hope of its sectarian ranks to liberate the church from secular control.

When the Protectorate Parliament met in January 1659, the members saw in the presence of the relatively weak Richard Cromwell the opportunity to bring the military once more under their control. Their proposal that the army should be directed jointly by Parliament and the Protector was one of the factors that precipitated the dissolution of both institutions that spring. When the members of the Rump resumed their seats, they attempted to return the arrangement to one similar to that which had prevailed under the Commonwealth. They accepted Fleetwood as commander-in-chief but delegated control of the military to a committee of Parliamentary commissioners on which he sat as only one member. Fleetwood reluctantly acquiesced to this arrangement, which prevailed until the officers took matters into their own hands and dissolved Parliament in October. When the Rump tried to impose the

---

25. It is interesting to note that the constitution of 1657, *The Humble Petition and Advice*, made provision for the separation of the two offices after Cromwell's death (Gardiner, *Constitutional Documents*, 453).

same structure on Monk the following February, he responded by forcing them to admit the excluded members.

Evidence of Milton's concept of the place of the army in his "Free Commonwealth" is scant but suggestive. In *A Letter to a Friend* he recognizes, and assumes that the military does as well, that they are "insufficient to discharge at once both military & civill offices" (7:329); and he proposes that they either recall the Rump or constitute a Council of State suitable to assume the civil authority. His only thought on the disposition of the military is that its officers, like members of Parliament, should be confirmed in their posts "during life." He adds nothing to this arrangement in *Proposalls* and avoids the issue entirely in the first edition of *The Readie and Easie Way*, making no mention of life tenure for officers and stipulating only that his "Grand Council must have the forces by sea and land in thir power" (7:368). He is scarcely more forthcoming in the second edition but the additions to the text reveal the direction of his thought on the matter.

There were two separate bodies of troops to be provided for in any constitutional settlement of the time, the standing army and the militia. The former served at the will of the central government; the latter, consisting of the various Trained Bands throughout the country, were local citizen units under the jurisdiction of city and county magistrates. These units could be called up in times of national emergency, as they were during the civil wars, but they showed a marked reluctance to serve outside their home territories. They were not well trained, certainly no match for regular units, but they had to be taken into consideration, especially the six regiments of London Trained Bands.

In the second edition of *The Readie and Easie Way* Milton states unequivocally that there will be a standing army, for "there must be then as necessarily as now" (7:454), but he does not say who is to control it. In a significant revision of the earlier text, rather than "have the forces by land and sea in thir power," the Grand Council will now have the military "committed to them for the preservation of the common peace and libertie" (7:432–33). In two other passages added to the second edition, however, he clearly states that the military will be in the hands of "the people":

> Neither do I think a perpetual Senat, especially chosen and entrusted by the people, much in this land to be feard, where the well-affected either in a standing armie, or in a setled militia have thir arms in thir own hands. (7:435)

It is an element of his argument which he feels bears repeating:

> And when we have our forces by sea and land, either of a faith-
> ful Armie or a setl'd Militia, in our own hands to the firm
> establishment of a free Commonwealth . . . what can a perpet-
> ual senat have then wherein to grow corrupt, wherein to en-
> croach upon us or usurp; or if they do, wherein to be formida-
> ble?[26] (7:461)

Both passages appear in sections of the tract in which Milton is seeking to allay fears that the perpetual senate will wax too powerful and
assume dictatorial powers; and he is reassuring his readers that nothing
of the like can happen so long as control of the army is "in our own
hands." The military, then, "either of a faithful Armie or a settl'd Militia," will act as a safeguard against tyranny, certainly against the reim-
position of the monarchy, as it had in its opposition to the crowning of
Cromwell. This contention seems to contradict Milton's earlier statement about the relationship between the Grand Council and the military, and one can only conjecture about his thought on the subject. The
revision of the wording of the first edition is suggestive, however, for
there is a marked difference between a statement that the Grand Council will "have the forces by sea and land in thir power" and one that
they will "have the forces by sea and land committed to them." It is
difficult to fathom Milton's meaning here but the latter phrase unquestionably represents an erosion of the Council's authority. It would appear that, since he insists that "the people" control the standing army in
some undefined way, he intends that they can exercise the option of
"committing" the military to the central government in times of national emergency and presumably have it returned to their "hands"
when the need is past.

The military, in brief, will stand outside the central government structure, serving as insurance that the Grand Council will not encroach
upon the rights and liberties of the people.[27] It will occupy roughly the
same political position it had during the Protectorate and one similar to
that proposed by the military during the Anarchy when they petitioned
for the appointment of a commander-in-chief unhampered by Parlia-

---

26. Milton discusses the issue at some length in the first *Defence*, countering the argument that the king exercises exclusive authority over the military. "Thus it is quite clear,"
as he puts it, "that the armed forces of the realm, as well as their leaders, were of old (and
ought to be) controlled by the people, not the king" (4:501).

27. Christopher Hill's suggestion that Milton was anxious about how "military inter-
vention [was] to be prevented" needs reexamination in this light. I can find nothing in the
tract to substantiate his assertion that the militia "would guard against the influence of
the army at the center" (*Milton and the English Revolution* 200–201).

mentary oversight. The additions and revisions in the second edition do not necessarily represent a change in Milton's thinking, since the provision that "the people" are to have the military "in thir own hands" rather than leave it in the control of the Council may have been an element of his rhetorical strategy from the outset. If this is the case, he probably thought the issue too volatile for definition in his earlier tracts, which were designed to resolve already heated differences. He may well have avoided the issue in the first edition because in mid-February the outcome of the struggle between the two bodies was still in doubt, and he chose to address it in mid-March since by then Monk had firmly established his authority over the Parliament and acknowledgment of the general's autonomy may have seemed politic. On the other hand, it may simply be a matter which he was unable to resolve to his own satisfaction.

Milton clarifies his position somewhat in *The Present Means, and Brief Delineation of a Free Commonwealth* (7:392–95), a letter that he wrote to Monk, drawing the general's attention to "that Book," a reference to the first edition of *The Readie and Easie Way*, which he briefly summarizes in its lines. Milton apparently composed the letter some time in late February or early March; but it was not published at the time, nor is there any evidence that it was ever delivered. As a piece of private correspondence, however, intended perhaps for the general's eyes only, it offers a more intimate insight into the poet's thought. He repeats his argument for a Grand Council of limited political scope, one that will "have so little matter in thir Hands, or Power to endanger our Liberty" that "we shall have little cause to fear [their] perpetuity." As Robert Ayers notes, however, the letter is less a plea for Milton's free commonwealth than it is an effort to persuade Monk to manage the forthcoming elections.[28] Milton repeats his proposal that the Grand Council "with due Caution, [will] dispose of Forces, both by Sea and Land" but only *"under the conduct of your Excellency"* (7:394, emphasis mine). If Parliament meets, he goes on, and its members prove reluctant to accept Milton's settlement, "these fair and noble Offers of immediate Liberty, and happy Condition," as he puts it, then there are certainly sensible Englishmen "in every County who will thankfully accept them." In other words, "if these Gentlemen convocated" demonstrate any monarchist leanings, Monk should feel free to dissolve them and assemble a Parliament not so disposed. This he can do with ease, Milton advises, since he has "a faithful Veteran Army, so ready, and

28. *Prose* 7:393n.

glad to assist you in the prosecution thereof." At this stage Monk was well advanced in his design to restore the monarchy; but Milton may be forgiven for misjudging him so egregiously, for "Silent Old George" kept his purposes very close, an enigma to all.

In these proposals Milton is clearly reaching back into his experience, urging on Monk a role similar to Cromwell's in the spring of 1653. On that occasion the Lord General had dissolved Parliament and called for new elections, both of which Monk had stipulated as conditions for the admission of the secluded members. Cromwell had convened a committee of army officers, which Monk already had in place, to preside in the interim. That earlier committee had carefully screened nominations for the body in a manner comparable to that proposed by Milton (7:442–43); and when the Nominated Assembly first met in the Council-Chamber at Whitehall, all must have thought that it was indeed "a grand councel of ablest men." The Barebones Parliament disappointed both Cromwell and Milton, of course, and indeed the design might well fail in 1660 as it had in 1653, forcing Monk to pick up the mantle of the dead Protector. But would the poet have viewed this as a tragic development? Considering the alternative, one would assume not; and Milton said as much in public print. In his *Brief Notes upon a Late Sermon*, published that April in reply to a blatantly royalist sermon given by Dr. Matthew Griffin, he acknowledges that "chusing out of our own number one who hath best aided the people, and best merited against tyrannie, the space of a raign or two we may chance to live happily anough, or tolerably" (7:482). Indeed, had another Cromwell appeared in that distracted spring to rally a divided army against the threat poised across the Channel, who can doubt that Milton would have embraced him as warmly as he had the Lord Protector six years earlier?

In summary, Milton proposes that the standing army remain in the hands of "the people," to be committed "with Caution" to the Grand Council in times of national need. In setting up the military as an autonomous body in the state he is reaching back for his model to the Protectorate period when it served as a guard against the concentration of power in the executive and legislative branchs of government, dissuading Cromwell from accepting a crown and balancing the authority of Parliament. Under that system Cromwell kept control of the military firmly in his own hands; and in the crisis of 1660 Milton urged a similar role on General Monk, who with his "faithful Veteran Army" was all that stood between the promise of the Republic and the restoration of the king.

Such a conclusion, it must be said, runs counter to the judgment of many scholars, who find Milton unalterably opposed to the rule of any "single person" and conclude thereby that he repudiated the Lord Protector and distanced himself from his tainted regime. Their commentary focuses on the poet's frequently stated insistence that members of his Grand Council subscribe to an oath opposing the imposition of government by "single person and House of Lords." As Austin Woolrych puts it, "he completely reverses the position that he had taken up in 1654, when he justified the first expulsion of the Rump." Woolrych finds Milton reacting "against a whole regime rather than a single personality," indeed "applauding" the overthrow of the Protectorate.[29] Others do not go so far. Arthur Barker writes, however, that Milton's "official connection with Cromwell's government . . . should not be permitted to obscure his suspicion of the continued rule of a single person wielding all but regal power."[30] Even A.S.P. Woodhouse, who identified Milton as persisting "to the end" in his loyalty to the Protectorate, finds him in the final tracts opposed to "any form of single person rule—such as the Protectorate";[31] and Mary Ann Radzinowicz, who argues at length for his consistency, yet finds in *The Readie and Easie Way* that he "declines to continue an implicit endorsement of rule by a single man."[32]

The phrase "single person" had its origin early in the history of the Republic, when Parliament required that all men eighteen or older accept the Oath of Engagement, confirming their loyalty to the Commonwealth "without a King or a House of Lords."[33] The ardent republicans of the restored Rump required a similar oath; but with memories of Cromwell's usurpation still fresh, they expanded the phrase to "single person kingship or house of peers."[34] There is no doubt that the Rump had little love for the Protectorate, but to suggest that Milton shared these views in February 1660 is to rip his words out of historical context and identify him with one of the many divisive factions whose existence he deplored. It should be observed that in all his works of the period he never uses the full wording, "single person kingship or house of peers," but consistently abbreviates it to "single person or house of lords" or a similar expression.[35] He edited the phrase in this way be-

29. Woolrych, "Milton and Cromwell," 209, 212. In his introduction to volume 7 of *Prose*, Woolrych seems to soften his position that in opposing government by "single person" the poet is repudiating the Protectorate.

30. Barker 62.

31. A.S.P. Woodhouse, *The Heavenly Muse*, 212.

32. Mary Ann Radzinowicz, *Toward "Samson Agonistes,"* 146. See also pp. 82 and 145–51 for Milton's political thought.

33. Gardiner, *Constitutional Documents*, 391.

34. Godfrey Davies 102, quoting the Council Register of 25 May.

35. In *A Letter to a Friend* it is alternately "Abjuration of a single person" or "abjura-

cause he considered the full wording tautological; in his own mind the "single person" was always the "king."

The phrase appears frequently in *The Readie and Easie Way*, but given the circumstances under which the tract was written, the deterioration of both army and Parliament, the increasingly open expression of royalist sentiment, and the rampant rumors of invasion by Charles II, it is difficult to imagine Milton occupying his thoughts with the long-since-expired Protectorate. It is even more difficult contemplating him, at that time, condemning a regime that at the height of its power would have crushed such a threat with a word. Milton is looking to the uncertain future, not the dead past, and warning against consequences of Restoration, an event he believed would sweep the whole political experiment into the dust-bin of history and replace it all with the despised monarch and his stable of bishops. This was surely not an occasion to contemplate at leisure the inadequacies of the Protectorate, whatever he may have thought them to be. It is difficult again, to read *The Readie and Easie Way* without recognizing it as a warning against monarchy. It is subtitled, "The inconveniences and dangers of readmitting kingship in this nation"; some two-thirds of it is devoted to that subject; and the words, "king," "kingship," and "monarch" dot its pages as unmistakable landmarks of his meaning, appearing in almost every paragraph.

Indeed the words "king" and "single person" are so frequently juxtaposed as to leave little question of Milton's meaning: In *A Letter to a Friend* the phrase "Abjuration of a single person" is followed closely by "abjuration of Monarchy" (7:330–31). In *The Readie and Easie Way* the words are immediately juxtaposed, "And do they among them who are so forward to bring in the single person, think to be by him trusted or long regarded? So trusted they shall be and so regarded, as by kings are wont reconcil'd enemies" (7:453). He goes on to warn the army that they will be disbanded without pay and prosecuted for their acts in arms if kingship returns, the people that they will be deprived of liberty of conscience if kingship returns, the tradesmen that their commerce will languish if kingship returns, and the educators that their academies will fade, for "Monarchs will never permitt" the people to flourish. Woolrych is fond of reading between the lines: "He nowhere mentions Cromwell, but the achievements that he celebrates are those of the Long Parliament and the Commonwealth, not of the Protectorate."[36] The ar-

---

tion of Monarchy" (7:330–31), in *Proposalls* "a single person & house of Lords" (7:337), and in *The Readie and Easie Way* variations on "a free Commonwealth without single person or house of lords" (7:429, 432).

36. Woolrych, "Milton and Cromwell," 210.

gument is unpersuasive as well as somewhat inaccurate, for Milton makes specific reference to the "ten or twelve years prosperous warr and contestation with tyrannie" (7:428), a span that includes the entire existence of the Republic. But even this is beside the point. He does not mention Cromwell and the Protectorate simply because they are far from his thoughts. *The Readie and Easie Way* is an argument for a free Commonwealth as preferable to a restored monarchy; and the "single person" he warns against is not the long-dead Lord Protector, but the very-much-alive Charles II, waiting at Breda for the word to embark.

Some conclusions may be drawn concerning Milton's view of government and the influence of his experience as a public official on the design of his "Free Commonwealth." His is essentially a federal system in which responsibility and authority are decentralized to form a nation of "many Commonwealths under one united and entrusted Sovrantie." County and city governments are to have "in thir own election and within thir own hands" the administration of justice, education, religion, and the local militia, along with the necessary tax authority to support them (7:461). The central government will have the "sovrantie," or power to rule, not "transferred, but delegated only" to it (7:432); but it will have limited scope in the exercise of that power.

> . . . yet know withal
> Since thy original lapse, true Liberty
> Is lost.
>
> (*PL* 12:82–84)

There is a basic contradiction in Milton's design. Governments, he believed, are a legacy of the Fall; and only insofar as a people are able to achieve a state of spiritual virtue can they release themselves from the burden of that legacy. It was his judgment that those who can govern themselves stand less in need of governing by others. In brief, people get the government they deserve; and those who decline from virtue can expect to find themselves living under tyrants. Milton proposes that England adopt a system of limited government so that the people may grow and prosper; but at the same time he despairs of his fellow citizens, the "perverse inhabitants" of the land even then clamoring for the rule of a king. If they are not worthy of limited rule, how can he conceive of them living under it?

This dilemma raises the question of the origins of Milton's design. His argument is founded on two principles, the rejection of kingship and the delegation of sovereignty to a permanent senate. In the fall of 1659 his chief concern was the breach between the army and Parliament, a clash he considered a threat to the ability of the Republic to resist the growing sentiment for the restoration of the king; and he hoped to resolve their differences by confirming members of both bodies secure in their positions "during life." By early December he found it necessary to defend his resolution against fears that any ruling body that did not have to return to the electorate from time to time would wax too powerful in the land; and in *Proposalls* he sketched out a series of limitations to be imposed on the central authority. In *The Readie and Easie Way* he provided some particulars about those limitations and pressed his argument that under his system such fears were groundless.

On tracing his thought as it evolved during the Anarchy, one receives the distinct impression that Milton, convinced that rule by a permanent body of many men was much to be preferred to that by a single permanent man, eventually became captive to his own conviction, and that his design of government simply flowed from it. In *The Readie and Easie Way* the entire weight of his argument and the shape of his design focus on one concern, to defend his Grand Council from fears that it will constitute a threat to liberty. In those few pages where he goes into detail about the division of powers between local and central governments, he concludes the description with a rhetorical question that sums up the principle upon which his design is based (quoted in part earlier):

> And when we have our forces by sea or land, either of a faithful Armie or a setl'd Militia, in our own hands to the firm establishment of a free Commonwealth, publick accounts under our own inspection, general laws and taxes with thir causes in our own domestic suffrages, judicial laws, offices and ornaments at home in our own ordering and administration, all distinction of lords and commoners, that may any way divide or sever the publick interest, remov'd, what can a perpetual senate have then wherin to grow corrupt, wherin to encroach upon us or usurp; or if they do, wherin to be formidable. (7:461)

The design, in brief, does not lead to, but derives from his argument for a Grand Council. It is a matter of cart and horse.

> Lest entering on the *Canaanite* alarm'd
> War terrify them inexpert, and fear
> Return them back to *Egypt*, choosing rather
> Inglorious life with servitude.
>   (PL 12:217–20)

Further, one must question whether Milton conceived of his settlement as the best form of government for the English people, despite his fervent assurances to that effect. All that can be said with any confidence is that he thought it the best way to prevent the return of the king. The election of a permanent senate was certainly a bold stroke, "Readie and Easie," "free and smooth" to implement as an immediate response to that threat; but one must wonder if he really believed a central government of such limited powers appropriate for a people who had declined "so low / From virtue" as to be "chusing them a captain back for *Egypt*" (7:463). It seems doubtful. Milton is caught up in the chain of his own logic: The king must not return. The best means to prevent it is to establish a permanent senate. The only way to make such a body acceptable is to limit its powers. Hence, his design limits its powers.

Scholars have sought out the origins of Milton's political thought in the works of authors ancient and contemporary; but given the turmoil of the Anarchy and the swift changes to which he was responding, it is doubtful that his free commonwealth was the product of studied contemplation. He was certainly at home in controversies involving abstract political theory; but he was not drawn to the particulars of constitutional design, as were his contemporaries, James Harrington and Thomas Hobbes. Scholars frequently refer to the influence of Harrington's *Commonwealth of Oceana* on Milton's thought, some suggesting that the poet may have attended meetings of the ROTA, a discussion group that met privately under Harrington's direction from November 1659 to February 1660 to debate constitutional issues.[37] Harrington proposed a legislature one-third of whose members would retire every two or three years, a device that Milton found cumbersome and unnecessary (7:435, 440–41, 444). With one exception he brings the notion up only to dismiss it, at times rather scornfully, preferring his own proposal of decentralized authority as a better means "to prevent setling of too much absolute power" on the body (7:434). The exception is of interest. At the very end of the entire body of his argument, the last sentence before his peroration, he acknowledges that if "the fear and envie of a perpetual sitting" is too pervasive, perhaps "to change a third part of them yearly or every two or three years" might be acceptable (7:461). It was clearly inserted as an afterthought; it does not appear in the first edition, although he does mention it in his letter to Monk (7:395). It is a poignant note. After devoting months of thought

37. Masson 5:481–86; Barker 266–71; Wolfe 304–10; Parker 1:537–39; Davies 291; and Woolrych, Introduction, 209–11.

to the issue and employing all his considerable rhetorical skills to persuade readers that a perpetual senate is the surest guard against monarchy, in the end he must admit that it might not be politically realistic,
a judgment endorsed by centuries of readers since.

His commonwealth was, to use Arthur Barker's phrase, "a crazy
structure hastily raised" under the pressure of events; and he threw it
together using bits and pieces of the governments of his experience
more frequently than those of his reading. As he evolved his concept of
a Grand Council, he drew on his memory of a similar, though smaller,
body "sitting perpetual," which presided over a nation blessed with
prosperity and comparative domestic peace, during a time when the
states of Europe both feared and courted the power of England. The
Protectorate Council, it will be recalled, was composed of members appointed for life and remained little changed during Cromwell's rule.
Milton's Grand Council resembles Cromwell's further in that both
bodies exercise executive authority, though the latter shared those
powers with the Lord Protector. Milton makes provisions for his perpetual senate to elect a Council of State, to which it would delegate
certain of its executive functions; but his sketchy description leaves the
clear impression that it will remain essentially subordinate to the parent
body. His insistence on a weak executive may reflect a preference for
the arrangement under the Commonwealth, when a Parliament jealous
of its prerogatives annually elected the members of the Council of State
"out of thir own number and others," as will Milton's Grand Council
(7:433).

Those years as Latin Secretary may also be reflected in his frequent
allusions to the Dutch, for whom he repeats his long-held admiration.
He holds up the United Netherlands as an example of the benefits of a
republic (7:427) and the advantage they have of being ruled by "a
standing Senat, without succession," a body which they regard as "the
main prop of thir liberty" (7:437). His proposed settlement will even be
superior to theirs, however, in that it will have no "house of *Nassaw*"
to worry about (7:446), and the individual "counties or commonalities"
will not have veto power over decisions of his Grand Council, as the
Dutch provinces do over those of the States General (7:459).[38]

Although he drew on the memory of former years, Milton was obviously influenced in his design by more immediate events. His permanent
senate resembles in some respects the "other House" of the later Protectorate Parliaments, and he may well have consulted the restrictions

38. There are also a number of allusions to the Waldensians in the tracts (7:291, 306,
308).

placed on that body's legal jurisdiction by *The Humble Petition and Advice* of 1657 in shaping the similar limits he imposes on his Grand Council.[39] Though the "other House" had no executive functions, it was just such a senate that the army proposed in its various petitions to the Rump in 1659, intending it as a check on the excesses of a popular assembly.[40] The army's concept understandably found little favor in the Rump but the petitions may have impressed Milton with the advantages of a perpetual body. At any rate, after wavering in October between "an annuall democracy or a perpetuall Aristocracy," he settled in *Proposalls* on a body of members who "retaine their places during life." This was but one provision of a settlement he advanced as an immediate solution to the rift between the Rump and the officers of the army, who were to be given the same security of serving "during life"; but the conviction apparently grew on him between December and February that such a body offered the best chance of saving the Republic. He was living in radically unstable times and whatever dangers such a Grand Council might pose to liberty, it at least promised stability.

Milton's provisions for control of the military are unclear. As we have seen, in urging Monk to employ his "faithful Veteran Army" to control elections for a new Parliament in 1660, he was hoping for a reenactment of the authority exercised by Cromwell in 1653. It was the kind of proposal the poet felt free to make in a private letter; but, given Parliament's often stated opposition to rule by a "single person," he could not proclaim it publically. Even if he did entertain a nostalgia for that earlier time, he was cautious not to include any office in his free commonwealth that might call for the services of a king.

His provisions for a standing army, however vaguely sketched, leave the unmistakable impression that he was tentatively thinking of it as an autonomous body in the scheme of things, an arrangement resembling that which prevailed during the Protectorate when the army was a power unto itself, guarding against the threat of tyranny from within and without. The essential difference, of course, is that Milton's commonwealth is to have no single head of state; and the poet leaves undefined the relationship between the military commander-in-chief and the Grand Council. This is a dangerously unstable arrangement in that it sets up a separation of powers with no intermediary agency, such as

39. Gardiner, *Constitutional Documents*, 452.

40. See Godfrey Davies. The various petitions were: the Wallingford House party's conditions for restoring the Rump, 2 May (76–77); the *Petition and Address* of the army, 12 May (97–98); Lambert's Derby petition of September; and Desborough's of 5 October (147–50).

that provided by Cromwell himself during the Protectorate, to resolve
differences between the two bodies, duplicating the situation that prevailed in the summer of 1659, which proved so incendiary and destruc-
tive to the Republic. Milton is optimistic, however; he assumes that in a
settlement which ends state control of the church, an issue he considers
at the heart of all the conflicts between the two bodies, "ambitious
leaders of armies would then have no hypothetical pretences so ready at
hand to contest with Parliaments" (7:380).[41]

It would be difficult to single out any of Milton's proposals as entirely original. The manner in which he combined them is an impressive
accomplishment; but they had all been suggested by others in one form
or another during that era of constitutional experimentation or were
features of the governments he had served. Modern scholars, with the
benefit of hindsight and two hundred years of experience with demo-
cratic rule, will dismiss some of them as highly impractical and surely
unwise. Milton's arguments for a permanent senate, which failed to
move his contemporaries, are unconvincing to modern ears as well, although it must be said that the rate of retention of incumbents in recent
elections to the U.S. Congress has created a legislative body not far
removed from permanent.[42] Controlled elections with candidates nominated by a small group of the "rightly qualifi'd [and] others of better
breeding" (7:443) have proven corrupting time and time again. But
Milton's experience had made him contemptuous of "the noise and
shouting of a rude multitude," and he was sufficiently attuned to the
political realities of 1660 as to leave little doubt in his mind that only a
carefully selected body of like-minded legislators could be counted on
the preserve the Republic. His notion to place control of the military
rather vaguely in the hands of "the people" was but a thinly disguised
device to keep it out of the hands of the central government. His own
experience should have told him that this kind of separation of powers
was unstable, but such was his faith in the radical religious convictions
of the soldiers that his vision was clouded. Armies today are more likely
to establish tyrannies than they are to deter them; and if constitutions

41. This passage appears in a section of the first edition that Milton later deleted from
the text. In the second edition he is considerably less harsh on the military, the only
reference to "ambitious leaders in the Armie" expressing confidence that they are very
much a minority whose actions are contrary "to the mind and approbation of the Armie it
self and thir other Commanders" (7:430).

42. The elections of 1988 and 1990 come to mind, though at this sitting the pundits
predict that 1992 will be different.

have provisions for the separation of powers, it is achieved by setting up a strong executive and an independent judiciary.

One could go on cataloging the impracticalities of Milton's free commonwealth but this would only be an injustice to his political vision. His system was admittedly unworkable, but it was in many ways prophetic. The principle of separation of church and state, which was central to his thought, has been embraced by most modern nations, excepting of course those in the world of Islam and systems that solve the problem by abolishing religion altogether. Although religious belief remains a strong cultural influence in the world, Western states seem to have learned the lessons of the Thirty Years War and take pains to insulate the political process from the kind of single-minded fervor that characterizes religious movements.[43] His proposals that the national government be hedged about with limitations and that matters such as education and the prosecution of the law remain in the hands of local authorities foreshadow features of modern federal systems. Milton's cumbersome legislative process, whereby laws passed at the national level must be ratified by provincial legislatures, is preserved in the U.S. Constitution only in its provisions for amending the document (Art. 5). And although the direction of the military is a responsibility of the head of government in present-day states, as it was during the Protectorate and the monarchy before it, the armed forces are in the hands of "the people" insofar as they control appropriations through their elected representatives. His insistence that the people "have thir arms in thir own hands" eventually found its way into the Bill of Rights (Art. 2).

Milton's experience in government, then, can be said to have had a strong influence on the shaping of his political thought. There can be little doubt that his constitutional settlement would have been radically different had he been able to contemplate the design at leisure rather than respond to the pressure of swiftly changing events. We can be grateful for those events, however, for were it not for them, in all likelihood he would never have turned his mind to such matters in the first place.

The second edition of *The Readie and Easie Way* raises questions about Milton's political acumen. Surely he knew it was all over. What could have possessed him? The first had done him enough harm but it might have been overlooked as yet another voice in the din of public

---

43. Roland Mushat Frye has recently discussed the importance of Milton's thought on church and state to the American experience. His emphasis, like Sensabaugh's, is on the influence of *Areopagitica* ("The Dissidence of Dissent" 482–88).

outcry lamenting the demise of the Republic. The second, however, expanded to twice the length of the former and its antimonarchical rhetoric raised to new heights of invective, could not be ignored. It had to be condemned and its author arrested, his fate placed in doubt by a Convention Parliament heatedly debating who should be excluded and who not from the general pardon declared by Charles at Breda.[44] *Paradise Lost* was but a fragment and in danger of remaining so had the full weight of vengeance been visited upon one who had raged so vehemently against the evils of kingship. Had all those years in political life not taught him something about "the art of the possible"? They had, of course, but for him liberty of conscience lay at the heart of life itself, indeed of eternal life; and in that adamant conviction is to be found both his strength and his weakness as a politician and a political thinker.

44. Gardiner, *Constitutional Documents*, 465–67.

APPENDIXES

Appendix A

Companion Letters

Cromwell's campaign, in May–June 1655, to rally the Protestant nations of Europe to the cause of the Vaudois resulted in nine of Milton's letters to heads of state. Four were individualized messages to the states immediately involved in the massacre and its aftermath, those to France, Savoy, and Geneva, and five to others not involved but whose aid Cromwell sought to enlist, those to Sweden, Denmark, the Swiss Protestant Cantons, the United Netherlands, and Transylvania. These last five are markedly similar in style and content, and in their similarities they offer an insight into how companion letters were composed.

The message of the five letters follows the same pattern. They open with a dramatic description of the plight of the Vaudois. This is followed by the other elements of the appeal, organized with some few exceptions *in the same sequence*: Cromwell pleads the cause of Protestants in general, announces that he has written to the duke personally, encourages the addressee to do so as well, warns that the attack constitutes a threat to all Protestants, expresses the hope that the duke will relent, and suggests that, should he not, the concerned states should hold "Consultations" on what further action might be appropriate.

Phillips's translations of a passage describing the plight of the Vaudois will serve to illustrate the practice of sending the same message but altering the text so that each letter employs different language in artful variations on a theme. Four of the documents open with this passage. Since the letter to Transylvania is Cromwell's first to that prince, the passage is buried in the text, following avowals of "Alliance and Friendship" and a shared commitment to "the common Defence of the Protestant Religion."

To Sweden (W53, P74):

> We make no question but that the fame of that most rigid Edict has reach'd your Dominions, whereby the Duke of *Savoy* has totally Ruin'd his Protestant Subjects Inhabiting the *Alpine* Valleys, and commanded 'em to be exterminated from their Native Seats and Habitations, unless they give security to renounce their Religion receiv'd from their Forefathers, in exchange for the *Roman* Catholick Superstition, and that within Twenty days at farthest; so that many being kill'd, the rest Strip to their Skins and expos'd to most certain destruction, are now forc'd to wander over desert Mountains and through perpetual Winter, together with their Wives and Children, half dead with Cold and Hunger.

To the United Netherlands (W54, P75):

> We make no question but that you have already bin inform'd of the Duke of *Savoy's* Edict, set forth against his Subjects Inhabiting the Valleys at the feet of the *Alps*, Ancient Professors of the Orthodox Faith; by which Edict they are commanded to abandon their Native Habitations, stript of all their fortunes, unless within Twenty days they embrace the *Roman Faith*; and with what Cruelty the Authority of this Edict has rag'd against a needy and harmless People, many being slain by the Soldiers, the rest Plunder'd and driven from their Houses together with their Wives and Children, to combat Cold and Hunger among desert Mountains, and perpetual Snow.

To the Protestant Swiss (W55, P76):

> We make no question but the late Calamity of the *Piemontois*, Professing our Religion, reached your Ears, before the unwelcome News of it arriv'd with us. Who being a People under the Protection and Jurisdiction of the Duke of *Savoy*, and by a severe Edict of their Prince Commanded to depart their Native Habitations, unless within Three days they gave security to embrace the *Roman* Religion, soon after were assail'd by Armed Violence, that turn'd their Dwellings into Slaughter-houses, while others, without Number, were terrifi'd into Banishment, where now Naked and Afflicted, without House or Home, or any Covering from the Weather, and ready to perish through Hunger and Cold, they miserably wander through desert

Mountains, and depths of Snow, together with their Wives and Children.

To Denmark (W58, P77):

With what a severe and unmerciful Edict *Immanuel* Duke of *Savoy* has expell'd from their Native Seats his Subjects inhabiting the Valleys of *Piemont*, men otherwise harmless, onely for many years remarkably famous for embracing the Purity of Religion; and after a dreadful Slaughter of some numbers, how he has expos'd the rest to the hardships of those desert Mountains, Stript to their Skins, and barr'd from all relief, we believe your Majesty has long since heard.

To Transylvania (W52, P80):

[We put] your Highness in mind how unmercifully the Duke of *Savoy* has Persecuted his own Subjects, Professing the Orthodox faith, in certain Valleys at the feet of the *Alps*. Whom he has not only constrain'd by a most severe Edict as many as refuse to embrace the Catholick Religion, to forsake their Native Habitations, Goods and Estates, but has fall'n upon 'em with his Army, put several most Cruelly to the Sword, others more Barbarously Tormented to Death, and driven the greatest number to the Mountains, there to be consum'd with Cold and Hunger, exposing their Houses to the Fury, and their Goods to the Plunder of his Executioners.

A glance at the Latin of two of these appeals will demonstrate the common use of words and phrases that identify them as companion letters.

To Sweden (W53, P74):

Pervenisse nuper in regna vestra illius Edicti acerbissimi famam quo dux *Sabaudiae* subjectos sibi Alpinos incolas, *Reformatam* Religionem profitentes, funditus afflixit, & nisi religione Romanâ suam mutare fidem à Majoribus acceptam intra dies viginti velint, patriis sedibus exterminari jussit, unde multis interfectis, caeteri spoliati, & ad interitum certissimum expositi, per incultissimos montes, hyememque perpetuam fame & frigore confecti cum conjugibus ac parvulis jam nunc aberrant, & haec graviter tulisse Majestatem vestram nobis persuassimum est.

To the United Provinces (W54, P75):

> Edictum *Ducis Sabaudiae* nuperrimum in subjectos sibi *Alpinos*
> incolas, Orthodoxam Religionem antiquitùs profitentes, quo illi
> edicto, ni intra dies viginti fidem *Romanam* amplectantur, exuti
> fortunis omnibus, patriae quoque sedes relinquere jubentur, &
> quantâ crudelitate in homines innoxios atque inopes nostros-
> que, quod maximè refert, in *Christo* fratres illius edicti auc-
> toritas grassata sit, occisis permultis ab exercitûs parte contra
> eos missâ, direptis reliquis atque domo expulsis, unde illi cum
> conjugibus ac liberis fame & frigore conflictari inter asperrimos
> montes, nivesque perpetuas jamdui coacti sunt, rumore & vi-
> cinis undique ex locis creberrimis literis ac nuntiis cognovisse
> vos jamdudum existimamus.

Cromwell was, at the time, considering military action against Savoy,
inquiring about suitable landing sites in the area of Villafranca and Nice
(Masson 5:43). The closing lines of the letters include a passage which
guardedly proposes that the Protestant powers consult over what further is to be done.

To Sweden:

> But if he [the Duke] rather chuse to listen to his Anger then our
> joynt Intreaties and Intercessions, . . . upon Consultations duly
> first communicated to your Majesty and the chief of Protestant
> Princes, some other course is to be speedily taken, that such a
> numerous multitude of our Innocent Brethren may not misera-
> bly Perish for want of Succour and Assistance.

To the United Netherlands:

> But if he persist in the same obstinate Resolutions . . . we are
> ready to take such other Course and Counsels with your selves,
> in common with the rest of our Reformed Friends and Confed-
> erates, as may be most necessary for the preservation of Just
> and Good men upon the brink of inevitable Ruin, and to make
> the Duke himself sensible, that we can no longer neglect the
> heavy Oppressions and Calamities of our Orthodox Brethren.

To the Protestant Swiss:

> But if his mind be obstinately bent to other determinations, we
> are ready to communicate our Consultations with yours, by

what most prevalent means to relieve and re-establish most Innocent men, and our most dearly beloved Brethren in Christ, tormented and overlaid with so many Wrongs and Oppressions; and preserve'em from inevitable and undeserved Ruin.

To Denmark:

Or if he persist in his Determinations, we protest our selves ready, together with your Majesty, and the rest of our Confederates of the Reformed Religion, to take such speedy methods as may enable us, as far in us lies, to relieve the distresses of so many miserable Creatures, and provide for their Liberty and Safety.

These similarities serve to illustrate that it was not necessary that Milton have an English draft for *each* of the companion letters and closely related groups for which he was responsible. He needed but one initially and from it he could easily compose the others, incorporating what slight variations might be called for by the circumstances of the addressee. The letter to the prince of Transylvania, for example, omits the reference contained in the others to future "Consultations" on what action to take should the duke not relent, this obviously because that prince lived at such a distance as to preclude his participation in any action agreed upon. But such variations could easily be effected by verbal instructions to an experienced Latin Secretary, particularly one who made it his business to keep abreast of developments in any single issue or set of negotiations.

Appendix B

The Seventeenth-Century Manuscripts

Doctrine which we would know whence learnt.
(PL 5:856)

As far as is known, in the seventeenth century three manuscripts of Milton's State Papers were transcribed from the documents he had in his possession.[1] The Columbia MS was prepared in 1659 or 1660 by an unknown amanuensis, and the Skinner MS sometime before 1674 by Daniel Skinner, the poet's amanuensis at the time. These have both survived. A third has not, but it was published as *Literae Pseudo-Senatus Anglicani* in 1676. Milton retained copies of his letters as a personal archive for reference in the performance of his official duties as Latin Secretary; and since that collection remained in his possession until his death, it must be assumed that the first two were transcribed certainly with his knowledge and almost certainly under his supervision. The *Literae* manuscript probably dates from after Milton's death, hence there is no evidence that he had a hand in its preparation.[2] It cannot escape notice, however, that the order of the letters in the volume follows roughly the same scheme as those in the Skinner MS, which Milton certainly supervised. Both are divided into three books, one containing letters written during the Commonwealth period (1649–53), a second letters during Cromwell's Protectorate (1654–58), and a third those written thereafter (1658–59). The similarity is surely more than coincidence, implying either that the editor of *Literae* was familiar with the

---

1. Other manuscripts were in circulation. Shawcross argues that the fifty letters in Gregorio Leti's *Historia* (1692) were not copied from *Literae* ("Survey" 357); and Miller states confidently that the 113 in Johan Christian Lünig's *Literae Procurem Europae* (1712) came from "a different manuscript collection from any hitherto known" ("Milton's State Letters" 413).

2. *Works* cites "three collections of state papers, compiled obviously with his approval (in one case with his certain, in the others his probable supervision)" (594).

Skinner MS or that he had in his possession the collection of documents ordered in that manner, from which it had been transcribed.[3]

The three manuscripts differ in important respects, for they appear to have been compiled at different times, for different purposes, and independently of one another. Both the Columbia and Skinner MSS, for example, include letters not in the other two, and *Literae* has letters not in Skinner. These circumstances strongly suggest that each manuscript represents a *selection* of letters from Milton's archives, which were available to all three transcribers.[4]

The Columbia MS

This manuscript[5] was prepared in order to preserve, rather than to publish the documents, as was the case with the other two, at some time between 20 October 1659, when the English Republic began to come unraveled, and the Restoration the following May. The manuscript was in all likelihood compiled in anticipation of the latter event, hence, although there is no direct evidence for it, almost certainly under Milton's supervision. He could reasonably expect that the new government would order him to turn over to the State Paper Office the copies of official documents he had accumulated over ten years of public service, even as Georg Weckherlin had been instructed to deliver his papers to Milton in 1650 and John Bradshaw his to Thurloe in 1652. The authorities ordered Thurloe to surrender his papers in 1660 and he was forced to comply, though he did so only in part; but for some reason it seems that Milton's were overlooked, perhaps because they were only copies, and he was able to retain his collection.

The manuscript shows signs of having been compiled in some haste. The letters are in haphazard sequence, although in several instances those addressed to any single nation are grouped together. Among others, letters 1–6 and 14–26 are to France; 106–10 to the Spanish ambassador; 133–43 to the Hanseatic League (with the exception of

3. The Skinner MS is organized into "*Libri Tres.*": "Lib:1:^min": nos. 1 (10 August 1649)–25 (8 October 1653); "*Liber secundus*": nos. 26 (29 June 1654)–111 (August 1658); and "*Liber tertius*": nos. 123 (5 September 1658)–139 (15 May 1659). There are differences, of course. Skinner, for example, included a separate category of eleven letters for which he had no dates (nos. 112–122), and the editor of *Literae* placed them in roughly chronological order.

4. For a more detailed account of the history and content of the manuscripts, see Shawcross, "Survey," 347–54, and *Prose* 5:470–75.

5. Rare Book and Manuscript Library, Butler Library, Columbia University, no. X823M64S62.

138); and 150–56 to the United Netherlands. The only semblance of order in their sequence, therefore, seems to be a consequence of Milton's practice of keeping the letters of any single state in a separate file; hence during the process of transcription each letter or group of letters was simply copied down as he came upon them while going through his records. The numerous exceptions to this organization in the manuscript suggest that he did not have them in very good order in the first place and time did not permit him to sort them out.[6]

The manuscript itself suggests further evidence of haste. It is a crudely bound notebook of unusual size (6 1/2" by 15"), which quite obviously belonged to *someone else*. The first nineteen pages are a commonplace book consisting of entries, mostly on political matters, in which Milton could have had little interest. One cannot imagine his taking the time, for example, to list the ranks of English nobility, "The differences of all degrees and ye order of their goeing" (5–6), or to keep a record of the duties of the Constable of England (8–11), or the powers of the King's Lord Chancellor (13–16).[7] Immediately preceding the letters are *Proposals of certaine expedients* (19–21) and *Letter to a Friend* (21–23; although not titled), which are either drafts or copies later transcribed, again to preserve them. These features suggest that the booklet either belonged to the unnamed amanuensis or was simply lying about in Milton's office and snatched up for the purpose when the need arose to have his papers transcribed.[8]

---

6. Some notion of the disorder may be seen in the following representative sequence:

Letter nos.	Addressee
28–29	Spain
30–31	France
32–33	Portugal
35–36	Hamburg
37–38	Spain
39	France
40–44	Portugal
45	Spain
46–47	Portugal

This group apparently was copied from a file of Iberian correspondence, among which other letters had been intermingled.

7. *Works* prints two entries, "Of Statues & Antiquities" and "A breif description of Genoa," but with serious reservations about attribution (18:258–62, 519–20). The latter is a detailed report on the fortifications and armaments of the city, obviously intended for the information of the Admiralty during the Spanish War. It concludes, "The King of Spaine hath continually in Genoa 13 gallies (for his service) in his pay."

8. According to a printed reference inside the front cover, the notebook was later used "by Bernard Gardiner, Warden of All Soul's College in 1703, and keeper of the Archives

All of the Latin letters in the Columbia MS appear in one or the other of the other two sources; it is, however, the only source for ten in English. Of significant note is the absence of four that appear in the Skinner MS.[9] The existence of these four is one indication that those Milton had transcribed in 1659–60 represent only a selection of the number he possessed. As he reviewed his letters, he apparently chose some for preservation and dismissed others, again perhaps because time was short.

Literae Pseudo-Senatus Anglicani

This collection, which contains 136 letters arranged in chronological order, was published twice in the fall of 1676, first in October in Amsterdam, and second, in a pirated edition, shortly thereafter in Brussels (Shawcross, *Milton, A Bibliography*, 88). Milton's biographers generally agree that his nephew, Edward Phillips, was the source of the documents published in *Literae*, although the only evidence for this is a note by Aubrey, who visited Milton's widow seven years after his death and reported her as saying that she had given "all his papers" to Phillips (Masson 6:806; Parker 1:651). One feature of the volume clearly indicates that the editor was more familiar with the letters than was Daniel Skinner. When Milton's young amanuensis, then in his mid-twenties, compiled his manuscript, he made a separate category of letters for which he had no dates. *Literae*, on the other hand, inserts these documents among the others in roughly chronological order, indicating that the editor had some knowledge of when they were written. There is reason to believe that Phillips had assisted his uncle in his official duties during the Interregnum and so would be privy to that knowledge.[10]

Daniel Skinner observed only that a London bookseller, Moses Pitt, had bought them "of a poor fellow that had formerly surrepticiously

---

of Oxford University." Gardiner inverted the book and started on the final page. He intended it for a commonplace book, for which he prepared an elaborate index but made only eight entries. The balance of his notes are a hodgepodge of inventories (126–57).

    9. Skinner included the following four not in the Columbia MS:

        W139, P78—Cromwell to the king of France, 25 May 1655
        W140, P88—Cromwell to the king of France, 13 January 1656
        W141, P101—Romswinkel Passport, 13 June 1656
        W142, P102—Cromwell to the king of Sweden, 13 June 1656

    10. *Works* suggests that Phillips "was a contemporary and in Milton's confidence, and may even have discussed passages with him and been the amanuensis who wrote some of the letters at Milton's dictation" (18:600).

got them from Milton" himself, rather than from his widow (Masson 6:794; SP 29/386/65). Whoever the "poor fellow" was, there is some question whether he sold Pitt the actual papers (Masson 6:806; Parker 1:611) or a transcript of them (*Prose* 5:472). Whichever the case, certainly at some point prior to publication a manuscript of the documents was prepared, in either London or Amsterdam. *Literae* contains thirteen letters not in the Skinner MS, eleven of them dated in 1652,[11] and lacks fourteen that appear in Skinner, twelve of them dated in 1655–59.[12] Although there may be a rationale for the absence of the 1652 letters from the Skinner MS (see below), it is difficult to understand why the 1655–59 letters were omitted from *Literae*. Either Milton chose to exclude them from the original manuscript, or the editor found it impolitic to publish them; the contents offer no clue.

Literae opens with a preface that praises Milton's Latin and deplores his politics; he had, as it is phrased, "soiled the eloquence of his style

11. The *Literae* letters not in Skinner are:
    W17, P29—Parliament to the duke of Tuscany, 20 January 1652
    W18, P37—Parliament to Hamburg, 12 March 1652
    W19, P36—Parliament to the queen of Sweden, 11 March 1652
    W22, P61—Council to the duke of Venice, 2 February 1653
    W23, P40—Council to the Spanish ambassador, 31 March 1652
    W24, P41—Parliament to the king of Denmark, 13 April 1652
    W26, P42—Parliament to Hamburg, 16 April 1652
    W28, P48—Council to the Spanish ambassador, 10 August 1652
    W29, P50—Council to the Danish ambassadors, 13 September 1652
    W30, P51—Council to the Danish ambassadors, 13 September 1652
    W32, P53—Council to the Spanish ambassador, 11 November 1652
    W43a, P39—Demands for damages to the Dutch, 15 March 1652
    W97, P131—Cromwell to Lübeck, 20 August 1657
12. The Skinner letters not in *Literae* are:
    W137, P8—Parliament to the king of Spain, 25 January 1650
    W138, P45—Parliament to the duke of Savoy, 8 May 1652
    W139, P78—Cromwell to the king of France, 25 May 1655
    W140, P88—Cromwell to the king of France, 13 January 1656
    W141, P101—Romswinckel Passport, 13 June 1656
    W142, P102—Cromwell to the king of Sweden, 13 June 1656
    W143, P156—Cromwell to the king of France, 1 July 1658
    W144, P157—Cromwell to Mazarin, 1 July 1658
    W145, P93—Cromwell to the king of France, 9 April 1656
    W146, P94—Cromwell to Mazarin, 9 April 1656
    W147, P171—R. Cromwell to the duke of Tuscany, 19 April 1659
    W148, P172—R. Cromwell to the duke of Tuscany, 19 April 1659
    W149, P170—R. Cromwell to the king of Portugal, 19 April 1659
    W150, P173—R. Cromwell to the king of Sweden, 25 April 1659

with most wretched manners" (*Works* 3). Skinner, writing to promote his own forthcoming volume and perhaps to defend his dead mentor, characterized the volume as "a little imperfect book" and promised to publish "the true and more perfect copy, with many other papers." There is some justification for his remarks, for the collection is limited. For example, the editor had access to some of the elaborate salutations and signatures that are absent from the other two manuscripts, but by no means all of them. In this respect, Cromwell's letters are most irregular. Some have his name first, some last, some in both places, and others not at all. Among the Commonwealth letters, some have the name of the addressee first, some have it last, and others abbreviate it severely, e.g., "*Hamburgensis*" (16) and "*Internuntio Portugallico*" (21). Though limited and imperfect, the volume has provided the source for later editions. Edward Phillips translated its Latin for his *Letters of State* in 1694, the source for the English of the present study, and *Works* prints the letters in the order in which they appear therein (W1–136).

The Skinner MS

This document and its editorial history contain material relevant to our study, although not so much in what the collection includes as in what it does not.[13] The manuscript itself, in Skinner's hand, contains 139 letters, of which, as mentioned, 4 are absent from the Columbia MS and 14 from *Literae*. They are arranged in three books in chronological order, except for 11 (nos. 112–22) that have no dates. It does not attempt the elaborate salutations of *Literae* but names the addressee only briefly, occasionally using "*eidem*" where the sequence allows. "*Joannis Miltoni Angli Epistolae*" appears as a heading for every two pages in open leaf, which seems an unnecessary detail for such a document.

As to its history, in the early 1670s Milton decided to publish his letters, both private and public, and had a manuscript prepared for the purpose. The Licenser would not permit the public letters to appear in print, however, so he substituted his early Latin *Prolusions* and published the collection in 1674 as *Epistolarum Familiarium Liber Unus*.[14]

---

13. SP 9/194.

14. The original title is not known, but when the State Letters were withdrawn and the *Prolusions* included, doubtless *Familiarium* was added. *Liber Unus* is difficult to explain, as there is no *Liber Secundus*.

Since the manuscript is in Skinner's hand, most scholars agree that it is
the one originally prepared for the volume, that he inherited it on Milton's death, and that it is the same one he later intended to have published.[15] Masson chronicles Skinner's abortive efforts to publish Milton's letters, and Shawcross has since unearthed additional letters
exchanged by several hands involved in the incident.[16] Briefly, in 1675
Skinner sent a manuscript, presumably the surviving document, to the
Dutch printer, Daniel Elzevir, along with a copy of *De Doctrina Chris-
tiana*, which he had also inherited, with the intention of having both
published. In this enterprise he ran afoul of Sir Joseph Williamson, the
Secretary of State, who was unalterably opposed to the printing of the
letters. Skinner, who was seeking public office at the time and stood in
need of Williamson's good will, stopped publication and surrendered
both documents to him, whereupon they disappeared into the State Paper Office, to reemerge a century and a half later, discovered there by
Robert Lemon in 1823.[17]

The correspondence associated with the incident gives clear evidence
that Skinner had in his possession and intended to publish more documents than are to be found in the manuscript as it has come down to
us. When *Literae* appeared in October 1676, he saw it as a threat to his
own prospective volume and undertook to diminish its importance. As
noted, he called it, "a little imperfect book" and promised "the true and
more perfect copy, with many other papers." In a Latin prospectus prepared for the *London Gazette* he disparaged the volume as "imperfect
and crude" and offered his own, to use Masson's wording, "the full,
true, and perfect edition in elegant type . . . to be accompanied by
copies of the Spanish, Portuguese, French, and Dutch Treaties and other
illustrative documents, German, Danish, and Swedish."[18]

15. Masson 6:791; Parker 1:637; *Prose* 5:471. These seem reasonable assumptions;
and if the transcription of the private letters were available and found to be in Skinner's
hand also, it would be unquestionably confirmed. Meanwhile, the only certainty is that it
is the manuscript Elzevir returned to Williamson in 1677.

16. Masson 6:790–806. In his useful "Survey," Shawcross cites sixteen separate pieces
of correspondence related to Skinner's plan to publish the letters (348–49), a list which he
subsequently expanded (*Milton, A Bibliography* 238–39, 242–43; "A Contemporary Letter" 119–20).

17. William B. Hunter questions Milton's authorship of *Christian Doctrine* and in the
process raises doubts that the poet "thought so highly of [Skinner] that he entrusted to
him copies of the yet-unpublished *State Papers* and *Christian Doctrine*" ("Provenance"
136). Hunter does not, however, question Milton's authorship of the *State Papers*. Barbara Lewalski and John Shawcross offer persuasive rebuttals to Hunter's argument
("Provenance" 143–62).

18. Masson 6:796. The prospectus is in SP 84/204/120 and is printed in *Works*

The prospectus has important implications for our study. It demonstrates, first, that the Skinner MS is but a part of the original collection of documents that he had in his possession. Further, it implies strongly that among the "many other papers" he inherited from Milton and intended to publish were copies of the four treaties and additional documents related to correspondence with Germany, Denmark, and Sweden. It is difficult to imagine where Skinner could have secured such sensitive papers other than from Milton, and their existence may partially explain Williamson's adamant insistence that they not be published. The existence of additional papers in Skinner's possession casts doubt on the remark of Milton's widow that she gave "all his papers" to Edward Phillips. Indeed, another collection, a file of Cromwell's private papers alleged to have been in Milton's possession, came into the hands of Thomas Ellwood.[19] Elizabeth Milton's "all" doubtless meant "all that were left."

It certainly cannot be claimed, on the basis of the prospectus alone, that Milton was responsible for these additional documents, since they may have been papers from other sources that he kept on file for reference in the preparation of letters. There is other evidence, however, that he was involved in the negotiations that led to three of the treaties mentioned (the French excepted), and their presence among the papers that Skinner inherited from him will serve to strengthen the position that he was, at least in part, responsible for those three. One must wonder what became of them and the "other illustrative documents" cited in the prospectus, for they were not mentioned when the package was discovered in 1823. One can only conjecture that they were separated from the letters when Skinner had them returned to Williamson and deposited in their appropriate files in the Paper Office.

The presence of the treaties among the papers intended for publication may also explain a curious feature of the Skinner MS, the absence of so many letters from the year 1652. During that year England was engaged in treaty negotiations with four of the nations mentioned,

---

18:648, where the Latin reads: "Quae una cum Articulis, Hispanicis, Portugallicis, Gallicis, Belgicis in ista rerum inclinatione nobiscum initis & percussis, pluribusque chartis Germanicis, Danicis, Suevicis scitissime scriptus." *Works* indicates that it "was issued by the Elzevirs," but Masson remarks that Williamson would not permit Skinner to print it in the *Gazette* (6:795). The language is similar enough to that in Skinner's correspondence to suggest that he wrote it as well.

19. Masson 6:815. They were published by John Nickolls in 1743 as *Original Letters and Papers of State, addressed to Oliver Cromwell*. The original documents are on deposit with the Society of Antiquaries, London.

Spain, Portugal, Denmark, and the United Netherlands, and letters relating directly to the negotiations with three of these four, while present in the other manuscripts, are absent from Skinner's, the three to the Spanish ambassador, the three to Denmark, and the one to the Dutch.[20] Assuming that he had these documents available, why did he not include them among the letters? On the assumption that the transcript Skinner prepared for the volume of letters in 1674 is the same one he sent to Elzevir in 1675, it would appear that the decision to omit them was Milton's.

He may have done so for either or both of two reasons. On a practical level, if Milton hoped to get his volume of letters past the Licenser, and he had already had problems with *Paradise Lost*, it would have been politic to omit any reference to international agreements. Governments are very sensitive about who publishes their official documents. The title page of the Dutch *Declaration* of 9 July 1652, for example, includes the following injunction: "ORdered by the Parliament, *That no person whatsoever, without particular License from the Parliament, do presume to Print the Declaration . . . Nor any the Papers therewith printed, other than the Printer to the Parliament*" (Shawcross, *Milton, A Bibliography*, 37). These papers may have been omitted also because the original volume was intended to be a collection of *letters* and so was not to include the longer and less than interesting treaties. Even a cursory glance at the letters written during the negotiations will persuade the reader that they are virtually unintelligible without access to the documents they cite. Hence, if the treaties were not to be included, it would have been wise to omit the letters associated with them. Skinner, on the other hand, intended to publish the treaties and, if he had copies of the omitted letters, may well have decided to include them in the missing section, where the reader would have readily available the documents to which they refer. This is only conjecture, of course, though it is clear that Skinner had a sizable bundle of Milton's papers; and this being the case, one must wonder how many additional Miltonic letters associated with these treaties were in that missing section, later to be withdrawn and scattered throughout the Public Records with them.

20. There are no letters from the Portuguese negotiations in any of the manuscripts. There is one to a German state, the County of Oldenburg, but it is a routine *recreditif* releasing the envoy, Hermann Mylius, for return home (W39, P34). No letters exchanged *during the Oldenburg negotiations* appear in any of the sources, nor does the Safeguard itself (W152, P35).

Appendix C

The Spanish Treaty of 12 November 1652

Save for a handful of obvious printing errors, the text is that as printed in the 1702 edition of *Original Letters of his Excellency Sir Richard Fanshaw* (486–510), which is faithful to the original in SP 103/65/216–26. *Original Letters*, in fact, prints the entire "Transactions between *England* and *Spain*, from the Year 1650" (405–510), including the annotated version of the 1630 treaty. At the Restoration, Charles II appointed Sir Richard Fanshawe to succeed Milton as Secretary for Foreign Languages (Masson 6:297). He advanced rapidly in public service, as had Philip Meadows during the Protectorate, and doubtless as the poet would have also had it not been for his blindness. In 1664 Fanshawe was designated the envoy to Spain and in preparation for his mission was instructed to familiarize himself with documents pertaining to past relations between the two powers, including an examination of "the Transactions betwixt D. Alonso de Cardenas, and the Usurpers here" (Fanshawe 4). A copy of the manuscript remained among his papers and was published with them.

The treaty is dated 12 November in both the transcript and *Original Letters*, hence the wording of the articles is as they were presented to Cardenas on that day. A secretary to the Council of State entered into the margin by each article a notation of the ambassador's exceptions and revisions, or his acceptance of the wording as written. Thurloe may have done so himself or assigned the task to Milton, since Cardenas's comments were almost certainly submitted in Latin. The marginal notations reflect the debate that ensued, ending on occasion with the remark "and so this Article was agreed." The treaty in the transcript represents the status of the negotiations as of September 1653, for the text concludes as follows:

77 572 *Nov: 12. 1652*

Artickles for the renewing of a Peace and
Friendship between the Parlmt. of the Comonwea
-lth of England, and his most serene Matie. the
King of Spaine, offerd by the Counsell of State
to the Ambr. of the sd King.

This artickle the Ambr. assented to, reserving the point of precedency to be setled last of all.	1. That there be from henceforth between the Comonwealth of England, and his Matie. the King of Spaine, a good generall, sin =cere, true, firm & perfect peace to endure for ever, and inviolably to be observed aswell by Land, at sea and Freshwaters, And alsoe between the Countries, Lands, Kingdomes & Dominions and Countries associated to them & under their obedience, and the subjects People & Inhabitants of them respectively, of whatsoever condition, place or degree they be so as the sd People & subjects respectively from henceforth do mutually aide, assist & shew all manner of Civility & offices of Friendship to each other
This assented to by the Ambr. wth this addition in the end of the Artickle . In manner and according as shalbe agreed in the 5th Artickle of the Treaty	2. Neither of the sd Parties or respective people, subjects or Inhabts. shall not upon any account whatsoever either secretly or openly doe, act, or attempt any thing against the other in any place by Land or water, nor in the Ports or Ryvers of each other but shall treat each other wth all love & Friendship, and may come

First page of draft Spanish Treaty, 12 November 1652. Courtesy, Public Record Office. Crown copyright, reproduced with the permission of the Controller of Her Majesty's Stationery Office, London.

In this state the Treaty stood the 19/9 of *September*, 1653. And the Ambassador by a Paper of the 10/20 of *October* after pressed for a Resolution of the Council, whether they would conclude the Treaty upon the Articles, as consented to by him; yet it doth not appear that they returned any Answer, or that the Subsequent Government made any proceeding therein. (Fanshawe 510)

The wording of Cardenas's additions to Article XIX suggest that it was the rock upon which the negotiations foundered. He required, as he had in the draft treaty submitted the year before, that Parliament set aside the provisions of the Navigation Act concerning imports, which the English adamantly refused to do.

The text of the treaty is as follows:

ARTICLES for the Renewing of a Peace and Friendship between the Parliament of the Commonwealth of England, and his most Serene Majesty the King of Spain; offered by the Council of State to the Ambassador of the said King.

I. That there be from henceforth between the Commonwealth of *England*, and his Majesty the King of *Spain*, a good, general, sincere, true, firm, and perfect Amity, League, and Peace, to endure for Ever, and inviolably to be observed, as well by Land as Sea, and fresh Waters; and also between the Countries, Lands, Kingdoms, Dominions, and Countries [*sic*] associated to them and under their Obedience, and the Subjects, People, and Inhabitants of them respectiviely, of whatsoever Condition, Place, or Degree they be; so as the said People and Subjects respectively, from henceforth do mutually aid, assist and shew all manner of Civility and offices of Friendship to each other.

This Article the Ambassador assented to; reserving the point of Precedency to be settled last of all.

II. Neither of the Parties, nor their respective People, Subjects, or Inhabitants shall not upon any account whatsoever, either secretly, or openly, do, act, or attempt any thing against the other, in any place by Land or Water, nor in the Ports or Rivers of each other, but shall treat each other with all Love and Friendship, and may come by Water and Land, safely and freely into each other's Countries, Lands, Kingdoms, Dominions, Islands, Cities, Towns, Villages, walled or unwalled, fortified or unfortified, their Havens and Roads; and there remain and tarry, and thence depart at their pleasure.

This assented to by the Ambassador, with this addition in the end of the Article: In manner, and according as shall be agreed in the eighth Article of the Treaty.

III. That the Parliament of the Commonwealth of *England*, and the King of *Spain*, take care, that their respective People and Subjects, from henceforth, abstain from all force and wrong doing, and if it shall happen that any violence or injury be offered by the Commonwealth, or King aforesaid, or by the People or Subjects of either of them, against the People or Subjects of the other, either against any of the Articles of this League, or against Common Right. Nevertheless, no Letters of Reprizal, Mark or Countermark, shall be granted by either of the Confederates, until Justice be first sought in the ordinary course of Law, but if Justice be either delayed or denied, then demand thereof shall be made from the Supreme Power of the Commonwealth, or the Kingdom whose People and Inhabitants have received wrong from that Commonwealth or Kingdom, by whom, as is said, the Justice is either delayed or denied, or from such Commissioners which by either part shall be appointed to hear and receive such demands, to the end that all such differences may be either Friendly, or according to Law composed; but if yet there shall be delays and no Right be done, nor satisfaction given, within *Three* Months after demand made, then Letters of Reprizal, Mark, or Countermark may be granted. And all Commissions, Letters of Reprizal and Mark, and otherwise, containing Letters to take Prizes; which either part heretofore, without observing the aforesaid Rules, have, to the prejudice of the Commonwealth, or Kingdom, or either of their People or Inhabitants, granted either to the Subjects or Inhabitants, or to Strangers, shall be hereafter void and of no force, as they likewise by this Treaty are declared to be.

The Spanish *Ambassador adds, after the word* (denied) longer than the cause shall require, having regard to the distance of the place where the proofs are to be made.

The Ambassador adds, six Months after, &c.

With the Two Amendments aforesaid, the Ambassador consents to this Article.

IV. That between the Commonwealth of *England* and the King of *Spain*, and their respective People, Inhabitants and Subjects, as well by Land as Sea, and fresh Waters, in all and singular their Countries, Dominions, Lands, Territories, Provinces, Islands, Plantations, Cities, Towns, Villages, Ports, Rivers, Creeks, Harbours and Districts, there shall be free Trade and Comerce, in such sort and manner, that without any Safe-conduct or Licence, general or special, the People and Subjects of each party, may freely, as well by Land as Sea, and fresh Waters, go, enter, and sayl into the said Countries, Kingdoms, Dominions, and all the Cities, Ports, Shoars, Roads, Streights, and other places thereof, and put themselves into whatsoever Havens of the same with their Ships, laden or unladen, Carriages and Draughts wherewith, they bring their Commodities; and there to buy and sell as much as they will, and in the same places, upon just prises, furnish themselves with Victuals, and other Necessaries for their Sustenances and Voyages; as also, as need shall require, Repair their Ships and Carriages; and from thence with their Merchandises, Goods, and other Commodities, freely to depart and return into their own Countries, or other Places, as they think good, without any let or molestation; provided they, and every of them, on each side, do pay the Customs and Tolls expressed in the following Article, and conform their Trade and Traffick to the Laws and Ordinances of each place respectively, during the time they Traffick there.

The Ambassador adds here these words, after the word (Districts,) [In manner and according as shall be declared in the 8th Article of this Treaty] *And with this Addition the Ambassador consents to this Article.*

V. That the People and Inhabitants of the Commonwealth of *England*, trading in the Kingdoms, Territories, Islands, Ports, or other Places whatever, within the Dominions of the King of *Spain*, shall not hereafter pay any Custom, Subsidy or Toll, neither shall any thing be imposed upon them, but only the Customs called in *Spanish Alcavalla*, as they are now imposed, according to the Law of the Place where such Customs or *Alcavallas* are to be paid. In like manner the King of *Spain's* Subjects, trading in any of the Countries, Island, Ports, or Places, of the Commonwealth of *England*, shall not pay any Custom or Toll, nor any thing be imposed upon them, but only the Custom and Excise, as they are laid in every place where they are used to be paid; and all other Tributes, Subsidies, and Payments, imposed by either part upon the People of the other, be they upon the account of private or publick Commodity, shall be henceforth taken away and declared void, and no other Tolls than those which are already mentioned, shall either be imposed or exacted by either party, for the time to come.

Instead of this Article, the Ambassador propounded this following; That the People, Inhabitants, and Subjects of the aforesaid Confederates, trading in the respective Kingdoms, Dominions, Islands, Ports, Havens, and Places whatsoever, belonging unto, or in the Possession of the one or of the other party, shall be treated and dealt withal as the respective Natives; so as no time, or upon any occasion (altho' the same be for publick or particular Necessity) they shall be put to pay, or be

burdened with any Impositions, Taxes, or other Charges whatsoever,
excepting only the Customs, Alcavallas, *or Excise, which are paid by*
the Natives of the respective Dominions of the said Commonwealth and
King, and that all other Impositions, Taxes, and Charges, set or im-
posed by the one side or the other, upon the People of either, whether
for publick or particular use, are hereby abolished and declared Null;
nor shall any other Duties than as aforesaid, be set, or imposed, or
taken, by either side, in any time to come.

VI. And that no Office or Minister, in any of the Cities, Towns, or
Places of the said Commonwealth, or King, do demand, take, or exact,
greater Tolls, Customs, Payments, Rewards, Gifts, or other Charges
whatever, from the Merchants and the People of the other, than ought
to be taken by the virtue of the precedent Articles. And that the said
Merchants and People may understand and know certainly what is ordained in all things relating hereunto, it is agreed there shall be Tables
hung up in all the Publick Custom-Houses in the several Cities, Towns,
and Places of the Commonwealth of *England*, and of the King of *Spain*,
where such Custom and Excise, or *Alcavallas* are paid; wherein how
much and of what sort such Customs and Tolls are, whereof mention is
made in the foregoing Article, shall be set down in writing and declared,
as well for Wares Imported as Exported. Furthermore if any Officer or
other in their Names, shall upon any pretence openly or secretly demand or receive of any Merchant or People respectively, any summ or
summs of Mony, or other thing in the Name of Toll, Custom, Gift,
Stipend, or Reward, than what is set down in the said Tables, although
it were offered *Gratis*, that then such Officer, or their Deputy being
guilty as aforesaid, and convicted before a Competent Judge, in the
Country where the Crime was commited, shall be Imprisoned for three
Months, and shall forfeit triple the Mony or thing they took, as
aforesaid, whereof one half shall go to the said Parliament, or King, and
the other to the Informer; for which he may sue before any Competent
Judge in the Country where the Fault was commited.
   The Ambassador assented to this Article.

VII. That is shall be lawful for the People of the Common-Wealth of
England to transport and bring into *Spain,* and other the Countries and
Dominions of the King, and traffick therewith all sorts of Goods and
Wares of this Common-Wealth, or the Manufactures of the Islands,
Places and Plantations thereunto belonging, or such as are brought by
any *English* Factors from on this side, or beyond the *Cape of Good*

Hope. And again at their pleasure depart from the Dominions of the King of *Spain*, with any Commodities and Merchandizes, into any of the Territories, Islands and Dominions of the said Common-Wealth, *or any other place*, paying those Customs and Tributes which are mentioned in the preceding Articles, or otherwise Ratably according to their Proportion, and that all Goods, Wares, or Ships brought into the Territories of this Common-Wealth as Prize, and so adjudged, shall be taken for *English* Goods, which is the meaning of this Article.

The Ambassador adds before all sorts of Goods, &c. these Words, [like and according as it shall be declared in the insuing Article.] And leaves out the Words, [or any other place.]

VIII. That the People of the Common-Wealth of *England*, and the Subjects of the King of *Spain*, may freely without any Licence or Safe-Conduct, General or Special, Sail into each others Islands, Countries, Ports, Towns, or Villages, and Places possessed by either of them respectively and other Parts, as well in *America*, as *Asia* or *Africa*, and there to Traffick, Remain and Trade with all sorts of Wares and Merchandizes, and them at their Pleasure, in their own Ships, to Transport to any other Place or Country, any Law made and published by either part to the contrary thereof notwithstanding.

The Ambassador propounds instead of this the following Article, That the Subjects of Spain, *and the People of* England *respectively, may freely without any Licence or Safe-Conduct, General or Special, Sail into the Kingdoms, Dominions, Ports, Havens, Towns, and Villages of each other, and that there be free Comerce, except, as hitherto, in the Kingdoms, Provinces, Islands, Ports and Places strengthned with Forts, Lodges, or Castles, and all other possessed by the one or the other Party in the* East *or* West Indies, *or other Parts as well in* America, *as in* Asia *or* Africa, *so as the Subjects of* Spain *shall not Sail nor Trade into the Ports, Islands, Dominions and Plantations which* England *possesseth in the said Parts, nor the People of* England *into the Kingdoms, Islands and Dominions which in all the aforesaid Parts are possessed by and belong to* Spain.

IX. That the People of the Common-Wealth of *England*, Trading in any of the Kingdoms, Dominions, Islands, Territories or Plantations of the said King, be obliged to bring with them Certificates Signed and Sealed by the Officers of the Custom-Houses of the place where their Ships shall be laden, that may certifie the Ships Lading, or from such Persons as the Parliament shall to that purpose appoint, and such Certificates being produced, shall without difficulty be allowed and admitted by the Officers and Ministers of the King of *Spain*, and the Goods and Merchandizes therein mentioned held and reputed for lawful Goods.

The Ambassador desired that this Article may be made reciprocal, and that the following words be added after the word King, [like and according as is declared in the Precedent Article,] and consents to the rest.

X. And that the Officers of the Custom-House of both Parties, or other Persons that shall make Certificates, as is expressed in the foregoing Article, shall not commit Fraud herein, and if they do offend herein they shall lose their Places, and have farther Punishment inflicted upon them according to Law.

The Ambassador consents to this Article.

XI. That the People, Inhabitants and Subjects of either part, shall not upon any colour or pretence of Comerce, carry or send, directly or indirectly, to the Enemies or Rebels of the other, any *Contrabanda* or Prohibited Goods or Commodities, to wit, any kind of Guns, or Locks, or Iron Barrels, or any other Fire-works made for the use of War, Powder, Match, Bullets, Pikes, Swords, Javelins, Halbards, Musketts, Cannons, or other Instruments of War, as Morterpeices, Petardes, Granadoes, Rests, Bandaliers, Saltpetre, Bullets, Helmets, Headpieces, Caskets, Cuiriasses, Coats of Mail, or such like; nor Soldiers, Horse or Horse Furniture, Holsters, Rapiers, Belts, and all Furniture fashioned and made for use of War: Provided that under the Name of *Contrabanda* and Prohibited Goods, be not comprehended Wheat, Rye, or any other kind of Grain; neither Salt, Wine, Oyle, or any thing else that serves for the preservation of the Life of Men, which shall be free, and may be carried to the Places belonging to the Rebels and Enemies of either; as also all other Commodities which are not particularly abovenamed. And that if any of the forementioned Prohibited Goods shall be found upon the Ships of either part, going to the Rebels or Enemies of the one side or the other, they shall after due proof be made confiscate, and adjudged Prize to him that takes them, nevertheless the Ship on which such *Contrabanda* Goods are found, nor the other Wares and Goods, nor Owner or Mariners shall be molested or detained.

The Ambassador insisted to have added amongst Contrabanda Goods, all kinds of Mony, Gold, Silver, or Plate wrought or unwrought. As also these Words added after the word abovenamed, [except to such Towns and Places as are Besieged, block'd up, or assailed by the Arms and Power of either Party.] This Amendment was con-

sented to by the Counsel, and the former waved by himself, and so the Article was agreed.

XII. That the Ships of the Common-Wealth Sailing into the Dominions of the King of *Spain*, or any of his Ports, shall not be visited by the Ministers of the Inquisition, or Judge of *Contrabanda* Goods, or any others by their Authority; neither shall they put upon them Soldiers or Armed Men, for the Custody of them; neither shall the Officers of the Customs on either side search the Ships of the People or Subjects of either, that shall come into their respective Ports, Countries or Dominions, while their Ships are unlading, until they have put on Shoar all their Goods, but may in mean time have Officers on board the Ships, to see that the Goods be duly delivered, yet without any Charge to the Ship or Ships, or Owners thereof. And if any other Goods or Merchandizes be found on board the Ship or Ships, or Vessels, than are expressed in the Bill of Lading, and are discovered before the Ship be unladen, leave shall be given to make a post-Entry to save the Forfeiture. And in case Entry or Manifestation be not made within the time aforesaid, that then the particular Goods so taken shall be forfeited, and no other, nor other trouble or punishment inflicted upon the Merchants and Owners aforesaid.

Instead of this Article the Ambassador propounded the following Article. That the Ships and Vessels on either side, Sailing into the Dominions of the other, or their respective Ports or Havens shall be visited by the Officers and Ministers according the Custom and Practice used with the People and Subjects on both sides, so as the said Visits and Searches be made without any Molestation or Charges to the Ship or Ships, or Owners thereof; and that Entry be made of the Lading of the said Ship or Ships in the Custom-House, according to the usual form, which done, if any more Goods be found in the said Ship or ships, than are already entred, a term of four days shall be granted, beginning from the first unlading of the said Ships, to the end they make a post-Entry to safe the Forfeiture; and in case Entry or Manifestation be not made within the time aforesaid, that then the particular Goods so taken (though the unlading be not yet ended) shall be Forfeited, and no other Trouble or Punishment inflicted upon the Merchant and Owner aforesaid.

XIII. That the Ship or Ships belonging to the one Party or the other, or their respective People and Subjects, which shall come into each others Countries or Dominions, and unlade any part of their Goods and Merchandizes in any Port or Haven, being bound with the rest unto other

Parts, either without or within the aforesaid Dominions, shall not be compelled to enter or pay Custom for any other Goods and Merchandizes, than such as shall Land in such Port or Haven, nor constrained to give any Security for the Goods they carry elsewhere, nor other Security unless it be in case of Debt, Felony, Murther, Treason, or other Capital Offence.

The Ambassador consented to this Article.

XIV. That the People and Subjects, respectively of the one being in the Dominions, Territories, Countries, or Collonies of the other, be not compelled to sell their Merchandize for Brass Mony, or change them for other Monies, or things than they are willing, or having sold the same, to receive Payment in any other Specie than they contracted for any Law or Custom to the contrary of this Article notwithstanding.

This Article consented to.

XV. That it shall be lawful for the People and Subjects of both sides, to have access into their respective Ports, and there remain, and from thence to depart with the same Liberty, not only with their Ships of Merchandizes, and Ships of Burden, but also with their other Shipping furnished for War, armed and prepared to withstand the Face of Enemies, whether they shall arrive there by force of Tempest, or for repairing their Ships, or for Provision of Victuals, so as if they come in on their own accord, they be not such a number that may give just occasion of suspition, nor that they continue in the Havens, or about the Ports longer than they shall have just cause for the repairing of their Ships, or Provision of other Necessaries, lest they should be any occasion of interruption unto the free Commerce and Entercourse of other Friends and Nations, in Amity. And whenever unusual number of Ships of War come by accident to such Ports, it shall not be lawful for them to make any entrance into any the said Ports and Havens, unless they first obtain leave from them unto whom the said Ports do belong, unless they be driven so to do by Tempest, or some other necessity for avoiding the danger of the Sea, and in such case they shall forthwith make known to the Governour, or chief Magistrate of the Place the cause of the coming, neither shall they stay longer there than such Governour or Magistrate shall think fit, nor do any Hostile Act in those Ports, that may be prejudicial either to the said Common-Wealth or King.

The Ambassador desired that the number of Eight Ships of War might be Inserted instead of the indefinite number which was admited. As also that in the end of the Article might be added these Words [nor to their respective Enemies, which may chance to be in the Ports of either side, for as long as they shall continue there] which was admitted, and to this Article was agreed.

XVI. That neither the said Common-Wealth, nor King of *Spain*, shall by any Command General or Particular, or for any cause whatsoever Imbargue, Stop, Arrest, or Seize into their respective Service any Merchants, Masters of Ships, Pilots, or Mariners, their Ships, Merchandize, Wares, or other Goods belonging to them, of either of the other, being in their Ports or Waters, unless the Parliament, or said King, or the Parties to whom the said Ships appertain, be first admonished thereof, and shall also yeild his or their consent thereto; provided that thereby shall not be excluded the Arrests and Seisures in the ordinary way of Justice.

This Article was assented to.

XVII. That the Merchants on both sides, their Factors, Servants, as also their Ship-Masters and Mariners may, as well travelling and returning by Sea, and other Waters, as in the Havens of each other respectively, carry and use all sorts of Arms for Defence and Offence, without being compelled to Register the same, and also on Shoar wear and use Arms for their defence, according to the Custom of the Place.

This Article was consented to.

XVIII. That it shall be lawful for the Ships of the People or Subjects of the one side or the other to ride at Anchor in the Sea, or in any Road belonging to either, without being compelled to come into Port. And in case they be necessitated thereunto by Tempest, pursuits of Enemies or Pyrates, or any other Reason or Accident: It shall be lawful for them to depart again at their pleasure with their Ships and Merchandizes; provided they break not Bulk, nor expose any thing to Sale; neither shall they, riding at Anchor or entering in Port as aforesaid, be molested or searched; but it shall be sufficient for them in this case to shew their Pass-ports and Sea Letters, which the Officers of the said Common-Wealth or King respectively having seen, they may freely depart again with their Ships whither they please, without any further Impediment or Molestation.

The Ambassador consented to this Article with the addition following in the end thereof. But if there happen to be some suspicion that they carry Merchandizes of Contrabanda *to the Enemy of the one or the other Party: In that case they shall not only be obliged to shew their Pass-ports and Sea Letters unto the Officers as before, but likewise to*

give a particular Specification of their Lading, which being seen, and
found that there is no Contrabanda *Goods in the said Ship or Ships,*
they may freely depart, as aforesaid.

XIX. That all Goods, Wares, and Merchandizes whatsoever of the said
Common-Wealth or King, or their respective People and Subjects, laden
or unladen, on board any Ship or Ships belonging to the Enemy on the
one side or the other, shall be Confiscate and Prize, as well as the Ships.
But all Goods and Merchandizes whatsoever belonging to the Enemies
of the one side or the other, and laden or found on board the Ships and
Vessels of either of the said Parties, or the People or Subjects of either
shall be free, unless the same be *Contrabanda* Goods, and is expressed
in the former Article.

The Ambassador consented to this Article upon condition the follow-
ing Clause were admited, which takes in the substance of the last Article
of those 24 which he formerly delivered in. The Clause is this. And here
it is declared, that whatsoever Goods, Commodities, or Merchandizes,
growing, produced or made in any part of the King of Spain's *Domin-*
ions and Territories whatsoever, belonging to the Subjects of the said
King, may be carried and transported to the Dominions of the Com-
mon-Wealth of England, *in any Ship or Ships whatsoever that shall*
belong to the said King, or to his Subjects, though they be not of the
same Place, where the said Commodities or Merchandizes are made or
grown, any Law, Statute or Custom to the contrary notwithstanding.

XX. To the end that the greater Advantage may by this concord accrue
to the respective People and Subjects of the said Common-Wealth, and
King of *Spain*, in their Kingdoms and Dominions, each of them shall
endeavour jointly and severally that their People and Subjects respectively have not the Passages stopp'd or letted unto any of their Ports,
Kingdoms and Dominions, nor that their Ports or Rivers be shut; but
that they may with their Ships, Merchandizes, and Carriages freely and
without Impediment come and go (paying the Customs and Tolls, as in
the precedent Articles be expressed) to and from the said Kingdoms,
Countries, Cities, Ports, and Places; and with the like Liberty to depart;
and particularly the King of *Spain* shall do his utmost to open the Passage by the River *Skelde* to *Antwerp*.

The Ambassador offered his consent to this Article, adding these
Words, [except into the Ports and Rivers where heretofore there was no
free access] after the word shut. *And omitting that Clause concerning*
the River Skelde, *in the latter end of the Article.*

XXI. And to the end all Impediments may be taken away, and the Merchant Adventurers of this Common-Wealth permitted to return into *Brabant* and *Flanders*, and the other Provinces of the Low Countries, under the Jurisdiction of the said King. All Laws, Edicts and Acts whatever, whereby the Importation of Cloaths or other Woollen Manufactures that are either Dyed or Undyed, Dressed or Rough, into *Flanders*, or the said other Provinces are forbidden, or whereby any Custom, Tribute, Tax, Charge or Monies are by Permission or any other manner laid or imposed upon Cloath or other the aforesaid Woollen Manufactures that are carried into the said Countries or Cities, except that antient Tribute of two___upon every peice of Cloath, and so proportionably upon every such Woollen Manufactures, shall be henceforth utterly Null and Void: And such like Taxes and Impositions shall not hereafter at any time be Let or Laid upon such Cloaths or Manufactures, upon any pretences soever. And all *English* Merchants trading in any the said Provinces or Cities, and Places thereof, and their Factors, Commissaries or Servants, shall hereafter enjoy all Privileges, Exemptions, Immunities, and Benefits which heretofore were agreed and granted by antient Treaties made between the then Kings of *England* and the Dukes of *Burgundy* and Governours of the Low Countries. And moreover other Privileges, Immunities and Exemptions suitable to the present state of Affairs, shall be granted for the Encouragement of the said Merchants and Security of Trade, according as it shall be agreed in a special Treaty to be made hereupon between both Parties.

The Ambassador objected against this Article, that it was against the Privileges granted to the Subjects of Flanders, *and therefore could not be granted. And upon the debate thereof the Council was willing to wave it, if the Ambassador thought it not for the advantage of* Spain; *but the Ambassador acknowledging it beneficial to their Subjects, said, That though the whole could not be now granted, yet it might be convenient to have something done therein, and propounded in the stead thereof the ensuing Article.*

And as concerning the antient Treaty of Entercourse and Commerce which have sometimes been betwixt the Kingdoms of England, Scotland *and* Ireland, *and the Dominions of the Dukes of* Burgundy, *and Princes of the Low Countries, which in some times of trouble might have been in some points intermitted. It is agreed by way of Provision between the said Parties, that they shall retain and have their antient Force and Authority; and that they shall be used on both parts, as they were before the War between* Don Philip II. *King of* Spain, *and* Elizabeth *Queen of* England, *according as it was agreed on in the Treaties of Peace, and particularly in the Year 1604. in the 22d Article, and in the Year 1630. in the 18th Article, reserving to a farther Treaty the Adjustation of the Privileges, Immunities and Exemptions which shall be thought convenient to be reciprocally granted for the Encouragement and Security of the respective Merchants Adventurers of the Common Wealth of* England, *into* Brabant *and* Flanders, *and those other Provinces of the* Netherlands *under the King of* Spain.

XXII. And for that the Rights of Commerce which do ensue by Peace, should be rendered unprofitable, as they would be if the People and Inhabitants of *England* should be troubled upon the account of their Religion, whilst they do remain in the Kingdoms and Dominions of *Spain*. Therefore to the intent that their Traffick may be safe without danger, it is agreed and concluded, by and between the said Common-Wealth and King of *Spain*, that no trouble or molestation be given to the People of the said Common-wealth Trading in any of the Kingdoms or Countries of the King of *Spain*'s Dominions, for the cause of Religion, but that it be free and lawful for the said People, either in their own Houses, or in the Houses of other *English* dwelling there, or in their Ships, to worship God, and exercise their Religion, in their own manner and form, according to their Consciences; and also read *English* Bibles, or any other Books, without Let or Molestation, either from the Inquisition or their Ministers, and other Judges; and that neither their Bodies nor Estates be seized on by the Inquisitions, or Imprisoned, nor for any of the said Causes liable to their Jurisdiction.

   Instead of this Article the Ambassador propounded this following. And for that the Right of Commerce which do ensue by Peace, ought not to be made unfruitful, as they would be, if the People and Inhabitants of the Common-Wealth of England, *whilest they have recourse to and from the Kingdoms and Dominions of the King of* Spain, *and do remain there for Commerce, or their own Business, should be molested in the cause of Conscience. Therefore to the intent their Traffick may be safe, and without danger, both at Sea and Land, the said King of* Spain *shall (that the People of the said Common Wealth be not troubled and molested for the said cause of Conscience contrary to the Laws of Commerce, so as they give no Scandal) and the said Common-Wealth shall also provide for the same Reasons, that in none of their Dominions the Subjects of said King be troubled or molested, contrary to the Laws, so as they give no Scandal.*

XXIII. That the Captain, Officers and Mariners of the Ships belonging to the People and Subjects of the Common-Wealth, being within the

Kingdoms, Governments or Islands of the said King of *Spain*, shall not commence any Action or procure any trouble against the Ships of the People of the said Common-Wealth for their Wages and Salleries, upon pretence that they are of the *Romish* Religion; neither shall they upon the same or like Pretext, put themselves under the King of *Spains* Protection, or take up Arms for him, but if any Controversie arise between the Merchants and Masters of Ships, or between the Masters and Mariners, the decision thereof shall be left only to the Consul of the Nation, so as notwithstanding he which will not submit to his Arbitrement may appeal into *England*.

The Ambassador propounded a Reciprocation in this Article. 2dly, That the Words Romish Religion *be omitted, and instead thereof under any colour or pretext whatsoever. 3dly, That the appeal to* England *might be omitted as needless, which was not much gainsaid, and so this Article was agreed.*

XXIV. That in case of seisure upon the Estate of any Person or Persons within the Lands and Territories of the said King, by the Inquisitions, or other Tribunal or Minister of Justice, the Estates and Debts which, *bona fide*, belong to the People of this Common-Wealth, and shall happen to be in the possession of such Criminals, shall not be forfeited, but restored to the right owner in Specie, if they be remaining, or otherwise the just value of them, according to the Contract or the Summ which was contracted for betwixt the Parties, within one Month after such Seisure or Proscription.

This Article was agreed to, taking away the Word Inquisition, *as being comprehended in these Words, whatsoever Tribunal, and that instead of one Month, there be allowed three Months for Satisfaction and making it Reciprocal.*

XXV. If any prohibited Goods or Merchandizes shall happen to be Exported out of the Dominions, Kingdoms or Territories of either part, by the respective People or Subjects of the one or the other, that in such case the prohibited Goods only shall be Confiscate, and no other, nor any other Punishment inflicted upon the Delinquent.

The Ambassador consents with this addition in the close, Except in case of Exporting without Licence out of the respective Dominions, of the one or the other side, any Gold or Plate, wrought or unwrought, in which case any Person so offending, shall be subject to the Penalties of the Laws of either their respective Dominions,

XXVI. That the Goods and Estates of the People or Subjects of the one Party, dying within the Countries and Dominions of the other, be preserved to the lawful Heirs and Successors of the Deceased, the right of a third Party always reserved.

This Article consented to.

XXVII. That the Goods and Estates of the People of this Common-Wealth dying intestate in the Dominions of the King of *Spain* be Inventoried, with their Papers and Writings, and Books of Account, by the Consul, and put into the Hands of two or three Merchants, to be named by the same Consul, to be kept for the Proprietors and Creditors; neither shall the Crusada or any of the King's Subjects interpose therein.

This Article was consented to by the Ambassador, with this Variation in the latter end, after the word Creditors, And in such cases as it shall belong to the Cruzada, in the Dominions of the King of Spain, *to name the said Depositaries, that it be done with satisfaction of the* English *Consul.*

XXVIII. That the Immunities and Privileges given by former Treaties and Grants to the Merchants and Subjects of either Nation shall wholly be revived, and have their full Force and Strength. And that the People of this Common-Wealth, Trading or Dwelling in any of the Kingdoms, Governments, Islands, Ports or Territories of the said King of *Spain* have, use and enjoy those Privileges and Immunities, which the said King granted and confirmed to the *English* Merchants remaining in *Andaluzia*, by Writing bearing date the 19th of *March*, and 9th of *November*, 1645.

The first Point of this Article the Ambassador agreed to, for renewing Antient Privileges, so as they be not contrary to what is settled in this Treaty. For the Second Part he Pen'd it thus, And likewise that the Privileges, Infranchisements, Liberties and Immunities as were granted and confirmed by the said King of Spain, *his Schedules of the* 19th *of* March, *and* 9th *of* November, 1645. *to the* English *Merchants residing in* Andaluzia *be renewed and confirmed, whereby be refuseth to extend those Privileges to the* English *Merchants in general, which were granted to those in* Andaluzia, *which was the scope of the Councils Article.*

XXIX. That if it shall happen hereafter, that any displeasure ariseth between the said Common-Wealth and King of *Spain*, that may endanger the interruption of mutual Commerce and Intercourse, the respective People of either Party shall have such timely notice or monition to Transport their Merchandizes, without any Arrest, Restraint, Molestation, or Disturbance in the mean Season, to be done or given unto them, or their Persons or Merchandizes.

The Ambassador consents to this Article.

XXX. That the Merchants of both Nations, and their Factors, Servants, Families, Commissaries, or others by them imployed; as also the Masters of Ships, Pilots and Mariners, freely shall and may safely abide in the Dominions, Countries and Territories of the said Common-Wealth or King; and also in their Ports and Shoars. And that the People and Subjects of the one may have and hold in the Countries and Dominions of the other Party, their own Houses to dwell in, and their Warehouses for their Goods and Merchandizes, for such time as they shall take them, without any Molestation whatever.

This Article consented to.

XXXI. That if any Controversie happen to be moved in the Dominions of either Party, by any Person not being under the Dominion of, nor Subject to either Party, for or upon occasion of any Depredations or Spoil committed upon them at Sea, the cause shall be referred to the Judge of the Jurisdiction under the said Common Wealth or King, against whose People or Subjects the Suit is commenced.

The Ambassador agrees to this Article.

XXXII. The People and Subjects of the one side and the other shall have and enjoy, in each others Countries and Territories, safely, as ample Privileges, Security and Freedom as are granted and allowed to the People and Subjects of any other Common-Wealth or Kingdom whatsoever.

The Ambassador agrees to this Article.

XXXIII. The Consuls who shall hereafter reside in any part of the King of *Spains* Dominions, for the Aid and Protection of the People of this Common-Wealth, shall for the time to come be named by the Parliament of the Common-Wealth of *England*, and being so named shall have and exercise the same Power and Authority in the execution of their Charges, as any of the former Consuls have done.

The Ambassador agreed to this Article, so it be Reciprocal, and so his Majesty may name his own Subjects for Consuls in any part of the Dominions of the Common-Wealth of England.

XXXIV. The People of this Common-Wealth residing in *Spain*, shall not be compeled to keep their Accounts in the *Spanish* Tongue, nor to shew the Books and Papers of Accounts to any Person, unless it be for Evidence for desiding of Controversies, neither shall they be seized upon, arrested, or taken out of their Possession upon any pretence whatsoever. And the Subjects of the said King shall throughout all the Dominions of *England* enjoy the like Liberty and Immunities.

The Ambassador agreed to this Article.

XXXV. That convenient place shall be ordained and granted for the burying of the Bodies of such of the People of this Common-Wealth as shall die within any of the Dominions of the King of *Spain*.

The Ambassador consented to this Article.

Appendix D

The Shadow Secretariat

The men appointed to secretariat positions in the area of foreign affairs, those such as Georg Weckherlin, John Thurloe, Philip Meadows, and Andrew Marvell, are discussed in the text as they enter the narrative. Another group, a "shadow secretariat" of sorts, although they did not receive official appointments, played an important role in the conduct of relations with foreign states; they were called upon as the need arose and apparently paid generously for their services.

The presence of other translators in the governments of the Republic is significant to our study in that it lends weight to the position that Milton's superiors used him selectively in correspondence, relying on him in exchanges with particular cities and states over a period of time. From 1650 to 1652, for example, while Theodore Haak was available for correspondence with the Dutch and René Augier with the French, Milton could focus his efforts on Hamburg and the Iberian States. The disarray within the secretariat in early 1652, occasioned by Milton's blindness and Frost's death and exacerbated by the flood of foreign diplomats on English shores, doubtless temporarily upset this practice of divided labor; but Thurloe soon returned order to the process.

The English Republic was able to attract to public service a diverse and richly talented group of individuals at the third and fourth tier of the government structure, men who, although they did not work under Milton's direction, surely looked to the Secretary for Foreign Languages as a model of sacrifice and dedication to the "grand old cause." Samuel Hartlib, for example, will be remembered for prompting the poet to write *Of Education* and attracting John Amos Comenius to England in 1641. Further, in the late 1640s he and Theodore Haak, another member of the shadow secretariat, were active in the "Invisible College," which met in London and from which grew the Royal Society. Thus,

Milton shared duties with a group of highly accomplished men, whom he must have encountered almost daily as he fulfilled the obligations of his office.

One of the more revealing of the entries in the Order Books of the Council is that of 26 June 1650, which reads, "The declaration to be translated into Latin by Mr. Milton, Dutch by Theodore Haak, and French by Mons. Augier." The last named, René Augier, was Parliament's agent in France from 1644 until he was recalled in March 1650; and he had in fact, like Georg Weckherlin, served King Charles in his office for some years prior to committing himself to the Parliamentary cause. A year after his recall Council took the unusual step of officially recognizing his loyalty to the Republic, although admittedly in somewhat subdued terms; those years in Paris, the order reads, demonstrate that "by his good services he made his affection to the commonwealth apparent."[1] Because of those services and his knowledge of French affairs, he was employed in various ways by Council and became acquainted with Milton. It was through Augier that the poet learned of Leonard Philaras's admiration for the first *Defence*, and on writing to Philaras he referred to his coworker as "a man renowned here for his remarkable fidelity in transacting the diplomatic business of this state."[2] Augier continued on the payroll until at least 17 April 1655, when he fell victim to the same belt-tightening order that reduced Milton's income. His annual salary of £182 was one of those "taken away" by Council on that occasion, and it would appear that his dismissal was permanent, for on the same day Thurloe was instructed to "put the part of the Intelligence which is managed by Rene Augier into the Common Charge of intelligence and to order it for the future."[3]

Augier's name appears in the record now and again, most frequently in reference to his petitions for arrears in pay, one of which he addressed from debtor's prison. The Council seemed reluctant to allow what was owed him; and they delayed by shuttling his requests from one committee to another until he finally died, whereupon they authorized his widow a pension of 60 shillings a week.[4] Augier's term of service is suggestive in that it came to an end at precisely the time when Milton's French correspondence began. He was dismissed on 17 April 1655 and the poet's first letters to Louis XIV and Cardinal Mazarin were dated 25 May.

1. *CSPD* 3:209.
2. *Prose* 4:852. See also French 3:220–24, 372.
3. *CSPD* 8:127, 128; SP 25/76/31.
4. E403/2608/277.

Theodore Haak, an ordained deacon, had been employed during the 1640s by both the Westminster Assembly and Parliament to translate Dutch publications into English; and he appears to have undertaken diplomatic missions late in the decade, for Weckherlin wrote to him in Germany, the United Netherlands, and Scandinavia. The Republic retained his services as a translator very early on. In July 1649 the Council ordered that he receive the same stipend as Samuel Hartlib, Peter Sterry, and others, that is, £100 a year; and apparently this salary was no sinecure. He was frequently engaged by the Council; the following year both he and Hartlib were awarded £50 "for many good services in their correspondence beyond seas, and to enable them to continue" it. Two years later he received an additional £100 "for translating a book out of Dutch into English"; and it is clear that he remained in good favor with the Council, for on 19 March 1656 they authorized him "a pension of 100 per annum and the arrears thereof for 3 years and 3 quarters, being 375."[5]

This evidence strongly suggests that Haak was regularly employed in correspondence with the United Netherlands, which may help to explain why Milton was not. There are only a handful of letters to the Dutch in the seventeenth-century sources of the State Papers, and they are for the most part routine petitions and letters of credential. Obviously, a good many more were written, for the United Netherlands was enormously important in shaping the Republic's foreign policy; but Haak's is the only name in the Order Books associated with Dutch translations. After the Restoration he was admitted as a fellow of the Royal Society in 1663 and later translated parts of his colleague's *Paradise Lost* into High Dutch.

It is not as easy to identify Samuel Hartlib with correspondence to any particular nation as it is Augier and Haak, since he seems to have been engaged in a variety of activities. As has been noted, he and Haak were awarded £100 for unspecified services in 1649 and an additional £50 the following year "to enable them to continue" their "many good services" in foreign correspondence; and payments to Hartlib were continued in 1651, another £100 for "intelligence and correspondence maintained by him abroad." Subsequently his salary was raised to £200 a year and as late as January 1659 he was still on the payroll.[6] There is nothing in the Order Books to indicate what he did for the money, since "correspondence maintained by him abroad" might refer to personal contacts rather than the kind of work in which Milton was engaged. At

5. *CSPD* 1:177, 233; 2:292; 4:619. The pension is recorded in E403/2608/36.
6. *CSPD* 2:292; 4:27, 488, 502; 5:489; 7:44; 12:585.

one point he "attended the Council of Trade . . . in reference to the tanners and skinners of London," for which services the Council undertook "to consider what should be given him for encouragement of his public undertakings"; and during the Protectorate he carried on essential diplomatic correspondence during Thurloe's frequent illnesses.[7] He was simply one of those immensely useful hangers-on who was never appointed to a post in government but managed to receive handsome rewards for his many talents.

There were others who performed secretarial duties from time to time: John Dury, an ordained minister, was appointed librarian at St. James at a salary of £200 a year; and there were added benefits. When he translated *Eikonoklastes* into French, Thurloe was instructed "to consider a fit reward" for the effort.[8] In 1654 Cromwell sent him to Switzerland on a mission to unify the various Protestant churches there, and for the next three years he traveled throughout Germany and the United Netherlands encouraging the cause of Christian unity.[9]

On 2 February 1652, "Mons. Rosin" was engaged "for translating French papers into English for the Committee for Foreign Affairs," perhaps while Augier was in prison. Leo Miller is persuaded that Lewis Rosin assisted Milton in the Dutch negotiations of 1652 and cites Aitzema's diary, which states that Rosin translated the Dutch Declaration into French.[10]

John Hall was employed by the Council as early as May 1649 and awarded £100 "for answering pamphlets against the commonwealth"; and when he petitioned for the continuation of his pension in May 1654, he based his case on the claim that he had "been a constant servant of several Councils." Although it is uncertain just what his services were, on that plea presumably he received the pension, for his was one of those "taken away" the following April.[11]

Last, the public record reflects a payment of £50 on 19 October 1657 to "John Driden" for unspecified services.[12]

7. *CSPD* 4:488; Vaughan 2:433–40.

8. *CSPD* 3:208; 4:492.

9. *Prose* 5:875. Cromwell's letter of 27 March 1654 to the Geneva Senate, informing them of Dury's mission, has been attributed by some to Milton, though there is no evidence for it (*Works* 13:643; *Prose* 5:875). In March 1657 Milton prepared Cromwell's letter to the landgrave of Hesse in which he praises Dury's long effort to forward "the same Reconciliation" (W88, P121). In 1668 Dury's daughter, Dora Katherina, married Milton's good friend, Henry Oldenburg.

10. Miller, *John Milton's Writings*, 30–59; "New Milton Texts" 286. Miller located the diary in the Algemeen Rijksarchief, Collectie Aitzema, Invent. nr. 46.

11. *CSPD* 1:139; 7:163; 8:217.

12. SP 18/180/193.

Appendix E

The Letters of State

The State Papers are listed below under two heads. In Table 1 the sequence is that adopted by *Works* 13, which in general follows the order of *Literae*. In Table 2 the documents are listed chronologically by country. For a chronological arrangement of the entire collection, readers may consult *Prose* 5: ix–xiv. Both *Works* and *Prose* add a number of documents not in the seventeenth-century sources, however, and each includes several not in the other edition. *Prose* occasionally lists a document only to dismiss it. Letters marked "*" are not cited in the text. Those marked "#" are doubtfully attributed to Milton. Letters are indexed to the text.

Table 1

W1, P5—Parliament to Hamburg, 10 August 1649: 35n, 36.

W2, P6—Parliament to Hamburg, 4 January 1650: 37.

W3, P12—Parliament to the king of Spain, 4 February 1650: 89, 90.

W4, P11—Parliament to the king of Spain, 4 February 1650: 36n, 39, 89n, 90.

W5, P10—Parliament to the king of Portugal, 4 February 1650: 36n, 43, 44n.

W6, P7—Parliament to the king of Portugal, 24 February 1650: 44, 44n.

W7, P24—Parliament to the king of Spain, 30 January 1652: 92, 92n, 94, 94n.

W8, P33—Council of State to the Spanish ambassador, 30 January 1652: 52, 91, 94, 94n.

*W9, P13—Council of State to the archduke of Austria, 28 March 1650.

W10, P15—Parliament to the king of Portugal, 27 April 1650: 44, 45n.

W11, P14—Parliament to Hamburg, 2 April 1650: 37, 89n.

W12, P16—Parliament to Hamburg, 31 May 1650: 40, 41.

W13, P17—Parliament to the king of Spain, 28 June 1650: 91, 93, 94n.

W14, P19—Council of State to the governors of Andalusia and Galicia, 7 November 1650: 10n, 45.

*W15, P25—Parliament to the Senate of Danzig, 6 February 1651.

W16, P20—Council of State to the Portuguese envoy, 19 December 1650: 40, 46.

P26—Anglo-Portuguese negotiations, February–June 1651: 53.

W17, P29—Parliament to the duke of Tuscany, 20 January 1652: 10, 112n, 224n.

W18, P37—Parliament to Hamburg, 12 March 1652: 35n, 40, 41, 224n.

W19, P36—Parliament to the queen of Sweden, 11 March 1652: 163n, 224n.

W20—Omitted as virtually identical to W17, P29.

W21, P28—Parliament to the king of Spain, 14 July 1651: 93.

W22, P61—Council of State to the duke of Venice, 2 February 1653: 224n.

W23, P40—Council of State to the Spanish ambassador, 31 March 1652: 52n, 94, 224n.

W24, P41—Parliament to the king of Denmark, 13 April 1652: 70n, 101, 101n, 224n.

W25, P43—Parliament to the Hanse Towns, 13 April 1652: 35n, 42, 42n.

W26, P42—Parliament to Hamburg, 13 April 1652: 35n, 42, 42n, 224n.

W27, P46—Council of State to the duke of Tuscany, 29 July 1652: 83, 112.

W28, P48—Council of State to the Spanish ambassador, 10 August 1652: 52n, 95n, 224n.

W29, P50—Council of State to the Danish ambassadors, 13 September 1652: 52n, 101, 104, 224n.

W30, P51—Council of State to the Danish ambassadors, 13 September 1652: 52n, 101, 104, 224n.

W31, P49—Council of State to the duke of Tuscany, 16 September 1652: 112.

W32, P54—Council of State to the Spanish ambassador, 11 November 1652: 93, 97, 98n, 224n.

W33, P53—Council of State to the Spanish ambassador, 11 November 1652: 90, 97, 98n, 112n.

*W60, P86—Cromwell to the duke of Venice, December 1655.

W61, P85—Cromwell to the king of France, December 1655: 156n.

W62, P87—Cromwell to the Swiss Protestant Cantons, January 1656: 99, 164n.

W63, P89—Cromwell to the king of Sweden, 7 February 1656: 164.

W64, P122—Cromwell to the king of Denmark, March 1657: 172n.

W65, P67—Cromwell to the king of Portugal, 25 July 1654: 47n, 50, 89n, 110n.

W66, P92—Cromwell to the United Netherlands, 1 April 1656: 86n.

W67, P95—Cromwell to the king of Sweden, 19 April 1656: 63n, 89n, 172n.

W68, P97—Cromwell to the king of France, 14 May 1656: 156n.

W69, P99—Cromwell to the United Netherlands, 31 May 1656: 86n.

W70, P98—Cromwell to the United Netherlands, 30 May 1656: 86n.

W71, P103—Cromwell to the king of Portugal, July 1656: 51n.

W72, P104—Cromwell to the king of Sweden, 30 July 1656: 63n, 89n, 172n.

W73, P111—Cromwell to the king of France, 25 September 1656: 152, 152n, 157n.

W74, P113—Cromwell to Cardinal Mazarin, 25 September 1656: 152n, 153, 157, 159n.

W75, P109—Cromwell to the United Netherlands, 21 August 1656: 86, 164.

W76, P105—Cromwell to the king of Portugal, August 1656: 50.

W77, P106—Cromwell to the king of Portugal, August 1656: 50.

W78, P107—Cromwell to Conde d'Odemira, August 1656: 50.

W79, P108—Cromwell to the king of Sweden, 21(?) August 1656: 152n, 164, 192n.

W80, P110—Cromwell to Holland, 10 September 1656: 86n.

W81, P112—Cromwell to the king of France, 25(?) September 1656: 156n.

W82, P114—Cromwell to the king of Portugal, October 1656: 51n, 89, 89n.

W83, P117—Cromwell to the king of Sweden, 22 October 1656: 172n.

W84, P115—Cromwell to the king of Portugal, October 1656: 51n.

*W85, P116—Cromwell to the Senate of Hamburg, 16 October 1656.

W86, P120—Cromwell to the king of France, *after* 1 January 1657: 153, 156n.

W87, P119—Cromwell to the king of Denmark, 4 December 1656: 39, 110n, 164n, 192.

W88, P121—Cromwell to the landgrave of Hesse, March 1657: 162n, 250n.

W89, P142—Cromwell to the duke of Courland, March 1658: 166n.
W90, P125—Cromwell to Danzig, 10 April 1657: 172n.
W91, P124—Cromwell to the emperor of Russia, 10 April 1657: 89n, 166.
W92, P127—Cromwell to the king of Sweden, 20 August 1657: 39n, 135n, 167.
W93, P126—Council of State to the French ambassador, August 1657: 157n.
W94, P128—Cromwell to the elector of Brandenburg, 20 August 1657: 39n, 89, 135n, 167.
W95, P129—Cromwell to Hamburg, 20 August 1657: 10, 39n, 89, 135n, 167.
W96, P130—Cromwell to Bremen, 20 August 1657: 10, 39n, 89, 135n, 167.
W97, P131—Cromwell to Lübeck, 20 August 1657: 10, 39, 89, 135n, 167, 224n.
W98, P133—Cromwell to Hamburg, 20 August 1657: 39, 89, 135n, 167.
W99, P132—Cromwell to the duke of Holstein, 20 August 1657: 39n, 89, 135n.
W100, P134—Cromwell to the duke of Tuscany, 10 September 1657: 120.
W101, P135—Cromwell to the elector of Brandenburg, 23(?) September 1657: 89, 168.
W102, P136—Council of State to the French ambassador, October 1657: 157n.
W103, P137—Cromwell to the duke of Venice, 22 October 1657: 63n.
W104, P138—Cromwell to the United Netherlands, 12 November 1657: 63n, 86n, 89n.
W105, P141—Cromwell to the United Netherlands, 17 December 1657: 86n, 89n.
W106, P140—Cromwell to Holland, December 1657: 86n, 89n, 135n.
W107, P139—Cromwell to the duke of Tuscany, December 1657: 120.
W108, P143—Cromwell to the king of Sweden, 30 March 1658: 168, 192.
W109, P144—Cromwell to the duke of Tuscany, 7 April 1658: 121.
W110, P151—Cromwell to the king of France, 26 May 1658: 151, 151n, 156n, 157.
W111, P152—Cromwell to the Swiss Protestant Cantons, 26 May 1658: 151.
W112, P79—Cromwell to Cardinal Mazarin, 25 May 1655: 142,143n, 147n, 151, 152n, 158n.

W113, P146—Cromwell to the king of France, May 1658: 89n, 152n, 154.

W114, P147—Cromwell to Cardinal Mazarin, May 1658: 89n, 152n, 154.

W115, P149—Cromwell to Cardinal Mazarin, May 1658: 89n, 152n, 154.

P150—Cromwell to Cardinal Mazarin, 20 May 1658: 154, 159n.

W116, P148—Cromwell to the king of France, May 1658: 89n, 152n, 154.

W117, P145—Cromwell to the duke of Tuscany, 14 May 1658: 121.

W118, P154—Cromwell to the king of France, 19 June 1658: 152n, 155.

W119, P155—Cromwell to Cardinal Mazarin, 19 June 1658: 152n, 155.

W120, P153—Cromwell to the king of Sweden, 4 June 1658: 172n.

W121, P158—Cromwell to the king of Portugal, August 1658: 51n.

*W122, P66—Cromwell to the archduke of Austria, 18 July 1654.

*W123, *Prose 5*: 874—Commissioners of the Great Seal to the Parliament of Paris, n.d.

W124, P159—R. Cromwell to the king of France, 6 September 1658: 11, 87n, 152n, 157, 169.

W125, P160—R. Cromwell to Cardinal Mazarin, 6 September 1658: 11, 87n, 152n, 153, 157, 159n, 169.

W126, P161—R. Cromwell to the king of Sweden, October 1658: 169.

W127, P163—R. Cromwell to the king of Sweden, 13 November 1658: 39, 169.

W128, P162—R. Cromwell to the king of Sweden, 26 October 1658: 172n.

W129, P165—R. Cromwell to the king of Sweden, 28 January 1659: 172n.

W130, P164—R. Cromwell to West Friesland, 27 January 1659: 86n.

W131, P166—R. Cromwell to the king of France, 18 February 1659: 156n, 157.

W132, P167—R. Cromwell to Cardinal Mazarin, 19 February 1659: 156, 157n.

W133, P169—R. Cromwell to the king of Portugal, 23 February 1659: 51n.

W134, P168—R. Cromwell to Cardinal Mazarin, 22 February 1659: 156, 157n.

W135, P174—Parliament to the king of Sweden, 15 May 1659: 11, 36n, 39, 171, 178.

W159, P118—King of Denmark to Cromwell, 16 February 1656: 110n, 164n, 176n.

*W160, *Prose* 5: 876—Cromwell to Sir Thomas Bendish, 19 April 1656.

*W161, P90—Cromwell to Hamet Bashaw, April 1656.

*W162, P91—Cromwell to the Council of Algiers, April 1656.

*W163, P100—Cromwell to the Council of Algiers, June 1656.

W164, P123—Instructions for the agent to Russia, 10 April 1657: 89, 150, 154n, 166.

*W165, P3—Princess Sophie to the Prince Maurice, 13 April 1649.

W167A, P4—Dutch ambassador to Parliament, 18 May 1649: 77.

W167B, P30—Dutch ambassadors to the Council of State, 24 January 1652: 77.

W167C, P32—Council of State to the Dutch ambassadors, 29 January 1652: 78, 78n, 80.

W167D, P31—Council of State to the Dutch ambassadors, 29 January 1652: 78, 78n.

W167E, P38—Council of State to the Dutch ambassadors, 15 March 1652: 52, 79, 110n.

#W167F, P44—Dutch ambassadors to the Council of State, 12 April 1652: 80.

W167H, P27—Council of State to the Spanish ambassador, June 1651: 93.

#W169, P84—A Declaration of the Lord Protector, 26 October 1655: 88.

W170, P96—Anglo-Swedish Treaty, 17 July 1656: 174.

Note: W167C–F are published in *Works* 18: 80–127.

Table 2

This list contains duplications since letters from one country to another often relate to the affairs of a third, such as those to various European heads of state on the Piedmont Massacre and Sweden's War in the North.

Hamburg and the Hanse Towns

W151, P1—Parliament to Hamburg, 2 April 1649: 34, 35, 35n, 44n, 89, 89n.

P2—Parliament to Hamburg, 2 April 1649: 36, 44n, 89.

W1, P5—Parliament to Hamburg, 10 August 1649: 35n, 36.

W2, P6—Parliament to Hamburg, 4 January 1650: 37.

W159, P118—King of Denmark to Cromwell, 16 February 1656: 110n, 164n, 176n.

*W160, *Prose 5*: 876—Cromwell to Sir Thomas Bendish, 19 April 1656.

*W161, P90—Cromwell to Hamet Bashaw, April 1656.

*W162, P91—Cromwell to the Council of Algiers, April 1656.

*W163, P100—Cromwell to the Council of Algiers, June 1656.

W164, P123—Instructions for the agent to Russia, 10 April 1657: 89, 150, 154n, 166.

*W165, P3—Princess Sophie to the Prince Maurice, 13 April 1649.

W167A, P4—Dutch ambassador to Parliament, 18 May 1649: 77.

W167B, P30—Dutch ambassadors to the Council of State, 24 January 1652: 77.

W167C, P32—Council of State to the Dutch ambassadors, 29 January 1652: 78, 78n, 80.

W167D, P31—Council of State to the Dutch ambassadors, 29 January 1652: 78, 78n.

W167E, P38—Council of State to the Dutch ambassadors, 15 March 1652: 52, 79, 110n.

#W167F, P44—Dutch ambassadors to the Council of State, 12 April 1652: 80.

W167H, P27—Council of State to the Spanish ambassador, June 1651: 93.

#W169, P84—A Declaration of the Lord Protector, 26 October 1655: 88.

W170, P96—Anglo-Swedish Treaty, 17 July 1656: 174.

Note: W167C–F are published in *Works* 18: 80–127.

Table 2

This list contains duplications since letters from one country to another often relate to the affairs of a third, such as those to various European heads of state on the Piedmont Massacre and Sweden's War in the North.

Hamburg and the Hanse Towns

W151, P1—Parliament to Hamburg, 2 April 1649: 34, 35, 35n, 44n, 89, 89n.

P2—Parliament to Hamburg, 2 April 1649: 36, 44n, 89.

W1, P5—Parliament to Hamburg, 10 August 1649: 35n, 36.

W2, P6—Parliament to Hamburg, 4 January 1650: 37.

W89, P142—Cromwell to the duke of Courland, March 1658: 166n.

W90, P125—Cromwell to Danzig, 10 April 1657: 172n.

W91, P124—Cromwell to the emperor of Russia, 10 April 1657: 89n, 166.

W92, P127—Cromwell to the king of Sweden, 20 August 1657: 39n, 135n, 167.

W93, P126—Council of State to the French ambassador, August 1657: 157n.

W94, P128—Cromwell to the elector of Brandenburg, 20 August 1657: 39n, 89, 135n, 167.

W95, P129—Cromwell to Hamburg, 20 August 1657: 10, 39n, 89, 135n, 167.

W96, P130—Cromwell to Bremen, 20 August 1657: 10, 39n, 89, 135n, 167.

W97, P131—Cromwell to Lübeck, 20 August 1657: 10, 39, 89, 135n, 167, 224n.

W98, P133—Cromwell to Hamburg, 20 August 1657: 39, 89, 135n, 167.

W99, P132—Cromwell to the duke of Holstein, 20 August 1657: 39n, 89, 135n.

W100, P134—Cromwell to the duke of Tuscany, 10 September 1657: 120.

W101, P135—Cromwell to the elector of Brandenburg, 23(?) September 1657: 89, 168.

W102, P136—Council of State to the French ambassador, October 1657: 157n.

W103, P137—Cromwell to the duke of Venice, 22 October 1657: 63n.

W104, P138—Cromwell to the United Netherlands, 12 November 1657: 63n, 86n, 89n.

W105, P141—Cromwell to the United Netherlands, 17 December 1657: 86n, 89n.

W106, P140—Cromwell to Holland, December 1657: 86n, 89n, 135n.

W107, P139—Cromwell to the duke of Tuscany, December 1657: 120.

W108, P143—Cromwell to the king of Sweden, 30 March 1658: 168, 192.

W109, P144—Cromwell to the duke of Tuscany, 7 April 1658: 121.

W110, P151—Cromwell to the king of France, 26 May 1658: 151, 151n, 156n, 157.

W111, P152—Cromwell to the Swiss Protestant Cantons, 26 May 1658: 151.

W112, P79—Cromwell to Cardinal Mazarin, 25 May 1655: 142, 143n, 147n, 151, 152n, 158n.

Portugal

W78, P107—Cromwell to Conde d'Odemira, August 1656: 50.

W82, P114—Cromwell to the king of Portugal, October 1656: 51n, 89, 89n.

W84, P115—Cromwell to the king of Portugal, October 1656: 51n.

W121, P158—Cromwell to the king of Portugal, August 1658: 51n.

W133, P169—R. Cromwell to the king of Portugal, 23 February 1659: 51n.

W149, P170—R. Cromwell to the king of Portugal, 19 April 1659(?): 51n, 224n.

Oldenburg

W39, P34—Parliament to the count of Oldenburg, 17 February 1652: 54, 228n.

W152, P35—The Oldenburg Safeguard, 17 February 1652: 56, 228n.

W44, P64—Cromwell to the count of Oldenburg, 29 June 1654: 60, 63n, 89n.

W45, P65—Cromwell to the count of Oldenburg, 29 June 1654: 60.

United Netherlands

W167A, P4—Dutch ambassador to Parliament, 18 May 1649: 77.

W167B, P30—Dutch ambassadors to the Council of State, 24 January 1652: 77.

W167C, P32—Council of State to the Dutch ambassadors, 29 January 1652: 78, 78n, 80.

W167D, P31—Council of State to the Dutch ambassadors, 29 January 1652: 78, 78n.

W167E, P38—Council of State to the Dutch ambassadors, 15 March 1652: 79, 110n.

#W167F, P44—Dutch ambassadors to the Council of State, 12 April 1652: 80.

W43a, P39—Council of State to the Dutch ambassadors, 15 March 1652: 52n, 79, 224n.

Works 18: 8–79; P47—Declaration against the Dutch, 9 July 1652: 82.

W40, P63—Parliament to the Swiss Protestant Cantons, 28 November 1653: xiiin, 107.

W54, P75—Cromwell to the United Provinces, 25 May 1655: 86, 145, 146n, 216, 218.

W66, P92—Cromwell to the United Netherlands, 1 April 1656: 86n.

W69, P99—Cromwell to the United Netherlands, 31 May 1656: 86n.

W70, P98—Cromwell to the United Netherlands, 30 May 1656: 86n.

Spain

W43, P59—Council of State to the Spanish ambassador, 14 January 1653: 97.

W41, P57—Council of State to the Spanish ambassador, 1653(?): 97.

W42, P56—Council of State to the marquis of Leida, 1653(?): 97.

*W122, P66—Cromwell to the archduke of Austria, 18 July 1654.

W47, P69—Cromwell to the Spanish prime minister, 4 September 1654: 91, 99.

#W169, P84—A Declaration of the Lord Protector, 26 October 1655: 88.

Denmark

W24, P41—Parliament to the king of Denmark, 13 April 1652: 70n, 101, 101n, 224n.

W29, P50—Council of State to the Danish ambassadors, 13 September 1652: 52n, 101, 104, 224.

W30, P51—Council of State to the Danish ambassadors, 13 September 1652: 52n, 101, 104, 224n.

W35, P52—Parliament to the king of Denmark, 9 November 1652: 89n, 107.

W58, P77—Cromwell to the king of Denmark, 25 May 1655: 110n, 147n, 217.

W159, P118—King of Denmark to Cromwell, 16 February 1656: 110n, 164, 176n.

W87, P119—Cromwell to the king of Denmark, 4 December 1656: 39, 110n, 164n, 192.

W64, P122—Cromwell to the king of Denmark, March 1657: 172n.

W136, P175—Parliament to the king of Denmark, 15 May 1659: 11, 36n, 39, 110n, 171, 178.

Tuscany

W17, P29—Parliament to the duke of Tuscany, 20 January 1652: 10, 112n, 224n.

W27, P46—Council of State to the duke of Tuscany, 29 July 1652: 83, 112.

W31, P49—Council of State to the duke of Tuscany, 16 September 1652: 112n.

W33, P53—Council of State to the Spanish ambassador, 11 November 1652: 90, 97, 98n, 112n.

Savoy and the Piedmont Massacre

W111, P152—Cromwell to the Swiss Protestant Cantons, 26 May 1658: 151.

France

W139, P78—Cromwell to the king of France, 25 May 1655: 141, 147n, 151, 158n, 223n, 224n.

W112, P79—Cromwell to Cardinal Mazarin, 25 May 1655: 142, 143n, 147n, 151, 152n, 158n.

W56, P82—Cromwell to the king of France, 31 July 1655: 89n, 147n, 152n, 158n.

W57, P83—Cromwell to Cardinal Mazarin, 31 July 1655: 89, 89n, 147n, 150, 152, 152n, 157n, 158n.

W61, P85—Cromwell to the king of France, December 1655: 156n.

W140, P88—Cromwell to the king of France, 13 January 1656: 156n, 223n, 224n.

W145, P93—Cromwell to the king of France, 14 April 1656: 89n, 152n, 160n, 224n.

W146, P94—Cromwell to Cardinal Mazarin, 14 April 1656: 89n, 152n, 158n, 160n, 224n.

W68, P97—Cromwell to the king of France, 14 May 1656: 156n.

W73, P111—Cromwell to the king of France, 25 September 1656: 152, 152n, 157.

W74, P113—Cromwell to Cardinal Mazarin, 25 September 1656: 152n, 153, 157, 159n.

W81, P112—Cromwell to the king of France, 25 (?) September 1656: 156n.

W86, P120—Cromwell to the king of France, *after* 1 January 1657: 153, 156n.

W93, P126—Council of State to the French ambassador, August 1657: 157n.

W102, P136—Council of State to the French ambassador, October 1657: 157n.

W110, P151—Cromwell to the king of France, 26 May 1658: 151, 151n, 156n, 157.

W113, P146—Cromwell to the king of France, May 1658: 89n, 152n, 154.

W114, P147—Cromwell to Cardinal Mazarin, May 1658: 89n, 152n, 154.

W115, P149—Cromwell to Cardinal Mazarin, May 1658: 89n, 152n, 154.

P150—Cromwell to Cardinal Mazarin, 20 May 1658: 154, 159.

Sweden and the War in the North

Miscellaneous

Appendix F

Additional Attributions

The following representative list of documents consists of some that have been located in the public record and some that have not, as well as some that have been attributed to Milton by one or more of his biographers and editors but contested by others. It is not exhaustive, nor is it in any way prescriptive; and it includes only individual documents cited in the text and notes of this study, to which it is indexed. I have made no effort to catalogue the numerous documents that Milton translated from Latin to English. The categories—Certain, Near Certain, Probable, Possible—are entirely arbitrary and will not survive scrutiny for semantic precision. Readers should feel at liberty to question such categories or to move individual documents up and down within the chain of certainty as seems best to them. The list is offered simply as a convenience to interested readers and as a road map for those who would continue the journey.

The classification of individual documents draws on evidence of three kinds presented in the text and notes—historic, archival, and textual. At times all three combine, as in Morland's speech, to argue for unquestionable attribution; at others two are so compelling as to appear irrefutable, as in the historic and archival evidence for the French companion letters and Meadows's credential letter to Frederick III. Leo Miller has proposed additions to the canon in some cases on the basis of textual analysis alone, and his judgments are honored below.

The attribution of any single document or groups of documents may surely be questioned—and indeed later research may prove some wrong—but the inescapable conclusion of the evidence offered is that Milton was responsible for many more Letters of State than have hitherto been acknowledged his.

Groups and Pairs

Milton prepared at least one document in the diplomatic packet of each of the following envoys. Since it highly likely that he was responsible for all the routine documents for any single mission (with the exception of the Set of Instructions in English), additional documents from any individual packet may be attributed to him with varying degrees of certainty: (see pp. 89–90)

Richard Bradshaw to Hamburg, 1650	Certain
Charles Vane to Portugal, 1650	Near Certain
Anthony Ascham to Spain, 1650	Certain
Samuel Morland to Savoy, 1655	Certain
Thomas Maynard to Portugal, 1656	Near Certain
William Lockhart to France, 1656	Near Certain
William Jephson to Sweden, 1657	Certain
Philip Meadows to Denmark, 1657	Certain
George Downing to the United Netherlands, 1656	Near Certain
Thomas Fauconberg to France, 1658	Certain

Records indicate that Milton was involved in negotiations held in London with envoys from the following states. Documents associated with these negotiations may be attributed to him with varying degrees of certainty:

Portugal, 1651	Certain
Oldenburg, 1652	Certain
United Netherlands, 1652	Near Certain
Denmark, 1652	Near Certain
Spain, 1652–53	Certain
Sweden, 1656	Certain

Since the distribution of known letters indicates that Milton was at times responsible for correspondence with specific cities and states over a period of time, any letters addressed to the following during the years indicated may be considered his:

Hamburg, 1649–50	Possible
Portugal, 1650–51	Possible
Spain, 1650–53	Probable
Tuscany, 1652–58	Possible
France, 1655–59	Probable
Sweden, 1655–59	Probable

On the same basis, letters associated with the following events may be attributed to him:

The Piedmont Massacre, 1655–58	Certain
The War in the North, 1655–59	Near Certain

Individual Documents

The following documents may be attributed to Milton to the degree indicated:

Certain

The Oldenburg Safeguard, 17 February 1652: 21, 53–59
The Dutch Declaration, 9 July 1652: 82–83
Council of State to the governor of Porto Longone, 11 November 1652: 97–98n, 113n
The Spanish treaty, 12 November 1652: 93–98, Appendix C
Morland's speech to the duke of Savoy, 25 May 1655: 144–50
Letters of Safe-Conduct for Peter Romswinckel, 13 June 1656: 172n
The Swedish treaty, 17 July 1656: 172–75
Companions of known letters to Louis XIV and Mazarin, 1655–59: 11, 156–60
Meadows's credential letter to Frederick III, 20 August 1657: 167, 172

Near Certain

Council of State to the Dutch ambassadors, 16 April 1652: 81
Council of State to the Danish ambassadors, 8 July 1652 (2): 102–3, 108–9
Council of State to the Danish ambassadors, 5 October 1652: 105–6, 108–9
Letters to envoys in London on holding Mass, 12 January 1653: 97
Safeguards to the German states, 1652–54: 59–60
Letters dealing with capture and transfer of Dunkirk, May–June 1658: 153–56
Cromwell to Frederick III, 19 October 1657: 167n

Probable

Council of State to Leo ab Aitzema, 8 April 1652: 42n
Parliament to the Danish ambassadors, 8 July 1652 (on war): 107
Council of State to the Danish ambassadors, 19 October 1652 (on war): 107

Council of State to the Dutch ambassadors, 13 July 1653: 85
Council of State to the Dutch ambassadors, 1 August 1653: 85
Richard Cromwell's first letters, confirming succession, 6 September
1658: 21, 87n, 169n, 169

Possible

Cromwell to Geneva Senate, 27 March 1654: 250n
Cromwell to the duke of Tuscany, 6 May 1658: 121
Cromwell to the duke of Tuscany, 12 June 1658: 121
The Rump's first letters, confirming succession, 15 May 1659: 178
Sets of instructions in English in diplomatic packets: 90, 134n, 167–
68n, 172–173

Works Cited

ORIGINAL SOURCES

Milton's State Papers: See Appendix E.

Editions

Birch, Thomas, ed. *A Compleat Collection of the Historical, Political, and Miscellaneous Works of John Milton*. London, 1738.

Hamilton, W. Douglas. *Original Papers Illustrative of the Life and Writings of John Milton, Including Sixteen Letters of State Written by Him, Now Published from MSS. in the State Paper Office*. London, 1859.

Hughes, Merritt Y. *John Milton, Complete Poems and Major Prose*. New York: Odyssey Press, 1957.

Milton, John. *Complete Prose Works of John Milton*. 8 vols. Ed. Don M. Wolfe et al. New Haven: Yale University Press, 1953–83.

———. *Literae Pseudo-Senatus Anglicani Cromwelii, Reliquorumque Perduellium Nomine as Jussu Conscriptae A Joanne Miltono*. Amsterdam, 1676.

———. *Milton's Republican-Letters Or a Collection of such as were written by Command of the Late Commonwealth of England; from the Year 1648. to the Year 1659*. 1682.

———. *The Works of John Milton*. 18 vols. Ed. Frank Allen Patterson et al. New York: Columbia University Press, 1931–38.

Phillips, Edward, ed. *Letters of State. Written by Mr. John Milton. To most of the Sovereign Princes and Republicks of Europe. From the Year 1649, Till the Year 1659*. London, 1694.

Public Record Office Files

C82/2246–49, Chancery Warrants for the Great Seal.
E403/1756–57, Issue Books (Pells').
E403/2180–2258, Debenture Books (Auditor's).
E403/2415–16, Register of Certificates, Reports, etc.

E403/2444–2511, Patent Books (Auditor's).
E403/2523, Patent Books (Pells').
E403/2570–71, Privy Seal Books (Auditor's).
E403/2590–91, Enrollment of Privy Seals (Auditor's).
E403/2608, Privy Seal Books (Pells').
E403/2761, Order Books (Pells').
E403/2815–16, Order Books (Auditor's).
E403/2981–3039, Warrant Books (Pells').
E403/3040–3115, Warrant Books (Auditor's).
E404/157–58, Privy Seals & Warrants for Issue.
E404/238, Orders and Warrants.
E405/213–322, Certificate Books (Pells').
E405/477–561, Accounts of Receipts and Issues.
E406/45–80, Assignments Books (Auditor's).
E407/1–2, Gentlemen Pensioners' Rolls.
PRO 31/3/1–203, Baschet's Transcripts.
SP 9/194, State Papers, Miscellaneous.
SP 18, State Papers Domestic, Interregnum.
SP 25/1–61, Order Books of the Council of State (Draft).
SP 25/62–79, Order Books of the Council of State (Fair).
SP 25/107, Warrant Books of the Council of State.
SP 25/121–22, Businesses Referred to Committee.
SP 25/131–33, Order Books of the Committee for Trade and Foreign Affairs.
SP 28/1–352, Commonwealth Exchequer Papers.
SP 29/386, State Papers Domestic, Charles II.
SP 45/20, State Papers Domestic, Various.
SP 71–113, State Papers Foreign, Interregnum.
SP 75/16, State Papers Foreign, Denmark.
SP 78/113–14, State Papers Foreign, France.
SP 81/54, State Papers Foreign, Germany (States).
SP 82/7 and 8, State Papers Foreign, Hamburg and Hanse Towns.
SP 84/159–62, 204, State Papers Foreign, Holland.
SP 89/4, State Papers Foreign, Portugal.
SP 92/24, State Papers Foreign, Savoy.
SP 94/43, State Papers Foreign, Spain.
SP 95/5A and 5B, State Papers Foreign, Sweden.
SP 96/6, State Papers Foreign, Switzerland.
SP 98/3 and 4, State Papers Foreign, Tuscany.
SP 103/3, State Papers Foreign, Treaty Papers, Denmark.
SP 103/12, State Papers Foreign, Treaty Papers, France.
SP 103/24, State Papers Foreign, Treaty Papers, Germany (States).
SP 103/31, State Papers Foreign, Treaty Papers, Hamburg and Hanse Towns.
SP 103/45 and 46, State Papers Foreign, Treaty Papers, Holland.
SP 103/57, State Papers Foreign, Treaty Papers, Portugal.
SP 103/65, State Papers Foreign, Treaty Papers, Spain.
SP 103/69, State Papers Foreign, Treaty Papers, Sweden.

SP 104, Entry Books.
SP 108/32, State Papers Foreign, Treaties, Denmark.
SP 108/54–56, State Papers Foreign, Treaties, France.
SP 108/300–301, State Papers Foreign, Treaties, Holland.
SP 108/386, State Papers Foreign, Treaties, Portugal.
SP 108/516, State Papers Foreign, Treaties, Sweden.

Miscellaneous

Abbott, Wilbur Cortez, ed. *The Writings and Speeches of Oliver Cromwell.* 4 vols. Cambridge: Harvard University Press, 1937–47.

Appleton, Henry. *A Remonstrance of the Fight in Legorn-Road Between the English and the Dutch, With all the Passages of the Treaty held by the Great Duke of Florence before the Same. Also many other Particulars, as they were presented to by His Excellency the Lord General Cromwell, and the Right Honorable The Council of State.* London, Printed by John Field, Printer to the Parliament of England, 1653. Thomason Tracts, E 1068 (5). British Library, London.

Badiley, Richard. *Capt. Badiley's Answer unto Capt. Appleton's Remonstrance, Given in To his Excellency the Lord General Cromwell and the Right Honourable, the Council of State. As also: His true Relation of what past between the Great Duke of Tuscany, and himselfe.* London, Printed by M. Simmons, in Aldersgate-street, 1653. Thomason Tracts, E 1952 (9). British Library, London.

———. *Capt. Badiley's Reply to Certaine Declarations from Capt. Seaman, Capt. Ell[is], & Capt. Fisher.* London, Printed by Matthew Simmons, in Aldersgate-streete, 1653. Thomason Tracts, E 1952 (9). British Library, London.

Baschet, M. Armand. "Lists of Despatches of Ambassadors from France to England; Henry VIII.–George I.; 1509–1714; with Remarks on their Correspondence." *The Thirty-ninth Annual Report of the Deputy Keeper of the Public Records.* Appendix 8. London, 1878.

Bodleian Library, Nalson MS 10, 17, 18.

Bodleian Library, Rawlinson MS A 1–73, 260–61.

Bodleian Library, Tanner MS 52–56, 114, 118.

British Library, Add MS 4157.

Calendar of State Papers, Colonial Series, 1575–1660. Ed. Noel Sainsbury. Reprint. Vaduz, Liechtenstein: Kraus Reprints, 1964.

Calendar of State Papers, Domestic Series, Commonwealth. 13 vols. Ed. Mary Ann Everett Green. Reprint. Vaduz, Liechtenstein: Kraus Reprints, 1965.

Casas, Bartolome de las. *The Tears of the Indians: being an historical . . . account of the cruel massacres and slaughter of above twenty-millions of innocent people. Written in Spanish by Caseus . . . and made English by J[ohn] P[hillips].* J.C. for Nath. Brook. London, 1656. British Library, London.

Columbia Manuscript. Rare Book and Manuscript Library, Columbia University, no. X823M64S62.

Detailed List of Paris Archives, Baschet's Transcripts (PRO 31/3). Rebound for the Literary Search Room, 1923. PRO Round Room, 19/42. Public Record Office, London.

Fanshawe, Richard. *Original Letters of his Excellency Sir Richard Fanshaw, During his Embassies in Spain and Portugal.* London, 1702.

The Fifth Report of the Deputy Keeper of the Public Records. London, 1844.

Firth, C. H., ed. *The Clarke Papers. Selections from the Papers of William Clarke.* 4 vols. London: Longmans, 1891–1901.

The Fourth Report of the Deputy Keeper of the Public Records. London, 1843.

French, J. Milton. *The Life Records of John Milton.* 5 vols. New Brunswick: Rutgers University Press, 1949–58.

Gardiner, Samuel Rawson. *The Constitutional Documents of the Puritan Revolution, 1625–1660.* 3d ed., rev. Oxford: Clarendon Press, 1906.

Harrington, James. *The Commonwealth of Oceana. The Political Works of James Harrington.* Ed. J.G.A. Pocock. Cambridge: Cambridge University Press, 1977.

Historical Manuscripts Commission. Thirteenth Report. Appendix, Part I, The Manuscripts of his Grace the Duke of Portland, Preserved at Welbeck Abbey. Vol. 1. London, 1891.

The Journal of the House of Commons. 17 vols. London, n.d.

Leti, Gregorio, ed. *Historia, E Memorie Recondite Sopra Alla Vita Di Oliviero Cromvele.* Amsterdam, 1692.

Ludlow, Edmund. *The Memoirs of Edmund Ludlow.* Ed. C. H. Firth. 2 vols. London, 1894.

Lünig, Johan Christian, ed. *Literae Procerum Europae.* Leipsic, 1712.

Master, Benjamin. *Sabaudiensis in Reformatam Religionem Persecutionis Brevis Narratio.* London, 1655.

Meadows, Philip. *A Narrative of the Principal Actions Occurring in the Wars Betwixt Sueden and Denmark Before and After Roschild Treaty.* London, 1677.

Morland, Samuel. *The History of the Evangelical Churches of the Valley of Piemont.* London, 1658.

Nickolls, John, ed. *Original Letters and Papers of State, addressed to Oliver Cromwell; concerning the affairs of Great Britain from the year 1649 to 1658. Found among the Political collections of Mr. John Milton.* London, 1743.

Roberts, Michael, ed. and trans. *Swedish Diplomats at Cromwell's Court 1655–1656.* Camden Fourth Series, vol. 36. London: Royal Historical Society, 1988.

Sixth Report of the Royal Commission on Historical Manuscripts. Reprint. Vaduz, Liechtenstein: Kraus Reprints, 1979.

Skinner Manuscript. Public Record Office, SP 9/194.

Stouppe, J[ean] B[aptiste]. *A Collection of Several Papers Sent to his Highness* the Lord Protector . . . Concerning the Bloody and Barbarous Massacres. Published by Command of his Highness. London, 1655.

The Thirty-Seventh Annual Report of the Deputy Keeper of the Public Records. London, 1876.

The Thirty-Sixth Annual Report of the Deputy Keeper of the Public Records. London, 1875.

Thurloe, John. A Collection of the State Papers of John Thurloe, Esq; Secretary, First to the Council of State, and afterwards to the Two Protectors, Oliver and Richard Cromwell. 7 vols. Ed. Thomas Birch. London, 1742.

Trumbull Papers. Students' Room of the Department of Manuscripts of the British Library, vol. 22.

Whitelocke, Bulstrode. Memorials of the English Affairs from the Beginning of the Reign of Charles the First to the Happy Restoration of King Charles II. Oxford, 1853.

SECONDARY SOURCES

Aubrey, Philip. Mr. Secretary Thurloe. London: Athlone Press, 1990.

Aylmer, G. E. The King's Servants: The Civil Service of Charles I, 1625–1642. London: Routledge & Kegan Paul, 1974.

———. The State's Servants: The Civil Service of the English Republic, 1649–1660. London: Routledge & Kegan Paul, 1973.

Barker, Arthur. Milton and the Puritan Dilemma, 1641–1660. Toronto: University of Toronto Press, 1942.

Beal, Peter. The Trumbull Papers, Property of the most Honorable the Marquess of Downshire. Catalogue prepared for Southby's, 1989.

Bennett, Joan S. Reviving Liberty: Radical Christian Humanism in Milton's Great Poems. Cambridge: Harvard University Press, 1989.

Bidwell, William. "The Committees and Legislation of the Rump Parliament, 1648–1653: A Quantitative Study." Ph.D. diss., University of Rochester, 1977.

Cole, Charles Woolsey. Colbert and a Century of French Mercantilism. 2 vols. New York: Columbia University Press, 1932.

Davies, Godfrey. The Restoration of Charles II, 1658–1660. Oxford: Oxford University Press, 1969.

Davies, Stevie. Images of Kingship in "Paradise Lost": Milton's Politics and Christian Liberty. Columbia: University of Missouri Press, 1983.

DiSalvo, Jackie. "The Lord's Battells': Samson Agonistes and the Puritan Revolution." In Milton Studies 4, ed. James D. Simmonds, 39–62. Pittsburgh: Pittsburgh University Press, 1972.

Fallon, Robert Thomas. Captain or Colonel: The Soldier in Milton's Life and Art. Columbia: University of Missouri Press, 1984.

———. "Filling the Gaps: New Perspectives on Mr. Secretary Milton." In Milton Studies 12, ed. James D. Simmonds, 165–95. Pittsburgh: Pittsburgh University Press, 1979.

———. "Miltonic Documents in the Public Record Office, London." In *Studies in Bibliography* 32, ed. Fredson Bowers, 82–100. Charlottesville: University of Virginia Press, 1979.

———. "Milton in the Anarchy, 1659–60: A Question of Consistency." *Studies in English Literature* 21 (Winter 1981): 123–46.

———. Review of Leo Miller, *John Milton and the Oldenburg Safeguard. Renaissance Quarterly* 40 (Summer 1987): 377–80.

Fixler, Michael. *Milton and the Kingdoms of God*. London: Faber and Faber, 1964.

Fraser, Antonia. *Cromwell, The Lord General*. New York: Knopf, 1974.

Frye, Roland Mushat. "The Dissidence of Dissent and the Origins of Religious Freedom in America: John Milton and the Puritans." *Proceedings of the American Philosophical Society* 133 (December 1989): 475–88.

Gardiner, Samuel Rawson. *History of the Commonwealth and Protectorate, 1649–1656*. 4 vols. Reprint. New York: AMS Press, 1965.

Gaunt, Peter G. "The Councils of the Protectorate, from December 1653 to September 1658." Ph.D. diss., University of Exeter, 1983.

Grierson, H.J.C. *Milton and Wordsworth, Poets and Prophets*. London: Chatto and Windus, 1960.

Hanford, James Holly. *John Milton, Englishman*. New York: Crown, 1949.

Hanson, Michael. *2000 Years of London*. London: Billing and Sons, 1967.

Hill, Christopher. *God's Englishman: Oliver Cromwell and the English Revolution*. London: Weidenfeld and Nicolson, 1970.

———. *Milton and the English Revolution*. New York: Viking Press, 1977.

———. "Milton and the English Revolution." In *Perspectives on Literature and Society in Eastern and Western Europe*, ed. Geoffrey A. Hosking and George F. Cushing, 23–36. London: Macmillan, 1989.

Hinton, R.W.K. *The Eastland Trade and the Common Weal in the Seventeenth Century*. Cambridge: Cambridge University Press, 1959.

Hirst, Derek. "The Lord Protector, 1653–1658." In *Oliver Cromwell and the English Revolution*, ed. John Morrill, 119–48. London: Longman, 1990.

Howard, Donald R. "Flying Through Space: Chaucer and Milton." In *Milton and the Line of Vision*, ed. Joseph Anthony Wittreich, Jr., 3–23. Madison: University of Wisconsin Press, 1975.

Howat, G.M.D. *Stuart and Cromwellian Foreign Policy*. New York: St. Martin's Press, 1974.

Hughes, Merritt Y. *Ten Perspectives on Milton*. New Haven: Yale University Press, 1965.

Hunter, William B., Jr. "Milton and Richard Cromwell." *ELN* 3 (June 1966): 252–59.

———. "The Provenance of *Christian Doctrine*." *Studies in English Literature* 32 (1992): 129–66.

Levin, Richard. "The Poetics and Politics of Bardicide." *PMLA* 105 (May 1990): 491–504.

Lewalski, Barbara K. "Milton: Political Beliefs and Polemical Methods, 1659–1660." *PMLA* 74 (June 1959): 191–202.

Masson, David. *The Life of John Milton.* 6 vols. Reprint. Gloucester, Mass.: Peter Smith, 1965.

Miller, Leo. *John Milton and the Oldenburg Safeguard.* New York: Loewenthal Press, 1985.

―――. *John Milton's Writings in the Anglo-Dutch Negotiations 1651–1654.* Pittsburgh: Duquesne University Press, 1992.

―――. "Lexicographer Milton Leads Us To Recover His Unknown Works." *Milton Quarterly* 24 (May 1990): 58–62.

―――. "Milton's State Letters: The Lünig Version." *Notes and Queries* 17 (November 1970): 412–14.

―――. "New Milton Texts and Data from the Aitzema Mission, 1652." *Notes and Queries* 37 (September 1990): 279–88.

―――. Review of *The Miltonic State Papers, 1649–1659. Notes and Queries* 19 (December 1972): 474–78.

Morand, Paul P. *The Effects of His Political Life on John Milton.* Paris: Didier, 1939.

Muir, Kenneth. *John Milton.* London: Longmans, 1955.

Nardo, Anna K. *Milton's Sonnets and the Ideal Community.* Lincoln: University of Nebraska Press, 1979.

Parker, William Riley. *Milton: A Biography.* 2 vols. Oxford: Clarendon Press, 1968.

Pechter, Edward. "The New Historicism and Its Discontents: Politicizing Renaissance Drama." *PMLA* 102 (May 1987): 292–303.

Peck, Francis. *Memoirs of the Life of . . . Cromwell.* London, 1740.

Pinto, Vivian de Sala. *Peter Sterry, Platonist and Puritan.* Cambridge: Cambridge University Press, 1934.

Radzinowicz, Mary Ann. *Toward "Samson Agonistes": The Growth of Milton's Mind.* Princeton: Princeton University Press, 1978.

Roberts, Michael. "Cromwell and the Baltic." *The English Historical Review* 76, no. 300 (July 1961): 402–46. Reprinted in *Essays in Swedish History*, ed. Michael Roberts, 138–94. London: Wiedenfeld and Nicolson, 1967.

Saillens, Emile. *John Milton, Man, Poet, Polemicist.* New York: Barnes and Noble, 1964.

Saurat, Denis. *Milton, Man and Thinker.* New York: Dial Press, 1925.

Sensabaugh, George F. *That Grand Whig Milton.* Stanford: Stanford University Press, 1952.

Shawcross, John T. "A Contemporary Letter Concerning Milton's State Papers." *Milton Quarterly* 15 (December 1981): 119–20.

―――. *Milton, A Bibliography for the Years 1624–1700.* Binghamton, N.Y.: Medieval & Renaissance Texts and Studies, 1984.

―――. "A Survey of Milton's Prose Works." In *Achievements of the Left Hand, Essays on the Prose of John Milton*, ed. Michael Lieb and John T. Shawcross, 291–391. Amherst: University of Massachusetts Press, 1974.

Smart, James S. *The Sonnets of Milton.* Oxford: Clarendon Press, 1966.

Spalding, Thomas Alfred. *A Life of Richard Badiley, Vice Admiral of the Fleet*. Westminster: Archibald Constable, 1899.

Stern, Alfred. *Milton und seine Zeit*. 2 vols. Leipzig, 1877–79.

Summers, Joseph H. "Milton and the Cult of Conformity." In *Milton: Modern Judgments*, ed. Alan Rudrum, 29–43. London: Macmillan, 1968.

Tillyard, E.M.W. *Shakespeare's History Plays*. New York: Macmillan, 1947.

Trevor-Roper, Hugh. *Catholics, Anglicans, and Puritans*. London: Fontana, 1989.

Tuchman, Barbara. *The First Salute*. New York: Knopf, 1988.

Vaughan, Robert. *The Protectorate of Oliver Cromwell and the State of Europe*. 2 vols. London, 1839.

Wolfe, Don M. *Milton in the Puritan Revolution*. New York: Humanities Press, 1941.

Woodhouse, A.S.P. *The Heavenly Muse: A Preface to Milton*. Ed. Hugh MacCallum. Toronto: University of Toronto Press, 1972.

Woolrych, Austin. "Milton and Cromwell: 'A Short but Scandalous Night of Interruption,'" In *Achievements of the Left Hand, Essays on the Prose of John Milton*, ed. Michael Lieb and John T. Shawcross, 185–218. Amherst: University of Massachusetts Press, 1974.

———. Introduction to vol. 7 of *The Complete Prose Works of John Milton*. Ed. Robert W. Ayers. New Haven: Yale University Press, 1980.

Index

Textual reference to individuals is omitted in instances when they are cited simply as signatory or addressee of specific letters. See Appendix E for an index of the Letters of State.

9.95